Hard Press

WITH LORD BRAYBROOKE'S NOTES

EDITED WITH ADDITIONS BY

HENRY B. WHEATLEY F.S.A.

Diaryof Samuel Pepys

1663 N.S. *Complete*

January& February
1662-1663

January 1st, 1662-63.

Lay with my wife at my Lord's lodgings, where I have been these two nights, till 10 o'clock with great pleasure talking, then I rose and to White Hall, where I spent a little time walking among the courtiers, which I perceive I shall be able to do with great confidence, being now beginning to be pretty well known among them. Then to my wife again, and found Mrs. Sarah with us in the chamber we lay in. Among other discourse, Mrs. Sarah tells us how the King sups at least four or [five] times every week with my Lady Castlemaine; and most often stays till the morning with her, and goes home through the garden all alone privately, and that so as the very centrys take notice of it and speak of it. She tells me, that about a month ago she [Lady Castlemaine] quickened at my Lord Gerard's at dinner, and cried out that she was undone; and all the lords and men were fain to quit the room, and women called to help her. In fine, I find that there is nothing almost but bawdry at Court from top to bottom, as, if it were fit, I could instance, but it is not necessary; only they say my Lord Chesterfield, groom of the stole to the Queen, is either gone or put away from the Court upon the score of his lady's having smitten the Duke of York, so as that he is watched by the Duchess of York, and his lady is retired into the country upon it. How much of this is true, God knows, but it is common talk. After dinner I did reckon with Mrs. Sarah for what we have eat and drank here, and gave her a crown, and so took coach, and to the Duke's House, where we saw "The Villaine" again; and the more I see it, the more I am offended at my first undervaluing the play, it being very good and pleasant, and yet a true and allowable tragedy. The house was full of citizens, and so the less pleasant, but that I was willing to make an end of my gaddings, and to set to my business for all the year again tomorrow. Here we saw the old Roxalana in the chief box, in a velvet gown, as the fashion is, and very handsome, at which I was glad. Hence by coach home, where I find all well, only Sir W. Pen they say ill again. So to my office to set down these two or three days' journall, and to close the last year therein, and so that being done, home to supper, and to bed, with great pleasure talking and discoursing with my wife of our late observations abroad.

2nd. Lay long in bed, and so up and to the office, where all the morning alone doing something or another. So dined at home with my wife, and in the afternoon to the Treasury office, where Sir W. Batten was paying off tickets, but so simply and arbitrarily, upon a dull pretence of doing right to the King, though to the wrong of poor people (when I know there is no man that means the King less right than he, or would trouble himself less about it, but only that he sees me stir, and so he would appear doing something, though to little purpose), that I was weary of it. At last we broke up, and walk home together, and I to see Sir W. Pen, who is fallen sick again. I staid a while talking with him, and so to my office, practising some arithmetique, and so home to supper and bed, having sat up late talking to my poor wife with great content.

3rd. Up and to the office all the morning, and dined alone with my wife at noon, and then to my office all the afternoon till night, putting business in order with great content in my mind. Having nothing now in my mind of trouble in the world, but quite the contrary, much joy, except only the ending of our difference with my uncle Thomas, and the getting of the bills well over for my building of my house here, which however are as small and less than any of the others. Sir W. Pen it seems is fallen very ill again. So to my arithmetique again to-night, and so home to supper and to bed.

4th (Lord's day). Up and to church, where a lazy sermon, and so home to dinner to a good piece of powdered beef, but a little too salt. At dinner my wife did propound my having of my sister Pall at my house again to be her woman, since one we must have, hoping that in that quality possibly she may prove better than she did before, which I take very well of her, and will consider of it, it being a very great trouble to me that I should have a sister of so ill a nature, that I must be forced to spend money upon a stranger when it might better be upon her, if she were good for anything. After dinner I and she walked, though it was dirty, to White Hall (in the way calling at the Wardrobe to see how Mr. Moore do, who is pretty well, but not cured yet), being much afeard of being seen by anybody, and was, I think, of Mr. Coventry, which so troubled me that I made her go before, and I ever after loitered behind. She to Mr. Hunt's, and I to White Hall Chappell, and then up to walk up and down the house, which now I am well known there, I shall forbear to do, because I would not be thought a lazy body by Mr. Coventry and others by being seen, as I have lately been, to walk up and down doing nothing. So to Mr. Hunt's, and there was most prettily and kindly entertained by him and her, who are two as good people as I hardly know any, and so neat and kind one to another. Here we staid late, and so to my Lord's to bed.

5th. Up and to the Duke, who himself told me that Sir J. Lawson was come home to Portsmouth from the Streights, who is now come with great renown among all men, and, I perceive, mightily esteemed at Court by all. The Duke did not stay long in his chamber; but to the King's chamber, whither by and by the Russia Embassadors come; who, it seems, have a custom that they will not come to have any treaty with our or any King's Commissioners, but they will themselves see at the time the face of the King himself, be it forty days one after another; and so they did to-day only go in and see the King; and so out again to the Council-chamber. The Duke returned to his chamber, and so to his closett, where Sir G. Carteret, Sir J. Minnes, Sir W. Batten, Mr. Coventry, and myself attended him about the business of the Navy; and after much discourse and pleasant talk he went away. And I took Sir W. Batten and Captain Allen into the wine cellar to my tenant (as I call him, Serjeant Dalton), and there drank a great deal of variety of wines, more than I have drunk at one time, or shall again a great while, when I come to return to my oaths, which I intend in a day or two. Thence to my Lord's lodging, where Mr. Hunt and Mr. Creed dined with us, and were very merry. And after dinner he and I to White Hall, where the Duke and the Commissioners for Tangier met, but did not do much: my Lord Sandwich not being in town, nobody making it their business. So up, and Creed and I to my wife again, and after a game or two at cards, to the Cockpitt, where we saw "Claracilla," a poor play, done by the King's house (but neither the King nor Queen were there, but only the Duke and Duchess, who did show some impertinent and, methought, unnatural dalliances there, before the whole world, such as kissing, and leaning upon one another); but to my very little content, they not acting in any degree like the Duke's people. So home (there being here this night Mrs. Turner and Mrs. Martha Batten of our office) to my Lord's lodgings again, and to a game at cards, we three and Sarah, and so to supper and some apples and ale, and to bed with great pleasure, blessed be God!

6th (Twelfth Day). Up and Mr. Creed brought a pot of chocolate ready made for our morning draft, and then he and I to the Duke's, but I was not very willing to be seen at this end of the town, and so returned to our lodgings, and took my wife by coach to my brother's, where I set her down, and Creed and I to St. Paul's Church-yard, to my bookseller's, and looked over several books with good discourse, and then into St. Paul's Church, and there finding Elborough, my old schoolfellow at Paul's, now a parson, whom I know to be a silly fellow, I took him out and walked with him, making Creed and myself sport with talking with him, and so sent him away, and we to my office and house to see all well, and thence to the Exchange, where we met with Major Thomson, formerly of our office, who do talk very highly of liberty of conscience, which now he hopes for by the King's declaration, and that he doubts not that if he will give him, he will find more and better friends than the Bishopps can be to him, and that if he do not, there will many thousands in a little time go out of England, where they may have it. But he says that they are well contented that if the King thinks it good, the Papists may have the same liberty with them. He tells me, and so do others, that Dr. Calamy is this day sent to Newgate for preaching, Sunday was se'nnight, without leave, though he did it only to supply the place; when otherwise the people must have gone away without ever a sermon, they being disappointed of a minister but the Bishop of London will not take that as an excuse. Thence into Wood Street, and there bought a fine table for my dining-room, cost me 50s.; and while we were buying it, there was a scare-fire

[Scar-fire or scarefire. An alarm of fire. One of the little pieces in Herrick's "Hesperides" is entitled "The Scar-fire," but the word sometimes was used, as in the text, for the fire itself. Fuller, in his "Worthies," speaks of quenching scare-fires.]

in an ally over against us, but they quenched it. So to my brother's, where Creed and I and my wife dined with Tom, and after dinner to the Duke's house, and there saw "Twelfth Night"

[Pepys saw "Twelfth Night" for the first time on September 11th, 1661, when he supposed it was a new play, and "took no pleasure at all in it."]

acted well, though it be but a silly play, and not related at all to the name or day. Thence Mr. Battersby the apothecary, his wife, and I and mine by coach together, and setting him down at his house, he paying his share, my wife and I home, and found all well, only myself somewhat vexed at my wife's neglect in leaving of her scarf, waistcoat, and night-dressings in the coach today that brought us from Westminster, though, I confess, she did give them to me to look after, yet it was her fault not to see that I did take them out of the coach. I believe it might be as good as 25s. loss or thereabouts. So to my office, however, to set down my last three days' journall, and writing to my Lord Sandwich to give him an account of Sir J. Lawson's being come home, and to my father about my sending him some wine and things this week, for his making an entertainment of some friends in the country, and so home. This night making an end wholly of Christmas, with a mind fully satisfied with the great pleasures we have had by being abroad from home, and I do find my mind so apt to run to its old want of pleasures, that it is high time to betake myself to my late vows, which I will to-morrow, God willing, perfect and bind myself to, that so I may, for a great while, do my duty, as I have well begun, and increase my good name and esteem in the world, and get money, which sweetens all things, and whereof I have much need. So home to supper and to bed, blessing God for his mercy to bring me home, after much pleasure, to my house and business with health and resolution to fall hard to work again.

7th. Up pretty early, that is by seven o'clock, it being not yet light before or then. So to my office all the morning, signing the Treasurer's ledger, part of it where I have not put my hand, and then eat a mouthful of pye at home to stay my stomach, and so with Mr. Waith by water to Deptford, and there among other things viewed old pay-books, and found that the Commanders did never heretofore receive any pay for the rigging time, but only for seatime, contrary to what Sir J. Minnes and Sir W. Batten told the Duke the other day. I also searched all the ships in the Wett Dock for fire, and found all in good order, it being very dangerous for the King that so many of his ships lie together there. I was among the canvass in stores also, with Mr. Harris, the saylemaker, and learnt the difference between one sort and another, to my great content, and so by water home again, where my wife tells me stories how she hears that by Sarah's going to live at Sir W. Pen's, all our affairs of my family are made known and discoursed of there and theirs by my people, which do trouble me much, and I shall take a time to let Sir W. Pen know how he has dealt in taking her without our full consent. So to my office, and by and by home to supper, and so to prayers and bed.

8th. Up pretty early, and sent my boy to the carrier's with some wine for my father, for to make his feast among his Brampton friends this Christmas, and my muff to my mother, sent as from my wife. But before I sent my boy out with them, I beat him for a lie he told me, at which his sister, with whom we have of late been highly displeased, and warned her to be gone, was angry, which vexed me, to see the girl I loved so well, and my wife, should at last turn so much a fool and unthankful to us. So to the office, and there all the morning, and though without and a little against the advice of the officers did, to gratify him, send Thomas Hater to-day towards Portsmouth a day or two before the rest of the clerks, against the Pay next week. Dined at home; and there being the famous new play acted the first time to-day, which is called "The Adventures of Five Hours," at the Duke's house, being, they say, made or translated by Colonel Tuke, I did long to see it; and so made my wife to get her ready, though we were forced to send for a smith, to break open her trunk, her mayde Jane being gone forth with the keys, and so we went; and though early, were forced to sit almost out of sight, at the end of one of the lower forms, so full was the house. And the play, in one word, is the best, for the variety and the most excellent continuance of the plot to the very end, that ever I saw, or think ever shall, and all possible, not only to be done in the time, but in most other respects very admittable, and without one word of ribaldry; and the house, by its frequent plaudits, did show their sufficient approbation. So home; with much ado in an hour getting a coach home, and, after writing letters at my office, I went home to supper and to bed, now resolving to set up my rest as to plays till Easter, if not Whitsuntide next, excepting plays at Court.

9th. Waking in the morning, my wife I found also awake, and begun to speak to me with great trouble and tears, and by degrees from one discourse to another at last it appears that Sarah has told somebody that has told my wife of my meeting her at my brother's and making her sit down by me while she told me stories of my wife, about her giving her scallop to her brother, and other things, which I am much vexed at, for I am sure I never spoke any thing of it, nor could any body tell her but by Sarah's own words. I endeavoured to excuse my silence herein hitherto by not believing any thing she told me, only that of the scallop which she herself told me of. At last we pretty good friends, and my wife begun to speak again of the necessity of her keeping somebody to bear her company; for her familiarity with her other servants is it that spoils them all, and other company she hath none, which is too true, and called for Jane to reach her out of her trunk, giving her the keys to that purpose, a bundle of papers, and pulls out a paper, a copy of what, a pretty while since, she had wrote in a discontent to me, which I would not read, but burnt. She now read it, and it was so piquant, and wrote in English, and most of it true, of the retiredness of her life, and how unpleasant it was; that being wrote in English, and so in danger of being met with and read by others, I was vexed at it, and desired her and then commanded her to tear it. When she desired to be excused it, I forced it from her, and tore it, and withal took her other bundle of papers from her, and leapt out of the bed and in my shirt clapped them into the pocket of my breeches, that she might not get them from me, and having got on my stockings and breeches and gown, I pulled them out one by one and tore them all before her face, though it went against my heart to do it, she crying and desiring me not to do it, but such was my passion and trouble to see the letters of my love to her, and my Will wherein I had given her all I have in the world, when I went to sea with my Lord Sandwich, to be joyned with a paper of so much disgrace to me and dishonour, if it should have been found by any body. Having torn them all, saving a bond of my uncle Robert's, which she hath long had in her hands, and our marriage license, and the first letter that ever I sent her when I was her servant,

> [The usual word at this time for a lover. We have continued the
> correlative term "mistress," but rejected that of "servant."]

I took up the pieces and carried them into my chamber, and there, after many disputes with myself whether I should burn them or no, and having picked up, the pieces of the paper she read to-day, and of my Will which I tore, I burnt all the rest, and so went out to my office troubled in mind. Hither comes Major Tolhurst, one of my old acquaintance in Cromwell's time, and sometimes of our clubb, to see me, and I could do no less than carry him to the Mitre, and having sent for Mr. Beane, a merchant, a neighbour of mine, we sat and talked, Tolhurst telling me the manner of their collierys in the north. We broke up, and I home to dinner. And to see my folly, as discontented as I am, when my wife came I could not forbear smiling all dinner till she began to speak bad words again, and then I began to be angry again, and so to my office. Mr. Bland came in the evening to me hither, and sat talking to me about many things of merchandise, and I should be very happy in his discourse, durst I confess my ignorance to him, which is not so fit for me to do. There coming a letter to me from Mr. Pierce, the surgeon, by my desire appointing his and Dr. Clerke's coming to dine with me next Monday, I went to my wife and agreed upon matters, and at last for my honour am forced to make her presently a new Moyre gown to be seen by Mrs. Clerke, which troubles me to part with so much money, but, however, it sets my wife and I to friends again, though I and she never were so heartily angry in our lives as to-day almost, and I doubt the heartburning will not [be] soon over, and the truth is I am sorry for the tearing of so many poor loving letters of mine from sea and elsewhere to her. So to my office again, and there the Scrivener brought me the end of the manuscript which I am going to get together of things of the Navy, which pleases me much. So home, and mighty friends with my wife again, and so to bed.

10th. Up and to the office. From thence, before we sat, Sir W. Pen sent for me to his bedside to talk (indeed to reproach me with my not owning to Sir J. Minnes that he had my advice in the blocking up of the garden door the other day, which is now by him out of fear to Sir J. Minnes opened again), to which I answered him so indifferently that I think he and I shall be at a distance, at least to one another, better than ever we did and love one another less, which for my part I think I need not care for. So to the office, and sat till noon, then rose and to dinner, and then to the office again, where Mr. Creed sat with me till late talking very good discourse, as he is full of it, though a cunning knave in his heart, at least not to be too much trusted, till Sir J. Minnes came in, which at last he did, and so beyond my expectation he was willing to sign his accounts, notwithstanding all his objections, which really were very material, and yet how like a doting coxcomb he signs the accounts without the least satisfaction, for which we both sufficiently laughed at him and Sir W. Batten after they had signed them and were gone, and so sat talking together till 11 o'clock at night, and so home and to bed.

11th (Lord's day). Lay long talking pleasant with my wife, then up and to church, the pew being quite full with strangers come along with Sir W. Batten and Sir J. Minnes, so after a pitifull sermon of the young Scott, home to dinner. After dinner comes a footman of my Lord Sandwich's (my Lord being come to town last night) with a letter from my father, in which he presses me to carry on the business for Tom with his late mistress, which I am sorry to see my father do, it being so much out of our power or for his advantage, as it is clear to me it is, which I shall think of and answer in my next. So to my office all the afternoon writing orders myself to have ready against to-morrow, that I might not appear negligent to Mr. Coventry. In the evening to Sir W. Pen's, where Sir J. Minnes and Sir W. Batten, and afterwards came Sir G. Carteret. There talked about business, and afterwards to Sir W. Batten's, where we staid talking and drinking Syder, and so I went away to my office a little, and so home and to bed.

12th. Up, and to Sir W. Batten's to bid him and Sir J. Minnes adieu, they going this day towards Portsmouth, and then to Sir W. Pen's to see Sir J. Lawson, who I heard was there, where I found him the same plain man that he was, after all his success in the Straights, with which he is come loaded home. Thence to Sir G. Carteret, and with him in his coach to White Hall, and first I to see my Lord Sandwich (being come now from Hinchingbrooke), and after talking a little with him, he and I to the Duke's chamber, where Mr. Coventry and he and I into the Duke's closett and Sir J. Lawson discoursing upon business of the Navy, and particularly got his consent to the ending some difficulties in Mr. Creed's accounts. Thence to my Lord's lodgings, and with Mr. Creed to the King's Head ordinary, but people being set down, we went to two or three places; at last found some meat at a Welch cook's at Charing Cross, and here dined and our boys. After dinner to the 'Change to buy some linen for my wife, and going back met our two boys. Mine had struck down Creed's boy in the dirt, with his new suit on, and the boy taken by a gentlewoman into a house to make clean, but the poor boy was in a pitifull taking and pickle; but I basted my rogue soundly. Thence to my Lord's lodging, and Creed to his, for his papers against the Committee. I found my Lord within, and he and I went out through the garden towards the Duke's chamber, to sit upon the Tangier matters; but a lady called to my Lord out of my Lady Castlemaine's lodging, telling him that the King was there and would speak with him. My Lord could not tell what to bid me say at the Committee to excuse his absence, but that he was with the King; nor would suffer me to go into the Privy Garden (which is now a through-passage, and common), but bid me to go through some other way, which I did; so that I see he is a servant of the King's pleasures too, as well as business. So I went to the Committee, where we spent all this night attending to Sir J. Lawson's description of Tangier and the place for the Mole,

[The construction of this Mole or breakwater turned out a very costly undertaking. In April, 1663, it was found that the charge for one year's work was L13,000. In March, 1665, L36,000 had been spent upon it. The wind and sea exerted a very destructive influence over this structure, although it was very strongly built, and Colonel Norwood reported in 1668 that a breach had been made in the Mole, which cost a considerable sum to repair.]

of which he brought a very pretty draught. Concerning the making of the Mole, Mr. Cholmely did also discourse very well, having had some experience in it. Being broke up, I home by coach to Mr. Bland's, and there discoursed about sending away of the merchant ship which hangs so long on hand for Tangier. So to my Lady Batten's, and sat with her awhile, Sir W. Batten being gone out of town; but I did it out of design to get some oranges for my feast to-morrow of her, which I did. So home, and found my wife's new gown come home, and she mightily pleased with it. But I appeared very angry that there were no more things got ready against to-morrow's feast, and in that passion sat up long, and went discontented to bed.

13th. So my poor wife rose by five o'clock in the morning, before day, and went to market and bought fowls and many other things for dinner, with which I was highly pleased, and the chine of beef was down also before six o'clock, and my own jack, of which I was doubtfull, do carry it very well. Things being put in order, and the cook come, I went to the office, where we sat till noon and then broke up, and I home, whither by and by comes Dr. Clerke and his lady, his sister, and a she-cozen, and Mr. Pierce and his wife, which was all my guests. I had for them, after oysters, at first course, a hash of rabbits, a lamb, and a rare chine of beef. Next a great dish of roasted fowl, cost me about 30s., and a tart, and then fruit and cheese. My dinner was noble and enough. I had my house mighty clean and neat; my room below with a good fire in it; my dining-room above, and my chamber being made a withdrawing-chamber; and my wife's a good fire also. I find my new table very proper, and will hold nine or ten people well, but eight with great room. After dinner the women to cards in my wife's chamber, and the Dr. and Mr. Pierce in mine, because the dining-room smokes unless I keep a good charcoal fire, which I was not then provided with. At night to supper, had a good sack posset and cold meat, and sent my guests away about ten o'clock at night, both them and myself highly pleased with our management of this day; and indeed their company was very fine, and Mrs. Clerke a very witty, fine lady, though a little conceited and proud. So weary, so to bed. I believe this day's feast will cost me near L5.

14th. Lay very long in bed, till with shame forced to rise, being called up by Mr. Bland about business. He being gone I went and staid upon business at the office and then home to dinner, and after dinner staid a little talking pleasant with my wife, who tells me of another woman offered by her brother that is pretty and can sing, to which I do listen but will not appear over forward, but I see I must keep somebody for company sake to my wife, for I am ashamed she should live as she do. So to the office till 10 at night upon business, and numbering and examining part of my sea-manuscript with great pleasure, my wife sitting working by me. So home to supper and to bed.

15th. Up and to my office preparing things, by and by we met and sat Mr. Coventry and I till noon, and then I took him to dine with me, I having a wild goose roasted, and a cold chine of beef and a barrel of oysters. We dined alone in my chamber, and then he and I to fit ourselves for horseback, he having brought me a horse; and so to Deptford, the ways being very dirty. There we walked up and down the Yard and Wett Dock, and did our main business, which was to examine the proof of our new way of the call-books, which we think will be of great use. And so to horse again, and I home with his horse, leaving him to go over the fields to Lambeth, his boy at my house taking home his horse. I vexed, having left my keys in my other pocket in my chamber, and my door is shut, so that I was forced to set my boy in at the window, which done I shifted myself, and so to my office till late, and then home to supper, my mind being troubled about Field's business and my uncle's, which the term coming on I must think to follow again. So to prayers and to bed, and much troubled in mind this night in my dreams about my uncle Thomas and his son going to law with us.

16th. Lay long talking in bed with my wife. Up, and Mr. Battersby, the apothecary, coming to see me, I called for the cold chine of beef and made him eat, and drink wine, and talked, there being with us Captain Brewer, the paynter, who tells me how highly the Presbyters do talk in the coffeehouses still, which I wonder at. They being gone I walked two or three hours with my brother Tom, telling him my mind how it is troubled about my father's concernments, and how things would be with them all if it should please God that I should die, and therefore desire him to be a good husband and follow his business, which I hope he do. At noon to dinner, and after dinner my wife began to talk of a woman again, which I have a mind to have, and would be glad Pall might please us, but she is quite against having her, nor have I any great mind to it, but only for her good and to save money flung away upon a stranger. So to my office till 9 o'clock about my navy manuscripts, and there troubled in my mind more and more about my uncle's business from a letter come this day from my father that tells me that all his tenants are sued by my uncle, which will cost me some new trouble, I went home to supper and so to bed.

17th. Waked early with my mind troubled about our law matters, but it came into my mind that [sayings] of Epictetus, which did put me to a great deal of ease, it being a saying of great reason. Up to the office, and there sat Mr. Coventry, Mr. Pett, new come to town, and I. I was sorry for signing a bill and guiding Mr. Coventry to sign a bill to Mr. Creed for his pay as Deputy Treasurer to this day, though the service ended 5 or 6 months ago, which he perceiving did blot out his name afterwards, but I will clear myself to him from design in it. Sat till two o'clock and then home to dinner, and Creed with me, and after dinner, to put off my mind's trouble, I took Creed by coach and to the Duke's playhouse, where we did see "The Five Hours" entertainment again, which indeed is a very fine play, though, through my being out of order, it did not seem so good as at first; but I could discern it was not any fault in the play. Thence with him to the China alehouse, and there drank a bottle or two, and so home, where I found my wife and her brother discoursing about Mr. Ashwell's daughter, whom we are like to have for my wife's woman, and I hope it may do very well, seeing there is a necessity of having one. So to the office to write letters, and then home to supper and to bed.

18th (Lord's day). Up, and after the barber had done, and I had spoke with Mr. Smith (whom I sent for on purpose to speak of Field's business, who stands upon L250 before he will release us, which do trouble me highly), and also Major Allen of the Victualling Office about his ship to be hired for Tangier, I went to church, and thence home to dinner alone with my wife, very pleasant, and after dinner to church again, and heard a dull, drowsy sermon, and so home and to my office, perfecting my vows again for the next year, which I have now done, and sworn to in the presence of Almighty God to observe upon the respective penalties thereto annexed, and then to Sir W. Pen's (though much against my will, for I cannot bear him, but only to keep him from complaint to others that I do not see him) to see how he do, and find him pretty well, and ready to go abroad again.

19th. Up and to White Hall, and while the Duke is dressing himself I went to wait on my Lord Sandwich, whom I found not very well, and Dr. Clerke with him. He is feverish, and hath sent for Mr. Pierce to let him blood, but not being in the way he puts it off till night, but he stirs not abroad to-day. Then to the Duke, and in his closett discoursed as we use to do, and then broke up. That done, I singled out Mr. Coventry into the Matted Gallery, and there I told him the complaints I meet every day about our Treasurer's or his people's paying no money, but at the goldsmith's shops, where they are forced to pay fifteen or twenty sometimes per cent. for their money, which is a most horrid shame, and that which must not be suffered. Nor is it likely that the Treasurer (at least his people) will suffer Maynell the Goldsmith to go away with L10,000 per annum, as he do now get, by making people pay after this manner for their money. We were interrupted by the Duke, who called Mr. Coventry aside for half an hour, walking with him in the gallery, and then in the garden, and then going away I ended my discourse with Mr. Coventry. But by the way Mr. Coventry was saying that there remained nothing now in our office to be amended but what would do of itself every day better and better, for as much as he that was slowest, Sir W. Batten, do now begin to look about him and to mind business. At which, God forgive me! I was a little moved with envy, but yet I am glad, and ought to be, though it do lessen a little my care to see that the King's service is like to be better attended than it was heretofore. Thence by coach to Mr. Povy's, being invited thither by [him] came a messenger this morning from him, where really he made a most excellent and large dinner, of their variety, even to admiration, he bidding us, in a frolique, to call for what we had a mind, and he would undertake to give it us: and we did for prawns, swan, venison, after I had thought the dinner was quite done, and he did immediately produce it, which I thought great plenty, and he seems to set off his rest in this plenty and the neatness of his house, which he after dinner showed me, from room to room, so beset with delicate pictures, and above all, a piece of perspective in his closett in the low parler; his stable, where was some most delicate horses, and the very-racks painted, and mangers, with a neat leaden painted cistern, and the walls done with Dutch tiles, like my chimnies. But still, above all things, he bid me go down into his wine-cellar, where upon several shelves there stood bottles of all sorts of wine, new and old, with labells pasted upon each bottle, and in the order and plenty as I never saw books in a bookseller's shop; and herein, I observe, he puts his highest content, and will accordingly commend all that he hath, but still they deserve to be so. Here dined with me Dr. Whore and Mr. Scawen. Therewith him and Mr. Bland, whom we met by the way, to my Lord Chancellor's, where the

King was to meet my Lord Treasurer, &c., many great men, to settle the revenue of Tangier. I staid talking awhile there, but the King not coming I walked to my brother's, where I met my cozen Scotts (Tom not being at home) and sent for a glass of wine for them, and having drunk we parted, and I to the Wardrobe talking with Mr. Moore about my law businesses, which I doubt will go ill for want of time for me to attend them. So home, where I found Mrs. Lodum speaking with my wife about her kinswoman which is offered my wife to come as a woman to her. So to the office and put things in order, and then home and to bed, it being my great comfort that every day I understand more and more the pleasure of following of business and the credit that a man gets by it, which I hope at last too will end in profit. This day, by Dr. Clerke, I was told the occasion of my Lord Chesterfield's going and taking his lady (my Lord Ormond's daughter) from Court. It seems he not only hath been long jealous of the Duke of York, but did find them two talking together, though there were others in the room, and the lady by all opinions a most good, virtuous woman. He, the next day (of which the Duke was warned by somebody that saw the passion my Lord Chesterfield was in the night before), went and told the Duke how much he did apprehend himself wronged, in his picking out his lady of the whole Court to be the subject of his dishonour; which the Duke did answer with great calmness, not seeming to understand the reason of complaint, and that was all that passed but my Lord did presently pack his lady into the country in Derbyshire, near the Peake; which is become a proverb at Court, to send a man's wife to the Devil's arse a' Peake, when she vexes him. This noon I did find out Mr. Dixon at Whitehall, and discoursed with him about Mrs. Wheatly's daughter for a wife for my brother Tom, and have committed it to him to enquire the pleasure of her father and mother concerning it. I demanded L300.

20th. Up betimes and to the office, where all the morning. Dined at home, and Mr. Deane of Woolwich with me, talking about the abuses of the yard. Then to the office about business all the afternoon with great pleasure, seeing myself observed by every body to be the only man of business of us all, but Mr. Coventry. So till late at night, and then home to supper and bed.

21st. Up early leaving my wife very ill in bed . . . and to my office till eight o'clock, there coming Ch. Pepys

> [Charles Pepys was second son of Thomas Pepys, elder brother of
> Samuel's father. Samuel paid part of the legacy to Charles and his
> elder brother Thomas on May 25th, 1664.]

to demand his legacy of me, which I denied him upon good reason of his father and brother's suing us, and so he went away. Then came Commissioner Pett, and he and I by agreement went to Deptford, and after a turn or two in the yard, to Greenwich, and thence walked to Woolwich. Here we did business, and I on board the Tangier-merchant, a ship freighted by us, that has long lain on hand in her despatch to Tangier, but is now ready for sailing. Back, and dined at Mr. Ackworth's, where a pretty dinner, and she a pretty, modest woman; but above all things we saw her Rocke, which is one of the finest things done by a woman that ever I saw. I must have my wife to see it. After dinner on board the Elias, and found the timber brought by her from the forest of Deane to be exceeding good. The Captain gave each of us two barrels of pickled oysters put up for the Queen mother. So to the Dock again, and took in Mrs. Ackworth and another gentlewoman, and carried them to London, and at the Globe tavern, in Eastcheap, did give them a glass of wine, and so parted. I home, where I found my wife ill in bed all day, and her face swelled with pain. My Will has received my last two quarters salary, of which I am glad. So to my office till late and then home, and after the barber had done, to bed.

22nd. To the office, where Sir W. Batten and Sir J. Minnes are come from Portsmouth. We sat till dinner time. Then home, and Mr. Dixon by agreement came to dine, to give me an account of his success with Mr. Wheatly for his daughter for my brother; and in short it is, that his daughter cannot fancy my brother because of his imperfection in his speech, which I am sorry for, but there the business must die, and we must look out for another. There came in also Mrs. Lodum, with an answer from her brother Ashwell's daughter, who is likely to come to me, and with her my wife's brother, and I carried Commissioner Pett in with me, so I feared want of victuals, but I had a good dinner, and mirth, and so rose and broke up, and with the rest of the officers to Mr. Russell's buriall, where we had wine and rings, and a great and good company of aldermen and the livery of the Skinners' Company. We went to St. Dunstan's in the East church, where a sermon, but I staid not, but went home, and, after writing letters, I took coach to Mr. Povy's, but he not within I left a letter there of Tangier business, and so to my Lord's, and there find him not sick, but expecting his fit to-night of an ague. Here was Sir W. Compton, Mr. Povy, Mr. Bland, Mr. Gawden and myself; we were very busy about getting provisions sent forthwith to Tangier, fearing that by Mr. Gawden's neglect they might want bread. So among other ways thought of to supply them I was empowered by the Commissioners of Tangier that were present to write to Plymouth and direct Mr. Lanyon to take up vessels great or small to the quantity of 150 tons, and fill them with bread of Mr. Gawden's lying ready there for Tangier, which they undertake to bear me out in, and to see the freight paid. This I did. About 10 o'clock we broke up, and my Lord's fit was coming upon him, and so we parted, and I with Mr. Creed, Mr. Pierce, Win. Howe and Captn. Ferrers, who was got almost drunk this afternoon, and was mighty capricious and ready to fall out with any body, supped together in the little chamber that was mine heretofore upon some fowls sent by Mr. Shepley, so we were very merry till 12 at night, and so away, and I lay with Mr. Creed at his lodgings, and slept well.

23rd. Up and hastened him in despatching some business relating to Tangier, and I away homewards, hearing that my Lord had a bad fit to-night, called at my brother's, and found him sick in bed, of a pain in the sole of one of his feet, without swelling, knowing not how it came, but it will not suffer him to stand these two days. So to Mr. Moore, and Mr. Lovell, our proctor, being there, discoursed of my law business. Thence to Mr. Grant, to bid him come for money for Mr. Barlow, and he and I to a coffee-house, where Sir J. Cutler was;

[Citizen and grocer of London; most severely handled by Pope. Two statues were erected to his memory—one in the College of Physicians, and the other in the Grocers' Hall. They were erected and one removed (that in the College of Physicians) before Pope stigmatized "sage Cutler." Pope says that Sir John Cutler had an only daughter; in fact, he had two: one married to Lord Radnor; the other, mentioned afterwards by Pepys, the wife of Sir William Portman.—B.]

and in discourse, among other things, he did fully make it out that the trade of England is as great as ever it was, only in more hands; and that of all trades there is a greater number than ever there was, by reason of men taking more 'prentices, because of their having more money than heretofore. His discourse was well worth hearing. Coming by Temple Bar I bought "Audley's Way to be Rich," a serious pamphlett and some good things worth my minding. Thence homewards, and meeting Sir W. Batten, turned back again to a coffee-house, and there drunk more till I was almost sick, and here much discourse, but little to be learned, but of a design in the north of a rising, which is discovered, among some men of condition, and they sent for up. Thence to the 'Change, and so home with him by coach, and I to see how my wife do, who is pretty well again, and so to dinner to Sir W. Batten's to a cod's head, and so to my office, and after stopping to see Sir W. Pen, where was Sir J. Lawson and his lady and daughter, which is pretty enough, I came back to my office, and there set to business pretty late, finishing the margenting my Navy-Manuscript. So home and to bed.

24th. Lay pretty long, and by lying with my sheet upon my lip, as I have of old observed it, my upper lip was blistered in the morning. To the office all the morning, sat till noon, then to the Exchange to look out for a ship for Tangier, and delivered my manuscript to be bound at the stationer's. So to dinner at home, and then down to Redriffe, to see a ship hired for Tangier, what readiness she was in, and found her ready to sail. Then home, and so by coach to Mr. Povy's, where Sir W. Compton, Mr. Bland, Gawden, Sir J. Lawson and myself met to settle the victualling of Tangier for the time past, which with much ado we did, and for a six months' supply more. So home in Mr. Gawden's coach, and to my office till late about business, and find that it is business that must and do every day bring me to something.—[In earlier days Pepys noted for us each few pounds or shillings of graft which he annexed at each transaction in his office.]—So home to supper and to bed.

25th (Lord's day). Lay till 9 a-bed, then up, and being trimmed by the barber, I walked towards White Hall, calling upon Mr. Moore, whom I found still very ill of his ague. I discoursed with him about my Lord's estate against I speak with my Lord this day. Thence to the King's Head ordinary at Charing Cross, and sent for Mr. Creed, where we dined very finely and good company, good discourse. I understand the King of France is upon consulting his divines upon the old question, what the power of the Pope is? and do intend to make war against him, unless he do right him for the wrong his Embassador received;

[On the 20th of August, the Duc de Crequi, then French ambassador at Rome, was insulted by the Corsican armed police, a force whose ignoble duty it was to assist the Sbirri; and the pope, Alexander *vii.*, at first refused reparation for the affront offered to the French. Louis, as in the case of D'Estrades, took prompt measures. He ordered the papal nuncio forthwith to quit France; he seized upon Avignon, and his army prepared to enter Italy. Alexander found it necessary to submit. In fulfilment of a treaty signed at Pisa in 1664, Cardinal Chigi, the pope's nephew, came to Paris, to tender the pope's apology to Louis. The guilty individuals were punished; the Corsicans banished for ever from the Roman States; and in front of the guard-house which they had occupied a pyramid was erected, bearing an inscription which embodied the pope's apology. This pyramid Louis permitted Clement IX. to destroy on his accession.-B.]

and banish the Cardinall Imperiall,

[Lorenzo Imperiali, of Genoa. He had been appointed Governor of Rome by Innocent X., and he had acted in that capacity at the time of the tumult.—B.]

which I understand this day is not meant the Cardinall belonging or chosen by the Emperor, but the name of his family is Imperiali. Thence to walk in the Park, which we did two hours, it being a pleasant sunshine day though cold. Our discourse upon the rise of most men that we know, and observing them to be the results of chance, not policy, in any of them, particularly Sir J. Lawson's, from his declaring against Charles Stuart in the river of Thames, and for the Rump. Thence to my Lord, who had his ague fit last night, but is now pretty well, and I staid talking with him an hour alone in his chamber, about sundry publique and private matters. Among others, he wonders what the project should be of the Duke's going down to Portsmouth just now with his Lady, at this time of the year: it being no way, we think, to increase his popularity, which is not great; nor yet safe to do it, for that reason, if it would have any such effect. By and by comes in my Lady Wright, and so I went away, end after talking with Captn. Ferrers, who tells me of my Lady Castlemaine's and Sir Charles Barkeley being the great favourites at Court, and growing every day more and more; and that upon a late dispute between my Lord Chesterfield, that is the Queen's Lord Chamberlain, and Mr. Edward Montagu, her Master of the Horse, who should have the precedence in taking the Queen's upperhand abroad out of the house, which Mr. Montagu challenges, it was given to my Lord Chesterfield. So that I perceive he goes down the wind in honour as well as every thing else, every day. So walk to my brother's and talked with him, who tells me that this day a messenger is come, that tells us how Collonel Honiwood, who was well yesterday at Canterbury, was flung by his horse in getting up, and broke his scull, and so is dead. So home and to the office, despatching some business, and so home to supper, and then to prayers and to bed.

26th. Up and by water with Sir W. Batten to White Hall, drinking a glass of wormewood wine at the Stillyard, and so up to the Duke, and with the rest of the officers did our common service; thence to my Lord Sandwich's, but he was in bed, and had a bad fit last night, and so I went to, Westminster Hall, it being Term time, it troubling me to think that I should have any business there to trouble myself and thoughts with. Here I met with Monsieur Raby, who is lately come from France. [He] tells me that my Lord Hinchingbroke and his brother do little improve there, and are much neglected in their habits and other things; but I do believe he hath a mind to go over as their tutour, and so I am not apt to believe what he says therein. But I had a great deal of very good discourse with him, concerning the difference between the French and the Pope, and the occasion, which he told me very particularly, and to my great content; and of most of the chief affairs of France, which I did enquire: and that the King is a most excellent Prince, doing all business himself; and that it is true he hath a mistress, Mademoiselle La Valiere, one of the Princess Henriette's women, that he courts for his pleasure every other day, but not so as to make him neglect his publique affairs. He tells me how the King do carry himself nobly to the relations of the dead Cardinall,—[Cardinal Mazarin died March 9th, 1661.]—and will not suffer one pasquill to come forth against him; and that he acts by what directions he received from him before his death. Having discoursed long with him, I took him by coach and set him down at my Lord Crew's, and myself went and dined at Mr. Povy's, where Orlando Massam, Mr. Wilks, a Wardrobe man, myself and Mr. Gawden, and had just such another dinner as I had the other day there. But above all things I do the most admire his piece of perspective especially, he opening me the closett door, and there I saw that there is nothing but only a plain picture hung upon the wall. After dinner Mr. Gauden and I to settle the business of the Tangier victualling, which I perceive none of them yet have hitherto understood but myself. Thence by coach to White Hall, and met upon the Tangier Commission, our greatest business the discoursing of getting things ready for my Lord Rutherford to go about the middle of March next, and a proposal of Sir J. Lawson's and Mr. Cholmely's concerning undertaking the Mole, which is referred to another time. So by coach home, being melancholy, overcharged with business, and methinks I fear that I have some ill offices done to Mr. Coventry, or else he observes that of late I have not despatched business so as I did use to do, which I confess I do acknowledge. But it may be it is but my fear only, he is not so fond as he used to be of me. But I do believe that Sir W. Batten has made him believe that I do too much crow upon having his kindness, and so he may on purpose to countenance him seem a little more strange to me, but I will study hard to bring him back again to the same degree of kindness. So home, and after a little talk with my wife, to the office, and did a great deal of business there till very late, and then home to supper and to bed.

27th. Up and to the office, where sat till two o'clock, and then home to dinner, whither by and by comes Mr. Creed, and he and I talked of our Tangier business, and do find that there is nothing in the world done with true integrity, but there is design along with it, as in my Lord Rutherford, who designs to have the profit of victualling of the garrison himself, and others to have the benefit of making the Mole, so that I am almost discouraged from coming any more to the Committee, were it not that it will possibly hereafter bring me to some acquaintance of great men. Then to the office again, where very busy till past ten at night, and so home to supper and to bed. I have news this day from Cambridge that my brother hath had his bachelor's cap put on; but that which troubles me is, that he hath the pain of the stone, and makes bloody water with great pain, it beginning just as mine did. I pray God help him.

28th. Up and all the morning at my office doing business, and at home seeing my painters' work measured. So to dinner and abroad with my wife, carrying her to Unthank's, where she alights, and I to my Lord Sandwich's, whom I find missing his ague fit to-day, and is pretty well, playing at dice (and by this I see how time and example may alter a man; he being now acquainted with all sorts of pleasures and vanities, which heretofore he never thought of nor loved, nor, it may be, hath allowed) with Ned Pickering and his page Laud. Thence to the Temple to my cozen Roger Pepys, and thence to Serjt. Bernard to advise with him and retain him against my uncle, my heart and head being very heavy with the business. Thence to Wotton's, the shoemaker, and there bought another pair of new boots, for the other I bought my last would not fit me, and here I drank with him and his wife, a pretty woman, they broaching a vessel of syder a-purpose for me. So home, and there found my wife come home, and seeming to cry; for bringing home in a coach her new ferrandin

[Ferrandin, which was sometimes spelt farendon, was a stuff made of silk mixed with some other material, like what is now called poplin. Both mohair and farendon are generally cheap materials; for in the case of Manby v. Scott, decided in the Exchequer Chamber in 1663, and reported in the first volume of "Modern Reports," the question being as to the liability of a husband to pay for goods supplied against his consent to his wife, who had separated from him, Mr. Justice Hyde (whose judgment is most amusing) observes, in putting various supposed cases, that "The wife will have a velvet gown and a satin petticoat, and the husband thinks a mohair or farendon for a gown, and watered tabby for a petticoat, is as fashionable, and fitter for her quality."—B.]

waistecoate, in Cheapside, a man asked her whether that was the way to the Tower; and while she was answering him, another, on the other side, snatched away her bundle out of her lap, and could not be recovered, but ran away with it, which vexes me cruelly, but it cannot be helped. So to my office, and there till almost 12 at night with Mr. Lewes, learning to understand the manner of a purser's account, which is very hard and little understood by my fellow officers, and yet mighty necessary. So at last with great content broke up and home to supper and bed.

29th. Lay chiding, and then pleased with my wife in bed, and did consent to her having a new waistcoate made her for that which she lost yesterday. So to the office, and sat all the morning. At noon dined with Mr. Coventry at Sir J. Minnes his lodgings, the first time that ever I did yet, and am sorry for doing it now, because of obliging me to do the like to him again. Here dined old Captn. Marsh of the Tower with us. So to visit Sir W. Pen, and then to the office, and there late upon business by myself, my wife being sick to-day. So home and to supper and to bed.

30th. A solemn fast for the King's murther, and we were forced to keep it more than we would have done, having forgot to take any victuals into the house. I to church in the forenoon, and Mr. Mills made a good sermon upon David's heart smiting him for cutting off the garment of Saul.

> [Samuel, chap. xxiv. v. 5, "And it came to pass afterward, that David's heart smote him, because he bad cut off Saul's skirt."]

Home, and whiled away some of the afternoon at home talking with my wife. So to my office, and all alone making up my month's accounts, which to my great trouble I find that I am got no further than L640. But I have had great expenses this month. I pray God the next may be a little better, as I hope it will. In the evening my manuscript is brought home handsomely bound, to my full content; and now I think I have a better collection in reference to the Navy, and shall have by the time I have filled it, than any of my predecessors. So home and eat something such as we have, bread and butter and milk, and so to bed.

31st. Up and to my office, and there we sat till noon. I home to dinner, and there found my plate of the Soverayne with the table to it come from Mr. Christopher Pett, of which I am very glad. So to dinner late, and not very good, only a rabbit not half roasted, which made me angry with my wife. So to the office, and there till late, busy all the while. In the evening examining my wife's letter intended to my Lady, and another to Mademoiselle; they were so false spelt that I was ashamed of them, and took occasion to fall out about them with my wife, and so she wrote none, at which, however, I was, sorry, because it was in answer to a letter of Madam about business. Late home to supper and to bed.

Diary of Samuel Pepys.
February
1662-1663

February 1st (Lord's day). Up and to church, where Mr. Mills, a good sermon, and so home and had a good dinner with my wife, with which I was pleased to see it neatly done, and this troubled me to think of parting with Jane, that is come to be a very good cook. After dinner walked to my Lord Sandwich, and staid with him in the chamber talking almost all the afternoon, he being not yet got abroad since his sickness. Many discourses we had; but, among others, how Sir R. Bernard is turned out of his Recordership of Huntingdon by the Commissioners for Regulation, &c., at which I am troubled, because he, thinking it is done by my Lord Sandwich, will act some of his revenge, it is likely, upon me in my business, so that I must cast about me to get some other counsel to rely upon. In the evening came Mr. Povey and others to see my Lord, and they gone, my Lord and I and Povey fell to the business of Tangier, as to the victualling, and so broke up, and I, it being a fine frost, my boy lighting me I walked home, and after supper up to prayers, and then alone with my wife and Jane did fall to tell her what I did expect would become of her since, after so long being my servant, she had carried herself so as to make us be willing to put her away, and desired God to bless [her], but bid her never to let me hear what became of her, for that I could never pardon ingratitude. So I to bed, my mind much troubled for the poor girl that she leaves us, and yet she not submitting herself, for some words she spoke boldly and yet I believe innocently and out of familiarity to her mistress about us weeks ago, I could not recall my words that she should stay with me. This day Creed and I walking in White Hall garden did see the King coming privately from my Lady Castlemaine's; which is a poor thing for a Prince to do; and I expressed my sense of it to Creed in terms which I should not have done, but that I believe he is trusty in that point.

2nd. Up, and after paying Jane her wages, I went away, because I could hardly forbear weeping, and she cried, saying it was not her fault that she went away, and indeed it is hard to say what it is, but only her not desiring to stay that she do now go. By coach with Sir J. Minnes and Sir W. Batten to the Duke; and after discourse as usual with him in his closett, I went to my Lord's: the King and Duke being gone to chappell, it being collar-day, it being Candlemas-day; where I staid with him a while until towards noon, there being Jonas Moore talking about some mathematical businesses, and thence I walked at noon to Mr. Povey's, where Mr. Gawden met me, and after a neat and plenteous dinner as is usual, we fell to our victualling business, till Mr. Gawden and I did almost fall out, he defending himself in the readiness of his provision, when I know that the ships everywhere stay for them. Thence Mr. Povey and I walked to White Hall, it being a great frost still, and after a turn in the Park seeing them slide, we met at the Committee for Tangier, a good full Committee, and agreed how to proceed in the dispatching of my Lord Rutherford, and treating about this business of Mr. Cholmely and Sir J. Lawson's proposal for the Mole. Thence with Mr. Coventry down to his chamber, where among other discourse he did tell me how he did make it not only his desire, but as his greatest pleasure, to make himself an interest by doing business truly and justly, though he thwarts others greater than himself, not striving to make himself friends by addresses; and by this he thinks and observes he do live as contentedly (now he finds himself secured from fear of want), and, take one time with another, as void of fear or cares, or more, than they that (as his own termes were) have quicker pleasures and sharper agonies than he. Thence walking with Mr. Creed homewards we turned into a house and drank a cup of Cock ale and so parted, and I to the Temple, where at my cozen Roger's chamber I met Madam Turner, and after a little stay led her home and there left her, she and her daughter having been at the play to-day at the Temple, it being a revelling time with them.

[The revels were held in the Inner Temple Hall. The last revel in any of the Inns of Court was held in the Inner Temple in 1733.]

Thence called at my brother's, who is at church, at the buriall of young Cumberland, a lusty young man. So home and there found Jane gone, for which my wife and I are very much troubled, and myself could hardly forbear shedding tears for fear the poor wench should come to any ill condition after her being so long with me. So to my office and setting papers to rights, and then home to supper and to bed. This day at my Lord's I sent for Mr. Ashwell, and his wife came to me, and by discourse I perceive their daughter is very fit for my turn if my family may be as much for hers, but I doubt it will be to her loss to come to me for so small wages, but that will be considered of.

3rd. To the office all the morning, at noon to dinner, where Mr. Creed dined with me, and Mr. Ashwell, with whom after dinner I discoursed concerning his daughter coming to live with us. I find that his daughter will be very fit, I think, as any for our turn, but the conditions I know not what they will be, he leaving it wholly to her, which will be agreed on a while hence when my wife sees her. After an hour's discourse after dinner with them, I to my office again, and there about business of the office till late, and then home to supper and to bed.

4th. Up early and to Mr. Moore, and thence to Mr. Lovell about my law

business, and from him to Paul's School, it being Apposition-day there. I heard some of their speeches, and they were just as schoolboys' used to be, of the seven liberal sciences; but I think not so good as ours were in our time. Away thence and to Bow Church, to the Court of Arches, where a judge sits, and his proctors about him in their habits, and their pleadings all in Latin. Here I was sworn to give a true answer to my uncle's libells, and so paid my fee for swearing, and back again to Paul's School, and went up to see the head forms posed in Latin, Greek, and Hebrew, but I think they did not answer in any so well as we did, only in geography they did pretty well: Dr. Wilkins and Outram were examiners. So down to the school, where Dr. Crumlum did me much honour by telling many what a present I had made to the school, shewing my Stephanus, in four volumes, cost me L4 10s. He also shewed us, upon my desire, an old edition of the grammar of Colett's, where his epistle to the children is very pretty; and in rehearsing the creed it is said "borne of the cleane Virgin Mary." Thence with Mr. Elborough (he being all of my old acquaintance that I could meet with here) to a cook's shop to dinner, but I found him a fool, as he ever was, or worse. Thence to my cozen Roger Pepys and Mr. Phillips about my law businesses, which stand very bad, and so home to the office, where after doing some business I went home, where I found our new mayde Mary, that is come in Jane's place.

5th. Up and to the office, where we sat all the morning, and then home to dinner, and found it so well done, above what I did expect from my mayde Susan, now Jane is gone, that I did call her in and give her sixpence. Thence walked to the Temple, and there at my cozen Roger Pepys's chamber met by appointment with my uncle Thomas and his son Thomas, and there I shewing them a true state of my uncle's estate as he has left it with the debts, &c., lying upon it, we did come to some quiett talk and fair offers against an agreement on both sides, though I do offer quite to the losing of the profit of the whole estate for 8 or 10 years together, yet if we can gain peace, and set my mind at a little liberty, I shall be glad of it. I did give them a copy of this state, and we are to meet tomorrow with their answer. So walked home, it being a very great frost still, and to my office, there late writing letters of office business, and so home to supper and to bed.

6th. Up and to my office about business, examining people what they could swear against Field, and the whole is, that he has called us cheating rogues and cheating knaves, for which we hope to be even with him. Thence to Lincoln's Inn Fields; and it being too soon to go to dinner, I walked up and down, and looked upon the outside of the new theatre, now a-building in Covent Garden, which will be very fine. And so to a bookseller's in the Strand, and there bought Hudibras again, it being certainly some ill humour to be so against that which all the world cries up to be the example of wit; for which I am resolved once again to read him, and see whether I can find it or no. So to Mr. Povy's, and there found them at dinner, and dined there, there being, among others, Mr. Williamson, Latin Secretary, who, I perceive, is a pretty knowing man and a scholler, but, it may be, thinks himself to be too much so. Thence, after dinner, to the Temple, to my cozen Roger Pepys, where met us my uncle Thomas and his son; and, after many high demands, we at last came to a kind of agreement upon very hard terms, which are to be prepared in writing against Tuesday next. But by the way promising them to pay my cozen Mary's' legacys at the time of her marriage, they afterwards told me that she was already married, and married very well, so that I must be forced to pay it in some time. My cozen Roger was so sensible of our coming to agreement that he could not forbear weeping, and, indeed, though it is very hard, yet I am glad to my heart that we are like to end our trouble. So we parted for to-night, and I to my Lord Sandwich and there staid, there being a Committee to sit upon the contract for the Mole, which I dare say none of us that were there understood, but yet they agreed of things as Mr. Cholmely and Sir J. Lawson demanded, who are the undertakers, and so I left them to go on to agree, for I understood it not. So home, and being called by a coachman who had a fare in him, he carried me beyond the Old Exchange, and there set down his fare, who would not pay him what was his due, because he carried a stranger with him, and so after wrangling he was fain to be content with 6d., and being vexed the coachman would not carry me home a great while, but set me down there for the other 6d., but with fair words he was willing to it, and so I came home and to my office, setting business in order, and so to supper and to bed, my mind being in disorder as to the greatness of this day's business that I have done, but yet glad that my trouble therein is like to be over.

7th. Up and to my office, whither by agreement Mr. Coventry came before the time of sitting to confer about preparing an account of the extraordinary charge of the Navy since the King's coming, more than is properly to be applied and called the Navy charge. So by and by we sat, and so till noon. Then home to dinner, and in the afternoon some of us met again upon something relating to the victualling, and thence to my writing of letters late, and making my Alphabet to my new Navy book very pretty. And so after writing to my father by the post about the endeavour to come to a composition with my uncle, though a very bad one, desiring him to be contented therewith, I went home to supper and to bed.

8th (Lord's day). Up, and it being a very great frost, I walked to White Hall, and to my Lord Sandwich's by the fireside till chapel time, and so to chappell, where there preached little Dr. Duport, of Cambridge, upon Josiah's words,—"But I and my house, we will serve the Lord." But though a great scholler, he made the most flat dead sermon, both for matter and manner of delivery, that ever I heard, and very long beyond his hour, which made it worse. Thence with Mr. Creed to the King's Head ordinary, where we dined well, and after dinner Sir Thomas Willis and another stranger, and Creed and I, fell a-talking; they of the errours and corruption of the Navy, and great expence thereof, not knowing who I was, which at last I did undertake to confute, and disabuse them: and they took it very well, and I hope it was to good purpose, they being Parliament-men. By and by to my Lord's, and with him a good while talking upon his want of money, and ways of his borrowing some, &c., and then by other visitants, I withdrew and away, Creed and I and Captn. Ferrers to the Park, and there walked finely, seeing people slide, we talking all the while; and Captn. Ferrers telling me, among other Court passages, how about a month ago, at a ball at Court, a child was dropped by one of the ladies in dancing, but nobody knew who, it being taken up by somebody in their handkercher. The next morning all the Ladies of Honour appeared early at Court for their vindication, so that nobody could tell whose this mischance should be. But it seems Mrs. Wells

[Winifred Wells, maid of honour to the Queen, who figures in the "Grammont Memoirs." The king is supposed to have been father of the child. A similar adventure is told of Mary Kirke (afterwards married to Sir Thomas Vernon), who figures in the "Grammont Memoirs" as Miss Warmestre.]

fell sick that afternoon, and hath disappeared ever since, so that it is concluded that it was her. Another story was how my Lady Castlemaine, a few days since, had Mrs. Stuart to an entertainment, and at night began a frolique that they two must be married, and married they were, with ring and all other ceremonies of church service, and ribbands and a sack posset in bed, and flinging the stocking; but in the close, it is said that my Lady Castlemaine, who was the bridegroom, rose, and the King came and took her place with pretty Mrs. Stuart. This is said to be very true. Another story was how Captain Ferrers and W. Howe both have often, through my Lady Castlemaine's window, seen her go to bed and Sir Charles Barkeley in the chamber all the while with her. But the other day Captn. Ferrers going to Sir Charles to excuse his not being so timely at his arms the other day, Sir Charles swearing and cursing told him before a great many other gentlemen that he would not suffer any man of the King's Guards to be absent from his lodging a night without leave. Not but that, says he, once a week or so I know a gentleman must go . . ., and I am not for denying it to any man, but however he shall be bound to ask leave to lie abroad, and to give account of his absence, that we may know what guard the King has to depend upon. The little Duke of Monmouth, it seems, is ordered to take place of all Dukes, and so to follow Prince Rupert now, before the Duke of Buckingham, or any else. Whether the wind and the cold did cause it or no I know not, but having been this day or two mightily troubled with an itching all over my body' which I took to be a louse or two that might bite me, I found this afternoon that all my body is inflamed, and my face in a sad redness and swelling and pimpled, so that I was before we had done walking not only sick but ashamed of myself to see myself so changed in my countenance, so that after we had thus talked we parted and I walked home with much ado (Captn. Ferrers with me as far as Ludgate Hill towards Mr. Moore at the Wardrobe), the ways being so full of ice and water by peoples' trampling. At last got home and to bed presently, and had a very bad night of it, in great pain in my stomach, and in great fever.

9th. Could not rise and go to the Duke, as I should have done with the rest, but keep my bed and by the Apothecary's advice, Mr. Battersby, I am to sweat soundly, and that will carry all this matter away which nature would of itself eject, but they will assist nature, it being some disorder given the blood, but by what I know not, unless it be by my late quantitys of Dantzic-girkins that I have eaten. In the evening came Sir J. Minnes and Sir W. Batten to see me, and Sir J. Minnes advises me to the same thing, but would not have me take anything from the apothecary, but from him, his Venice treacle being better than the others, which I did consent to and did anon take and fell into a great sweat, and about 10 or 11 o'clock came out of it and shifted myself, and slept pretty well alone, my wife lying in the red chamber above.

10th. In the morning most of my disease, that is, itching and pimples, were gone. In the morning visited by Mr. Coventry and others, and very glad I am to see that I am so much inquired after and my sickness taken notice of as I did. I keep my bed all day and sweat again at night, by which I expect to be very well to-morrow. This evening Sir W. Warren came himself to the door and left a letter and box for me, and went his way. His letter mentions his giving me and my wife a pair of gloves; but, opening the box, we found a pair of plain white gloves for my hand, and a fair state dish of silver, and cup, with my arms, ready cut upon them, worth, I believe, about L18, which is a very noble present, and the best I ever had yet. So after some contentful talk with my wife, she to bed and I to rest.

11th. Took a clyster in the morning and rose in the afternoon. My wife and I dined on a pullet and I eat heartily, having eat nothing since Sunday but water gruel and posset drink, but must needs say that our new maid Mary has played her part very well in her readiness and discretion in attending me, of which I am very glad. In the afternoon several people came to see me, my uncle Thomas, Mr. Creed, Sir J. Minnes (who has been, God knows to what end, mighty kind to me and careful of me in my sickness). At night my wife read Sir H. Vane's tryall to me, which she began last night, and I find it a very excellent thing, worth reading, and him to have been a very wise man. So to supper and to bed.

12th. Up and find myself pretty well, and so to the office, and there all the morning. Rose at noon and home to dinner in my green chamber, having a good fire. Thither there came my wife's brother and brought Mary Ashwell with him, whom we find a very likely person to please us, both for person, discourse, and other qualitys. She dined with us, and after dinner went away again, being agreed to come to us about three weeks or a month hence. My wife and I well pleased with our choice, only I pray God I may be able to maintain it. Then came an old man from Mr. Povy, to give me some advice about his experience in the stone, which I [am] beholden to him for, and was well pleased with it, his chief remedy being Castle soap in a posset. Then in the evening to the office, late writing letters and my Journall since Saturday, and so home to supper and to bed.

13th. Lay very long with my wife in bed talking with great pleasure, and then rose. This morning Mr. Cole, our timber merchant, sent me five couple of ducks. Our maid Susan is very ill, and so the whole trouble of the house lies upon our maid Mary, who do it very contentedly and mighty well, but I am sorry she is forced to it. Dined upon one couple of ducks to-day, and after dinner my wife and I by coach to Tom's, and I to the Temple to discourse with my cozen Roger Pepys about my law business, and so back again, it being a monstrous thaw after the long great frost, so that there is no passing but by coach in the streets, and hardly that. Took my wife home, and I to my office. Find myself pretty well but fearful of cold, and so to my office, where late upon business; Mr. Bland sitting with me, talking of my Lord Windsor's being come home from Jamaica, unlooked-for; which makes us think that these young Lords are not fit to do any service abroad, though it is said that he could not have his health there, but hath razed a fort of the King of Spain upon Cuba, which is considerable, or said to be so, for his honour. So home to supper and to bed. This day I bought the second part of Dr. Bates's Elenchus, which reaches to the fall of Richard, and no further, for which I am sorry. This evening my wife had a great mind to choose Valentines against to-morrow, I Mrs. Clerke, or Pierce, she Mr. Hunt or Captain Ferrers, but I would not because of getting charge both to me for mine and to them for her, which did not please her.

14th. Up and to my office, where we met and sate all the morning, only Mr. Coventry, which I think is the first or second time he has missed since he came to the office, was forced to be absent. So home to dinner, my wife and I upon a couple of ducks, and then by coach to the Temple, where my uncle Thomas, and his sons both, and I, did meet at my cozen Roger's and there sign and seal to an agreement. Wherein I was displeased at nothing but my cozen Roger's insisting upon my being obliged to settle upon them as the will do all my uncle's estate that he has left, without power of selling any for the payment of debts, but I would not yield to it without leave of selling, my Lord Sandwich himself and my cozen Thos. Pepys being judges of the necessity thereof, which was done. One thing more that troubles me was my being forced to promise to give half of what personal estate could be found more than L372, which I reported to them, which though I do not know it to be less than what we really have found, yet he would have been glad to have been at liberty for that, but at last I did agree to it under my own handwriting on the backside of the report I did make and did give them of the estate, and have taken a copy of it upon the backside of one that I have. All being done I took the father and his son Thos. home by coach, and did pay them L30, the arrears of the father's annuity, and with great seeming love parted, and I presently to bed, my head akeing mightily with the hot dispute I did hold with my cozen Roger and them in the business.

15th (Lord's day). This morning my wife did wake me being frighted with the noise I made in my sleep, being a dream that one of our sea maisters did desire to see the

St. John's Isle of my drawing, which methought I showed him, but methought he did handle it so hard that it put me to very horrid pain . . . . Which what a strange extravagant dream it was. So to sleep again and lay long in bed, and then trimmed by the barber, and so sending Will to church, myself staid at home, hanging up in my green chamber my picture of the Soveraigne, and putting some things in order there. So to dinner, to three more ducks and two teals, my wife and I. Then to Church, where a dull sermon, and so home, and after walking about the house awhile discoursing with my wife, I to my office there to set down something and to prepare businesses for tomorrow, having in the morning read over my vows, which through sicknesse I could not do the last Lord's day, and not through forgetfulness or negligence, so that I hope it is no breach of my vow not to pay my forfeiture. So home, and after prayers to bed, talking long with my wife and teaching her things in astronomy.

16th. Up and by coach with Sir W. Batten and Sir J. Minnes to White Hall, and, after we had done our usual business with the Duke, to my Lord Sandwich and by his desire to Sir W. Wheeler, who was brought down in a sedan chair from his chamber, being lame of the gout, to borrow L1000 of him for my Lord's occasions, but he gave me a very kind denial that he could not, but if any body else would, he would be bond with my Lord for it. So to Westminster Hall, and there find great expectation what the Parliament will do, when they come two days hence to sit again, in matters of religion. The great question is, whether the Presbyters will be contented to have the Papists have the same liberty of conscience with them, or no, or rather be denied it themselves: and the Papists, I hear, are very busy designing how to make the Presbyters consent to take their liberty, and to let them have the same with them, which some are apt to think they will. It seems a priest was taken in his vests officiating somewhere in Holborn the other day, and was committed by Secretary Morris, according to law; and they say the Bishop of London did give him thanks for it. Thence to my Lord Crew's and dined there, there being much company, and the above-said matter is now the present publique discourse. Thence about several businesses to Mr. Phillips my attorney, to stop all proceedings at law, and so to the Temple, where at the Solicitor General's I found Mr. Cholmely and Creed reading to him the agreement for him to put into form about the contract for the Mole at Tangier, which is done at 13s. the Cubical yard, though upon my conscience not one of the Committee, besides the parties concerned, do understand what they do therein, whether they give too much or too little. Thence with Mr. Creed to see Mr. Moore, who continues sick still, within doors, and here I staid a good while after him talking of all the things either business or no that came into my mind, and so home and to see Sir W. Pen, and sat and played at cards with him, his daughter, and Mrs. Rooth, and so to my office a while, and then home and to bed.

17th. Up and to my office, and there we sat all the morning, and at noon my wife being gone to Chelsey with her brother and sister and Mrs. Lodum, to see the wassell at the school, where Mary Ashwell is, I took home Mr. Pett and he dined with me all alone, and much discourse we had upon the business of the office, and so after dinner broke up and with much ado, it raining hard, which it has not done a great while now, but only frost a great while, I got a coach and so to the Temple, where discoursed with Mr. W. Montagu about borrowing some money for my Lord, and so by water (where I have not been a good while through cold) to Westminster to Sir W. Wheeler's, whom I found busy at his own house with the Commissioners of Sewers, but I spoke to him about my Lord's business of borrowing money, and so to my Lord of Sandwich, to give him an account of all, whom I found at cards with Pickering; but he made an end soon: and so all alone, he and I, after I had given him an account, he told me he had a great secret to tell me, such as no flesh knew but himself, nor ought; which was this: that yesterday morning Eschar, Mr. Edward Montagu's man, did come to him from his master with some of the Clerks of the Exchequer, for my Lord to sign to their books for the Embassy money; which my Lord very civilly desired not to do till he had spoke with his master himself. In the afternoon, my Lord and my Lady Wright being at cards in his chamber, in comes Mr. Montagu; and desiring to speak with my Lord at the window in his chamber, he begun to charge my Lord with the greatest ingratitude in the world: that he that had received his earldom, garter, L4000 per annum, and whatever he is in the world, from him, should now study him all the dishonour that he could; and so fell to tell my Lord, that if he should speak all that he knew of him, he could do so and so. In a word, he did rip up all that could be said that was unworthy, and in the basest terms they could be spoken in. To which my Lord answered with great temper, justifying himself, but endeavouring to lessen his heat, which was a strange temper in him, knowing that he did owe all he hath in the world to my Lord, and that he is now all that he is by his means and favour. But my Lord did forbear to increase the quarrel, knowing that it would be to no good purpose for the world to see a difference in the family; but did allay him so as that he fell to weeping. And after much talk (among other things Mr. Montagu telling him that there was a fellow in the town, naming me, that had done ill offices, and that if he knew it to be so, he would have him cudgelled) my Lord did promise him that, if upon account he saw that there was not many tradesmen unpaid, he would sign the books; but if there was, he could not bear with taking too great a debt upon him. So this day he sent him an account, and a letter assuring him there was not above L200 unpaid; and so my Lord did sign to the Exchequer books. Upon the whole, I understand fully what a rogue he is, and how my Lord do think and will think of him for the future; telling me that thus he has served his father my Lord Manchester, and his whole family, and now himself: and which is worst, that he hath abused, and in speeches every day do abuse, my Lord Chancellor, whose favour he hath lost; and hath no friend but Sir H. Bennet, and that (I knowing the rise of the friendship) only from the likeness of their pleasures, and acquaintance, and concernments, they have in the same matters of lust and baseness; for which, God forgive them! But he do flatter himself, from promises of Sir H. Bennet, that he shall have a pension of L2000 per annum, and be made an Earl. My Lord told me he expected a challenge from him, but told me there was no great fear of him, for there was no man lies under such an imputation as he do in the business of Mr. Cholmely, who, though a simple sorry fellow, do brave him and struts before him with the Queen, to the sport and observation of the whole Court. He did keep my Lord at the window, thus reviling and braving him above an hour, my Lady Wright being by; but my Lord tells me she could not hear every word, but did well know what their discourse was; she could hear enough to know that. So that he commands me to keep it as the greatest secret in the world, and bids me beware of speaking words against Mr. Montagu, for fear I should suffer by his passion thereby. After he had told me this I took coach and home, where I found my wife come home and in bed with her sister in law in the chamber with her, she not being able to stay to see the wassel, being so ill . . ., which I was sorry for. Hither we sent for her sister's viall, upon which she plays pretty well for a girl, but my expectation is much deceived in her, not only for that, but in her spirit, she being I perceive a very subtle witty jade, and one that will give her husband trouble enough as little as she is, whereas I took her heretofore for a very child and a simple fool. I played also, which I have not done this long time before upon any instrument, and at last broke up and I to my office a little while, being fearful of being too much taken with musique, for fear of returning to my old dotage thereon, and so neglect my business as I used to do. Then home and to bed. Coming home I brought Mr. Pickering as far as the Temple, who tells me the story is very true of a child being dropped at the ball at Court; and that the King had it in his closett a week after, and did dissect it; and making great sport of it, said that in his opinion it must have been a month and three hours old; and that, whatever others think, he hath the greatest loss (it being a boy, as he says), that hath lost a subject by the business. He tells me, too, that the other story, of my Lady Castlemaine's and Stuart's marriage, is certain, and that it was in order to the King's coming to Stuart, as is believed generally. He tells me that Sir H. Bennet is a Catholique, and how all the Court almost is changed to the worse since his coming in, they being afeard of him. And that the Queen-Mother's Court is now the greatest of all; and that our own Queen hath little or no company come to her, which I know also to be very true, and am sorry to see it.

18th. Up, leaving my wife sick as last night in bed. I to my office all the morning, casting up with Captain Cocke their accounts of 500 tons of hemp brought from Riga, and bought by him and partners upon account, wherein are many things worth my knowledge. So at noon to dinner, taking Mr. Hater with me because of losing them, and in the afternoon he and I alone at the office, finishing our account of the extra charge of the Navy, not properly belonging to the Navy, since the King's coming in to Christmas last; and all extra things being abated, I find that the true charge of the Navy to that time hath been after the rate of L374,743 a-year. I made an end by eleven o'clock at night, and so home to bed almost weary. This day the Parliament met again, after their long prorogation; but I know not any thing what they have done, being within doors all day.

19th. Up and to my office, where abundance of business all the morning. Dined by my wife's bedside, she not being yet well. We fell out almost upon my discourse of delaying the having of Ashwell, where my wife believing that I have a mind to have Pall, which I have not, though I could wish she did deserve to be had. So to my office, where by and by we sat, this afternoon being the first we have met upon a great while, our times being changed because of the parliament sitting. Being rose, I to my office till twelve at night, drawing out copies of the overcharge of the Navy, one to send to Mr. Coventry early to-morrow. So home and to bed, being weary, sleepy, and my eyes begin to fail me, looking so long by candlelight upon white paper. This day I read the King's speech to the Parliament yesterday; which is very short, and not very obliging; but only telling them his desire to have a power of indulging tender consciences, not that he will yield to have any mixture in the uniformity of the Church's discipline; and says the same for the Papists, but declares against their ever being admitted to have any offices or places of trust in the kingdom; but, God knows, too many have.

20th. Up and by water with Commissioner Pett to Deptford, and there looked over the yard, and had a call, wherein I am very highly pleased with our new manner of call-books, being my invention. Thence thinking to have gone down to Woolwich in the Charles pleasure boat, but she run aground, it being almost low water, and so by oars to the town, and there dined, and then to the yard at Mr. Ackworth's, discoursing with the officers of the yard about their stores of masts, which was our chief business, and having done something therein, took boat and to the pleasure boat, which was come down to fetch us back, and I could have been sick if I would in going, the wind being very fresh, but very pleasant it was, and the first time I have sailed in any one of them. It carried us to Cuckold's Point, and so by oars to the Temple, it raining hard, where missed speaking with my cosen Roger, and so walked home and to my office; there spent the night till bed time, and so home to supper and to bed.

21st. Up and to the office, where Sir J. Minnes (most of the rest being at the Parliament-house), all the morning answering petitions and other business. Towards noon there comes a man in as if upon ordinary business, and shows me a writ from the Exchequer, called a Commission of Rebellion, and tells me that I am his prisoner in Field's business; which methought did strike me to the heart, to think that we could not sit in the middle of the King's business. I told him how and where we were employed, and bid him have a care; and perceiving that we were busy, he said he would, and did withdraw for an hour: in which time Sir J. Minnes took coach and to Court, to see what he could do from thence; and our solicitor against Field came by chance and told me that he would go and satisfy the fees of the Court, and would end the business. So he went away about that, and I staid in my closett, till by and by the man and four more of his fellows came to know what I would do; I told them stay till I heard from the King or my Lord Chief Baron, to both whom I had now sent. With that they consulted, and told me that if I would promise to stay in the house they would go and refresh themselves, and come again, and know what answer I had: so they away, and I home to dinner, whither by chance comes Mr. Hawley and dined with me. Before I had dined, the bayleys come back again with the constable, and at the office knock for me, but found me not there; and I hearing in what manner they were come, did forbear letting them know where I was; so they stood knocking and enquiring for me. By and by at my parler-window comes Sir W. Batten's Mungo, to tell me that his master and lady would have me come to their house through Sir J. Minnes's lodgings, which I could not do; but, however, by ladders, did get over the pale between our yards, and so to their house, where I found them (as they have reason) to be much concerned for me, my lady especially. The fellows staid in the yard swearing with one or two constables, and some time we locked them into the yard, and by and by let them out again, and so kept them all the afternoon, not letting them see me, or know where I was. One time I went up to the top of Sir W. Batten's house, and out of one of their windows spoke to my wife out of one of ours; which methought, though I did it in mirth, yet I was sad to think what a sad thing it would be for me to be really in that condition. By and by comes Sir J. Minnes, who (like himself and all that he do) tells us that he can do no good, but that my Lord Chancellor wonders that we did not cause the seamen to fall about their ears: which we wished we could have done without our being seen in it; and Captain Grove being there, he did give them some affront, and would have got some seamen to have drubbed them, but he had not time, nor did we think it fit to have done it, they having executed their commission; but there was occasion given that he did draw upon one of them and he did complain that Grove had pricked him in the breast, but no hurt done; but I see that Grove would have done our business to them if we had bid him. By and by comes Mr. Clerke, our solicitor, who brings us a release from our adverse atturney, we paying the fees of the commission, which comes to five marks, and pay the charges of these fellows, which are called the commissioners, but are the most rake-shamed rogues that ever I saw in my life; so he showed them this release, and they seemed satisfied, and went away with him to their atturney to be paid by him. But before they went, Sir W. Batten and my lady did begin to taunt them, but the rogues answered them as high as themselves, and swore they would come again, and called me rogue and rebel, and they would bring the sheriff and untile his house, before he should harbour a rebel in his house, and that they would be here again shortly. Well, at last they went away, and I by advice took occasion to go abroad, and walked through the street to show myself among the neighbours, that they might not think worse than the business is. Being met by Captn. Taylor and Bowry, whose ship we have hired for Tangier, they walked along with me to Cornhill talking about their business, and after some difference about their prices we agreed, and so they would have me to a tavern, and there I drank one glass of wine and discoursed of something about freight of a ship that may bring me a little money, and so broke up, and I home to Sir W. Batten's again, where Sir J. Lawson, Captain Allen, Spragg, and several others, and all our discourse about the disgrace done to our office to be liable to this trouble, which we must get removed. Hither comes Mr. Clerke by and by, and tells me that he hath paid the fees of the Court for the commission; but the men are not contented with under; L5 for their charges, which he will not give them, and therefore advises me not to stir abroad till Monday that he comes or sends to me again, whereby I shall not be able to go to White Hall to the Duke of York, as I ought. Here I staid vexing, and yet pleased to see every body, man and woman, my Lady and Mr. Turner especially, for me, till 10 at night; and so home, where my people are mightily surprized to see this business, but it troubles me not very much, it being nothing touching my particular person or estate. Being in talk to-day with Sir W. Batten he tells me that little is done yet in the Parliament-house, but only this day it was moved and ordered that all the members of the House do subscribe to the renouncing of the Covenant, which is thought will try some of them. There is also a bill brought in for the wearing of nothing but cloth or stuffs of our own manufacture, and is likely to be passed. Among other talk this evening, my lady did speak concerning Commissioner Pett's calling the present King bastard, and other high words heretofore; and Sir W. Batten did tell us, that he did give the Duke or Mr. Coventry an account of that and other like matters in writing under oath, of which I was ashamed, and for which I was sorry, but I see there is an absolute hatred never to be altered there, and Sir J. Minnes, the old coxcomb, has got it by the end, which troubles me for the sake of the King's service, though I do truly hate the expressions laid to him. To my office and set down this day's journall, and so home with my mind out of order, though not very sad with it, but ashamed for myself something, and for the honour of the office much more. So home and to bed.

22d (Lord's day). Lay long in bed and went not out all day; but after dinner to Sir W. Batten's and Sir W. Pen's, where discoursing much of yesterday's trouble and scandal; but that which troubled me most was Sir J. Minnes coming from Court at night, and instead of bringing great comfort from thence (but I expected no better from him), he tells me that the Duke and Mr. Coventry make no great matter of it. So at night discontented to prayers, and to bed.

23d. Up by times; and not daring to go by land, did (Griffin going along with me for fear), slip to White Hall by water; where to Mr. Coventry, and, as we used to do, to the Duke; the other of my fellows being come. But we said nothing of our business, the Duke being sent for to the King, that he could not stay to speak with us. This morning came my Lord Windsor to kiss the Duke's hand, being returned from Jamaica. He tells the Duke, that from such a degree of latitude going thither he begun to be sick, and was never well till his coming so far back again, and then presently begun to be well. He told the Duke of their taking the fort of St. Jago, upon Cuba, by his men; but, upon the whole, I believe that he did matters like a young lord, and was weary of being upon service out of his own country, where he might have pleasure. For methought it was a shame to see him this very afternoon, being the first day of his coming to town, to be at a playhouse. Thence to my Lord Sandwich, who though he has been abroad again two or three days is falling ill again, and is let blood this morning, though I hope it is only a great cold that he has got. It was a great trouble to me (and I had great apprehensions of it) that my Lord desired me to go to Westminster Hall, to the Parliament-house door, about business; and to Sir Wm. Wheeler, which I told him I would do, but durst not go for fear of being taken by these rogues; but was forced to go to White Hall and take boat, and so land below the Tower at the Iron-gate; and so the back way over Little Tower Hill; and with my cloak over my face, took one of the watermen along with me, and staid behind a wall in the New-buildings behind our garden, while he went to see whether any body stood within the Merchants' Gate, under which we pass to go into our garden, and there standing but a little dirty boy before the gate, did make me quake and sweat to think he might be a Trepan. But there was nobody, and so I got safe into the garden, and coming to open my office door, something behind it fell in the opening, which made me start. So that God knows in what a sad condition I should be in if I were truly in the condition that many a poor man is for debt: and therefore ought to bless God that I have no such reall reason, and to endeavour to keep myself, by my good deportment and good husbandry, out of any such condition. At home I found Mr. Creed with my wife, and so he dined with us, I finding by a note that Mr. Clerke in my absence hath left here, that I am free; and that he hath stopped all matters in Court; I was very glad of it, and immediately had a light thought of taking pleasure to rejoice my heart, and so resolved to take my wife to a play at Court to-night, and the rather because it is my birthday, being this day thirty years old, for which let me praise God. While my wife dressed herself, Creed and I walked out to see what play was acted to-day, and we find it "The Slighted Mayde." But, Lord! to see that though I did know myself to be out of danger, yet I durst not go through the street, but round by the garden into Tower Street. By and by took coach, and to the

Duke's house, where we saw it well acted, though the play hath little good in it, being most pleased to see the little girl dance in boy's apparel, she having very fine legs, only bends in the hams, as I perceive all women do. The play being done, we took coach and to Court, and there got good places, and saw "The Wilde Gallant," performed by the King's house, but it was ill acted, and the play so poor a thing as I never saw in my life almost, and so little answering the name, that from beginning to end, I could not, nor can at this time, tell certainly which was the Wild Gallant. The King did not seem pleased at all, all the whole play, nor any body else, though Mr. Clerke whom we met here did commend it to us. My Lady Castlemaine was all worth seeing tonight, and little Steward.—[Mrs. Stuart]—Mrs. Wells do appear at Court again, and looks well; so that, it may be, the late report of laying the dropped child to her was not true. It being done, we got a coach and got well home about 12 at night. Now as my mind was but very ill satisfied with these two plays themselves, so was I in the midst of them sad to think of the spending so much money and venturing upon the breach of my vow, which I found myself sorry for, I bless God, though my nature would well be contented to follow the pleasure still. But I did make payment of my forfeiture presently, though I hope to save it back again by forbearing two plays at Court for this one at the Theatre, or else to forbear that to the Theatre which I am to have at Easter. But it being my birthday and my day of liberty regained to me, and lastly, the last play that is likely to be acted at Court before Easter, because of the Lent coming in, I was the easier content to fling away so much money. So to bed. This day I was told that my Lady Castlemaine hath all the King's Christmas presents, made him by the peers, given to her, which is a most abominable thing; and that at the great ball she was much richer in jewells than the Queen and Duchess put both together.

24th. Slept hard till 8 o'clock, then waked by Mr. Clerke's being come to consult me about Field's business, which we did by calling him up to my bedside, and he says we shall trounce him. Then up, and to the office, and at 11 o'clock by water to Westminster, and to Sir W. Wheeler's about my Lord's borrowing of money that I was lately upon with him, and then to my Lord, who continues ill, but will do well I doubt not. Among other things, he tells me that he hears the Commons will not agree to the King's late declaration, nor will yield that the Papists have any ground given them to raise themselves up again in England, which I perceive by my Lord was expected at Court. Thence home again by water presently, and with a bad dinner, being not looked for, to the office, and there we sat, and then Captn. Cocke and I upon his hemp accounts till 9 at night, and then, I not very well, home to supper and to bed. My late distemper of heat and itching being come upon me again, so that I must think of sweating again as I did before.

25th. Up and to my office, where with Captain Cocke making an end of his last night's accounts till noon, and so home to dinner, my wife being come in from laying out about L4 in provision of several things against Lent. In the afternoon to the Temple, my brother's, the Wardrobe, to Mr. Moore, and other places, called at about small businesses, and so at night home to my office and then to supper and to bed. The Commons in Parliament, I hear, are very high to stand to the Act of Uniformity, and will not indulge the Papists (which is endeavoured by the Court Party) nor the Presbyters.

26th. Up and drinking a draft of wormewood wine with Sir W. Batten at the Steelyard, he and I by water to the Parliament-house: he went in, and I walked up and down the Hall. All the news is the great odds yesterday in the votes between them that are for the Indulgence to the Papists and Presbyters, and those that are against it, which did carry it by 200 against 30. And pretty it is to consider how the King would appear to be a stiff Protestant and son of the, Church; and yet would appear willing to give a liberty to these people, because of his promise at Breda. And yet all the world do believe that the King would not have this liberty given them at all. Thence to my Lord's, who, I hear, has his ague again, for which I am sorry, and Creed and I to the King's Head ordinary, where much good company. Among the rest a young gallant lately come from France, who was full of his French, but methought not very good, but he had enough to make him think himself a wise man a great while. Thence by water from the New Exchange home to the Tower, and so sat at the office, and then writing letters till 11 at night. Troubled this evening that my wife is not come home from Chelsey, whither she is gone to see the play at the school where Ashwell is, but she came at last, it seems, by water, and tells me she is much pleased with Ashwell's acting and carriage, which I am glad of. So home and to supper and bed.

27th. Up and to my office, whither several persons came to me about office business. About 11 o'clock, Commissioner Pett and I walked to Chyrurgeon's Hall (we being all invited thither, and promised to dine there); where we were led into the Theatre; and by and by comes the reader, Dr. Tearne, with the Master and Company, in a very handsome manner: and all being settled, he begun his lecture, this being the second upon the kidneys, ureters, &c., which was very fine; and his discourse being ended, we walked into the Hall, and there being great store of company, we had a fine dinner and good learned company, many Doctors of Phisique, and we used with extraordinary great respect. Among other observables we drank the King's health out of a gilt cup given by King Henry *viii.* to this Company, with bells hanging at it, which every man is to ring by shaking after he hath drunk up the whole cup. There is also a very excellent piece of the King, done by Holbein, stands up in the Hall, with the officers of the Company kneeling to him to receive their Charter. After dinner Dr. Scarborough took some of his friends, and I went along with them, to see the body alone, which we did, which was a lusty fellow, a seaman, that was hanged for a robbery. I did touch the dead body with my bare hand: it felt cold, but methought it was a very unpleasant sight. It seems one Dillon, of a great family, was, after much endeavours to have saved him, hanged with a silken halter this Sessions (of his own preparing), not for honour only, but it seems, it being soft and sleek, it do slip close and kills, that is, strangles presently: whereas, a stiff one do not come so close together, and so the party may live the longer before killed. But all the Doctors at table conclude, that there is no pain at all in hanging, for that it do stop the circulation of the blood; and so stops all sense and motion in an instant. Thence we went into a private room, where I perceive they prepare the bodies, and there were the kidneys, ureters [&c.], upon which he read to-day, and Dr. Scarborough upon my desire and the company's did show very clearly the manner of the disease of the stone and the cutting and all other questions that I could think of . . . how the water [comes] into the bladder through the three skins or coats just as poor Dr. Jolly has heretofore told me. Thence with great satisfaction to me back to the

Company, where I heard good discourse, and so to the afternoon Lecture upon the heart and lungs, &c., and that being done we broke up, took leave, and back to the office, we two, Sir W. Batten, who dined here also, being gone before. Here late, and to Sir W. Batten's to speak upon some business, where I found Sir J. Minnes pretty well fuddled I thought: he took me aside to tell me how being at my Lord Chancellor's to-day, my Lord told him that there was a Great Seal passing for Sir W. Pen, through the impossibility of the Comptroller's duty to be performed by one man; to be as it were joynt-comptroller with him, at which he is stark mad; and swears he will give up his place, and do rail at Sir W. Pen the cruellest; he I made shift to encourage as much as I could, but it pleased me heartily to hear him rail against him, so that I do see thoroughly that they are not like to be great friends, for he cries out against him for his house and yard and God knows what. For my part, I do hope, when all is done, that my following my business will keep me secure against all their envys. But to see how the old man do strut, and swear that he understands all his duty as easily as crack a nut, and easier, he told my Lord Chancellor, for his teeth are gone; and that he understands it as well as any man in England; and that he will never leave to record that he should be said to be unable to do his duty alone; though, God knows, he cannot do it more than a child. All this I am glad to see fall out between them and myself safe, and yet I hope the King's service well done for all this, for I would not that should be hindered by any of our private differences. So to my office, and then home to supper and to bed.

28th. Waked with great pain in my right ear (which I find myself much subject to) having taken cold. Up and to my office, where we sat all the morning, and I dined with Sir W. Batten by chance, being in business together about a bargain of New England masts. Then to the Temple to meet my uncle Thomas, who I found there, but my cozen Roger not being come home I took boat and to Westminster, where I found him in Parliament this afternoon. The House have this noon been with the King to give him their reasons for refusing to grant any indulgence to Presbyters or Papists; which he, with great content and seeming pleasure, took, saying, that he doubted not but he and they should agree in all things, though there may seem a difference in judgement, he having writ and declared for an indulgence: and that he did believe never prince was happier in a House of Commons, than he was in them. Thence he and I to my Lord Sandwich, who continues troubled with his cold. Our discourse most upon the outing of Sir R. Bernard, and my Lord's being made Recorder of Huntingdon in his stead, which he seems well contented with, saying, that it may be for his convenience to have the chief officer of the town dependent upon him, which is very true. Thence he and I to the Temple, but my uncle being gone we parted, and I walked home, and to my office, and at nine o'clock had a good supper of an oxe's cheek, of my wife's dressing and baking, and so to my office again till past eleven at night, making up my month's account, and find that I am at a stay with what I was last, that is L640. So home and to bed. Coming by, I put in at White Hall, and at the Privy Seal I did see the docquet by which Sir W. Pen is made the Comptroller's assistant, as Sir J. Minnes told me last night, which I must endeavour to prevent.

After oysters, at first course, a hash of rabbits, a lamb
At last we pretty good friends

Before I sent my boy out with them, I beat him for a lie
Dr. Calamy is this day sent to Newgate for preaching
Eat a mouthful of pye at home to stay my stomach
Familiarity with her other servants is it that spoils them all
Feverish, and hath sent for Mr. Pierce to let him blood
Found him a fool, as he ever was, or worse
Goes down the wind in honour as well as every thing else
Had a good supper of an oxe's cheek
Hanged with a silken halter
How highly the Presbyters do talk in the coffeehouses still
I and she never were so heartily angry in our lives as to-day
Ill humour to be so against that which all the world cries up
Lady Castlemaine hath all the King's Christmas presents
Lay chiding, and then pleased with my wife in bed
Lay very long with my wife in bed talking with great pleasure
Liability of a husband to pay for goods supplied his wife
Many thousands in a little time go out of England
Money, which sweetens all things
Most flat dead sermon, both for matter and manner of delivery
Much discourse, but little to be learned
Nor will yield that the Papists have any ground given them
Nothing in the world done with true integrity
Once a week or so I know a gentleman must go . . . .
Pain of the stone, and makes bloody water with great pain
Rabbit not half roasted, which made me angry with my wife
Scholler, but, it may be, thinks himself to be too much so
See how time and example may alter a man
Servant of the King's pleasures too, as well as business
So home, and mighty friends with my wife again
So neat and kind one to another
Sorry for doing it now, because of obliging me to do the like
Talk very highly of liberty of conscience
The house was full of citizens, and so the less pleasant
There is no passing but by coach in the streets, and hardly that
These young Lords are not fit to do any service abroad
They were so false spelt that I was ashamed of them
Vexed at my wife's neglect in leaving of her scarf
Wine, new and old, with labells pasted upon each bottle
With much ado in an hour getting a coach home
Yet it was her fault not to see that I did take them

THE DIARY OF SAMUEL PEPYS M.A. F.R.S.

CLERK OF THE ACTS AND SECRETARY TO THE ADMIRALTY

Transcribed from the shorthand manuscript in the PEPYSIAN *library Magdalene College Cambridge by the Rev.* MYNORS *bright* M.A. *Late fellow and President of the College*

(Unabridged)

WITH LORD BRAYBROOKE'S NOTES

EDITED WITH ADDITIONS BY

HenryB. Wheatley F.S.A.

Diary of Samuel Pepys.
March & April
1662-1663

March 1st (Lord's day). Up and walked to White Hall, to the Chappell, where preached one Dr. Lewes, said heretofore to have been a great witt; but he read his sermon every word, and that so brokenly and so low, that nobody could hear at any distance, nor I anything worth hearing that sat near. But, which was strange, he forgot to make any prayer before sermon, which all wonder at, but they impute it to his forgetfulness. After sermon a very fine anthem; so I up into the house among the courtiers, seeing the fine ladies, and, above all, my Lady Castlemaine, who is above all, that only she I can observe for true beauty. The King and Queen being set to dinner I went to Mr. Fox's, and there dined with him. Much genteel company, and, among other things, I hear for certain that peace is concluded between the King of France and the Pope; and also I heard the reasons given by our Parliament yesterday to the King why they dissent from him in matter of Indulgence, which are very good quite through, and which I was glad to hear. Thence to my Lord Sandwich, who continues with a great cold, locked up; and, being alone, we fell into discourse of my uncle the Captain's death and estate, and I took the opportunity of telling my Lord how matters stand, and read his will, and told him all, what a poor estate he hath left, at all which he wonders strangely, which he may well do. Thence after singing some new tunes with W. Howe I walked home, whither came Will. Joyce, whom I have not seen here a great while, nor desire it a great while again, he is so impertinent a coxcomb, and yet good natured, and mightily concerned for my brother's late folly in his late wooing at the charge to no purpose, nor could in any probability a it. He gone, we all to bed, without prayers, it being washing day to-morrow.

2nd. Up early and by water with Commissioner Pett to Deptford, and there took the Jemmy yacht (that the King and the Lords virtuosos built the other day) down to Woolwich, where we discoursed of several matters both there and at the Ropeyard, and so to the yacht again, and went down four or five miles with extraordinary pleasure, it being a fine day, and a brave gale of wind, and had some oysters brought us aboard newly taken, which were excellent, and ate with great pleasure. There also coming into the river two Dutchmen, we sent a couple of men on board and bought three Hollands cheeses, cost 4d. a piece, excellent cheeses, whereof I had two and Commissioner Pett one. So back again to Woolwich, and going aboard the Hulke to see the manner of the iron bridles, which we are making of for to save cordage to put to the chain, I did fall from the shipside into the ship (Kent), and had like to have broke my left hand, but I only sprained some of my fingers, which, when I came ashore I sent to Mrs. Ackworth for some balsam, and put to my hand, and was pretty well within a little while after. We dined at the White Hart with several officers with us, and after dinner went and saw the Royal James brought down to the stern of the Docke (the main business we came for), and then to the Ropeyard, and saw a trial between Riga hemp and a sort of Indian grass, which is pretty strong, but no comparison between it and the other for strength, and it is doubtful whether it will take tarre or no. So to the yacht again, and carried us almost to London, so by our oars home to the office, and thence Mr. Pett and I to Mr. Grant's coffee-house, whither he and Sir J. Cutler came to us and had much discourse, mixed discourse, and so broke up, and so home where I found my poor wife all alone at work, and the house foul, it being washing day, which troubled me, because that tomorrow I must be forced to have friends at dinner. So to my office, and then home to supper and to bed.

3rd (Shrove Tuesday). Up and walked to the Temple, and by promise calling Commissioner Pett, he and I to White Hall to give Mr. Coventry an account of what we did yesterday. Thence I to the Privy Seal Office, and there got a copy of Sir W. Pen's grant to be assistant to Sir J. Minnes, Comptroller, which, though there be not much in it, yet I intend to stir up Sir J. Minnes to oppose, only to vex Sir W. Pen. Thence by water home, and at noon, by promise, Mrs. Turner and her daughter, and Mrs. Morrice, came along with Roger Pepys to dinner. We were as merry as I could be, having but a bad dinner for them; but so much the better, because of the dinner which I must have at the end of this month. And here Mrs. The. shewed me my name upon her breast as her Valentine, which will cost me 20s. After dinner I took them down into the wine-cellar, and broached my tierce of claret for them. Towards the evening we parted, and I to the office awhile, and then home to supper and to bed, the sooner having taken some cold yesterday upon the water, which brings me my usual pain. This afternoon Roger Pepys tells me, that for certain the King is for all this very highly incensed at the Parliament's late opposing the Indulgence; which I am sorry for, and fear it will breed great discontent.

4th. Lay long talking with my wife about ordering things in our family, and then rose and to my office, there collecting an alphabet for my Navy Manuscript, which, after a short dinner, I returned to and by night perfected to my great content. So to other business till 9 at night, and so home to supper and to bed.

5th. Rose this morning early, only to try with intention to begin my last summer's course in rising betimes. So to my office a little, and then to Westminster by coach with Sir J. Minnes and Sir W. Batten, in our way talking of Sir W. Pen's business of his patent, which I think I have put a stop to wholly, for Sir J. Minnes swears he will never consent to it. Here to the Lobby, and spoke with my cozen Roger, who is going to Cambridge to-morrow. In the Hall I do hear that the Catholiques are in great hopes for all this, and do set hard upon the King to get Indulgence. Matters, I hear, are all naught in Ireland, and that the Parliament has voted, and the people, that is, the Papists, do cry out against the Commissioners sent by the King; so that they say the English interest will be lost there. Thence I went to see my Lord Sandwich, who I found very ill, and by his cold being several nights hindered from sleep, he is hardly able to open his eyes, and is very weak and sad upon it, which troubled me much. So after talking with Mr. Cooke, whom I found there, about his folly for looking and troubling me and other friends in getting him a place (that is, storekeeper of the Navy at Tangier) before there is any such thing, I returned to the Hall, and thence back with the two knights home again by coach, where I found Mr. Moore got abroad, and dined with me, which I was glad to see, he having not been able to go abroad a great while. Then came in Mr. Hawley and dined with us, and after dinner I left them, and to the office, where we sat late, and I do find that I shall meet with nothing to oppose my growing great in the office but Sir W. Pen, who is now well again, and comes into the office very brisk, and, I think, to get up his time that he has been out of the way by being mighty diligent at the office, which, I pray God, he may be, but I hope by mine to weary him out, for I am resolved to fall to business as hard as I can drive, God giving me health. At my office late, and so home to supper and to bed.

6th. Up betimes, and about eight o'clock by coach with four horses, with Sir J. Minnes and Sir W. Batten, to Woolwich, a pleasant day. There at the yard we consulted and ordered several matters, and thence to the rope yard and did the like, and so into Mr. Falconer's, where we had some fish, which we brought with us, dressed; and there dined with us his new wife, which had been his mayde, but seems to be a genteel woman, well enough bred and discreet. Thence after dinner back to Deptford, where we did as before, and so home, good discourse in our way, Sir J. Minnes being good company, though a simple man enough as to the business of his office, but we did discourse at large again about Sir W. Pen's patent to be his assistant, and I perceive he is resolved never to let it pass. To my office, and thence to Sir W. Batten's, where Major Holmes was lately come from the Streights, but do tell me strange stories of the faults of Cooper his master, put in by me, which I do not believe, but am sorry to hear and must take some course to have him removed, though I believe that the Captain is proud, and the fellow is not supple enough to him. So to my office again to set down my Journall, and so home and to bed. This evening my boy Waynman's brother was with me, and I did tell him again that I must part with the boy, for I will not keep him. He desires my keeping him a little longer till he can provide for him, which I am willing for a while to do. This day it seems the House of Commons have been very high against the Papists, being incensed by the stir which they make for their having an Indulgence; which, without doubt, is a great folly in them to be so hot upon at this time, when they see how averse already the House have showed themselves from it. This evening Mr. Povy was with me at my office, and tells me that my Lord Sandwich is this day so ill that he is much afeard of him, which puts me to great pain, not more for my own sake than for his poor family's.

7th. Up betimes, and to the office, where some of us sat all the morning. At noon Sir W. Pen began to talk with me like a counterfeit rogue very kindly about his house and getting bills signed for all our works, but he is a cheating fellow, and so I let him talk and answered nothing. So we parted. I to dinner, and there met The. Turner, who is come on foot in a frolique to beg me to get a place at sea for John, their man, which is a rogue; but, however, it may be, the sea may do him good in reclaiming him, and therefore I will see what I can do. She dined with me; and after dinner I took coach, and carried her home; in our way, in Cheapside, lighting and giving her a dozen pair of white gloves as my Valentine. Thence to my Lord Sandwich, who is gone to Sir W. Wheeler's for his more quiet being, where he slept well last night, and I took him very merry, playing at cards, and much company with him. So I left him, and Creed and I to Westminster Hall, and there walked a good while. He told me how for some words of my Lady Gerard's

[Jane, wife of Lord Gerard (see ante, January 1st, 1662-63). The king had previously put a slight upon Lady Gerard, probably at the instigation of Lady Castlemaine, as the two ladies were not friends. On the 4th of January of this same year Lady Gerard had given a supper to the king and queen, when the king withdrew from the party and proceeded to the house of Lady Castlemaine, and remained there throughout the evening (see Steinman's "Memoir of Barbara, Duchess of Cleveland," 1871, p. 47).]

against my Lady Castlemaine to the Queen, the King did the other day affront her in going out to dance with her at a ball, when she desired it as the ladies do, and is since forbid attending the Queen by the King; which is much talked of, my Lord her husband being a great favourite. Thence by water home and to my office, wrote by the post and so home to bed.

8th (Lord's day). Being sent to by Sir J. Minnes to know whether I would go with him to White Hall to-day, I rose but could not get ready before he was gone, but however I walked thither and heard Dr. King, Bishop of Chichester, make a good and eloquent sermon upon these words, "They that sow in tears, shall reap in joy." Thence (the chappell in Lent being hung with black, and no anthem sung after sermon, as at other times), to my Lord Sandwich at Sir W. Wheeler's. I found him out of order, thinking himself to be in a fit of an ague, but in the afternoon he was very cheery. I dined with Sir William, where a good but short dinner, not better than one of mine commonly of a Sunday. After dinner up to my Lord, there being Mr. Kumball. My Lord, among other discourse, did tell us of his great difficultys passed in the business of the Sound, and of his receiving letters from the King there, but his sending them by Whetstone was a great folly; and the story how my Lord being at dinner with Sydney, one of his fellow plenipotentiarys and his mortal enemy, did see Whetstone, and put off his hat three times to him, but the fellow would not be known, which my Lord imputed to his coxcombly humour (of which he was full), and bid Sydney take notice of him too, when at the very time he had letters in his pocket from the King, as it proved afterwards. And Sydney afterwards did find it out at Copenhagen, the Dutch Commissioners telling him how my Lord Sandwich had hired one of their ships to carry back Whetstone to Lubeck, he being come from Flanders from the King. But I cannot but remember my Lord's aequanimity in all these affairs with admiration. Thence walked home, in my way meeting Mr. Moore, with whom I took a turn or two in the street among the drapers in Paul's Churchyard, talking of business, and so home to bed.

9th. Up betimes, to my office, where all the morning. About noon Sir J. Robinson, Lord Mayor, desiring way through the garden from the Tower, called in at the office and there invited me (and Sir W. Pen, who happened to be in the way) to dinner, which we did; and there had a great Lent dinner of fish, little flesh. And thence he and I in his coach, against my will (for I am resolved to shun too great fellowship with him) to White Hall, but came too late, the Duke having been with our fellow officers before we came, for which I was sorry. Thence he and I to walk one turn in the Park, and so home by coach, and I to my office, where late, and so home to supper and bed. There dined with us to-day Mr. Slingsby, of the Mint, who showed us all the new pieces both gold and silver (examples of them all), that are made for the King, by Blondeau's' way; and compared them with those made for Oliver. The pictures of the latter made by Symons, and of the King by one Rotyr, a German, I think, that dined with us also. He extolls those of Rotyr's above the others; and, indeed, I think they are the better, because the sweeter of the two; but, upon my word, those of the Protector are more like in my mind, than the King's, but both very well worth seeing. The crowns of Cromwell are now sold, it seems, for 25s. and 30s. apiece.

10th. Up and to my office all the morning, and great pleasure it is to be doing my business betimes. About noon Sir J. Minnes came to me and staid half an hour with me in my office talking about his business with Sir W. Pen, and (though with me an old doter) yet he told me freely how sensible he is of Sir W. Pen's treachery in this business, and what poor ways he has taken all along to ingratiate himself by making Mr. Turner write out things for him and then he gives them to the Duke, and how he directed him to give Mr. Coventry L100 for his place, but that Mr. Coventry did give him L20 back again. All this I am pleased to hear that his knavery is found out. Dined upon a poor Lenten dinner at home, my wife being vexed at a fray this morning with my Lady Batten about my boy's going thither to turn the watercock with their maydes' leave, but my Lady was mighty high upon it and she would teach his mistress better manners, which my wife answered aloud that she might hear, that she could learn little manners of her. After dinner to my office, and there we sat all the afternoon till 8 at night, and so wrote my letters by the post and so before 9 home, which is rare with me of late, I staying longer, but with multitude of business my head akes, and so I can stay no longer, but home to supper and to bed.

11th. Up betimes, and to my office, walked a little in the garden with Sir W. Batten, talking about the difference between his Lady and my wife yesterday, and I doubt my wife is to blame. About noon had news by Mr. Wood that Butler, our chief witness against Field, was sent by him to New England contrary to our desire, which made me mad almost; and so Sir J. Minnes, Sir W. Pen, and I dined together at Trinity House, and thither sent for him to us and told him our minds, which he seemed not to value much, but went away. I wrote and sent an express to Walthamstow to Sir W. Pen, who is gone thither this morning, to tell him of it. However, in the afternoon Wood sends us word that he has appointed another to go, who shall overtake the ship in the Downes. So I was late at the office, among other things writing to the Downes, to the Commander-in-Chief, and putting things into the surest course I could to help the business. So home and to bed.

12th. Up betimes and to my office all the morning with Captain Cocke ending their account of their Riga contract for hemp. So home to dinner, my head full of business against the office. After dinner comes my uncle Thomas with a letter to my father, wherein, as we desire, he and his son do order their tenants to pay their rents to us, which pleases me well. In discourse he tells me my uncle Wight thinks much that I do never see them, and they have reason, but I do apprehend that they have been too far concerned with my uncle Thomas against us, so that I have had no mind hitherto, but now I shall go see them. He being gone, I to the office, where at the choice of maisters and chyrurgeons for the fleet now going out, I did my business as I could wish, both for the persons I had a mind to serve, and in getting the warrants signed drawn by my clerks, which I was afeard of. Sat late, and having done I went home, where I found Mary Ashwell come to live with us, of whom I hope well, and pray God she may please us, which, though it cost me something, yet will give me much content. So to supper and to bed, and find by her discourse and carriage to-night that she is not proud, but will do what she is bid, but for want of being abroad knows not how to give the respect to her mistress, as she will do when she is told it, she having been used only to little children, and there was a kind of a mistress over them. Troubled all night with my cold, I being quite hoarse with it that I could not speak to be heard at all almost.

13th. Up pretty early and to my office all the morning busy. At noon home to dinner expecting Ashwell's father, who was here in the morning and promised to come but he did not, but there came in Captain Grove, and I found him to be a very stout man, at least in his discourse he would be thought so, and I do think that he is, and one that bears me great respect and deserves to be encouraged for his care in all business. Abroad by water with my wife and Ashwell, and left them at Mr. Pierce's, and I to Whitehall and St. James's Park (there being no Commission for Tangier sitting to-day as I looked for) where I walked an hour or two with great pleasure, it being a most pleasant day. So to Mrs. Hunt's, and there found my wife, and so took them up by coach, and carried them to Hide Park, where store of coaches and good faces. Here till night, and so home and to my office to write by the post, and so to supper and to bed.

14th. Up betimes and to my office, where we sat all the morning, and a great rant I did give to Mr. Davis, of Deptford, and others about their usage of Michell, in his Bewpers,—[Bewpers is the old name for bunting.]—which he serves in for flaggs, which did trouble me, but yet it was in defence of what was truth. So home to dinner, where Creed dined with me, and walked a good while in the garden with me after dinner, talking, among other things, of the poor service which Sir J. Lawson did really do in the Streights, for which all this great fame and honour done him is risen. So to my office, where all the afternoon giving maisters their warrants for this voyage, for which I hope hereafter to get something at their coming home. In the evening my wife and I and Ashwell walked in the garden, and I find she is a pretty ingenuous

[For ingenious. The distinction of the two words ingenious and ingenuous by which the former indicates mental, and the second moral qualities, was not made in Pepys's day.]

girl at all sorts of fine work, which pleases me very well, and I hope will be very good entertainment for my wife without much cost. So to write by the post, and so home to supper and to bed.

15th (Lord's day). Up and with my wife and her woman Ashwell the first time to church, where our pew was so full with Sir J. Minnes's sister and her daughter, that I perceive, when we come all together, some of us must be shut out, but I suppose we shall come to some order what to do therein. Dined at home, and to church again in the afternoon, and so home, and I to my office till the evening doing one thing or other and reading my vows as I am bound every Lord's day, and so home to supper and talk, and Ashwell is such good company that I think we shall be very lucky in her. So to prayers and to bed. This day the weather, which of late has been very hot and fair, turns very wet and cold, and all the church time this afternoon it thundered mightily, which I have not heard a great while.

16th. Up very betimes and to my office, where, with several Masters of the King's ships, Sir J. Minnes and I advising upon the business of Slopps, wherein the seaman is so much abused by the Pursers, and that being done, then I home to dinner, and so carried my wife to her mother's, set her down and Ashwell to my Lord's lodging, there left her, and I to the Duke, where we met of course, and talked of our Navy matters. Then to the Commission of Tangier, and there, among other things, had my Lord Peterborough's Commission read over; and Mr. Secretary Bennet did make his querys upon it, in order to the drawing one for my Lord Rutherford more regularly, that being a very extravagant thing. Here long discoursing upon my Lord Rutherford's despatch, and so broke up, and so going out of the Court I met with Mr. Coventry, and so he and I walked half an hour in the long Stone Gallery, where we discoursed of many things, among others how the Treasurer doth intend to come to pay in course, which is the thing of the world that will do the King the greatest service in the Navy, and which joys my heart to hear of. He tells me of the business of Sir J. Minnes and Sir W. Pen, which I knew before, but took no notice or little that I did know it. But he told me it was chiefly to make Mr. Pett's being joyned with Sir W. Batten to go down the better, and do tell me how he well sees that neither one nor the other can do their duties without help. But however will let it fall at present without doing more in it to see whether they will do their duties themselves, which he will see, and saith they do not. We discoursed of many other things to my great content and so parted, and I to my wife at my Lord's lodgings, where I heard Ashwell play first upon the harpsicon, and I find she do play pretty well, which pleaseth me very well. Thence home by coach, buying at the Temple the printed virginal-book for her, and so home and to my office a while, and so home and to supper and to bed.

17th. Up betimes and to my office a while, and then home and to Sir W. Batten, with whom by coach to St. Margaret's Hill in Southwark, where the judge of the

Admiralty came, and the rest of the Doctors of the Civill law, and some other Commissioners, whose Commission of Oyer and Terminer was read, and then the charge, given by Dr. Exton, which methought was somewhat dull, though he would seem to intend it to be very rhetoricall, saying that justice had two wings, one of which spread itself over the land, and the other over the water, which was this Admiralty Court. That being done, and the jury called, they broke up, and to dinner to a tavern hard by, where a great dinner, and I with them; but I perceive that this Court is yet but in its infancy (as to its rising again), and their design and consultation was, I could overhear them, how to proceed with the most solemnity, and spend time, there being only two businesses to do, which of themselves could not spend much time. In the afternoon to the court again, where, first, Abraham, the boatswain of the King's pleasure boat, was tried for drowning a man; and next, Turpin, accused by our wicked rogue Field, for stealing the King's timber; but after full examination, they were both acquitted, and as I was glad of the first, for the saving the man's life, so I did take the other as a very good fortune to us; for if Turpin had been found guilty, it would have sounded very ill in the ears of all the world, in the business between Field and us. So home with my mind at very great ease, over the water to the Tower, and thence, there being nobody at the office, we being absent, and so no office could be kept. Sir W. Batten and I to my Lord Mayor's, where we found my Lord with Colonel Strangways and Sir Richard Floyd, Parliament-men, in the cellar drinking, where we sat with them, and then up; and by and by comes in Sir Richard Ford. In our drinking, which was always going, we had many discourses, but from all of them I do find Sir R. Ford a very able man of his brains and tongue, and a scholler. But my Lord Mayor I find to be a talking, bragging Bufflehead, a fellow that would be thought to have led all the City in the great business of bringing in the King, and that nobody understood his plots, and the dark lanthorn he walked by; but led them and plowed with them as oxen and asses (his own words) to do what he had a mind when in every discourse I observe him to be as very a coxcomb as I could have thought had been in the City. But he is resolved to do great matters in pulling down the shops quite through the City, as he hath done in many places, and will make a thorough passage quite through the City, through Canning-street, which indeed will be very fine. And then his precept, which he, in vain-glory, said he had drawn up himself, and hath printed it, against coachmen and carrmen affronting of the gentry in the street; it is drawn so like a fool, and some faults were openly found in it, that I believe he will have so much wit as not to proceed upon it though it be printed. Here we staid talking till eleven at night, Sir R. Ford breaking to my Lord our business of our patent to be justices of the Peace in the City, which he stuck at mightily; but, however, Sir R. Ford knows him to be a fool, and so in his discourse he made him appear, and cajoled him into a consent to it: but so as I believe when he comes to his right mind tomorrow he will be of another opinion; and though Sir R. Ford moved it very weightily and neatly, yet I had rather it had been spared now. But to see how he do rant, and pretend to sway all the City in the Court of Aldermen, and says plainly that they cannot do, nor will he suffer them to do, any thing but what he pleases; nor is there any officer of the City but of his putting in; nor any man that could have kept the City for the King thus well and long but him. And if the country can be preserved, he will undertake that the City shall not dare to stir again. When I am confident there is no man almost in the City cares a turd for him, nor hath he brains to outwit any ordinary tradesman.

So home and wrote a letter to Commissioner Pett to Chatham by all means to compose the business between Major Holmes and Cooper his master, and so to bed.

18th. Wake betimes and talk a while with my wife about a wench that she has hired yesterday, which I would have enquired of before she comes, she having lived in great families, and so up and to my office, where all the morning, and at noon home to dinner. After dinner by water to Redriffe, my wife and Ashwell with me, and so walked and left them at Halfway house; I to Deptford, where up and down the storehouses, and on board two or three ships now getting ready to go to sea, and so back, and find my wife walking in the way. So home again, merry with our Ashwell, who is a merry jade, and so awhile to my office, and then home to supper, and to bed. This day my tryangle, which was put in tune yesterday, did please me very well, Ashwell playing upon it pretty well.

19th. Up betimes and to Woolwich all alone by water, where took the officers most abed. I walked and enquired how all matters and businesses go, and by and by to the Clerk of the Cheque's house, and there eat some of his good Jamaica brawne, and so walked to Greenwich. Part of the way Deane walking with me; talking of the pride and corruption of most of his fellow officers of the yard, and which I believe to be true. So to Deptford, where I did the same to great content, and see the people begin to value me as they do the rest. At noon Mr. Wayth took me to his house, where I dined, and saw his wife, a pretty woman, and had a good fish dinner, and after dinner he and I walked to Redriffe talking of several errors in the Navy, by which I learned a great deal, and was glad of his company. So by water home, and by and by to the office, where we sat till almost 9 at night. So after doing my own business in my office, writing letters, &c., home to supper, and to bed, being weary and vexed that I do not find other people so willing to do business as myself, when I have taken pains to find out what in the yards is wanting and fitting to be done.

20th. Up betimes and over the water, and walked to Deptford, where up and down the yarde, and met the two clerks of the Cheques to conclude by our method their callbooks, which we have done to great perfection, and so walked home again, where I found my wife in great pain abed.... I staid and dined by her, and after dinner walked forth, and by water to the Temple, and in Fleet Street bought me a little sword, with gilt handle, cost 23s., and silk stockings to the colour of my riding cloth suit, cost I 5s., and bought me a belt there too, cost 15s., and so calling at my brother's I find he has got a new maid, very likely girl, I wish he do not play the fool with her. Thence homewards, and meeting with Mr. Kirton's kinsman in Paul's Church Yard, he and I to a coffee-house; where I hear how there had like to have been a surprizall of Dublin by some discontented protestants, and other things of like nature; and it seems the Commissioners have carried themselves so high for the Papists that the others will not endure it. Hewlett and some others are taken and clapped up; and they say the King hath sent over to dissolve the Parliament there, who went very high against the Commissioners. Pray God send all well! Hence home and in comes Captain Ferrers and by and by Mr. Bland to see the and sat talking with me till 9 or to at night, and so good night. The Captain to bid my wife to his child's christening. So my wife being pretty well again and Ashwell there we spent the evening pleasantly, and so to bed.

21st. Up betimes and to my office, where busy all the morning, and at noon, after a very little dinner, to it again, and by and by, by appointment, our full board met, and Sir Philip Warwick and Sir Robert Long came from my Lord Treasurer to speak with us about the state of the debts of the Navy; and how to settle it, so as to begin upon the new foundation of L200,000 per annum, which the King is now resolved not to exceed. This discourse done, and things put in a way of doing, they went away, and Captain Holmes being called in he began his high complaint against his Master Cooper, and would have him forthwith discharged. Which I opposed, not in his defence but for the justice of proceeding not to condemn a man unheard, upon [which] we fell from one word to another that we came to very high terms, such as troubled me, though all and the worst that I ever said was that that was insolently or ill mannerdly spoken. When he told me that it was well it was here that I said it. But all the officers, Sir G. Carteret, Sir J. Minnes, Sir W. Batten, and Sir W. Pen cried shame of it. At last he parted and we resolved to bring the dispute between him and his Master to a trial next week, wherein I shall not at all concern myself in defence of any thing that is unhandsome on the Master's part nor willingly suffer him to have any wrong. So we rose and I to my office, troubled though sensible that all the officers are of opinion that he has carried himself very much unbecoming him. So wrote letters by the post, and home to supper and to bed.

22d (Lord's day). Up betimes and in my office wrote out our bill for the Parliament about our being made justices of Peace in the City. So home and to church, where a dull formall fellow that prayed for the Right Hon. John Lord Barkeley, Lord President of Connaught, &c. So home to dinner, and after dinner my wife and I and her woman by coach to Westminster, where being come too soon for the Christening we took up Mr. Creed and went out to take some ayre, as far as Chelsey and further, I lighting there and letting them go on with the coach while I went to the church expecting to see the young ladies of the school, Ashwell desiring me, but I could not get in far enough, and so came out and at the coach's coming back went in again and so back to Westminster, and led my wife and her to Captain Ferrers, and I to my Lord Sandwich, and with him talking a good while; I find the Court would have this Indulgence go on, but the Parliament are against it. Matters in Ireland are full of discontent. Thence with Mr. Creed to Captain Ferrers, where many fine ladies; the house well and prettily furnished. She [Mrs. Ferrers] lies in, in great state, Mr. G. Montagu, Collonel Williams, Cromwell that was,

[Colonel Williams—"Cromwell that was"—appears to have been Henry Cromwell, grandson of Sir Oliver Cromwell, and first cousin, once removed, to the Protector. He was seated at Bodsey House, in the parish of Ramsey, which had been his father's residence, and held the commission of a colonel. He served in several Parliaments for Huntingdonshire, voting, in 1660, for the restoration of the monarchy; and as he knew the name of Cromwell would not be grateful to the

Court, he disused it, and assumed that of Williams, which had belonged to his ancestors; and he is so styled in a list of knights of the proposed Order of the Royal Oak. He died at Huntingdon, 3rd August, 1673. (Abridged from Noble's "Memoirs of the Cromwells," vol. i., p. 70.)—B.]

and Mrs. Wright as proxy for my Lady Jemimah, were witnesses. Very pretty and plentiful entertainment, could not get away till nine at night, and so home. My coach cost me 7s. So to prayers, and to bed. This day though I was merry enough yet I could not get yesterday's quarrel out of my mind, and a natural fear of being challenged by Holmes for the words I did give him, though nothing but what did become me as a principal officer.

23rd. Up betimes and to my office, before noon my wife and I eat something, thinking to have gone abroad together, but in comes Mr. Hunt, who we were forced to stay to dinner, and so while that was got ready he and I abroad about 2 or 3 small businesses of mine, and so back to dinner, and after dinner he went away, and my wife and I and Ashwell by coach, set my wife down at her mother's and Ashwell at my Lord's, she going to see her father and mother, and I to Whitehall, being fearful almost, so poor a spirit I have, of meeting Major Holmes. By and by the Duke comes, and we with him about our usual business, and then the Committee for Tangier, where, after reading my Lord Rutherford's commission and consented to, Sir R. Ford, Sir W. Rider, and I were chosen to bring in some laws for the Civill government of it, which I am little able to do, but am glad to be joyned with them, for I shall learn something of them. Thence to see my Lord Sandwich, and who should I meet at the door but Major Holmes. He would have gone away, but I told him I would not spoil his visitt, and would have gone, but however we fell to discourse and he did as good as desire excuse for the high words that did pass in his heat the other day, which I was willing enough to close with, and after telling him my mind we parted, and I left him to speak with my Lord, and I by coach home, where I found Will. Howe come home to-day with my wife, and staid with us all night, staying late up singing songs, and then he and I to bed together in Ashwell's bed and she with my wife. This the first time that I ever lay in the room. This day Greatorex brought me a very pretty weather-glass for heat and cold.

[The thermometer was invented in the sixteenth century, but it is disputed who the inventor was. The claims of Santorio are supported by Borelli and Malpighi, while the title of Cornelius Drebbel is considered undoubted by Boerhaave. Galileo's air thermometer, made before 1597, was the foundation of accurate thermometry. Galileo also invented the alcohol thermometer about 1611 or 1612. Spirit thermometers were made for the Accademia del Cimento, and described in the Memoirs of that academy. When the academy was dissolved by order of the Pope, some of these thermometers were packed away in a box, and were not discovered until early in the nineteenth century. Robert Hooke describes the manufacture and graduation of thermometers in his "Micrographia" (1665).]

24th. Lay pretty long, that is, till past six o'clock, and them up and W. Howe and I very merry together, till having eat our breakfast, he went away, and I to my office. By and by Sir J. Minnes and I to the Victualling Office by appointment to meet several persons upon stating the demands of some people of money from the King. Here we went into their Bakehouse, and saw all the ovens at work, and good bread too, as ever I would desire to eat. Thence Sir J. Minnes and I homewards calling at Browne's, the mathematician in the Minnerys, with a design of buying White's ruler to measure timber with, but could not agree on the price. So home, and to dinner, and so to my office, where we sat anon, and among other things had Cooper's business tried against Captain Holmes, but I find Cooper a fuddling, troublesome fellow, though a good artist, and so am contented to have him turned out of his place, nor did I see reason to say one word against it, though I know what they did against him was with great envy and pride. So anon broke up, and after writing letters, &c., home to supper and to bed.

25th (Lady-day). Up betimes and to my office, where all the morning, at noon dined and to the Exchange, and thence to the Sun Tavern, to my Lord Rutherford, and dined with him, and some others, his officers, and Scotch gentlemen, of fine discourse and education. My Lord used me with great respect, and discoursed upon his business as with one that he did esteem of, and indeed I do believe that this garrison is likely to come to something under him. By and by he went away, forgetting to take leave of me, my back being turned, looking upon the aviary, which is there very pretty, and the birds begin to sing well this spring. Thence home and to my office till night, reading over and consulting upon the book and Ruler that I bought this morning of Browne concerning the lyne of numbers, in which I find much pleasure. This evening came Captain Grove about hiring ships for Tangier. I did hint to him my desire that I could make some lawfull profit thereof, which he promises that he will tell me of all that he gets and that I shall have a share, which I did not demand, but did silently consent to it, and money I perceive something will be got thereby. At night Mr. Bland came and sat with me at my office till late, and so I home and to bed. This day being washing day and my maid Susan ill, or would be thought so, put my house so out of order that we had no pleasure almost in anything, my wife being troubled thereat for want of a good cook-maid, and moreover I cannot have my dinner as I ought in memory of my being cut for the stone, but I must have it a day or two hence.

26th. Up betimes and to my office, leaving my wife in bed to take her physique, myself also not being out of some pain to-day by some cold that I have got by the sudden change of the weather from hot to cold. This day is five years since it pleased God to preserve me at my being cut of the stone, of which I bless God I am in all respects well. Only now and then upon taking cold I have some pain, but otherwise in very good health always. But I could not get my feast to be kept to-day as it used to be, because of my wife's being ill and other disorders by my servants being out of order. This morning came a new cook-maid at L4 per annum, the first time I ever did give so much, but we hope it will be nothing lost by keeping a good cook. She did live last at my Lord Monk's house, and indeed at dinner did get what there was very prettily ready and neat for me, which did please me much. This morning my uncle Thomas was with me according to agreement, and I paid him the L50, which was against my heart to part with, and yet I must be contented; I used him very kindly, and I desire to continue so voyd of any discontent as to my estate, that I may follow my business the better. At the Change I met him again, with intent to have met with my uncle Wight to have made peace with him, with whom by my long absence I fear I shall have a difference, but he was not there, so we missed. All the afternoon sat at the office about business till 9 or 10 at night, and so dispatch business and home to supper and to bed. My maid Susan went away to-day, I giving her something for her lodging and diet somewhere else a while that I might have room for my new maid.

27th. Up betimes and at my office all the morning, at noon to the Exchange, and there by appointment met my uncles Thomas and Wight, and from thence with them to a tavern, and there paid my uncle Wight three pieces of gold for himself, my aunt, and their son that is dead, left by my uncle Robert, and read over our agreement with my uncle Thomas and the state of our debts and legacies, and so good friendship I think is made up between us all, only we have the worst of it in having so much money to pay. Thence I to the Exchequer again, and thence with Creed into Fleet Street, and calling at several places about business; in passing, at the Hercules pillars he and I dined though late, and thence with one that we found there, a friend of Captain Ferrers I used to meet at the playhouse, they would have gone to some gameing house, but I would not but parted, and staying a little in Paul's Churchyard, at the foreign Bookseller's looking over some Spanish books, and with much ado keeping myself from laying out money there, as also with them, being willing enough to have gone to some idle house with them, I got home, and after a while at my office, to supper, and to bed.

28th. Up betimes and to my office, where all the morning. Dined at home and Creed with me, and though a very cold day and high wind, yet I took him by land to Deptford, my common walk, where I did some little businesses, and so home again walking both forwards and backwards, as much along the street as we could to save going by water. So home, and after being a little while hearing Ashwell play on the tryangle, to my office, and there late, writing a chiding letter—to my poor father about his being so unwilling to come to an account with me, which I desire he might do, that I may know what he spends, and how to order the estate so as to pay debts and legacys as far as may be. So late home to supper and to bed.

29th (Lord's day). Waked as I used to do betimes, but being Sunday and very cold I lay long, it raining and snowing very hard, which I did never think it would have done any more this year. Up and to church, home to dinner. After dinner in comes Mr. Moore, and sat and talked with us a good while; among other things telling me, that [neither] my Lord nor he are under apprehensions of the late discourse in the House of Commons, concerning resumption of Crowne lands, which I am very glad of. He being gone, up to my chamber, where my wife and Ashwell and I all the afternoon talking and laughing, and by and by I a while to my office, reading over some papers which I found in my man William's chest of drawers, among others some old precedents concerning the practice of this office heretofore, which I am glad to find and shall make use of, among others an oath, which the Principal Officers were bound to swear at their entrance into their offices, which I would be glad were in use still. So home and fell hard to make up my monthly accounts, letting my family go to bed after prayers. I staid up long, and find myself, as I think, fully worth L670. So with good comfort to bed, finding that though it be but little, yet I do get ground every month. I pray God it may continue so with me.

30th. Up betimes and found my weather-glass sunk again just to the same position which it was last night before I had any fire made in my chamber, which had made it rise in two hours time above half a degree. So to my office where all the morning and at the Glass-house, and after dinner by coach with Sir W. Pen I carried my wife and her woman to Westminster, they to visit Mrs. Ferrers and Clerke, we to the Duke, where we did our usual business, and afterwards to the Tangier Committee, where among other things we all of us sealed and signed the Contract for building the Mole with my Lord Tiviott, Sir J. Lawson, and Mr. Cholmeley. A thing I did with a very ill will, because a thing which I did not at all understand, nor any or few of the whole board. We did also read over the propositions for the Civill government and Law Merchant of the town, as they were agreed on this morning at the Glasshouse by Sir R. Ford and Sir W. Rider, who drew them, Mr. Povy and myself as a Committee appointed to prepare them, which were in substance but not in the manner of executing them independent wholly upon the Governor consenting to. Thence to see my Lord Sandwich, who I found very merry and every day better and better. So to my wife, who waited my coming at my Lord's lodgings, and took her up and by coach home, where no sooner come but to bed, finding myself just in the same condition I was lately by the extreme cold weather, my pores stopt and so my body all inflamed and itching. So keeping myself warm and provoking myself to a moderate sweat, and so somewhat better in the morning,

31st. And to that purpose I lay long talking with my wife about my father's coming, which I expect to-day, coming up with the horses brought up for my Lord. Up and to my office, where doing business all the morning, and at Sir W. Batten's, whither Mr. Gauden and many others came to us about business. Then home to dinner, where W. Joyce came, and he still a talking impertinent fellow. So to the office again, and hearing by and by that Madam Clerke, Pierce, and others were come to see my wife I stepped in and staid a little with them, and so to the office again, where late, and so home to supper and to bed.

Diary of Samuel Pepys.
April
1663

April 1st. Up betimes and abroad to my brother's, but he being gone out I went to the Temple to my Cozen Roger Pepys, to see and talk with him a little; who tells me that, with much ado, the Parliament do agree to throw down Popery; but he says it is with so much spite and passion, and an endeavour of bringing all Non-conformists into the same condition, that he is afeard matters will not yet go so well as he could wish. Thence back to my brother's, in my way meeting Mr. Moore and talking with him about getting me some money, and calling at my brother's they tell me that my brother is still abroad, and that my father is not yet up. At which I wondered, not thinking that he was come, though I expected him, because I looked for him at my house. So I up to his bedside and staid an hour or two talking with him. Among other things he tells me how unquiett my mother is grown, that he is not able to live almost with her, if it were not for Pall. All other matters are as well as upon so hard conditions with my uncle Thomas we can expect them. I left him in bed, being very weary, to come to my house to-night or tomorrow, when he pleases, and so I home, calling on the virginall maker, buying a rest for myself to tune my tryangle, and taking one of his people along with me to put it in tune once more, by which I learned how to go about it myself for the time to come. So to dinner, my wife being lazily in bed all this morning. Ashwell and I dined below together, and a pretty girl she is, and I hope will give my wife and myself good content, being very humble and active, my cook maid do also dress my meat very well and neatly. So to my office all the afternoon till night, and then home, calling at Sir W. Batten's, where was Sir J. Minnes and Sir W. Pen, I telling them how by my letter this day from Commissioner Pett I hear that his Stempeese

[Stemples, cross pieces which are put into a frame of woodwork to
cure and strengthen a shaft.]

he undertook for the new ship at Woolwich, which we have been so long, to our shame, in looking for, do prove knotty and not fit for service. Lord! how Sir J. Minnes, like a mad coxcomb, did swear and stamp, swearing that Commissioner Pett hath still the old heart against the King that ever he had, and that this was his envy against his brother that was to build the ship, and all the damnable reproaches in the world, at which I was ashamed, but said little; but, upon the whole, I find him still a fool, led by the nose with stories told by Sir W. Batten, whether with or without reason. So, vexed in my mind to see things ordered so unlike gentlemen, or men of reason, I went home and to bed.

2nd. Up by very betimes and to my office, where all the morning till towards noon, and then by coach to Westminster Hall with Sir W. Pen, and while he went up to the House I walked in the Hall with Mr. Pierce, the surgeon, that I met there, talking about my business the other day with Holmes, whom I told my mind, and did freely tell how I do depend upon my care and diligence in my employment to bear me out against the pride of Holmes or any man else in things that are honest, and much to that purpose which I know he will make good use of. But he did advise me to take as few occasions as I can of disobliging Commanders, though this is one that every body is glad to hear that he do receive a check. By and by the House rises and I home again with Sir W. Pen, and all the way talking of the same business, to whom I did on purpose tell him my mind freely, and let him see that it must be a wiser man than Holmes (in these very words) that shall do me any hurt while I do my duty. I to remember him of Holmes's words against Sir J. Minnes, that he was a knave, rogue, coward, and that he will kick him and pull him by the ears, which he remembered all of them and may have occasion to do it hereafter to his owne shame to suffer them to be spoke in his presence without any reply but what I did give him, which, has caused all this feud. But I am glad of it, for I would now and then take occasion to let the world know that I will not be made a novice. Sir W. Pen took occasion to speak about my wife's strangeness to him and his daughter, and that believing at last that it was from his taking of Sarah to be his maid, he hath now put her away, at which I am glad. He told me, that this day the King hath sent to the House his concurrence wholly with them against the Popish priests, Jesuits, &c., which gives great content, and I am glad of it. So home, whither my father comes and dines with us, and being willing to be merry with him I made myself so as much as I could, and so to the office, where we sat all the afternoon, and at night having done all my business I went home to my wife and father, and supped, and so to bed, my father lying with me in Ashwell's bed in the red chamber.

3rd. Waked betimes and talked half an hour with my father, and so I rose and to my office, and about 9 o'clock by water from the Old Swan to White Hall and to chappell, which being most monstrous full, I could not go into my pew, but sat among the quire. Dr. Creeton, the Scotchman, preached a most admirable, good, learned, honest and most severe sermon, yet comicall, upon the words of the woman concerning the Virgin, "Blessed is the womb that bare thee (meaning Christ) and the paps that gave thee suck; and he answered, Nay; rather is he blessed that heareth the word of God, and keepeth it." He railed bitterly ever and anon against John Calvin, and his brood, the Presbyterians, and against the present term, now in use, of "tender consciences." He ripped up Hugh Peters (calling him the execrable skellum—[A villain or scoundrel; the cant term for a thief.]—), his preaching and stirring up the maids of the city to bring in their bodkins and thimbles. Thence going out of White Hall, I met Captain Grove, who did give me a letter directed to myself from himself. I discerned money to be in it, and took it, knowing, as I found it to be, the proceed of the place I have got him to be, the taking up of vessels for Tangier. But I did not open it till I came home to my office, and there I broke it open, not looking into it till all the money was out, that I might say I saw no money in the paper, if ever I should be questioned about it. There was a piece in gold and L4 in silver. So home to dinner with my father and wife, and after dinner up to my tryangle, where I found that above my expectation Ashwell has very good principles of musique and can take out a lesson herself with very little pains, at which I am very glad. Thence away back again by water to Whitehall, and there to the Tangier Committee, where we find ourselves at a great stand; the establishment being but L70,000 per annum, and the forces to be kept in the town at the least estimate that my Lord Rutherford can be got to bring it is L53,000. The charge of this year's work of the Mole will be L13,000; besides L1000 a-year to my Lord Peterborough as a pension, and the fortifications and contingencys, which puts us to a great stand, and so unsettled what to do therein we rose, and I to see my Lord Sandwich, whom I found merry at cards, and so by coach home, and after supper a little to my office and so home and to bed. I find at Court that there is some bad news from Ireland of an insurrection of the Catholiques there, which puts them into an alarm. I hear also in the City that for certain there is an embargo upon all our ships in Spayne, upon this action of my Lord

Windsor's at Cuba, which signifies little or nothing, but only he hath a mind to say that he hath done something before he comes back again. Late tonight I sent to invite my uncle Wight and aunt with Mrs. Turner to-morrow.

4th. Up betimes and to my office. By and by to Lombard street by appointment to meet Mr. Moore, but the business not being ready I returned to the office, where we sat a while, and, being sent for, I returned to him and there signed to some papers in the conveying of some lands mortgaged by Sir Rob. Parkhurst in my name to my Lord Sandwich, which I having done I returned home to dinner, whither by and by comes Roger Pepys, Mrs. Turner her daughter, Joyce Norton, and a young lady, a daughter of Coll. Cockes, my uncle Wight, his wife and Mrs. Anne Wight. This being my feast, in lieu of what I should have had a few days ago for my cutting of the stone, for which the Lord make me truly thankful. Very merry at, before, and after dinner, and the more for that my dinner was great, and most neatly dressed by our own only maid. We had a fricasee of rabbits and chickens, a leg of mutton boiled, three carps in a dish, a great dish of a side of lamb, a dish of roasted pigeons, a dish of four lobsters, three tarts, a lamprey pie (a most rare pie), a dish of anchovies, good wine of several sorts, and all things mighty noble and to my great content. After dinner to Hide Park; my aunt, Mrs. Wight and I in one coach, and all the rest of the women in Mrs. Turner's; Roger being gone in haste to the Parliament about the carrying this business of the Papists, in which it seems there is great contest on both sides, and my uncle and father staying together behind. At the Park was the King, and in another coach my Lady Castlemaine, they greeting one another at every tour.

[The company drove round and round the Ring in Hyde Park. The following two extracts illustrate this, and the, second one shows how the circuit was called the Tour: "Here (1697) the people of fashion take the diversion of the Ring. In a pretty high place, which lies very open, they have surrounded a circumference of two or three hundred paces diameter with a sorry kind of balustrade, or rather with postes placed upon stakes but three feet from the ground; and the coaches drive round this. When they have turned for some time round one way they face about and turn t'other: so rowls the world!"—Wilson's Memoirs, 1719, p. 126.]
["It is in this Park where the Grand Tour or Ring is kept for the Ladies to take the air in their coaches, and in fine weather I have seen above three hundred at a time."—[Macky's] Journey through England, 1724, vol. i., p. 75.]

Here about an hour, and so leaving all by the way we home and found the house as clean as if nothing had been done there to-day from top to bottom, which made us give the cook 12d. a piece, each of us. So to my office about writing letters by the post, one to my brother John at Brampton telling him (hoping to work a good effect by it upon my mother) how melancholy my father is, and bidding him use all means to get my mother to live peaceably and quietly, which I am sure she neither do nor I fear can ever do, but frightening her with his coming down no more, and the danger of her condition if he should die I trust may do good. So home and to bed.

5th (Lord's day). Up and spent the morning, till the Barber came, in reading in my chamber part of Osborne's Advice to his Son (which I shall not never enough admire for sense and language), and being by and by trimmed, to Church, myself, wife, Ashwell, &c. Home to dinner, it raining, while that was prepared to my office to read over my vows with great affection and to very good purpose. So to dinner, and very well pleased with it. Then to church again, where a simple bawling young Scot preached. So home to my office alone till dark, reading some papers of my old navy precedents, and so home to supper, and, after some pleasant talk, my wife, Ashwell, and I to bed.

6th. Up very betimes and to my office, and there made an end of reading my book that I have of Mr. Barlow's of the Journal of the Commissioners of the Navy, who begun to act in the year 1628 and continued six years, wherein is fine observations and precedents out of which I do purpose to make a good collection. By and by, much against my will, being twice sent for, to Sir G. Carteret's to pass his accounts there, upon which Sir J. Minnes, Sir W. Batten, Sir W. Pen, and myself all the morning, and again after dinner to it, being vexed at my heart to see a thing of that importance done so slightly and with that neglect for which God pardon us, and I would I could mend it. Thence leaving them I made an excuse and away home, and took my wife by coach and left her at Madam Clerk's, to make a visit there, and I to the Committee of Tangier, where I found, to my great joy, my Lord Sandwich, the first time I have seen him abroad these some months, and by and by he rose and took leave, being, it seems, this night to go to Kensington or Chelsey, where he hath taken a lodging for a while to take the ayre. We staid, and after business done I got Mr. Coventry into the Matted Gallery and told him my whole mind concerning matters of our office, all my discontent to see things of so great trust carried so neglectfully, and what pitiful service the Controller and Surveyor make of their duties, and I disburdened my mind wholly to him and he to me his own, many things, telling me that he is much discouraged by seeing things not to grow better and better as he did well hope they would have done. Upon the whole, after a full hour's private discourse, telling one another our minds, we with great content parted, and with very great satisfaction for my [having] thus cleared my conscience, went to Dr. Clerk's and thence fetched my wife, and by coach home. To my office a little to set things in order, and so home to supper and to bed.

7th. Up very betimes, and angry with Will that he made no more haste to rise after I called him. So to my office, and all the morning there. At noon to the Exchange, and so home to dinner, where I found my wife had been with Ashwell to La Roche's to have her tooth drawn, which it seems aches much, but my wife could not get her to be contented to have it drawn after the first twich, but would let it alone, and so they came home with it undone, which made my wife and me good sport. After dinner to the office, where Sir J. Minnes did make a great complaint to me alone, how my clerk Mr. Hater had entered in one of the Sea books a ticket to have been signed by him before it had been examined, which makes the old fool mad almost, though there was upon enquiry the greatest reason in the world for it. Which though it vexes me, yet it is most to see from day to day what a coxcomb he is, and that so great a trust should lie in the hands of such a fool. We sat all the afternoon, and I late at my office, it being post night, and so home to supper, my father being come again to my house, and after supper to bed, and after some talk to sleep.

8th. Up betimes and to my office, and by and by, about 8 o'clock, to the Temple to Commissioner Pett lately come to town and discoursed about the affairs of our office, how ill they go through the corruption and folly of Sir W. Batten and Sir J. Minnes. Thence by water to White Hall, to chappell; where preached Dr. Pierce, the famous man that preached the sermon so much cried up, before the King against the Papists. His matter was the Devil tempting our Saviour, being carried into the Wilderness by the spirit. And he hath as much of natural eloquence as most men that ever I heard in my life, mixed with so much learning. After sermon I went up and saw the ceremony of the Bishop of Peterborough's paying homage upon the knee to the King, while Sir H. Bennet, Secretary, read the King's grant of the Bishopric of Lincoln, to which he is translated. His name is Dr. Lany. Here I also saw the Duke of Monmouth, with his Order of the Garter, the first time I ever saw it. I am told that the University of Cambridge did treat him a little while since with all the honour possible, with a comedy at Trinity College, and banquet; and made him Master of Arts there. All which, they say, the King took very well. Dr. Raynbow, Master of Magdalen, being now Vice-Chancellor. Home by water to dinner, and with my father, wife, and Ashwell, after dinner, by water towards Woolwich, and in our way I bethought myself that we had left our poor little dog that followed us out of doors at the waterside, and God knows whether he be not lost, which did not only strike my wife into a great passion but I must confess myself also; more than was becoming me. We immediately returned, I taking another boat and with my father went to Woolwich, while they went back to find the dog. I took my father on board the King's pleasure boat and down to Woolwich, and walked to Greenwich thence and turning into the park to show my father the steps up the hill, we found my wife, her woman, and dog attending us, which made us all merry again, and so took boats, they to Deptford and so by land to Half-way house, I into the King's yard and overlook them there, and eat and drank with them, and saw a company of seamen play drolly at our pence, and so home by water. I a little at the office, and so home to supper and to bed, after having Ashwell play my father and me a lesson upon her Tryangle.

9th. Up betimes and to my office, and anon we met upon finishing the Treasurer's accounts. At noon dined at home and am vexed to hear my wife tell me how our maid Mary do endeavour to corrupt our cook maid, which did please me very well, but I am resolved to rid the house of her as soon as I can. To the office and sat all the afternoon till 9 at night, and an hour after home to supper and bed. My father lying at Tom's to-night, he dining with my uncle Fenner and his sons and a great many more of the gang at his own cost to-day. To bed vexed also to think of Sir J. Minnes finding fault with Mr. Hater for what he had done the other day, though there be no hurt in the thing at all but only the old fool's jealousy, made worse by Sir W. Batten.

10th. Up very betimes and to my office, where most hard at business alone all the morning. At noon to the Exchange, where I hear that after great expectation from Ireland, and long stop of letters, there is good news come, that all is quiett after our great noise of troubles there, though some stir hath been as was reported. Off the Exchange with Sir J. Cutler and Mr. Grant to the Royall Oak Tavern, in Lumbard Street, where Alexander Broome the poet was, a merry and witty man, I believe, if he be not a little conceited, and here drank a sort of French wine, called Ho Bryan,

[Haut Brion, a claret; one of the first growths of the red wines of Medoc.]

that hath a good and most particular taste that I never met with. Home to dinner, and then by water abroad to Whitehall, my wife to see Mrs. Ferrers, I to Whitehall and the Park, doing no business. Then to my Lord's lodgings, met my wife, and walked to the New Exchange. There laid out 10s. upon pendents and painted leather gloves, very pretty and all the mode. So by coach home and to my office till late, and so to supper and to bed.

11th. Up betimes and to my office, where we sat also all the morning till noon, and then home to dinner, my father being there but not very well. After dinner in comes Captain Lambert of the Norwich, this day come from Tangier, whom I am glad to see. There came also with him Captain Wager, and afterwards in came Captain Allen to see me, of the Resolution. All staid a pretty while, and so away, and I a while to my office, then abroad into the street with my father, and left him to go to see my aunt Wight and uncle, intending to lie at Tom's to-night, or my cozen Scott's, where it seems he has hitherto lain and is most kindly used there. So I home and to my office very late making up my Lord's navy accounts, wherein I find him to stand debtor L1200. So home to supper and to bed.

12th (Lord's day). Lay till 8 o'clock, which I have not done a great while, then up and to church, where I found our pew altered by taking some of the hind pew to make ours bigger, because of the number of women, more by Sir J. Minnes company than we used to have. Home to dinner, and after dinner, intending to go to Chelsey to my Lord Sandwich, my wife would needs go with me, though she walked on foot to Whitehall. Which she did and staid at my Lord's lodgings while Creed and I took a turn at Whitehall, but no coach to be had, and so I returned to them and sat talking till evening, and then got a coach and to Gray's Inn walks, where some handsome faces, and so home and there to supper, and a little after 8 o'clock to bed, a thing I have not done God knows when. Coming home to-night, a drunken boy was carrying by our constable to our new pair of stocks to handsel them, being a new pair and very handsome.

13th. Up by five o'clock and to my office, where hard at work till towards noon, and home and eat a bit, and so going out met with Mr. Mount my old acquaintance, and took him in and drank a glass or two of wine to him and so parted, having not time to talk together, and I with Sir W. Batten to the Stillyard, and there eat a lobster together, and Wyse the King's fishmonger coming in we were very merry half an hour, and so by water to Whitehall, and by and by being all met we went in to the Duke and there did our business and so away, and anon to the Tangier Committee, where we had very fine discourse from Dr. Walker and Wiseman, civilians, against our erecting a court-merchant at Tangier, and well answered in many things by my Lord Sandwich (whose speaking I never till now observed so much to be very good) and Sir R. Ford. By and by the discourse being ended, we fell to my Lord Rutherford's dispatch, which do not please him, he being a Scott, and one resolved to scrape every penny that he can get by any way, which the Committee will not agree to. He took offence at something and rose away, without taking leave of the board, which all took ill, though nothing said but only by the Duke of Albemarle, who said that we ought to settle things as they ought to be, and if he will not go upon these terms another man will, no doubt. Here late, quite finishing things against his going, and so rose, and I walked home, being accompanied by Creed to Temple Bar, talking of this afternoon's passage, and so I called at the Wardrobe in my way home, and there spoke at the Horn tavern with Mr. Moore a word or two, but my business was with Mr. Townsend, who is gone this day to his country house, about sparing Charles Pepys some money of his bills due to him when he can, but missing him lost my labour. So walked home, finding my wife abroad, at my aunt, Wight's, who coming home by and by, I home to supper and to bed.

14th. Up betimes to my office, where busy till 8 o'clock that Sir W. Batten, Sir J. Minnes, Sir W. Pen and I down by barge to Woolwich, to see "The Royal James" launched, where she has been under repair a great while. We staid in the yard till almost noon, and then to Mr. Falconer's to a dinner of fish of our own sending, and when it was just ready to come upon the table, word is brought that the King and Duke are come, so they all went away to shew themselves, while I staid and had a little dish or two by myself, resolving to go home, and by the time I had dined they came again, having gone to little purpose, the King, I believe, taking little notice of them. So they to dinner, and I staid a little with them, and so good bye. I walked to Greenwich, studying the slide rule for measuring of timber, which is very fine. Thence to Deptford by water, and walked through the yard, and so walked to Redriffe, and so home pretty weary, to my office, where anon they all came home, the ship well launched, and so sat at the office till 9 at night, and I longer doing business at my office, and so home to supper, my father being come, and to bed. Sir G. Carteret tells me to-night that he perceives the Parliament is likely to make a great bustle before they will give the King any money; will call all things into question; and, above all, the expences of the Navy; and do enquire into the King's expences everywhere, and into the truth of the report of people being forced to sell their bills at 15 per cent. loss in the Navy; and, lastly, that they are in a very angry pettish mood at present, and not likely to be better.

15th. Up betimes, and after talking with my father awhile, I to my office, and there hard at it till almost noon, and then went down the river with Maynes, the purveyor, to show a ship's lading of Norway goods, and called at Sir W. Warren's yard, and so home to dinner. After dinner up with my wife and Ashwell a little to the Tryangle, and so I down to Deptford by land about looking out a couple of catches fitted to be speedily set forth in answer to a letter of Mr. Coventry's to me. Which done, I walked back again, all the way reading of my book of Timber measure, comparing it with my new Sliding Rule brought home this morning with great pleasure. Taking boat again I went to Shishe's yard, but he being newly gone out towards Deptford I followed him thither again, and there seeing him I went with him and pitched upon a couple, and so by water home, it being late, past 8 at night, the wind cold, and I a little weary. So home to my office, then to supper and bed.

16th. Up betimes and to my office, met to pass Mr. Pitt's (anon Sir J. Lawson's Secretary and Deputy Treasurer) accounts for the voyage last to the Streights, wherein the demands are strangely irregular, and I dare not oppose it alone for making an enemy and do no good, but only bring a review upon my Lord Sandwich, but God knows it troubles my heart to see it, and to see the Comptroller, whose duty it is, to make no more matter of it. At noon home for an hour to dinner, and so to the office public and private till late at night, so home to supper and bed with my father.

17th. Up by five o'clock as I have long done and to my office all the morning, at noon home to dinner with my father with us. Our dinner, it being Good Friday, was only sugarsopps and fish; the only time that we have had a Lenten dinner all this Lent. This morning Mr. Hunt, the instrument maker, brought me home a Basse Viall to see whether I like it, which I do not very well, besides I am under a doubt whether I had best buy one yet or no, because of spoiling my present mind and love to business. After dinner my father and I walked into the city a little, and parted and to Paul's Church Yard, to cause the title of my English "Mare Clausum"

[Selden's work was highly esteemed, and Charles I. made an order in council that a copy should be kept in the Council chest, another in the Court of Exchequer, and a third in the Court of Admiralty. The book Pepys refers to is Nedham's translation, which was entitled, "Of the Dominion or Ownership of the Sea. Two Books . . . , written at first in Latin and entituled Mare Clausum, by John Selden. Translated into English by Marchamont Nedham. London, 1652." This has the Commonwealth arms on the title-page and a dedication "To the Supreme Autoritie of the Nation-The Parliament of the Commonwealth of England." The dedication to Charles I. in Selden's original work was left out. Apparently a new title-page and dedication was prepared in 1663, but the copy in the British Museum, which formerly belonged to Charles Killigrew, does not contain these additions.]

to be changed, and the new title, dedicated to the King, to be put to it, because I am ashamed to have the other seen dedicated to the Commonwealth. So home and to my office till night, and so home to talk with my father, and supper and to bed, I have not had yet one quarter of an hour's leisure to sit down and talk with him since he came to town, nor do I know till the holidays when I shall.

18th. Up betimes and to my office, where all the morning. At noon to dinner. With us Mr. Creed, who has been deeply engaged at the office this day about the ending of his accounts, wherein he is most unhappy to have to do with a company of fools who after they have signed his accounts and made bills upon them yet dare not boldly assert to the Treasurer that they are satisfied with his accounts. Hereupon all dinner, and walking in the garden the afternoon, he and I talking of the ill management of our office, which God knows is very ill for the King's advantage. I would I could make it better. In the evening to my office, and at night home to supper and bed.

19th (Easter day). Up and this day put on my close-kneed coloured suit, which, with new stockings of the colour, with belt, and new gilt-handled sword, is very handsome. To church alone, and so to dinner, where my father and brother Tom dined with us, and after dinner to church again, my father sitting below in the chancel. After church done, where the young Scotchman preaching I slept all the while, my father and I to see my uncle and aunt Wight, and after a stay of an hour there my father to my brother's and I home to supper, and after supper fell in discourse of dancing, and I find that Ashwell hath a very fine carriage, which makes my wife almost ashamed of herself to see herself so outdone, but to-morrow she begins to learn to dance for a month or two. So to prayers and to bed. Will being gone, with my leave, to his father's this day for a day or two, to take physique these holydays.

20th. Up betimes as I use to do, and in my chamber begun to look over my father's accounts, which he brought out of the country with him by my desire, whereby I may see what he has received and spent, and I find that he is not anything extravagant, and yet it do so far outdo his estate that he must either think of lessening his charge, or I must be forced to spare money out of my purse to help him through, which I would willing do as far as L20 goes. So to my office the remaining part of the morning till towards noon, and then to Mr. Grant's. There saw his prints, which he shewed me, and indeed are the best collection of any things almost that ever I saw, there being the prints of most of the greatest houses, churches, and antiquitys in Italy and France and brave cutts. I had not time to look them over as I ought, and which I will take time hereafter to do, and therefore left them and home to dinner. After dinner, it raining very hard, by coach to Whitehall, where, after Sir G. Carteret, Sir J. Minnes, Mr. Coventry and I had been with the Duke, we to the Committee of Tangier and did matters there dispatching wholly my Lord Teviott, and so broke up. With Sir G. Carteret and Sir John Minnes by coach to my Lord Treasurer's, thinking to have spoken about getting money for paying the Yards; but we found him with some ladies at cards: and so, it being a bad time to speak, we parted, and Sir J. Minnes and I home, and after walking with my wife in the garden late, to supper and to bed, being somewhat troubled at Ashwell's desiring and insisting over eagerly upon her going to a ball to meet some of her old companions at a dancing school here in town next Friday, but I am resolved she shall not go. So to bed. This day the little Duke of Monmouth was marryed at White Hall, in the King's chamber; and tonight is a great supper and dancing at his lodgings, near Charing-Cross. I observed his coat at the tail of his coach he gives the arms of England, Scotland, and France, quartered upon some other fields, but what it is that speaks his being a bastard I know not.

21st. Up betimes and to my office, where first I ruled with red ink my English "Mare Clausum," which, with the new orthodox title, makes it now very handsome. So to business, and then home to dinner, and after dinner to sit at the office in the afternoon, and thence to my study late, and so home to supper to play a game at cards with my wife, and so to bed. Ashwell plays well at cards, and will teach us to play; I wish it do not lose too much of my time, and put my wife too much upon it.

22nd. Up betimes and to my office very busy all the morning there, entering things into my Book Manuscript, which pleases me very much. So to the Change, and so to my uncle Wight's, by invitation, whither my father, wife, and Ashwell came, where we had but a poor dinner, and not well dressed; besides, the very sight of my aunt's hands and greasy manner of carving, did almost turn my stomach. After dinner by coach to the King's Playhouse, where we saw but part of "Witt without mony," which I do not like much, but coming late put me out of tune, and it costing me four half-crowns for myself and company. So, the play done, home, and I to my office a while and so home, where my father (who is so very melancholy) and we played at cards, and so to supper and to bed.

23rd. St. George's day and Coronacion, the King and Court being at Windsor, at the installing of the King of Denmark by proxy and the Duke of Monmouth. I up betimes, and with my father, having a fire made in my wife's new closet above, it being a wet and cold day, we sat there all the morning looking over his country accounts ever since his going into the country. I find his spending hitherto has been (without extraordinary charges) at full L100 per annum, which troubles me, and I did let him apprehend it, so as that the poor man wept, though he did make it well appear to me that he could not have saved a farthing of it. I did tell him how things stand with us, and did shew my distrust of Pall, both for her good nature and housewifery, which he was sorry for, telling me that indeed she carries herself very well and carefully, which I am glad to hear, though I doubt it was but his doting and not being able to find her miscarriages so well nowadays as he could heretofore have done. We resolve upon sending for Will Stankes up to town to give us a right understanding in all that we have in Brampton, and before my father goes to settle every thing so as to resolve how to find a living for my father and to pay debts and legacies, and also to understand truly how Tom's condition is in the world, that we may know what we are like to expect of his doing ill or well. So to dinner, and after dinner to the office, where some of us met and did a little business, and so to Sir W. Batten's to see a little picture drawing of his by a Dutchman which is very well done. So to my office and put a few things in order, and so home to spend the evening with my father. At cards till late, and being at supper, my boy being sent for some mustard to a neat's tongue, the rogue staid half an hour in the streets, it seems at a bonfire, at which I was very angry, and resolve to beat him to-morrow.

24th. Up betimes, and with my salt eel

> [A salt eel is a rope's end cut from the piece to be used on the back of a culprit. "Yeow shall have salt eel for supper" is an emphatic threat.]

went down in the parler and there got my boy and did beat him till I was fain to take breath two or three times, yet for all I am afeard it will make the boy never the better, he is grown so hardened in his tricks, which I am sorry for, he being capable of making a brave man, and is a boy that I and my wife love very well. So made me ready, and to my office, where all the morning, and at noon home, whither came Captain Holland, who is lately come home from sea, and has been much harassed in law about the ship which he has bought, so that it seems in a despair he endeavoured to cut his own throat, but is recovered it; and it seems whether by that or any other persuasion (his wife's mother being a great zealot) he is turned almost a Quaker, his discourse being nothing but holy, and that impertinent, that I was weary of him. At last pretending to go to the Change we walked thither together, and there I left him and home to dinner, sending my boy by the way to enquire after two dancing masters at our end of the town for my wife to learn, of whose names the boy brought word. After dinner all the afternoon fiddling upon my viallin (which I have not done many a day) while Ashwell danced above in my upper best chamber, which is a rare room for musique, expecting this afternoon my wife to bring my cozen Scott and Stradwick, but they came not, and so in the evening we by ourselves to Half-way house to walk, but did not go in there, but only a walk and so home again and to supper, my father with us, and had a good lobster intended for part of our entertainment to these people to-day, and so to cards, and then to bed, being the first day that I have spent so much to my pleasure a great while.

25th. Up betimes and to my vyall and song book a pretty while, and so to my office, and there we sat all the morning. Among other things Sir W. Batten had a mind to cause Butler (our chief witness in the business of Field, whom we did force back from an employment going to sea to come back to attend our law sute) to be borne as a mate on the Rainbow in the Downes in compensation for his loss for our sakes. This he orders an order to be drawn by Mr. Turner for, and after Sir J. Minnes, Sir W. Batten, and Sir W. Pen had signed it, it came to me and I was going to put it up into my book, thinking to consider of it and give them my opinion upon it before I parted with it, but Sir W. Pen told me I must sign it or give it him again, for it should not go without my hand. I told him what I meant to do, whereupon Sir W. Batten was very angry, and in a great heat (which will bring out any thing which he has in his mind, and I am glad of it, though it is base in him to have a thing so long in his mind without speaking of it, though I am glad this is the worst, for if he had worse it would out as well as this some time or other) told me that I should not think as I have heretofore done, make them sign orders and not sign them myself. Which what ignorance or worse it implies is easy to judge, when he shall sign to things (and the rest of the board too as appears in this business) for company and not out of their judgment for. After some discourse I did convince them that it was not fit to have it go, and Sir W. Batten first, and then the rest, did willingly cancel all their hands and tear the order, for I told them, Butler being such a rogue as I know him, and we have all signed him to be to the Duke, it will be in his power to publish this to our great reproach, that we should take such a course as this to serve ourselves in wronging the King by putting him into a place he is no wise capable of, and that in an Admiral ship. At noon we rose, Sir W. Batten ashamed and vexed, and so home to dinner, and after dinner walked to the old Exchange and so all along to Westminster Hall, White Hall, my Lord Sandwich's lodgings, and going by water back to the Temple did pay my debts in several places in order to my examining my accounts tomorrow to my great content. So in the evening home, and after supper (my father at my brother's) and merrily practising to dance, which my wife hath begun to learn this day of Mr. Pembleton,

> [Pembleton, the dancing-master, made Pepys very jealous, and there are many allusions to him in the following pages. His lessons ceased on May 27th.]

but I fear will hardly do any great good at it, because she is conceited that she do well already, though I think no such thing. So to bed. At Westminster Hall, this day, I buy a book lately printed and licensed by Dr. Stradling, the Bishop of London's chaplin, being a book discovering the practices and designs of the papists, and the fears of some of our own fathers of the Protestant church heretofore of the return to Popery as it were prefacing it.

The book is a very good book; but forasmuch as it touches one of the Queenmother's fathers confessors, the Bishop, which troubles many good men and members of Parliament, hath called it in, which I am sorry for. Another book I bought, being a collection of many expressions of the great Presbyterian Preachers upon publique occasions, in the late times, against the King and his party, as some of Mr. Marshall, Case, Calamy, Baxter, &c., which is good reading now, to see what they then did teach, and the people believe, and what they would seem to believe now. Lastly, I did hear that the Queen is much grieved of late at the King's neglecting her, he having not supped once with her this quarter of a year, and almost every night with my Lady Castlemaine; who hath been with him this St. George's feast at Windsor, and came home with him last night; and, which is more, they say is removed as to her bed from her own home to a chamber in White Hall, next to the King's own; which I am sorry to hear, though I love her much.

26th (Lord's-day). Lay pretty long in bed talking with my wife, and then up and set to the making up of my monthly accounts, but Tom coming, with whom I was angry for botching my camlott coat, to tell me that my father and he would dine with me, and that my father was at our church, I got me ready and had a very good sermon of a country minister upon "How blessed a thing it is for brethren to live together in unity!" So home and all to dinner, and then would have gone by coach to have seen my Lord Sandwich at Chelsey if the man would have taken us, but he denying it we staid at home, and I all the afternoon upon my accounts, and find myself worth full L700, for which I bless God, it being the most I was ever yet worth in money. In the evening (my father being gone to my brother's to lie to-night) my wife, Ashwell, and the boy and I, and the dogg, over the water and walked to Half-way house, and beyond into the fields, gathering of cowslipps, and so to Half-way house, with some cold lamb we carried with us, and there supped, and had a most pleasant walk back again, Ashwell all along telling us some parts of their mask at Chelsey School, which was very pretty, and I find she hath a most prodigious memory, remembering so much of things acted six or seven years ago. So home, and after reading my vows, being sleepy, without prayers to bed, for which God forgive me!

27th. Up betimes and to my office, where doing business alone a good while till people came about business to me. Will Griffin tells me this morning that Captain Browne, Sir W. Batten's brother-in-law, is dead of a blow given him two days ago by a seaman, a servant of his, being drunk, with a stone striking him on the forehead, for which I am sorry, he having a good woman and several small children. At the office all the morning, at noon dined at home with my wife, merry, and after dinner by water to White Hall; but found the Duke of York gone to St. James's for this summer; and thence with Mr. Coventry, to whose chamber I went, and Sir W. Pen up to the Duke's closett. And a good while with him about our Navy business; and so I to White Hall, and there alone a while with my Lord Sandwich discoursing about his debt to the Navy, wherein he hath given me some things to resolve him in. Thence to my Lord's lodging, and thither came Creed to me, and he and I walked a great while in the garden, and thence to an alehouse in the market place to drink fine Lambeth ale, and so to Westminster Hall, and after walking there a great while, home by coach, where I found Mary gone from my wife, she being too high for her, though a very good servant, and my boy too will be going in a few days, for he is not for my family, he is grown so out of order and not to be ruled, and do himself, against his brother's counsel, desire to be gone, which I am sorry for, because I love the boy and would be glad to bring him to good. At home with my wife and Ashwell talking of her going into the country this year, wherein we had like to have fallen out, she thinking that I have a design to have her go, which I have not, and to let her stay here I perceive will not be convenient, for she expects more pleasure than I can give her here, and I fear I have done very ill in letting her begin to learn to dance. The Queen (which I did not know) it seems was at Windsor, at the late St. George's feast there; and the Duke of Monmouth dancing with her with his hat in his hand, the King came in and kissed him, and made him put on his hat, which every body took notice of. After being a while at my office home to supper and to bed, my Will being come home again after being at his father's all the last week taking physique.

28th. Up betimes and to my office, and there all the morning, only stepped up to see my wife and her dancing master at it, and I think after all she will do pretty well at it. So to dinner, Mr. Hunt dining with us, and so to the office, where we sat late, and then I to my office casting up my Lord's sea accounts over again, and putting them in order for payment, and so home to supper and to bed.

29th. Up betimes, and after having at my office settled some accounts for my Lord Sandwich, I went forth, and taking up my father at my brother's, took coach and towards Chelsey, 'lighting at an alehouse near the Gatehouse at Westminster to drink our morning draught, and so up again and to Chelsey, where we found my Lord all alone at a little table with one joynt of meat at dinner; we sat down and very merry talking, and mightily extolling the manner of his retirement, and the goodness of his diet, which indeed is so finely dressed: the mistress of the house, Mrs. Becke, having been a woman of good condition heretofore, a merchant's wife, and hath all things most excellently dressed; among others, her cakes admirable, and so good that my Lord's words were, they were fit to present to my Lady Castlemaine. From ordinary discourse my Lord fell to talk of other matters to me, of which chiefly the second part of the fray, which he told me a little while since of, between Mr. Edward Montagu and himself, which is that after that he had since been with him three times and no notice taken at all of any difference between them, and yet since that he hath forborn coming to him almost two months, and do speak not only slightly of my Lord every where, but hath complained to my Lord Chancellor of him, and arrogated all that ever my Lord hath done to be only by his direction and persuasion. Whether he hath done the like to the King or no, my Lord knows not; but my Lord hath been with the King since, and finds all things fair; and my Lord Chancellor hath told him of it, but with so much contempt of Mr. Montagu, as my Lord knows himself very secure against any thing the fool can do; and notwithstanding all this, so noble is his nature, that he professes himself ready to show kindness and pity to Mr. Montagu on any occasion. My Lord told me of his presenting Sir H. Bennet with a gold cupp of L100, which he refuses, with a compliment; but my Lord would have been glad he had taken it, that he might have had some obligations upon him which he thinks possible the other may refuse to prevent it; not that he hath any reason to doubt his kindness. But I perceive great differences there are at Court; and Sir H. Bennet and my Lord Bristol, and their faction, are likely to carry all things before them (which my Lord's judgment is, will not be for the best), and particularly against the Chancellor, who, he tells me, is irrecoverably lost: but, however, that he will not actually joyne in anything against the Chancellor, whom he do own to be his most sure friend, and to have been his greatest; and therefore will not openly act in either, but passively carry himself even. The Queen, my Lord tells me, he thinks he hath incurred some displeasure with, for his kindness to his neighbour, my Lady Castlemaine. My Lord tells me he hath no reason to fall for her sake, whose wit, management, nor interest, is not likely to hold up any man, and therefore he thinks it not his obligation to stand for her against his own interest. The Duke and Mr. Coventry my Lord says he is very well with, and fears not but they will show themselves his very good friends, specially at this time, he being able to serve them, and they needing him, which he did not tell me wherein. Talking of the business of Tangier, he tells me that my Lord Tiviott is gone away without the least respect paid to him, nor indeed to any man, but without his commission; and (if it be true what he says) having laid out seven or eight thousand pounds in commodities for the place; and besides having not only disobliged all the Commissioners for Tangier, but also Sir Charles Barkeley the other day, who, speaking in behalf of Colonel Fitz-Gerald, that having been deputy-governor there already, he ought to have expected and had the governorship upon the death or removal of the former governor. And whereas it is said that he and his men are Irish, which is indeed the main thing that hath moved the King and Council to put in Tiviott to prevent the Irish having too great and the whole command there under Fitz-Gerald; he further said that there was never an Englishman fit to command Tangier; my Lord Tiviott answered yes, that there were many more fit than himself or Fitz-Gerald either. So that Fitz-Gerald being so great with the Duke of York, and being already made deputy-governor, independent of my Lord Tiviott, and he being also left here behind him for a while, my Lord Sandwich do think that, putting all these things together, the few friends he hath left, and the ill posture of his affairs, my Lord Tiviott is not a man of the conduct and management that either people take him to be, or is fit for the command of the place. And here, speaking of the Duke of York and Sir Charles Barkeley, my Lord tells me that he do very much admire the good management, and discretion, and nobleness of the Duke, that whatever he may be led by him or Mr. Coventry singly in private, yet he did not observe that in publique matters, but he did give as ready hearing and as good acceptance to any reasons offered by any other man against the opinions of them, as he did to them, and would concur in the prosecution of it. Then we came to discourse upon his own sea accompts, and came to a resolution what and how to proceed in them; wherein he resolved, though I offered him a way of evading the greatest part of his debt honestly, by making himself debtor to the Parliament, before the King's time, which he might justly do, yet he resolved to go openly and nakedly in it, and put himself to the kindness of the King and Duke, which humour, I must confess, and so did tell him (with which he was not a little pleased) had thriven very well with him, being known to be a man of candid and open dealing, without any private tricks or hidden designs as other men commonly have in what they do. From that we had discourse of Sir G. Carteret, who he finds kind to him, but it may be a little envious, and most other men are, and of many others; and upon the whole do find that it is a troublesome thing for a man of any condition at Court to carry himself even, and without contracting enemys or envyers; and that much discretion and dissimulation is necessary to do it. My father staid a good while at the window and then sat down by himself while my Lord and I were thus an hour together or two after dinner discoursing, and by and by he took his leave, and told me he would stay below for me. Anon I took leave, and coming down found my father unexpectedly in great pain and desiring for God's sake to get him a bed to lie upon, which I did, and W. Howe and I staid by him, in so great pain as I never saw, poor wretch, and with that patience, crying only: Terrible, terrible pain, God help me, God help me, with the mournful voice, that made my heart ake. He desired to rest a little alone to see whether it would abate, and W. Howe and I went down and walked in the gardens, which are very fine, and a pretty fountayne, with which I was finely wetted, and up to a banquetting house, with a very fine prospect, and so back to my father, who I found in such pain that I could not bear the sight of it without weeping, never thinking that I should be able to get him from thence, but at last, finding it like to continue, I got him to go to the coach, with great pain, and driving hard, he all the while in a most unsufferable torment (meeting in the way with Captain Ferrers going to my Lord, to tell him that my Lady Jemimah is come to town, and that Will Stankes is come with my father's horses), not staying the coach to speak with any body, but once, in St. Paul's Churchyard, we were forced to stay, the jogging and pain making my father vomit, which it never had done before. At last we got home, and all helping him we got him to bed presently, and after half an hour's lying in his naked bed (it being a rupture [with] which he is troubled, and has been this 20 years, but never in half the pain and with so great swelling as now, and how this came but by drinking of cold small beer and sitting long upon a low stool and then standing long after it he cannot tell) .... After which he was at good ease, and so continued, and so fell to sleep, and we went down whither W. Stankes was come with his horses. But it is very pleasant to hear how he rails at the rumbling and ado that is in London over it is in the country, that he cannot endure it. He supped with us, and very merry, and then he to his lodgings at the Inne with the horses, and so we to bed, I to my father who is very well again, and both slept very well.

30th. Up, and after drinking my morning draft with my father and W. Stankes, I went forth to Sir W. Batten, who is going (to no purpose as he uses to do) to Chatham upon a survey. So to my office, where till towards noon, and then to the Exchange, and back home to dinner, where Mrs. Hunt, my father, and W. Stankes;

but, Lord! what a stir Stankes makes with his being crowded in the streets and wearied in walking in London, and would not be wooed by my wife and Ashwell to go to a play, nor to White Hall, or to see the lyons,

> [The Tower menagerie, with its famous lions, which was one of the chief sights of London, and gave rise to a new English word, was not abolished until the early part of the present century.]

though he was carried in a coach. I never could have thought there had been upon earth a man so little curious in the world as he is. At the office all the afternoon till 9 at night, so home to cards with my father, wife, and Ashwell, and so to bed.

> Academy was dissolved by order of the Pope
> After some pleasant talk, my wife, Ashwell, and I to bed
> And so to bed, my father lying with me in Ashwell's bed
> Dare not oppose it alone for making an enemy and do no good
> Dinner was great, and most neatly dressed
> Dog attending us, which made us all merry again
> Galileo's air thermometer, made before 1597
> I do not find other people so willing to do business as myself
> I was very angry, and resolve to beat him to-morrow
> Insurrection of the Catholiques there
> Justice of proceeding not to condemn a man unheard
> Matters in Ireland are full of discontent
> My maid Susan ill, or would be thought so
> Parliament do agree to throw down Popery
> Railed bitterly ever and anon against John Calvin
> She is conceited that she do well already
> So home to supper and bed with my father
> That he is not able to live almost with her
> That I might say I saw no money in the paper
> There is no man almost in the City cares a turd for him
> Though it be but little, yet I do get ground every month

THE DIARY OF SAMUEL PEPYS M.A. F.R.S.

CLERK OF THE ACTS AND SECRETARY TO THE ADMIRALTY

Transcribed from the shorthand manuscript in the PEPYSIAN *library Magdalene College Cambridge by the Rev.* MYNORS *bright* M.A. *Late fellow and President of the College*

(Unabridged)

WITH LORD BRAYBROOKE'S NOTES

EDITED WITH ADDITIONS BY

HenryB. Wheatley F.S.A.

Diaryof Samuel Pepys.
May & June
1663

May 1st. Up betimes and my father with me, and he and I all the morning and Will Stankes private, in my wife's closet above, settling our matters concerning our Brampton estate, &c., and I find that there will be, after all debts paid within L100, L50 per annum clear coming towards my father's maintenance, besides L25 per annum annuities to my Uncle Thomas and Aunt Perkins. Of which, though I was in my mind glad, yet thought it not fit to let my father know it thoroughly, but after he had gone out to visit my uncle Thomas and brought him to dinner with him, and after dinner I got my father, brother Tom, and myself together, I did make the business worse to them, and did promise L20 out of my own purse to make it L50 a year to my father, propounding that Stortlow may be sold to pay L200 for his satisfaction therein and the rest to go towards payment of debts and legacies. The truth is I am fearful lest my father should die before debts are paid, and then the land goes to Tom and the burden of paying all debts will fall upon the rest of the land. Not that I would do my brother any real hurt. I advised my father to good husbandry and to living within the compass of L50 a year, and all in such kind words, as not only made, them but myself to weep, and I hope it will have a good effect. That being done, and all things agreed on, we went down, and after a glass of wine we all took horse, and I, upon a horse hired of Mr. Game, saw him out of London, at the end of Bishopsgate Street, and so I turned and rode, with some trouble, through the fields, and then Holborn, &c., towards Hide Park, whither all the world, I think, are going, and in my going, almost thither, met W. Howe coming galloping upon a little crop black nag; it seems one that was taken in some ground of my Lord's, by some mischance being left by his master, a thief; this horse being found with black cloth ears on, and a false mayne, having none of his own; and I back again with him to the Chequer, at Charing Cross, and there put up my own dull jade, and by his advice saddled a delicate stone-horse of Captain Ferrers's, and with that rid in state to the Park, where none better mounted than I almost, but being in a throng of horses, seeing the King's riders showing tricks with their managed horses, which were very strange, my stone-horse was very troublesome, and begun to, fight with other horses, to the dangering him and myself, and with much ado I got out, and kept myself out of harm's way.. Here I saw nothing good, neither the King, nor my Lady Castlemaine, nor any great ladies or beauties being there, there being more pleasure a great deal at an ordinary day; or else those few good faces that there were choked up with the many bad ones, there being people of all sorts in coaches there, to some thousands, I think. Going thither in the highway, just by the Park gate, I met a boy in a sculler boat, carried by a dozen people at least, rowing as hard as he could drive, it seems upon some wager. By and by, about seven or eight o'clock, homeward; and changing my horse again, I rode home, coaches going in great crowds to the further end of the town almost. In my way, in Leadenhall Street, there was morris-dancing which I have not seen a great while. So set my horse up at Game's, paying 5s. for him. And so home to see Sir J. Minnes, who is well again, and after staying talking with him awhile, I took leave and went to hear Mrs. Turner's daughter, at whose house Sir J. Minnes lies, play on the harpsicon; but, Lord! it was enough to make any man sick to hear her; yet I was forced to commend her highly. So home to supper and to bed, Ashwell playing upon the tryangle very well before I went to bed. This day Captain Grove sent me a side of pork, which was the oddest present, sure, that was ever made any man; and the next, I remember I told my wife, I believe would be a pound of candles, or a shoulder of mutton; but the fellow do it in kindness, and is one I am beholden to. So to bed very weary, and a little galled for lack of riding, praying to God for a good journey to my father, of whom I am afeard, he being so lately ill of his pain.

2nd. Being weary last night, I slept till almost seven o'clock, a thing I have not done many a day. So up and to my office (being come to some angry words with my wife about neglecting the keeping of the house clean, I calling her beggar, and she me pricklouse, which vexed me) and there all the morning. So to the Exchange and then home to dinner, and very merry and well pleased with my wife, and so to the office again, where we met extraordinary upon drawing up the debts of the Navy to my Lord Treasurer. So rose and up to Sir W. Pen to drink a glass of bad syder in his new far low dining room, which is very noble, and so home, where Captain Ferrers and his lady are come to see my wife, he being to go the beginning of next week to France to sea and I think to fetch over my young Lord Hinchinbroke. They being gone I to my office to write letters by the post, and so home to supper and to bed.

3rd (Lord's day). Up before 5 o'clock and alone at setting my Brampton papers to rights according to my father's and my computation and resolution the other day to my good content, I finding that there will be clear saved to us L50 per annum, only a debt of it may be L100. So made myself ready and to church, where Sir W. Pen showed me the young lady which young Dawes, that sits in the new corner-pew in the church, hath stole away from Sir Andrew Rickard, her guardian, worth L1000 per annum present, good land, and some money, and a very well-bred and handsome lady: he, I doubt, but a simple fellow. However, he got this good luck to get her, which methinks I could envy him with all my heart. Home to dinner with my wife, who not being very well did not dress herself but staid at home all day, and so I to church in the afternoon and so home again, and up to teach Ashwell the grounds of time and other things on the tryangle, and made her take out a Psalm very well, she having a good ear and hand. And so a while to my office, and then home to supper and prayers, to bed, my wife and I having a little falling out because I would not leave my discourse below with her and Ashwell to go up and talk with her alone upon something she has to say. She reproached me but I had rather talk with any body than her, by which I find I think she is jealous of my freedom with Ashwell, which I must avoid giving occasion of.

4th. Up betimes and to setting my Brampton papers in order and looking over my wardrobe against summer, and laying things in order to send to my brother to alter. By and by took boat intending to have gone down to Woolwich, but seeing I could not get back time enough to dinner, I returned and home. Whither by and by the dancing-master' came, whom standing by, seeing him instructing my wife, when he had done with her, he would needs have me try the steps of a coranto, and what with his desire and my wife's importunity, I did begin, and then was obliged to give him entry-money 10s., and am become his scholler. The truth is, I think it a thing very useful for a gentleman, and sometimes I may have occasion of using it, and though it cost me what I am heartily sorry it should, besides that I must by my oath give half as much more to the poor, yet I am resolved to get it up some other way, and then it will not be above a month or two in a year. So though it be against my stomach yet I will try it a little while; if I see it comes to any great inconvenience or charge I will fling it off. After I had begun with the steps of half a coranto, which I think I shall learn well enough, he went away, and we to dinner, and by and by out by coach, and set my wife down at my Lord Crew's, going to see my Lady Jem. Montagu, who is lately come to town, and I to St. James's; where Mr. Coventry, Sir W. Pen and I staid a good while for the Duke's coming in, but not coming, we walked to White Hall; and meeting the King, we followed him into the Park, where Mr. Coventry and he talked of building a new yacht, which the King is resolved to have built out of his privy purse, he having some contrivance of his own. The talk being done, we fell off to White Hall, leaving the King in the Park, and going back, met the Duke going towards St. James's to meet us. So he turned back again, and to his closett at White Hall; and there, my Lord Sandwich present, we did our weekly errand, and so broke up; and I down into the garden with my Lord Sandwich (after we had sat an hour at the Tangier Committee); and after talking largely of his own businesses, we begun to talk how matters are at Court: and though he did not flatly tell me any such thing, yet I do suspect that all is not kind between the King and the Duke, and that the King's fondness to the little Duke do occasion it; and it may be that there is some fear of his being made heir to the Crown. But this my Lord did not tell me, but is my guess only; and that my Lord Chancellor is without doubt falling past hopes. He being gone to Chelsey by coach I to his lodgings, where my wife staid for me, and she from thence to see Mrs. Pierce and called me at Whitehall stairs (where I went before by land to know whether there was any play at Court to-night) and there being none she and I to Mr. Creed to the Exchange, where she bought something, and from thence by water to White Fryars, and wife to see Mrs. Turner, and then came to me at my brother's, where I did give him order about my summer clothes, and so home by coach, and after supper to bed to my wife, with whom I have not lain since I used to lie with my father till to-night.

5th. Up betimes and to my office, and there busy all the morning, among other things walked a good while up and down with Sir J. Minnes, he telling many old stories of the Navy, and of the state of the Navy at the beginning of the late troubles, and I am troubled at my heart to think, and shall hereafter cease to wonder, at the bad success of the King's cause, when such a knave as he (if it be true what he says) had the whole management of the fleet, and the design of putting out of my Lord Warwick, and carrying the fleet to the King, wherein he failed most fatally to the King's ruin. Dined at home, and after dinner up to try my dance, and so to the office again, where we sat all the afternoon. In the evening Deane of Woolwich went home with me and showed me the use of a little sliding ruler, less than that I bought the other day, which is the same with that, but more portable; however I did not seem to understand or even to have seen anything of it before, but I find him an ingenious fellow, and a good servant in his place to the King. Thence to my office busy writing letters, and then came Sir W. Warren, staying for a letter in his business by the post, and while that was writing he and I talked about merchandise, trade, and getting of money. I made it my business to enquire what way there is for a man bred like me to come to understand anything of trade. He did most discretely answer me in all things, shewing me the danger for me to meddle either in ships or merchandise of any sort or common stocks, but what I have to keep at interest, which is a good, quiett, and easy profit, and once in a little while something offers that with ready money you may make use of money to good profit. Wherein I concur much with him, and parted late with great pleasure and content in his discourse, and so home to supper and to bed. It has been this afternoon very hot and this evening also, and about 11 at night going to bed it fell a-thundering and lightening, the greatest flashes enlightening the whole body of the yard, that ever I saw in my life.

6th. Up betimes and to my office a good while at my new rulers, then to business, and towards noon to the Exchange with Creed, where we met with Sir J. Minnes coming in his coach from Westminster, who tells us, in great heat, that, by God, the Parliament will make mad work; that they will render all men incapable of any military or civil employment that have borne arms in the late troubles against the King, excepting some persons; which, if it be so, as I hope it is not, will give great cause of discontent, and I doubt will have but bad effects. I left them at the Exchange and walked to Paul's Churchyard to look upon a book or two, and so back, and thence to the Trinity House, and there dined, where, among other discourse worth hearing among the old seamen, they tell us that they have catched often in Greenland in fishing whales with the iron grapnells that had formerly been struck into their bodies covered over with fat; that they have had eleven hogsheads of oyle out of the tongue of a whale. Thence after dinner home to my office, and there busy till the evening. Then home and to supper, and while at supper comes Mr. Pembleton, and after supper we up to our dancing room and there danced three or four country dances, and after that a practice of my coranto I began with him the other day, and I begin to think that I shall be able to do something at it in time. Late and merry at it, and so weary to bed.

7th. Up betimes and to my office awhile, and then by water with my wife, leaving her at the new Exchange, and I to see Dr. Williams, and spoke with him about my business with Tom Trice, and so to my brother's, who I find very careful now-a-days, more than ordinary in his business and like to do well. From thence to Westminster, and there up and down from the Hall to the Lobby, the Parliament sitting. Sir Thomas Crew this day tells me that the Queen, hearing that there was L40,000 per annum brought into her account among the other expences of the Crown to the Committee of Parliament, she took order to let them know that she hath yet for the payment of her whole family received but L4,000, which is a notable act of spirit, and I believe is true. So by coach to my Lord Crew's, and there dined with him. He tells me of the order the House of Commons have made for the drawing an Act for the rendering none capable of preferment or employment in the State, but who have been loyall and constant to the King and Church; which will be fatal to a great many, and makes me doubt lest I myself, with all my innocence during the late times, should be brought in, being employed in the Exchequer; but, I hope, God will provide for me. This day the new Theatre Royal begins to act with scenes the Humourous Lieutenant, but I have not time to see it, nor could stay to see my Lady Jemimah lately come to town, and who was here in the house, but dined above with her grandmother. But taking my wife at my brother's home by coach, and the officers being at Deptford at a Pay we had no office, but I took my wife by water and so spent the evening, and so home with great pleasure to supper, and then to bed.

8th. Up very early and to my office, there preparing letters to my father of great import in the settling of our affairs, and putting him upon a way [of] good husbandry, I promising to make out of my own purse him up to L50 per annum, till either by my uncle Thomas's death or the fall of the Wardrobe place he be otherwise provided. That done I by water to the Strand, and there viewed the Queen-Mother's works at Somersett House, and thence to the new playhouse, but could not get in to see it. So to visit my Lady Jemimah, who is grown much since I saw her; but lacks mightily to be brought into the fashion of the court to set her off: Thence to the Temple, and there sat till one o'clock reading at Playford's in Dr. Usher's 'Body of Divinity' his discourse of the Scripture, which is as much, I believe, as is anywhere said by any man, but yet there is room to cavill, if a man would use no faith to the tradition of the Church in which he is born, which I think to be as good an argument as most is brought for many things, and it may be for that among others. Thence to my brother's, and there took up my wife and Ashwell to the Theatre Royall, being the second day of its being opened. The house is made with extraordinary good contrivance, and yet hath some faults, as the narrowness of the passages in and out of the Pitt, and the distance from the stage to the boxes, which I am confident cannot hear; but for all other things it is well, only, above all, the musique being below, and most of it sounding under the very stage, there is no hearing of the bases at all, nor very well of the trebles, which sure must be mended. The play was "The Humerous Lieutenant," a play that hath little good in it, nor much in the very part which, by the King's command, Lacy now acts instead of Clun. In the dance, the tall devil's actions was very pretty. The play being done, we home by water, having been a little shamed that my wife and woman were in such a pickle, all the ladies being finer and better dressed in the pitt than they used, I think, to be. To my office to set down this day's passage, and, though my oath against going to plays do not oblige me against this house, because it was not then in being, yet believing that at the time my meaning was against all publique houses, I am resolved to deny myself the liberty of two plays at Court, which are in arreare to me for the months of March and April, which will more than countervail this excess, so that this month of May is the first that I must claim a liberty of going to a Court play according to my oath. So home to supper, and at supper comes Pembleton, and afterwards we all up to dancing till late, and so broke up and to bed, and they say that I am like to make a dancer.

9th. Up betimes and to my office, whither sooner than ordinary comes Mr. Hater desiring to speak a word to me alone, which I was from the disorder of his countenance amused at, and so the poor man began telling me that by Providence being the last Lord's day at a meeting of some Friends upon doing of their duties, they were surprised, and he carried to the Counter, but afterwards released; however, hearing that Sir W. Batten do hear of [it,] he thought it good to give me an account of it, lest it might tend to any prejudice to me. I was extraordinary surprised with it, and troubled for him, knowing that now it is out it is impossible for me to conceal it, or keep him in employment under me without danger to myself. I cast about all I could, and did give him the best advice I could, desiring to know if I should promise that he would not for the time to come commit the same, he told me he desired that I would rather forbear to promise that, for he durst not do it, whatever God in His providence shall do with him, and that for my part he did bless God and thank me for all the love and kindness I have shewed him hitherto. I could not without tears in my eyes discourse with him further, but at last did pitch upon telling the truth of the whole to Mr. Coventry as soon as I could, and to that end did use means to prevent Sir W. Batten (who came to town last night) from going to that end to-day, lest he might doe it to Sir G. Carteret or Mr. Coventry before me; which I did prevail and kept him at the office all the morning. At noon dined at home with a heavy heart for the poor man, and after dinner went out to my brother's, and thence to Westminster, where at Mr. Jervas's, my old barber, I did try two or three borders and perriwiggs, meaning to wear one; and yet I have no stomach [for it,] but that the pains of keeping my hair clean is so great. He trimmed me, and at last I parted, but my mind was almost altered from my first purpose, from the trouble that I foresee will be in wearing them also. Thence by water home and to the office, where busy late, and so home to supper and bed, with my mind much troubled about T. Hater.

10th (Lord's day). Up betimes, and put on a black cloth suit, with white lynings under all, as the fashion is to wear, to appear under the breeches. So being ready walked to St. James's, where I sat talking with Mr. Coventry, while he made himself ready, about several businesses of the Navy, and afterwards, the Duke being gone out, he and I walked to White Hall together over the Park, I telling him what had happened to Tom Hater, at which he seems very sorry, but tells me that if it is not made very publique, it will not be necessary to put him away at present, but give him good caution for the time to come. However, he will speak to the Duke about it and know his pleasure. Parted with him there, and I walked back to St. James's, and was there at mass, and was forced in the crowd to kneel down; and mass being done, to the King's Head ordinary, whither I sent for Mr. Creed and there we dined, where many Parliament-men; and most of their talk was about the news from Scotland, that the Bishop of Galloway was besieged in his house by some woman, and had like to have been outraged, but I know not how he was secured; which is bad news, and looks just as it did in the beginning of the late troubles. From thence they talked of rebellion; and I perceive they make it their great maxime to be sure to master the City of London, whatever comes of it or from it. After that to some other discourse, and, among other things, talking of the way of ordinaries, that it is very convenient, because a man knows what he hath to pay: one did wish that, among many bad, we could learn two good things of France, which were that we would not think it below the gentleman, or person of honour at a tavern, to bargain for his meat before he eats it; and next, to take no servant without certificate from some friend or gentleman of his good behaviour and abilities. Hence with Creed into St. James's Park, and there walked all the afternoon, and thence on foot home, and after a little while at my office walked in the garden with my wife, and so home to supper, and after prayers to bed. My brother Tom supped with me, and should have brought my aunt Ellen with him; she was not free to go abroad.

11th. Up betimes, and by water to Woolwich on board the Royall James, to see in what dispatch she is to be carried about to Chatham. So to the yard a little, and thence on foot to Greenwich, where going I was set upon by a great dogg, who got hold of my garters, and might have done me hurt; but, Lord, to see in what a maze I was, that, having a sword about me, I never thought of it, or had the heart to make use of it, but might, for want of that courage, have been worried. Took water there and home, and both coming and going did con my lesson on my Ruler to measure timber, which I think I can well undertake now to do. At home there being Pembleton I danced, and I think shall come on to do something in a little time, and after dinner by coach with Sir W. Pen (setting down his daughter at Clerkenwell), to St. James's, where we attended the Duke of York: and, among other things, Sir G. Carteret and I had a great dispute about the different value of the pieces of eight rated by Mr. Creed at 4s. and 5d., and by Pitts at 4s. and 9d., which was the greatest husbandry to the King? he persisting that the greatest sum was; which is as ridiculous a piece of ignorance as could be imagined. However, it is to be argued at the Board, and reported to the Duke next week; which I shall do with advantage, I hope. Thence to the Tangier Committee, where we should have concluded in sending Captain Cuttance and the rest to Tangier to deliberate upon the design of the Mole before they begin to work upon it, but there being not a committee (my Lord intending to be there but was taken up at my Lady Castlemayne's) I parted and went homeward, after a little discourse with Mr. Pierce the surgeon, who tells me that my Lady Castlemaine hath now got lodgings near the King's chamber at Court; and that the other day Dr. Clerke and he did dissect two bodies, a man and a woman; before the King, with which the King was highly pleased. By water and called upon Tom Trice by appointment with Dr. Williams, but the Dr. did not come, it seems by T. Trice's desire, not thinking he should be at leisure. However, in general we talked of our business, and I do not find that he will come to any lower terms than L150, which I think I shall not give him but by law, and so we parted, and I called upon Mr. Crumlum, and did give him the 10s. remaining, not laid out of the L5 I promised him for the school, with which he will buy strings, and golden letters upon the books I did give them. I sat with him and his wife a great while talking, and she is [a] pretty woman, never yet with child, and methinks looks as if her mouth watered now and then upon some of her boys. Then upon Tom Pepys, the Turner, desiring his father and his letter to Piggott signifying his consent to the selling of his land for the paying of us his money, and so home, and finding Pembleton there we did dance till it was late, and so to supper and to bed.

12th. Up between four and five, and after dressing myself then to my office to prepare business against the afternoon, where all the morning, and dined at noon at home, where a little angry with my wife for minding nothing now but the dancing-master, having him come twice a day, which is a folly. Again, to my office. We sat till late, our chief business being the reconciling the business of the pieces of eight mentioned yesterday before the Duke of York, wherein I have got the day, and they are all brought over to what I said, of which I am proud. Late writing letters, and so home to supper and to bed. Here I found Creed staying for me, and so after supper I staid him all night and lay with me, our great discourse being the folly of our two doting knights, of which I am ashamed.

13th. Lay till 6 o'clock and then up, and after a little talk and mirth, he went away, and I to my office, where busy all the morning, and at noon home to dinner, and after dinner Pembleton came and I practised. But, Lord! to see how my wife will not be thought to need telling by me or Ashwell, and yet will plead that she has learnt but a month, which causes many short fallings out between us. So to my office, whither one-eyed Cooper came to see me, and I made him to show me the use of platts, and to understand the lines, and how to find how lands bear, &c., to my great content. Then came Mr. Barrow, storekeeper of Chatham, who tells me many things, how basely Sir W. Batten has carried himself to him, and in all things else like a passionate dotard, to the King's great wrong. God mend all, for I am sure we are but in an ill condition in the Navy, however the King is served in other places. Home to supper, to cards, and to bed.

14th. Up betimes and put up some things to send to Brampton. Then abroad to the Temple, and up and down about business, and met Mr. Moore; and with him to an alehouse in Holborn; where in discourse he told me that he fears the King will be tempted to endeavour the setting the Crown upon the little Duke, which may cause troubles; which God forbid, unless it be his due! He told me my Lord do begin to settle to business again, which I am glad of, for he must not sit out, now he has done his own business by getting his estate settled, and that the King did send for him the other day to my Lady Castlemaine's, to play at cards, where he lost L50; for which I am sorry, though he says my Lord was pleased at it, and said he would be glad at any time to lose L50 for the King to send for him to play, which I do not so well like. Thence home, and after dinner to the office, where we sat till night, and then made up my papers and letters by the post, and so home to dance with Pembleton. This day we received a baskett from my sister Pall, made by her of paper, which hath a great deal of labour in it for country innocent work. After supper to bed, and going to bed received a letter from Mr. Coventry desiring my coming to him to-morrow morning, which troubled me to think what the business should be, fearing it must be some bad news in Tom Hater's business.

15th. Up betimes and walked to St. James's, where Mr. Coventry being in bed I walked in the Park, discoursing with the keeper of the Pell Mell, who was sweeping of it; who told me of what the earth is mixed that do floor the Mall, and that over all there is cockle-shells powdered, and spread to keep it fast; which, however, in dry weather, turns to dust and deads the ball. Thence to Mr. Coventry; and sitting by his bedside, he did tell me that he sent for me to discourse upon my Lord Sandwich's allowances for his several pays, and what his thoughts are concerning his demands; which he could not take the freedom to do face to face, it being not so proper as by me: and did give me a most friendly and ingenuous account of all; telling me how unsafe, at this juncture, while every man's, and his actions particularly, are descanted upon, it is either for him to put the Duke upon doing, or my Lord himself to desire anything extraordinary, 'specially the King having been so bountifull already; which the world takes notice of even to some repinings. All which he did desire me to discourse with my Lord of; which I have undertook to do. We talked also of our office in general, with which he told me that he was now-a-days nothing so satisfied as he was wont to be. I confess I told him things are ordered in that way that we must of necessity break in a little time a pieces. After done with him about these things, he told me that for Mr. Hater the Duke's word was in short that he found he had a good servant, an Anabaptist, and unless he did carry himself more to the scandal of the office, he would bear with his opinion till he heard further, which do please me very much. Thence walked to Westminster, and there up and down in the Hall and the Parliament House all the morning; at noon by coach to my Lord Crew's, hearing that Lord Sandwich did dine there; where I told him what had passed between Mr. Coventry and myself; with which he was contented, though I could perceive not very well pleased. And I do believe that my Lord do find some other things go against his mind in the House; for in the motion made the other day in the House by my Lord Bruce, that none be capable of employment but such as have been loyal and constant to the King and Church, the General [Monk] and my Lord were mentioned to be excepted; and my Lord Bruce did come since to my Lord, to clear himself that he meant nothing to his prejudice, nor could it have any such effect if he did mean it. After discourse with my Lord; to dinner with him; there dining there my Lord Montagu of Boughton, Mr. William Montagu his brother, the Queen's Sollicitor, &c., and a fine dinner. Their talk about a ridiculous falling-out two days ago at my Lord of Oxford's house, at an entertainment of his, there being there my Lord of Albemarle, Lynsey, two of the Porters, my Lord Bellasses, and others, where there were high words and some blows, and pulling off of perriwiggs; till my Lord Monk took away some of their swords, and sent for some soldiers to guard the house till the fray was ended. To such a degree of madness the nobility of this age is come! After dinner I went up to Sir Thomas Crew, who lies there not very well in his head, being troubled with vapours and fits of dizziness: and there I sat talking with him all the afternoon from one discourse to another, the most was upon the unhappy posture of things at this time; that the King do mind nothing but pleasures, and hates the very sight or thoughts of business; that my Lady Castlemaine rules him, who, he says, hath all the tricks of Aretin

[An allusion to Aretin's infamous letters and sonnets accompanying the as infamous "Postures" engraved by Marc Antonio from the designs of Julio Romano (Steinman's "Memoir of Barbara, Duchess of Cleveland," privately printed, 1871).]

that are to be practised to give pleasure. In which he is too able . . . . but what is the unhappiness in that, as the Italian proverb says, "lazzo dritto non vuolt consiglio." If any of the sober counsellors give him good advice, and move him in anything that is to his good and honour, the other part, which are his counsellers of pleasure, take him when he is with my Lady Castlemaine, and in a humour of delight, and then persuade him that he ought not to hear nor listen to the advice of those old dotards or counsellors that were heretofore his enemies: when, God knows! it is they that now-a-days do most study his honour. It seems the present favourites now are my Lord Bristol, Duke of Buckingham, Sir H. Bennet, my Lord Ashley, and Sir Charles

Barkeley; who, among them, have cast my Lord Chancellor upon his back, past ever getting up again; there being now little for him to do, and he waits at Court attending to speak to the King as others do: which I pray God may prove of good effects, for it is feared it will be the same with my Lord Treasurer shortly. But strange to hear how my Lord Ashley, by my Lord Bristol's means (he being brought over to the Catholique party against the Bishopps, whom he hates to the death, and publicly rails against them; not that he is become a Catholique, but merely opposes the Bishopps; and yet, for aught I hear, the Bishopp of London keeps as great with the King as ever) is got into favour, so much that, being a man of great business and yet of pleasure, and drolling too, he, it is thought, will be made Lord Treasurer upon the death or removal of the good old man. My Lord Albemarle, I hear, do bear through and bustle among them, and will not be removed from the King's good opinion and favour, though none of the Cabinett; but yet he is envied enough. It is made very doubtful whether the King do not intend the making of the Duke of Monmouth legitimate;

[Thomas Ross, Monmouth's tutor, put the idea into his head that Charles *ii*. had married his mother. The report was sedulously spread abroad, and obtained some kind of credence, until, in June, 1678, the king set the matter at rest by publishing a declaration, which was entered in the Council book and registered in Chancery. The words of the declaration are: "That to avoid any dispute which might happen in time to come concerning the succession of the Crown, he (Charles) did declare, in the presence of Almighty God, that he never gave, nor made any contract of marriage, nor was married to Mrs. Barlow, alias Waters, the Duke of Monmouth's mother, nor to any other woman whatsoever, but to his present wife, Queen Catherine, then living."]

but surely the Commons of England will never do it, nor the Duke of York suffer it, whose lady, I am told, is very troublesome to him by her jealousy. But it is wonderful that Sir Charles Barkeley should be so great still, not [only] with the King, but Duke also; who did so stiffly swear that he had lain with her.

[The conspiracy of Sir Charles Berkeley, Lord Arran, Jermyn, Talbot, and Killigrew to traduce Anne Hyde was peculiarly disgraceful, and the conduct of all the actors in the affair of the marriage, from Lord Clarendon downwards, was far from creditable (see Lister's "Life of Clarendon," ii. 68-79)]

And another one Armour that he rode before her on horseback in Holland I think . . . . No care is observed to be taken of the main chance, either for maintaining of trade or opposing of factions, which, God knows, are ready to break out, if any of them (which God forbid!) should dare to begin; the King and every man about him minding so much their pleasures or profits. My Lord Hinchingbroke, I am told, hath had a mischance to kill his boy by his birding-piece going off as he was a-fowling. The gun was charged with small shot, and hit the boy in the face and about the temples, and he lived four days. In Scotland, it seems, for all the newes-books tell us every week that they are all so quiett, and everything in the Church settled, the old woman had like to have killed, the other day, the Bishop of Galloway, and not half the Churches of the whole kingdom conform. Strange were the effects of the late thunder and lightning about a week since at Northampton, coming with great rain, which caused extraordinary floods in a few hours, bearing away bridges, drowning horses, men, and cattle. Two men passing over a bridge on horseback, the arches before and behind them were borne away, and that left which they were upon: but, however, one of the horses fell over, and was drowned. Stacks of faggots carried as high as a steeple, and other dreadful things; which Sir Thomas Crew showed me letters to him about from Mr. Freemantle and others, that it is very true. The Portugalls have choused us,

[The word chouse appears to have been introduced into the language at the beginning of the seventeenth century. In 1609, a Chiaus sent by Sir Robert Shirley, from Constantinople to London, had chiaused (or choused) the Turkish and Persian merchants out of L4,000, before the arrival of his employer, and had decamped. The affair was quite recent in 1610, when Jonson's "Alchemist" appeared, in which it is alluded to .]

it seems, in the Island of Bombay, in the East Indys; for after a great charge of our fleets being sent thither with full commission from the King of Portugall to receive it, the Governour by some pretence or other will not deliver it to Sir Abraham Shipman, sent from the King, nor to my Lord of Marlborough; which the King takes highly ill, and I fear our Queen will fare the worse for it. The Dutch decay there exceedingly, it being believed that their people will revolt from them there, and they forced to give over their trade. This is talked of among us, but how true I understand not. Sir Thomas showed me his picture and Sir Anthony Vandike's, in crayon in little, done exceedingly well. Having thus freely talked with him, and of many more things, I took leave, and by coach to St. James's, and there told Mr. Coventry what I had done with my Lord with great satisfaction, and so well pleased home, where I found it almost night, and my wife and the dancing-master alone above, not dancing but talking. Now so deadly full of jealousy I am that my heart and head did so cast about and fret that I could not do any business possibly, but went out to my office, and anon late home again and ready to chide at every thing, and then suddenly to bed and could hardly sleep, yet durst not say any thing, but was forced to say that I had bad news from the Duke concerning Tom Hater as an excuse to my wife, who by my folly has too much opportunity given her with the man, who is a pretty neat black man, but married. But it is a deadly folly and plague that I bring upon myself to be so jealous and by giving myself such an occasion more than my wife desired of giving her another month's dancing. Which however shall be ended as soon as I can possibly. But I am ashamed to think what a course I did take by lying to see whether my wife did wear drawers to-day as she used to do, and other things to raise my suspicion of her, but I found no true cause of doing it.

16th. Up with my mind disturbed and with my last night's doubts upon me, for which I deserve to be beaten if not really served as I am fearful of being, especially since God knows that I do not find honesty enough in my own mind but that upon a small temptation I could be false to her, and therefore ought not to expect more justice from her, but God pardon both my sin and my folly herein. To my office and there sitting all the morning, and at noon dined at home. After dinner comes Pembleton, and I being out of humour would not see him, pretending business, but, Lord! with what jealousy did I walk up and down my chamber listening to hear whether they danced or no, which they did, notwithstanding I afterwards knew and did then believe that Ashwell was with them. So to my office awhile, and, my jealousy still reigning, I went in and, not out of any pleasure but from that only reason, did go up to them to practise, and did make an end of "La Duchesse," which I think I should, with a little pains, do very well. So broke up and saw him gone. Then Captain Cocke coming to me to speak about my seeming discourtesy to him in the business of his hemp, I went to the office with him, and there discoursed it largely and I think to his satisfaction. Then to my business, writing letters and other things till late at night, and so home to supper and bed. My mind in some better ease resolving to prevent matters for the time to come as much as I can, it being to no purpose to trouble myself for what is past, being occasioned too by my own folly.

17th (Lord's day). Up and in my chamber all the morning, preparing my great letters to my father, stating to him the perfect condition of our estate. My wife and Ashwell to church, and after dinner they to church again, and I all the afternoon making an end of my morning's work, which I did about the evening, and then to talk with my wife till after supper, and so to bed having another small falling out and myself vexed with my old fit of jealousy about her dancing-master. But I am a fool for doing it. So to bed by daylight, I having a very great cold, so as I doubt whether I shall be able to speak to-morrow at our attending the Duke, being now so hoarse.

18th. Up and after taking leave of Sir W. Batten, who is gone this day towards Portsmouth (to little purpose, God knows) upon his survey, I home and spent the morning at dancing; at noon Creed dined with us and Mr. Deane Woolwich, and so after dinner came Mr. Howe, who however had enough for his dinner, and so, having done, by coach to Westminster, she to Mrs. Clerke and I to St. James's, where the Duke being gone down by water to-day with the King I went thence to my Lord Sandwich's lodgings, where Mr. Howe and I walked a while, and going towards Whitehall through the garden Dr. Clerk and Creed called me across the bowling green, and so I went thither and after a stay went up to Mrs. Clerke who was dressing herself to go abroad with my wife. But, Lord! in what a poor condition her best chamber is, and things about her, for all the outside and show that she makes, but I found her just such a one as Mrs. Pierce, contrary to my expectation, so much that I am sick and sorry to see it. Thence for an hour Creed and I walked to White Hall, and into the Park, seeing the Queen and Maids of Honour passing through the house going to the Park. But above all, Mrs. Stuart is a fine woman, and they say now a common mistress to the King,

[The king said to 'la belle' Stuart, who resisted all his importunities, that he hoped he should live to see her "ugly and willing" (Lord Dartmouth's note to Burnet's "Own Time," vol. i., p. 436, ed. 1823).]

as my Lady Castlemaine is; which is a great pity. Thence taking a coach to Mrs. Clerke's, took her, and my wife, and Ashwell, and a Frenchman, a kinsman of hers, to the Park, where we saw many fine faces, and one exceeding handsome, in a white dress over her head, with many others very beautiful. Staying there till past eight at night, I carried Mrs. Clerke and her Frenchman, who sings well, home, and thence home ourselves, talking much of what we had observed to-day of the poor household stuff of Mrs. Clerke and mere show and flutter that she makes in the world; and pleasing myself in my own house and manner of living more than ever I did by seeing how much better and more substantially I live than others do. So to supper and bed.

19th. Up pretty betimes, but yet I observe how my dancing and lying a morning or two longer than ordinary for my cold do make me hard to rise as I used to do, or look after my business as I am wont. To my chamber to make an end of my papers to my father to be sent by the post to-night, and taking copies of them, which was a great work, but I did it this morning, and so to my office, and thence with Sir John Minnes to the Tower; and by Mr. Slingsby, and Mr. Howard, Controller of the Mint, we were shown the method of making this new money, from the beginning to the end, which is so pretty that I did take a note of every part of it and set them down by themselves for my remembrance hereafter. That being done it was dinner time, and so the Controller would have us dine with him and his company, the King giving them a dinner every day. And very merry and good discourse about the business we have been upon, and after dinner went to the Assay Office and there saw the manner of assaying of gold and silver, and how silver melted down with gold do part, just being put into aqua-fortis, the silver turning into water, and the gold lying whole in the very form it was put in, mixed of gold and silver, which is a miracle; and to see no silver at all but turned into water, which they can bring again into itself out of the water. And here I was made thoroughly to understand the business of the fineness and coarseness of metals, and have put down my lessons with my other observations therein. At table among other discourse they told us of two cheats, the best I ever heard. One, of a labourer discovered to convey away the bits of silver cut out pence by swallowing them down into his belly, and so they could not find him out, though, of course, they searched all the labourers; but, having reason to doubt him, they did, by threats and promises, get him to confess, and did find L7 of it in his house at one time. The other of one that got a way of coyning money as good and passable and large as the true money is, and yet saved fifty per cent. to himself, which was by getting moulds made to stamp groats like old groats, which is done so well, and I did beg two of them which I keep for rarities, that there is not better in the world, and is as good, nay, better than those that commonly go, which was the only thing that they could find out to doubt them by, besides the number that the party do go to put off, and then coming to the Comptroller of the Mint, he could not, I say, find out any other thing to raise any doubt upon, but only their being so truly round or near it, though I should never have doubted the thing neither. He was neither hanged nor burned, the cheat was thought so ingenious, and being the first time they could ever trap him in it, and so little hurt to any man in it, the money being as good as commonly goes. Thence to the office till the evening, we sat, and then by water (taking Pembleton with us), over the water to the Halfway House, where we played at nine-pins, and there my damned jealousy took fire, he and my wife being of a side and I seeing of him take her by the hand in play, though I now believe he did [it] only in passing and sport. Thence home and being 10 o'clock was forced to land beyond the Custom House, and so walked home and to my office, and having dispatched my great letters by the post to my father, of which I keep copies to show by me and for my future understanding, I went home to supper and bed, being late. The most observables in the making of money which I observed to-day, is the steps of their doing it.

1. Before they do anything they assay the bullion, which is done, if it be gold, by taking an equal weight of that and of silver, of each a small weight, which they reckon to be six ounces or half a pound troy; this they wrap up in within lead. If it be silver, they put such a quantity of that alone and wrap it up in lead, and then putting them into little earthen cupps made of stuff like tobacco pipes, and put them into a burning hot furnace, where, after a while, the whole body is melted, and at last the lead in both is sunk into the body of the cupp, which carries away all the copper or dross with it, and left the pure gold and silver embodyed together, of that which hath both been put into the cupp together, and the silver alone in these where it was put alone in the leaden case. And to part the silver and the gold in the first experiment, they put the mixed body into a glass of aqua-fortis, which separates them by spitting out the silver into such small parts that you cannot tell what it becomes, but turns into the very water and leaves the gold at the bottom clear of itself, with the silver wholly spit out, and yet the gold in the form that it was doubled together in when it was a mixed body of gold and silver, which is a great mystery; and after all this is done to get the silver together out of the water is as strange. But the nature of the assay is thus: the piece of gold that goes into the furnace twelve ounces, if it comes out again eleven ounces, and the piece of silver which goes in twelve and comes out again eleven and two pennyweight, are just of the alloy of the standard of England. If it comes out, either of them, either the gold above eleven, as very fine will sometimes within very little of what it went in, or the silver above eleven and two pennyweight, as that also will sometimes come out eleven and ten penny weight or more, they are so much above the goodness of the standard, and so they know what proportion of worse gold and silver to put to such a quantity of the bullion to bring it to the exact standard. And on the contrary, [if] it comes out lighter, then such a weight is beneath the standard, and so requires such a proportion of fine metal to be put to the bullion to bring it to the standard, and this is the difference of good and bad, better and worse than the standard, and also the difference of standards, that of Seville being the best and that of Mexico worst, and I think they said none but Seville is better than ours.

2. They melt it into long plates, which, if the mould do take ayre, then the plate is not of an equal heaviness in every part of it, as it often falls out.

3. They draw these plates between rollers to bring them to an even thickness all along and every plate of the same thickness, and it is very strange how the drawing it twice easily between the rollers will make it as hot as fire, yet cannot touch it.

4. They bring it to another pair of rollers, which they call adjusting it, which bring it to a greater exactness in its thickness than the first could be.

5. They cut them into round pieces, which they do with the greatest ease, speed, and exactness in the world.

6. They weigh these, and where they find any to be too heavy they file them, which they call sizeing them; or light, they lay them by, which is very seldom, but they are of a most exact weight, but however, in the melting, all parts by some accident not being close alike, now and then a difference will be, and, this filing being done, there shall not be any imaginable difference almost between the weight of forty of these against another forty chosen by chance out of all their heaps.

7. These round pieces having been cut out of the plates, which in passing the rollers are bent, they are sometimes a little crooked or swelling out or sinking in, and therefore they have a way of clapping 100 or 2 together into an engine, which with a screw presses them so hard that they come out as flat as is possible.

8. They blanch them.

9. They mark the letters on the edges, which is kept as the great secret by Blondeau, who was not in the way, and so I did not speak with him to-day.

[Professor W. C. Roberts-Austen, C.B., F.R.S., chemist to the Royal Mint, refers to Pepys's Diary and to Blondeau's machine in his Cantor Lectures on "Alloys used for Coinage," printed in the "journal of the Society of Arts" (vol. xxxii.). He writes, "The hammer was still retained for coining in the Mint in the Tower of London, but the question of the adoption of the screw-press by the Moneyers appears to have been revived in 1649, when the Council of State had it represented to them that the coins of the Government might be more perfectly and beautifully done, and made equal to any coins in Europe. It was proposed to send to France for Peter Blondeau, who had invented and improved a machine and method for making all coins 'with the most beautiful polish and equality on the edge, or with any proper inscription or graining.' He came on the 3rd of September, and although a Committee of the Mint reported in favour of his method of coining, the Company of Moneyers, who appear to have boasted of the success of their predecessors in opposing the introduction of the mill and screw-press in Queen Elizabeth's reign, prevented the introduction of the machinery, and consequently he did not produce pattern pieces until 1653 . . . . It is certain that Blondeau did not invent, but only improved the method of coining by the screw-press, and I believe his improvements related chiefly to a method for 'rounding the pieces before they are sized, and in making the edges of the moneys with letters and graining,' which he undertook to reveal to the king. Special stress is laid on the engines wherewith the rims were marked, 'which might be kept secret among few men.' I cannot find that there is any record in the Paris mint of Blondeau's employment there, and the only reference to his invention in the Mint records of this country refers to the 'collars,' or perforated discs of metal surrounding the 'blank' while it was struck into a coin. There is, however, in the British Museum a *Ms.* believed to be in Blondeau's hand, in which he claims his process, 'as a new invention, to make a handsome coyne, than can be found in all the world besides, *viz.*, that shall not only be stamped on both flat sides, but shall even be marked with letters on the thickness of the brim.' The letters were raised. The press Blondeau used was, I believe, the ordinary screw-press, and I suppose that the presses drawn in Akerman's well-known plate of the coining-room of the Mint in the Tower, published in 1803 ['Microcosm of London,' vol. ii., p. 202], if not actually the same machines, were similar to those erected in 1661-62 by Sir William Parkhurst and Sir Anthony St. Leger, wardens of the Mint, at a cost of L1400, Professor Roberts-Austen shows that Benvenuto Cellini used a similar press to that attributed to Blondeau, and he gives an illustration of this in his lecture (p. 810). In a letter to the editor the professor writes: "Pepys's account of the operations of coining, and especially of assaying gold and silver, is very interesting and singularly accurate considering that he could not have had technical knowledge of the subject."]

10. They mill them, that is, put on the marks on both sides at once with great exactness and speed, and then the money is perfect. The mill is after this manner: one of the dyes, which has one side of the piece cut, is fastened to a thing fixed below, and the other dye (and they tell me a payre of dyes will last the marking of L10,000 before it be worn out, they and all other their tools being made of hardened steel, and the Dutchman who makes them is an admirable artist, and has so much by the pound for every pound that is coyned to find a constant supply of dyes) to an

engine above, which is moveable by a screw, which is pulled by men; and then a piece being clapped by one sitting below between the two dyes, when they meet the impression is set, and then the man with his finger strikes off the piece and claps another in, and then the other men they pull again and that is marked, and then another and another with great speed. They say that this way is more charge to the King than the old way, but it is neater, freer from clipping or counterfeiting, the putting of the words upon the edges being not to be done (though counterfeited) without an engine of the charge and noise that no counterfeit will be at or venture upon, and it employs as many men as the old and speedier. They now coyne between L16 and L24,000 in a week. At dinner they did discourse very finely to us of the probability that there is a vast deal of money hid in the land, from this:—that in King Charles's time there was near ten millions of money coyned, besides what was then in being of King James's and Queene Elizabeth's, of which there is a good deal at this day in being. Next, that there was but L750,000 coyned of the Harp and Crosse money,

[The Commonwealth coins (stamped with the cross and harp, and the inscription, "The Commonwealth of England") were called in by proclamation, September, 1660, and when brought to the Mint an equal amount of lawful money was allowed for them, weight for weight, deducting only for the coinage (Ruding's "Annals of the Coinage," 18 19, vol. iii., p. 293). The harp was taken out of the naval flags in May, 1660.]

and of this there was L500,000 brought in upon its being called in. And from very good arguments they find that there cannot be less of it in Ireland and Scotland than L100,000; so that there is but L150,000 missing; and of that, suppose that there should be not above 650,000 still remaining, either melted down, hid, or lost, or hoarded up in England, there will then be but L100,000 left to be thought to have been transported. Now, if L750,000 in twelve years' time lost but a L100,000 in danger of being transported, then within thirty-five years' time will have lost but L3,888,880 and odd pounds; and as there is L650,000 remaining after twelve years' time in England, so after thirty-five years' time, which was within this two years, there ought in proportion to have been resting L6,111,120 or thereabouts, beside King James's and Queen Elizabeth's money. Now that most of this must be hid is evident, as they reckon, because of the dearth of money immediately upon the calling-in of the State's money, which was L500,000 that came in; and yet there was not any money to be had in this City, which they say to their own observation and knowledge was so. And therefore, though I can say nothing in it myself, I do not dispute it.

20th. Up and to my office, and anon home and to see my wife dancing with Pembleton about noon, and I to the Trinity House to dinner and after dinner home, and there met Pembleton, who I perceive has dined with my wife, which she takes no notice of, but whether that proceeds out of design, or fear to displease me I know not, but it put me into a great disorder again, that I could mind nothing but vexing, but however I continued my resolution of going down by water to Woolwich, took my wife and Ashwell; and going out met Mr. Howe come to see me, whose horse we caused to be set up, and took him with us. The tide against us, so I went ashore at Greenwich before, and did my business at the yard about putting things in order as to their proceeding to build the new yacht ordered to be built by Christopher Pett,

[In the minutes of the Royal Society is the following entry: "June 11, 1662. Dr. Pett's brother shewed a draught of the pleasure boat which he intended to make for the king" (Birch's "History of the Royal Society," vol. i., p. 85). Peter Pett had already built a yacht for the king at Deptford.]

and so to Woolwich town, where at an alehouse I found them ready to attend my coming, and so took boat again, it being cold, and I sweating, with my walk, which was very pleasant along the green come and pease, and most of the way sang, he and I, and eat some cold meat we had, and with great pleasure home, and so he took horse again, and Pembleton coming, we danced a country dance or two and so broke up and to bed, my mind restless and like to be so while she learns to dance. God forgive my folly.

21st. Up, but cannot get up so early as I was wont, nor my mind to business as it should be and used to be before this dancing. However, to my office, where most of the morning talking of Captain Cox of Chatham about his and the whole yard's difference against Mr. Barrow the storekeeper, wherein I told him my mind clearly, that he would be upheld against the design of any to ruin him, he being we all believed, but Sir W. Batten his mortal enemy, as good a servant as any the King has in the yard. After much good advice and other talk I home and danced with Pembleton, and then the barber trimmed me, and so to dinner, my wife and I having high words about her dancing to that degree that I did enter and make a vow to myself not to oppose her or say anything to dispraise or correct her therein as long as her month lasts, in pain of 2s. 6d. for every time, which, if God pleases, I will observe, for this roguish business has brought us more disquiett than anything [that] has happened a great while. After dinner to my office, where late, and then home; and Pembleton being there again, we fell to dance a country dance or two, and so to supper and bed. But being at supper my wife did say something that caused me to oppose her in, she used the word devil, which vexed me, and among other things I said I would not have her to use that word, upon which she took me up most scornfully, which, before Ashwell and the rest of the world, I know not now-a-days how to check, as I would heretofore, for less than that would have made me strike her. So that I fear without great discretion I shall go near to lose too my command over her, and nothing do it more than giving her this occasion of dancing and other pleasures, whereby her mind is taken up from her business and finds other sweets besides pleasing of me, and so makes her that she begins not at all to take pleasure in me or study to please me as heretofore. But if this month of her dancing were but out (as my first was this night, and I paid off Pembleton for myself) I shall hope with a little pains to bring her to her old wont. This day Susan that lived with me lately being out of service, and I doubt a simple wench, my wife do take her for a little time to try her at least till she goes into the country, which I am yet doubtful whether it will be best for me to send her or no, for fear of her running off in her liberty before I have brought her to her right temper again.

22nd. Up pretty betimes, and shall, I hope, come to myself and business again, after a small playing the truant, for I find that my interest and profit do grow daily, for which God be praised and keep me to my duty. To my office, and anon one tells me that Rundall, the house-carpenter of Deptford, hath sent me a fine blackbird, which I went to see. He tells me he was offered 20s. for him as he came along, he do so whistle. So to my office, and busy all the morning, among other things, learning to understand the course of the tides, and I think I do now do it. At noon Mr. Creed comes to me, and he and I to the Exchange, where I had much discourse with several merchants, and so home with him to dinner, and then by water to Greenwich, and calling at the little alehouse at the end of the town to wrap a rag about my little left toe, being new sore with walking, we walked pleasantly to Woolwich, in our way hearing the nightingales sing. So to Woolwich yard, and after doing many things there, among others preparing myself for a dispute against Sir W. Pen in the business of Bowyer's, wherein he is guilty of some corruption to the King's wrong, we walked back again without drinking, which I never do because I would not make my coming troublesome to any, nor would become obliged too much to any. In our going back we were overtook by Mr. Steventon, a purser, and uncle to my clerk Will, who told me how he was abused in the passing of his accounts by Sir J. Minnes to the degree that I am ashamed to hear it, and resolve to retrieve the matter if I can though the poor man has given it over. And however am pleased enough to see that others do see his folly and dotage as well as myself, though I believe in my mind the man in general means well.

Took boat at Greenwich and to Deptford, where I did the same thing, and found Davis, the storekeeper, a knave, and shuffling in the business of Bewpers, being of the party with Young and Whistler to abuse the King, but I hope I shall be even with them. So walked to Redriffe, drinking at the Half-way house, and so walked and by water to White Hall, all our way by water coming and going reading a little book said to be writ by a person of Quality concerning English gentry to be preferred before titular honours, but the most silly nonsense, no sense nor grammar, yet in as good words that ever I saw in all my life, but from beginning to end you met not with one entire and regular sentence. At White Hall Sir G. Carteret was out of the way, and so returned back presently, and home by water and to bed.

23rd. Waked this morning between four and five by my blackbird, which whistles as well as ever I heard any; only it is the beginning of many tunes very well, but there leaves them, and goes no further. So up and to my office, where we sat, and among other things I had a fray with Sir J. Minnes in defence of my Will in a business where the old coxcomb would have put a foot upon him, which was only in Jack Davis and in him a downright piece of knavery in procuring a double ticket and getting the wrong one paid as well as the second was to the true party. But it appeared clear enough to the board that Will was true in it. Home to dinner, and after dinner by water to the Temple, and there took my Lyra Viall book bound up with blank paper for new lessons. Thence to Greatorex's, and there seeing Sir J. Minnes and Sir W. Pen go by coach I went in to them and to White Hall; where, in the Matted Gallery, Mr. Coventry was, who told us how the Parliament have required of Sir G. Carteret and him an account what money shall be necessary to be settled upon the Navy for the ordinary charge, which they intend to report L200,000 per annum. And how to allott this we met this afternoon, and took their papers for our perusal, and so we parted. Only there was walking in the gallery some of the Barbary company, and there we saw a draught of the arms of the company, which the King is of, and so is called the Royall Company, which is, in a field argent an elephant proper, with a canton on which England and France is quartered, supported by two Moors. The crest an anchor winged, I think it is, and the motto too tedious: "Regio floret, patrocinio commercium, commercioque Regnum." Thence back by water to Greatorex's, and there he showed me his varnish which he had invented, which appears every whit as good, upon a stick which he hath done, as the Indian, though it did not do very well upon my paper ruled with musique lines, for it sunk and did not shine. Thence home by water, and after a dance with Pembleton to my office and wrote by the post to Sir W. Batten at Portsmouth to send for him up against next Wednesday, being our triall day against Field at Guildhall, in which God give us good end. So home: to supper and to bed.

24th (Lord's day). Having taken one of Mr. Holliard's pills last night it brought a stool or two this morning, and so forebore going to church this morning, but staid at home looking over my papers about Tom Trice's business, and so at noon dined, and my wife telling me that there was a pretty lady come to church with Peg Pen to-day, I against my intention had a mind to go to church to see her, and did so, and she is pretty handsome. But over against our gallery I espied Pembleton, and saw him leer upon my wife all the sermon, I taking no notice of him, and my wife upon him, and I observed she made a curtsey to him at coming out without taking notice to me at all of it, which with the consideration of her being desirous these two last Lord's days to go to church both forenoon and afternoon do really make me suspect something more than ordinary, though I am loth to think the worst, but yet it put and do still keep me at a great loss in my mind, and makes me curse the time that I consented to her dancing, and more my continuing it a second month, which was more than she desired, even after I had seen too much of her carriage with him. But I must have patience and get her into the country, or at least to make an end of her learning to dance as soon as I can. After sermon to Sir W. Pen's, with Sir J. Minnes to do a little business to answer Mr. Coventry to-night. And so home and with my wife and Ashwell into the garden walking a great while, discoursing what this pretty wench should be by her garb and deportment; with respect to Mrs. Pen she may be her woman, but only that she sat in the pew with her, which I believe he would not let her do. So home, and read to my wife a fable or two in Ogleby's AEsop, and so to supper, and then to prayers and to bed. My wife this evening discoursing of making clothes for the country, which I seem against, pleading lack of money, but I am glad of it in some respects because of getting her out of the way from this fellow, and my own liberty to look after my business more than of late I have done. So to prayers and to bed. This morning it seems Susan, who I think is distracted, or however is since she went from me taught to drink, and so gets out of doors 2 or 3 times a day without leave to the alehouse, did go before 5 o'clock to-day, making Griffin rise in his shirt to let her out to the alehouse, she said to warm herself, but her mistress, falling out with her about it, turned her out of doors this morning, and so she is gone like an idle slut. I took a pill also this night.

25th. Up, and my pill working a little I staid within most of the morning, and by and by the barber came and Sarah Kite my cozen, poor woman, came to see me and borrow 40s. of me, telling me she will pay it at Michaelmas again to me. I was glad it was no more, being indifferent whether she pays it me or no, but it will be a good excuse to lend her nor give her any more. So I did freely at first word do it, and give her a crown more freely to buy her child something, she being a good-natured and painful wretch, and one that I would do good for as far as I can that I might not be burdened. My wife was not ready, and she coming early did not see her, and I was glad of it. She gone, I up and then hear that my wife and her maid Ashwell had between them spilled the pot . . . . upon the floor and stool and God knows what, and were mighty merry making of it clean. I took no great notice, but merrily. Ashwell did by and by come to me with an errand from her mistress to desire money to buy a country suit for her against she goes as we talked last night, and so I did give her L4, and believe it will cost me the best part of 4 more to fit her out, but with peace and honour I am willing to spare anything so as to be able to keep all ends together, and my power over her undisturbed. So to my office and by and by home, where my wife and her master were dancing, and so I staid in my chamber till they had done, and sat down myself to try a little upon the Lyra viall, my hand being almost out, but easily brought to again. So by and by to dinner, and then carried my wife and Ashwell to St. James's, and there they sat in the coach while I went in, and finding nobody there likely to meet with the Duke, but only Sir J. Minnes with my Lord Barkely (who speaks very kindly, and invites me with great compliments to come now and then and eat with him, which I am glad to hear, though I value not the thing, but it implies that my esteem do increase rather than fall), and so I staid not, but into the coach again, and taking up my wife's taylor, it raining hard, they set me down, and who should our coachman be but Carleton the Vintner, that should have had Mrs. Sarah, at Westminster, my Lord Chancellor's, and then to Paternoster Row. I staid there to speak with my Lord Sandwich, and in my staying, meeting Mr. Lewis Phillips of Brampton, he and afterwards others tell me that news came last night to Court, that the King of France is sick of the spotted fever, and that they are struck in again; and this afternoon my Lord Mandeville is gone from the King to make him a visit; which will be great news, and of great import through Europe. By and by, out comes my Lord Sandwich, and he and I talked a great while about his business, of his accounts for his pay, and among other things he told me that this day a vote hath passed that the King's grants of land to my Lord Monk and him should be made good; which pleases him very well. He also tells me that things don't go right in the House with Mr. Coventry; I suppose he means in the business of selling of places; but I am sorry for it. Thence by coach home, where I found Pembleton, and so I up to dance with them till the evening, when there came Mr. Alsopp, the King's brewer, and Lanyon of Plymouth to see me. Mr. Alsopp tells me of a horse of his that lately, after four days' pain, voided at his fundament four stones, bigger than that I was cut of, very heavy, and in the middle of each of them either a piece of iron or wood. The King has two of them in his closett, and a third the College of Physicians to keep for rarity, and by the King's command he causes the turd of the horse to be every day searched to find more. At night to see Sir W. Batten come home this day from Portsmouth. I met with some that say that the King of France is poisoned, but how true that is is not known. So home to supper and to bed pleasant.

26th. Lay long in bed talking and pleasing myself with my wife. So up and to my office a while and then home, where I found Pembleton, and by many circumstances I am led to conclude that there is something more than ordinary between my wife and him, which do so trouble me that I know not at this very minute that I now write this almost what either I write or am doing, nor how to carry myself to my wife in it, being unwilling to speak of it to her for making of any breach and other inconveniences, nor let it pass for fear of her continuing to offend me and the matter grow worse thereby. So that I am grieved at the very heart, but I am very unwise in being so. There dined with me Mr. Creed and Captain Grove, and before dinner I had much discourse in my chamber with Mr. Deane, the builder of Woolwich, about building of ships. But nothing could get the business out of my head, I fearing that this afternoon by my wife's sending every [one] abroad and knowing that I must be at the office she has appointed him to come. This is my devilish jealousy, which I pray God may be false, but it makes a very hell in my mind, which the God of heaven remove, or I shall be very unhappy. So to the office, where we sat awhile. By and by my mind being in great trouble I went home to see how things were, and there I found as I doubted Mr. Pembleton with my wife, and nobody else in the house, which made me almost mad, and going up to my chamber after a turn or two I went out again and called somebody on pretence of business and left him in my little room at the door (it was the Dutchman, commander of the King's pleasure boats, who having been beat by one of his men sadly, was come to the office to-day to complain) telling him I would come again to him to speak with him about his business. So in great trouble and doubt to the office, and Mr. Coventry nor Sir G. Carteret being there I made a quick end of our business and desired leave to be gone, pretending to go to the Temple, but it was home, and so up to my chamber, and as I think if they had any intention of hurt I did prevent doing anything at that time, but I continued in my chamber vexed and angry till he went away, pretending aloud, that I might hear, that he could not stay, and Mrs. Ashwell not being within they could not dance. And, Lord! to see how my jealousy wrought so far that I went softly up to see whether any of the beds were out of order or no, which I found not, but that did not content me, but I staid all the evening walking, and though anon my wife came up to me and would have spoke of business to me, yet I construed it to be but impudence, and though my heart full yet I did say nothing, being in a great doubt what to do. So at night, suffered them to go all to bed, and late put myself to bed in great discontent, and so to sleep.

27th. So I waked by 3 o'clock, my mind being troubled, and so took occasion by making water to wake my wife, and after having lain till past 4 o'clock seemed going to rise, though I did it only to see what she would do, and so going out of the bed she took hold of me and would know what ailed me, and after many kind and some cross words I began to tax her discretion in yesterday's business, but she quickly told me my own, knowing well enough that it was my old disease of jealousy, which I denied, but to no purpose. After an hour's discourse, sometimes high and sometimes kind, I found very good reason to think that her freedom with him is very great and more than was convenient, but with no evil intent, and so after awhile I caressed her and parted seeming friends, but she crying in a great discontent. So I up and by water to the Temple, and thence with Commissioner Pett to St. James's, where an hour with Mr. Coventry talking of Mr. Pett's proceedings lately in the forest of Sherwood, and thence with Pett to my Lord Ashley, Chancellor of the Exchequer; where we met the auditors about settling the business of the accounts of persons to whom money is due before the King's time in the Navy, and the clearing of their imprests for what little of their debts they have received. I find my Lord, as he is reported, a very ready, quick, and diligent person. Thence I to Westminster Hall, where Term and Parliament make the Hall full of people; no further news yet of the King of France, whether he be dead or not. Here I met with my cozen Roger Pepys, and walked a good while with him, and among other discourse as a secret he hath committed to nobody but myself, and he tells me that his sister Claxton now resolving to give over the keeping of his house at Impington, he thinks it fit to marry again, and would have me, by the help of my uncle Wight or others, to look him out a widow between thirty and forty years old, without children, and with a fortune, which he will answer in any degree with a joynture fit for her fortune. A woman sober, and no high-flyer, as he calls it. I demanded his estate. He tells me, which he says also he hath not done to any, that his estate is not full L800 per annum, but it is L780 per annum, of which L200 is by the death of his last wife, which he will allot for a joynture for a wife, but the rest, which lies in Cambridgeshire, he is resolved to leave entire for his eldest son. I undertook to do what I can in it, and so I shall. He tells me that the King hath sent to them to hasten to make an end by midsummer, because of his going into the country; so they have set upon four bills to dispatch: the first of which is, he says, too devilish a severe act against conventicles; so beyond all moderation, that he is afeard it will ruin all: telling me that it is matter of the greatest grief to him in the world, that he should be put upon this trust of being a Parliament-man, because he says nothing is done, that he can see, out of any truth and sincerity, but mere envy and design. Thence by water to Chelsey, all the way reading a little book I bought of "Improvement of Trade," a pretty book and many things useful in it. So walked to Little Chelsey, where I found my Lord Sandwich with Mr. Becke, the master of the house, and Mr. Creed at dinner, and I sat down with them, and very merry. After dinner (Mr. Gibbons being come in also before dinner done) to musique, they played a good Fancy, to which my Lord is fallen again, and says he cannot endure a merry tune, which is a strange turn of his humour, after he has for two or three years flung off the practice of Fancies and played only fidlers' tunes. Then into the Great Garden up to the Banqueting House; and there by his glass we drew in the species very pretty. Afterwards to ninepins, where I won a shilling, Creed and I playing against my Lord and Cooke. This day there was great thronging to Banstead Downs, upon a great horse-race and foot-race. I am sorry I could not go thither. So home back as I came, to London Bridge, and so home, where I find my wife in a musty humour, and tells me before Ashwell that Pembleton had been there, and she would not have him come in unless I was there, which I was ashamed of; but however, I had rather it should be so than the other way. So to my office, to put things in order there, and by and by comes Pembleton, and word is brought me from my wife thereof that I might come home. So I sent word that I would have her go dance, and I would come presently. So being at a great loss whether I should appear to Pembleton or no, and what would most proclaim my jealousy to him, I at last resolved to go home, and took Tom Hater with me, and staid a good while in my chamber, and there took occasion to tell him how I hear that Parliament is putting an act out against all sorts of conventicles,

[16 Car. II., cap. 4, "An Act to prevent and suppresse seditious Conventicles." It was enacted that anyone of the age of sixteen or upwards present at an unlawful assembly or conventicle was to incur fine or imprisonment. A conventicle was defined as an assembly of more than five persons besides the members of a family met together for holding worship not according to the rites of the Church of England. The act was amended 22 Car. II., cap. i (1670), and practically repealed by the Toleration Act of 1689, but the act 22 Car. II., cap. i, was specially repealed 52 Geo. III., cap. 155, s. 1.]

and did give him good counsel, not only in his own behalf, but my own, that if he did hear or know anything that could be said to my prejudice, that he would tell me, for in this wicked age (specially Sir W. Batten being so open to my reproaches, and Sir J. Minnes, for the neglect of their duty, and so will think themselves obliged to scandalize me all they can to right themselves if there shall be any inquiry into the matters of the Navy, as I doubt there will) a man ought to be prepared to answer for himself in all things that can be inquired concerning him. After much discourse of this nature to him I sent him away, and then went up, and there we danced country dances, and single, my wife and I; and my wife paid him off for this month also, and so he is cleared. After dancing we took him down to supper, and were very merry, and I made myself so, and kind to him as much as I could, to prevent his discourse, though I perceive to my trouble that he knows all, and may do me the disgrace to publish it as much as he can. Which I take very ill, and if too much provoked shall witness it to her. After supper and he gone we to bed.

28th. Up this morning, and my wife, I know not for what cause, being against going to Chelsey to-day, it being a holy day (Ascension Day) and I at leisure, it being the first holy day almost that we have observed ever since we came to the office, we did give Ashwell leave to go by herself, and I out to several places about business. Among others to Dr. Williams, to reckon with him for physique that my wife has had for a year or two, coming to almost L4. Then to the Exchange, where I hear that the King had letters yesterday from France that the King there is in a [way] of living again, which I am glad to hear. At the coffee-house in Exchange Alley I bought a little book, "Counsell to Builders," by Sir Balth. Gerbier. It is dedicated almost to all the men of any great condition in England, so that the Epistles are more than the book itself, and both it and them not worth a turd, that I am ashamed that I bought it. Home and there found Creed, who dined with us, and after dinner by water to the Royall Theatre; but that was so full they told us we could have no room. And so to the Duke's House; and there saw "Hamlett" done, giving us fresh reason never to think enough of Betterton. Who should we see come upon the stage but Gosnell, my wife's maid? but neither spoke, danced, nor sung; which I was sorry for. But she becomes the stage very well. Thence by water home, after we had walked to and fro, backwards and forwards, six or seven times in the Temple walks, disputing whether to go by land or water. By land home, and thence by water to Halfway House, and there eat some supper we carried with us, and so walked home again, it being late we were forced to land at the dock, my wife and they, but I in a humour not willing to daub my shoes went round by the Custom House. So home, and by and by to bed, Creed lying with me in the red chamber all night.

29th. This day is kept strictly as a holy-day, being the King's Coronation. We lay long in bed, and it rained very hard, rain and hail, almost all the morning. By and by Creed and I abroad, and called at several churches; and it is a wonder to see, and by that to guess the ill temper of the City at this time, either to religion in general, or to the King, that in some churches there was hardly ten people in the whole church, and those poor people. So to a coffee-house, and there in discourse hear the King of France is likely to be well again. So home to dinner, and out by water to the Royall Theatre, but they not acting to-day, then to the Duke's house, and there saw "The Slighted Mayde," wherein Gosnell acted Pyramena, a great part, and did it very well, and I believe will do it better and better, and prove a good actor. The play is not very excellent, but is well acted, and in general the actors, in all particulars, are better than at the other house. Thence to the Cocke alehouse, and there having drunk, sent them with Creed to see the German Princess,

[Mary Moders, alias Stedman, a notorious impostor, who pretended to be a German princess. Her arrival as the German princess "at the Exchange Tavern, right against the Stocks betwixt the Poultry and Cornhill, at 5 in the morning . . . ., with her marriage to Carleton the taverner's wife's brother," are incidents fully narrated in Francis Kirkman's "Counterfeit Lady Unveiled," 1673 ("Boyne's Tokens," ed. Williamson, vol. i., p. 703). Her adventures formed the plot of a tragi-comedy by T. P., entitled "A Witty Combat, or the Female Victor," 1663, which was acted with great applause by persons of quality in Whitsun week. Mary Carleton was tried at the Old Bailey for bigamy and acquitted, after which she appeared on the stage in her own character as the heroine of a play entitled "The German Princess." Pepys went to the Duke's House to see her on April 15th, 1664. The rest of her life was one continued course of robbery and fraud, and in 1678 she was executed at Tyburn for stealing a piece of plate in Chancery Lane.]

at the Gatehouse, at Westminster, and I to my brother's, and thence to my uncle Fenner's to have seen my aunt James (who has been long in town and goes away to-morrow and I not seen her), but did find none of them within, which I was glad of, and so back to my brother's to speak with him, and so home, and in my way did take two turns forwards and backwards through the Fleete Ally to see a couple of pretty [strumpets] that stood off the doors there, and God forgive me I could scarce stay myself from going into their houses with them, so apt is my nature to evil after once, as I have these two days, set upon pleasure again. So home and to my office to put down these two days' journalls, then home again and to supper, and then Creed and I to bed with good discourse, only my mind troubled about my spending my time so badly for these seven or eight days; but I must impute it to the disquiet that my mind has been in of late about my wife, and for my going these two days to plays, for which I have paid the due forfeit by money and abating the times of going to plays at Court, which I am now to remember that I have cleared all my times that I am to go to Court plays to the end of this month, and so June is the first time that I am to begin to reckon.

30th. Up betimes, and Creed and I by water to Fleet Street, and my brother not being ready, he and I walked to the New Exchange, and there drank our morning draught of whay, the first I have done this year; but I perceive the lawyers come all in as they go to the Hall, and I believe it is very good. So to my brother's, and there I found my aunt James, a poor, religious, well-meaning, good soul, talking of nothing but God Almighty, and that with so much innocence that mightily pleased me. Here was a fellow that said grace so long like a prayer; I believe the fellow is a cunning fellow, and yet I by my brother's desire did give him a crown, he being in great want, and, it seems, a parson among the fanatiques, and a cozen of my poor aunt's, whose prayers she told me did do me good among the many good souls that did by my father's desires pray for me when I was cut of the stone, and which God did hear, which I also in complaisance did own; but, God forgive me, my mind was otherwise. I had a couple of lobsters and some wine for her, and so, she going out of town to-day, and being not willing to come home with me to dinner, I parted and home, where we sat at the office all the morning, and after dinner all the afternoon till night, there at my office getting up the time that I have of late lost by not following my business, but I hope now to settle my mind again very well to my business. So home, and after supper did wash my feet, and so to bed.

31st (Lord's day). Lay long in bed talking with my wife, and do plainly see that her distaste (which is beginning now in her again) against Ashwell arises from her jealousy of me and her, and my neglect of herself, which indeed is true, and I to blame; but for the time to come I will take care to remedy all. So up and to church, where I think I did see Pembleton, whatever the reason is I did not perceive him to look up towards my wife, nor she much towards him; however, I could hardly keep myself from being troubled that he was there, which is a madness not to be excused now that his coming to my house is past, and I hope all likelyhood of her having occasion to converse with him again. Home to dinner, and after dinner up and read part of the new play of "The Five Houres' Adventures," which though I have seen it twice; yet I never did admire or understand it enough, it being a play of the greatest plot that ever I expect to see, and of great vigour quite through the whole play, from beginning to the end. To church again after dinner (my wife finding herself ill . . . . did not go), and there the Scot preaching I slept most of the sermon. This day Sir W. Batten's son's child is christened in the country, whither Sir J. Minnes, and Sir W, Batten, and Sir W. Pen are all gone. I wonder, and take it highly ill that I am not invited by the father, though I know his father and mother, with whom I am never likely to have much kindness, but rather I study the contrary, are the cause of it, and in that respect I am glad of it. Being come from church, I to make up my month's accounts, and find myself clear worth L726, for which God be praised, but yet I might have been better by L20 almost had I forborne some layings out in dancing and other things upon my wife, and going to plays and other things merely to ease my mind as to the business of the dancing-master, which I bless God is now over and I falling to my quiet of mind and business again, which I have for a fortnight neglected too much. This month the greatest news is, the height and heat that the Parliament is in, in enquiring into the revenue, which displeases the Court, and their backwardness to give the King any money. Their enquiring into the selling of places do trouble a great many among the chief, my Lord Chancellor (against whom particularly it is carried), and Mr. Coventry; for which I am sorry. The King of France was given out to be poisoned and dead; but it proves to be the measles: and he is well, or likely to be soon well again. I find myself growing in the esteem and credit that I have in the office, and I hope falling to my business again will confirm me in it, and the saving of money which God grant! So to supper, prayers, and bed. My whole family lying longer this morning than was fit, and besides Will having neglected to brush my clothes, as he ought to do, till I was ready to go to church, and not then till I bade him, I was very angry, and seeing him make little matter of it, but seeming to make it a matter indifferent whether he did it or no, I did give him a box on the ear, and had it been another day should have done more. This is the second time I ever struck him.

Diary of Samuel Pepys.
June
1663

June 1st. Begun again to rise betimes by 4 o'clock, and made an end of "The Adventures of Five Houres," and it is a most excellent play. So to my office, where a while and then about several businesses, in my way to my brother's, where I dined (being invited) with Mr. Peter and Dean Honiwood, where Tom did give us a very pretty dinner, and we very pleasant, but not very merry, the Dean being but a weak man, though very good. I was forced to rise, being in haste to St. James's to attend the Duke, and left them to end their dinner; but the Duke having been a-hunting to-day, and so lately come home and gone to bed, we could not see him, and Mr. Coventry being out of the house too, we walked away to White Hall and there took coach, and I with Sir J. Minnes to the Strand May-pole; and there 'light out of his coach, and walked to the New Theatre, which, since the King's players are gone to the Royal one, is this day begun to be employed by the fencers to play prizes at. And here I came and saw the first prize I ever saw in my life: and it was between one Mathews, who did beat at all weapons, and one Westwicke, who was soundly cut several times both in the head and legs, that he was all over blood: and other deadly blows they did give and take in very good earnest, till Westwicke was in a most sad pickle. They fought at eight weapons, three bouts at each weapon. It was very well worth seeing, because I did till this day think that it has only been a cheat; but this being upon a private quarrel, they did it in good earnest; and I felt one of their swords, and found it to be very little, if at all blunter on the edge, than the common swords are. Strange to see what a deal of money is flung to them both upon the stage between every bout. But a woful rude rabble there was, and such noises, made my head ake all this evening. So, well pleased for once with this sight, I walked home, doing several businesses by the way. In my way calling to see Commissioner Pett, who lies sick at his daughter, a pretty woman, in Gracious Street, but is likely to be abroad again in a day or two. At home I found my wife in bed all this day . . . . I went to see Sir Wm. Pen, who has a little pain of his gout again, but will do well. So home to supper and to bed. This day I hear at Court of the great plot which was lately discovered in Ireland, made among the Presbyters and others, designing to cry up the Covenant, and to secure Dublin Castle and other places; and they have debauched a good part of the army there, promising them ready money.

[This was known as "Blood's Plot," and was named after Colonel Thomas Blood, afterwards notorious for his desperate attack upon the Duke of Ormond in St. James's Street (1670) and for his robbery of the crown jewels in the Tower (1671). He died August 24th, 1680.]

Some of the Parliament there, they say, are guilty, and some withdrawn upon it; several persons taken, and among others a son of Scott's, that was executed here for the King's murder. What reason the King hath, I know not; but it seems he is doubtfull of Scotland: and this afternoon, when I was there, the Council was called extraordinary; and they were opening the letters this last post's coming and going between Scotland and us and other places. Blessed be God, my head and hands are clear, and therefore my sleep safe. The King of France is well again.

2d. Up and by water to White Hall and so to St. James's, to Mr. Coventry; where I had an hour's private talk with him. Most of it was discourse concerning his own condition, at present being under the censure of the House, being concerned with others in the Bill for selling of offices. He tells me, that though he thinks himself to suffer much in his fame hereby, yet he values nothing more of evil to hang over him for that it is against no statute, as is pretended, nor more than what his predecessors time out of mind have taken; and that so soon as he found himself to be in an errour, he did desire to have his fees set, which was done; and since that he hath not taken a token more. He undertakes to prove, that he did never take a token of any captain to get him employed in his life beforehand, or demanded any thing: and for the other accusation, that the Cavaliers are not employed, he looked over the list of them now in the service, and of the twenty-seven that are employed, thirteen have been heretofore always under the King; two neutralls, and the other twelve men of great courage, and such as had either the King's particular commands, or great recommendation to put them in, and none by himself. Besides that, he says it is not the King's nor Duke's opinion that the whole party of the late officers should be rendered desperate. And lastly, he confesses that the more of the Cavaliers are put in, the less of discipline hath followed in the fleet; and that, whenever there comes occasion, it must be the old ones that must do any good, there being only, he says, but Captain Allen good for anything of them all. He tells me, that he cannot guess whom all this should come from; but he suspects Sir G. Carteret, as I also do, at least that he is pleased with it. But he tells me that he will bring Sir G. Carteret to be the first adviser and instructor of him what to make his place of benefit to him; telling him that Smith did make his place worth L5000 and he believed L7000 to him the first year; besides something else greater than all this, which he forbore to tell me. It seems one Sir Thomas Tomkins of the House, that makes many mad motions, did bring it into the House, saying that a letter was left at his lodgings, subscribed by one Benson (which is a feigned name, for there is no such man in the Navy), telling him how many places in the Navy have been sold. And by another letter, left in the same manner since, nobody appearing, he writes him that there is one Hughes and another Butler (both rogues, that have for their roguery been turned out of their places), that will swear that Mr. Coventry did sell their places and other things. I offered him my service, and will with all my heart serve him; but he tells me he do not think it convenient to meddle, or to any purpose, but is sensible of my love therein. So I bade him good morrow, he being out of order to speak anything of our office business, and so away to Westminster Hall, where I hear more of the plot from Ireland; which it seems hath been hatching, and known to the Lord Lieutenant a great while, and kept close till within three days that it should have taken effect. The term ended yesterday, and it seems the Courts rose sooner, for want of causes, than it is remembered to have done in the memory of man. Thence up and down about business in several places, as to speak with Mr. Phillips, but missed him, and so to Mr. Beacham, the goldsmith, he being one of the jury to-morrow in Sir W. Batten's case against Field. I have been telling him our case, and I believe he will do us good service there. So home, and seeing my wife had dined I went, being invited, and dined with Sir W. Batten, Sir J. Minnes, and others, at Sir W. Batten's, Captain Allen giving them a Foy' dinner, he being to go down to lie Admiral in the Downs this summer. I cannot but think it a little strange that having been so civil to him as I have been he should not invite me to dinner, but I believe it was but a sudden motion, and so I heard not of it. After dinner to the office, where all the afternoon till late, and so to see Sir W. Pen, and so home to supper and to bed. To-night I took occasion with the vintner's man, who came by my direction to taste again my tierce of claret, to go down to the cellar with him to consult about the drawing of it; and there, to my great vexation, I find that the cellar door hath long been kept unlocked, and above half the wine drunk. I was deadly mad at it, and examined my people round, but nobody would confess it; but I did examine the boy, and afterwards Will, and told him of his sitting up after we were in bed with the maids, but as to that business he denies it, which I can [not] remedy, but I shall endeavour to know how it went. My wife did also this evening tell me a story of Ashwell stealing some new ribbon from her, a yard or two, which I am sorry to hear, and I fear my wife do take a displeasure against her, that they will hardly stay together, which I should be sorry for, because I know not where to pick such another out anywhere.

3rd. Up betimes, and studying of my double horizontal diall against Dean Honiwood comes to me, who dotes mightily upon it, and I think I must give it him. So after talking with Sir W. Batten, who is this morning gone to Guildhall to his trial with Field, I to my office, and there read all the morning in my statute-book, consulting among others the statute against selling of offices, wherein Mr. Coventry is so much concerned; and though he tells me that the statute do not reach him, yet I much fear that it will. At noon, hearing that the trial is done, and Sir W. Batten come to the Sun behind the Exchange I went thither, where he tells me that he had much ado to carry it on his side, but that at last he did, but the jury, by the judge's favour, did give us but; L10 damages and the charges of the suit, which troubles me; but it is well it went not against us, which would have been much worse. So to the Exchange, and thence home to dinner, taking Deane of Woolwich along with me, and he dined alone with my wife being undressed, and he and I spent all the afternoon finely, learning of him the method of drawing the lines of a ship, to my great satisfaction, and which is well worth my spending some time in, as I shall do when my wife is gone into the country. In the evening to the office and did some business, then home, and, God forgive me, did from my wife's unwillingness to tell me whither she had sent the boy, presently suspect that he was gone to Pembleton's, and from that occasion grew so discontented that I could hardly speak or sleep all night.

4th. Up betimes, and my wife and Ashwell and I whiled away the morning up and down while they got themselves ready, and I did so watch to see my wife put on drawers, which poor soul she did, and yet I could not get off my suspicions, she having a mind to go into Fenchurch Street before she went out for good and all with me, which I must needs construe to be to meet Pembleton, when she afterwards told me it was to buy a fan that she had not a mind that I should know of, and I believe it is so. Specially I did by a wile get out of my boy that he did not yesterday go to Pembleton's or thereabouts, but only was sent all that time for some starch, and I did see him bringing home some, and yet all this cannot make my mind quiet. At last by coach I carried her to Westminster Hall, and they two to Mrs. Bowyer to go from thence to my wife's father's and Ashwell to hers, and by and by seeing my wife's father in the Hall, and being loth that my wife should put me to another trouble and charge by missing him to-day, I did employ a porter to go from a person unknown to tell him his daughter was come to his lodgings, and I at a distance did observe him, but, Lord! what a company of questions he did ask him, what kind of man I was, and God knows what. So he went home, and after I had staid in the Hall a good while, where I heard that this day the Archbishop of Canterbury, Juxon, a man well spoken of by all for a good man, is dead; and the Bishop of London is to have his seat. Home by water, where by and by comes Dean Honiwood, and I showed him my double horizontal diall, and promise to give him one, and that shall be it. So, without eating or drinking, he went away to Mr. Turner's, where Sir J. Minnes do treat my Lord Chancellor and a great deal of guests to-day with a great dinner, which I thank God I do not pay for; and besides, I doubt it is too late for any man to expect any great service from my Lord Chancellor, for which I am sorry, and pray God a worse do not come in his room. So I to dinner alone, and so to my chamber, and then to the office alone, my head aching and my mind in trouble for my wife, being jealous of her spending the day, though God knows I have no great reason. Yet my mind is troubled. By and by comes Will Howe to see us, and walked with me an hour in the garden, talking of my Lord's falling to business again, which I am glad of, and his coming to lie at his lodgings at White Hall again. The match between Sir J. Cutts and my Lady Jemimah, he says, is likely to go on; for which I am glad. In the Hall to-day Dr. Pierce tells me that the Queen begins to be brisk, and play like other ladies, and is quite another woman from what she was, of which I am glad. It may be, it may make the King like her the better, and forsake his two mistresses, my Lady Castlemaine and Stewart. He gone we sat at the office till night, and then home, where my wife is come, and has been with her father all the afternoon, and so home, and she and I to walk in the garden, giving ear to her discourse of her father's affairs, and I found all well, so after putting things in order at my office, home to supper and to bed.

5th. Up and to read a little, and by and by the carver coming, I directed him how to make me a neat head for my viall that is making. About 10 o'clock my wife and I, not without some discontent, abroad by coach, and I set her at her father's; but their condition is such that she will not let me see where they live, but goes by herself when I am out of sight. Thence to my brother's, taking care for a passage for my wife the next week in a coach to my father's, and thence to Paul's Churchyard, where I found several books ready bound for me; among others, the new Concordance of the Bible, which pleases me much, and is a book I hope to make good use of. Thence, taking the little History of England with me, I went by water to Deptford, where Sir J. Minnes and Sir W. Batten attending the Pay; I dined with them, and there Dr. Britton, parson of the town, a fine man and good company, dined with us, and good discourse. After dinner I left them and walked to Redriffe, and thence to White Hall, and at my Lord's lodgings found my wife, and thence carried her to see my Lady Jemimah, but she was not within. So to Mr. Turner's, and there saw Mr. Edward Pepys's lady, who my wife concurs with me to be very pretty, as most women we ever saw. So home, and after a walk in the garden a little troubled to see my wife take no more pleasure with Ashwell, but neglect her and leave her at home. Home to supper and to bed.

6th. Lay in bed till 7 o'clock, yet rose with an opinion that it was not 5, and so continued though I heard the clock strike, till noon, and would not believe that it was so late as it truly was. I was hardly ever so mistaken in my life before. Up and to Sir G. Carteret at his house, and spoke to him about business, but he being in a bad humour I had no mind to stay with him, but walked, drinking my morning draft of whay, by the way, to York House, where the Russia Embassador do lie; and there I saw his people go up and down louseing themselves: they are all in a great hurry, being to be gone the beginning of next week. But that that pleased me best, was the remains of the noble soul of the late Duke of Buckingham appearing in his house, in every place, in the doorcases and the windows. By and by comes Sir John Hebden, the Russia Resident, to me, and he and I in his coach to White Hall, to Secretary Morrice's, to see the orders about the Russia hemp that is to be fetched from Archangel for our King, and that being done, to coach again, and he brought me into the City and so I home; and after dinner abroad by water, and met by appointment Mr. Deane in the Temple Church, and he and I over to Mr. Blackbury's yard, and thence to other places, and after that to a drinking house, in all which places I did so practise and improve my measuring of timber, that I can now do it with great ease and perfection, which do please me mightily. This fellow Deane is a conceited fellow, and one that means the King a great deal of service, more of disservice to other people that go away with the profits which he cannot make; but, however, I learn much of him, and he is, I perceive, of great use to the King in his place, and so I shall give him all the encouragement I can. Home by water, and having wrote a letter for my wife to my Lady Sandwich to copy out to send this night's post, I to the office, and wrote there myself several things, and so home to supper and bed. My mind being troubled to think into what a temper of neglect I have myself flung my wife into by my letting her learn to dance, that it will require time to cure her of, and

I fear her going into the country will but make her worse; but only I do hope in the meantime to spend my time well in my office, with more leisure than while she is here. Hebden, to-day in the coach, did tell me how he is vexed to see things at Court ordered as they are by nobody that attends to business, but every man himself or his pleasures. He cries up my Lord Ashley to be almost the only man that he sees to look after business; and with that ease and mastery, that he wonders at him. He cries out against the King's dealing so much with goldsmiths, and suffering himself to have his purse kept and commanded by them. He tells me also with what exact care and order the States of Holland's stores are kept in their Yards, and every thing managed there by their builders with such husbandry as is not imaginable; which I will endeavour to understand further, if I can by any means learn.

7th (Lord's day). Whit Sunday. Lay long talking with my wife, sometimes angry and ended pleased and hope to bring our matters to a better posture in a little time, which God send. So up and to church, where Mr. Mills preached, but, I know not how, I slept most of the sermon. Thence home, and dined with my wife and Ashwell and after dinner discoursed very pleasantly, and so I to church again in the afternoon, and, the Scot preaching, again slept all the afternoon, and so home, and by and by to Sir W. Batten's, to talk about business, where my Lady Batten inveighed mightily against the German Princess, and I as high in the defence of her wit and spirit, and glad that she is cleared at the sessions. Thence to Sir W. Pen, who I found ill again of the gout, he tells me that now Mr. Castle and Mrs. Martha Batten do own themselves to be married, and have been this fortnight. Much good may it do him, for I do not envy him his wife. So home, and there my wife and I had an angry word or two upon discourse of our boy, compared with Sir W. Pen's boy that he has now, whom I say is much prettier than ours and she the contrary. It troubles me to see that every small thing is enough now-a-days to bring a difference between us. So to my office and there did a little business, and then home to supper and to bed. Mrs. Turner, who is often at Court, do tell me to-day that for certain the Queen hath much changed her humour, and is become very pleasant and sociable as any; and they say is with child, or believed to be so.

8th. Up and to my office a while, and thence by coach with Sir J. Minnes to St. James's to the Duke, where Mr. Coventry and us two did discourse with the Duke a little about our office business, which saved our coming in the afternoon, and so to rights home again and to dinner. After dinner my wife and I had a little jangling, in which she did give me the lie, which vexed me, so that finding my talking did but make her worse, and that her spirit is lately come to be other than it used to be, and now depends upon her having Ashwell by her, before whom she thinks I shall not say nor do anything of force to her, which vexes me and makes me wish that I had better considered all that I have of late done concerning my bringing my wife to this condition of heat, I went up vexed to my chamber and there fell examining my new concordance, that I have bought, with Newman's, the best that ever was out before, and I find mine altogether as copious as that and something larger, though the order in some respects not so good, that a man may think a place is missing, when it is only put in another place. Up by and by my wife comes and good friends again, and to walk in the garden and so anon to supper and to bed. My cozen John Angier the son, of Cambridge coming to me late to see me, and I find his business is that he would be sent to sea, but I dissuaded him from it, for I will not have to do with it without his friends' consent.

9th. Up and after ordering some things towards my wife's going into the country, to the office, where I spent the morning upon my measuring rules very pleasantly till noon, and then comes Creed and he and I talked about mathematiques, and he tells me of a way found out by Mr. Jonas Moore which he calls duodecimal arithmetique, which is properly applied to measuring, where all is ordered by inches, which are 12 in a foot, which I have a mind to learn. So he with me home to dinner and after dinner walk in the garden, and then we met at the office, where Coventry, Sir J. Minnes, and I, and so in the evening, business done, I went home and spent my time till night with my wife. Presently after my coming home comes Pembleton, whether by appointment or no I know not, or whether by a former promise that he would come once before my wife's going into the country, but I took no notice of, let them go up and Ashwell with them to dance, which they did, and I staid below in my chamber, but, Lord! how I listened and laid my ear to the door, and how I was troubled when I heard them stand still and not dance. Anon they made an end and had done, and so I suffered him to go away, and spoke not to him, though troubled in my mind, but showed no discontent to my wife, believing that this is the last time I shall be troubled with him. So my wife and I to walk in the garden, home and to supper and to bed.

10th. Up and all the morning helping my wife to put up her things towards her going into the country and drawing the wine out of my vessel to send. This morning came my cozen Thomas Pepys to desire me to furnish him with some money, which I could not do till his father has wrote to Piggott his consent to the sale of his lands, so by and by we parted and I to the Exchange a while and so home and to dinner, and thence to the Royal Theatre by water, and landing, met with Captain Ferrers his friend, the little man that used to be with him, and he with us, and sat by us while we saw "Love in a Maze." The play is pretty good, but the life of the play is Lacy's part, the clown, which is most admirable; but for the rest, which are counted such old and excellent actors, in my life I never heard both men and women so ill pronounce their parts, even to my making myself sick therewith. Thence, Creed happening to be with us, we four to the Half-Moon Tavern, I buying some sugar and carrying it with me, which we drank with wine and thence to the whay-house, and drank a great deal of whay, and so by water home, and thence to see Sir W. Pen, who is not in much pain, but his legs swell and so immoveable that he cannot stir them, but as they are lifted by other people and I doubt will have another fit of his late pain. Played a little at cards with him and his daughter, who is grown every day a finer and finer lady, and so home to supper and to bed. When my wife and I came first home we took Ashwell and all the rest below in the cellar with the vintner drawing out my wine, which I blamed Ashwell much for and told her my mind that I would not endure it, nor was it fit for her to make herself equal with the ordinary servants of the house.

11th. Up and spent most of the morning upon my measuring Ruler and with great pleasure I have found out some things myself of great dispatch, more than my book teaches me, which pleases me mightily. Sent my wife's things and the wine to-day by the carrier to my father's, but staid my boy from a letter of my father's, wherein he desires that he may not come to trouble his family as he did the last year. Dined at home and then to the office, where we sat all the afternoon, and at night home and spent the evening with my wife, and she and I did jangle mightily about her cushions that she wrought with worsteds the last year, which are too little for any use, but were good friends by and by again. But one thing I must confess I do observe, which I did not before, which is, that I cannot blame my wife to be now in a worse humour than she used to be, for I am taken up in my talk with Ashwell, who is a very witty girl, that I am not so fond of her as I used and ought to be, which now I do perceive I will remedy, but I would to the Lord I had never taken any, though I cannot have a better than her. To supper and to bed. The consideration that this is the longest day in the year is very unpleasant to me.—[It is necessary to note that this was according to the old style.]—This afternoon my wife had a visit from my Lady Jeminah and Mr. Ferrers.

12th. Up and my office, there conning my measuring Ruler, which I shall grow a master of in a very little time. At noon to the Exchange and so home to dinner, and abroad with my wife by water to the Royall Theatre; and there saw "The Committee," a merry but indifferent play, only Lacey's part, an Irish footman, is beyond imagination. Here I saw my Lord Falconbridge, and his Lady, my Lady Mary Cromwell, who looks as well as I have known her, and well clad; but when the House began to fill she put on her vizard,

[Masks were commonly used by ladies in the reign of Elizabeth, and when their use was revived at the Restoration for respectable women attending the theatre, they became general. They soon, however, became the mark of loose women, and their use was discontinued by women of repute. On June 1st, 1704, a song was sung at the theatre in Lincoln's Inn Fields called "The Misses' Lamentation for want of their Vizard Masques at the Theatre." Mr. R. W. Lowe gives several references to the use of vizard masks at the theatre in his interesting biography, "Thomas Betterton."]

and so kept it on all the play; which of late is become a great fashion among the ladies, which hides their whole face. So to the Exchange, to buy things with my wife; among others, a vizard for herself. And so by water home and to my office to do a little business, and so to see Sir W. Pen, but being going to bed and not well I could not see him. So home and to supper and bed, being mightily troubled all night and next morning with the palate of my mouth being down from some cold I took to-day sitting sweating in the playhouse, and the wind blowing through the windows upon my head.

13th. Up and betimes to Thames Street among the tarr men, to look the price of tarr and so by water to Whitehall thinking to speak with Sir G. Carteret, but he lying in the city all night, and meeting with Mr. Cutler the merchant, I with him in his coach into the city to Sir G. Carteret, but missing him there, he and I walked to find him at Sir Tho. Allen's in Bread Street, where not finding him he and I walked towards our office, he discoursing well of the business of the Navy, and particularly of the victualling, in which he was once I perceive concerned, and he and I parted and I to the office and there had a difference with Sir W. Batten about Mr. Bowyer's tarr, which I am resolved to cross, though he sent me last night, as a bribe, a barrel of sturgeon, which, it may be, I shall send back, for I will not have the King abused so abominably in the price of what we buy, by Sir W. Batten's corruption and underhand dealing. So from the office, Mr. Wayth with me, to the Parliament House, and there I spoke and told Sir G. Carteret all, with which he is well pleased, and do recall his willingness yesterday, it seems, to Sir W. Batten, that we should buy a great quantity of tarr, being abused by him. Thence with Mr. Wayth after drinking a cupp of ale at the Swan, talking of the corruption of the Navy, by water. I landed him at Whitefriars, and I to the Exchange, and so home to dinner, where I found my wife's brother, and thence after dinner by water to the Royall Theatre, where I resolved to bid farewell, as shall appear by my oaths tomorrow against all plays either at publique houses or Court till Christmas be over. Here we saw "The Faithfull Sheepheardesse," a most simple thing, and yet much thronged after, and often shown, but it is only for the scenes' sake, which is very fine indeed and worth seeing; but I am quite out of opinion with any of their actings, but Lacy's, compared with the other house. Thence to see Mrs. Hunt, which we did and were much made of; and in our way saw my Lady Castlemaine, who, I fear, is not so handsome as I have taken her for, and now she begins to decay something. This is my wife's opinion also, for which I am sorry. Thence by coach, with a mad coachman, that drove like mad, and down byeways, through Bucklersbury home, everybody through the street cursing him, being ready to run over them. So home, and after writing letters by the post, home to supper and bed. Yesterday, upon conference with the King in the Banqueting House, the Parliament did agree with much ado, it being carried but by forty-two voices, that they would supply him with a sum of money; but what and how is not yet known, but expected to be done with great disputes the next week. But if done at all, it is well.

14th (Lord's day). Lay long in bed. So up and to church. Then to dinner, and Tom dined with me, who I think grows a very thriving man, as he himself tells me. He tells me that his man John has got a wife, and for that he intends to part with him, which I am sorry for, and then that Mr. Armiger comes to be a constant lodger at his house, and he says has money in his purse and will be a good paymaster, but I do much doubt it. He being gone, I up and sending my people to church, my wife and I did even our reckonings, and had a great deal of serious talk, wherein I took occasion to give her hints of the necessity of our saving all we can. I do see great cause every day to curse the time that ever I did give way to the taking of a woman for her, though I could never have had a better, and also the letting of her learn to dance, by both which her mind is so devilishly taken off her business and minding her occasions, and besides has got such an opinion in her of my being jealous, that it is never to be removed, I fear, nor hardly my trouble that attends it; but I must have patience. I did give her 40s. to carry into the country tomorrow with her, whereof 15s. is to go for the coach-hire for her and Ashwell, there being 20s. paid here already in earnest. In the evening our discourse turned to great content and love, and I hope that after a little forgetting our late differences, and being a while absent one from another, we shall come to agree as well as ever. So to Sir W. Pen's to visit him, and finding him alone, sent for my wife, who is in her riding-suit, to see him, which she hath not done these many months I think. By and by in comes Sir J. Minnes and Sir W. Batten, and so we sat talking. Among other things, Sir J. Minnes brought many fine expressions of Chaucer, which he doats on mightily, and without doubt he is a very fine poet.

[Pepys continued through life an admirer of Chaucer, and we have the authority of Dryden himself for saying that we owe his character of the Good Parson to Pepys's recommendation.]

Sir W. Pen continues lame of the gout, that he cannot rise from his chair. So after staying an hour with him, we went home and to supper, and so to prayers and bed.

15th. Up betimes, and anon my wife rose and did give me her keys, and put other things in order and herself against going this morning into the country. I was forced to go to Thames Street and strike up a bargain for some tarr, to prevent being abused therein by Hill, who was with me this morning, and is mightily surprised that I should tell him what I can have the same tarr with his for. Thence home, but finding my wife gone, I took coach and after her to her inn, where I am troubled to see her forced to sit in the back of the coach, though pleased to see her company none but women and one parson; she I find is troubled at all, and I seemed to make a promise to get a horse and ride after them; and so, kissing her often, and Ashwell once, I bid them adieu. So home by coach, and thence by water to Deptford to the Trinity House, where I came a little late; but I found them reading their charter, which they did like fools, only reading here and there a bit, whereas they ought to do it all, every word, and then proceeded to the election of a maister, which was Sir W. Batten, without any control, who made a heavy, short speech to them, moving them to give thanks to the late Maister for his pains, which he said was very great, and giving them thanks for their choice of him, wherein he would serve them to the best of his power. Then to the choice of their assistants and wardens, and so rose. I might have received 2s. 6d. as a younger Brother, but I directed one of the servants of the House to receive it and keep it. Thence to church, where Dr. Britton preached a sermon full of words against the Nonconformists, but no great matter in it, nor proper for the day at all. His text was, "With one mind and one mouth give glory to God, the Father of our Lord Jesus Christ." That done, by water, I in the barge with the Maister, to the Trinity House at London; where, among others, I found my Lords Sandwich and Craven, and my cousin Roger Pepys, and Sir Wm. Wheeler. Anon we sat down to dinner, which was very great, as they always have. Great variety of talk. Mr. Prin, among many, had a pretty tale of one that brought in a bill in parliament for the empowering him to dispose his land to such children as he should have that should bear the name of his wife. It was in Queen Elizabeth's time. One replied that there are many species of creatures where the male gives the denomination to both sexes, as swan and woodcock, but not above one where the female do, and that is a goose. Both at and after dinner we had great discourses of the nature and power of spirits, and whether they can animate dead bodies; in all which, as of the general appearance of spirits, my Lord Sandwich is very scepticall. He says the greatest warrants that ever he had to believe any, is the present appearing of the Devil

[In 1664, there being a generall report all over the kingdom of Mr. Monpesson his house being haunted, which hee himself affirming to the King and Queene to be true, the King sent the Lord Falmouth, and the Queene sent mee, to examine the truth of; but wee could neither see nor heare anything that was extraordinary; and about a year after, his Majesty told me that hee had discovered the cheat, and that Mr. Monpesson, upon his Majesty sending for him, confessed it to him. And yet Mr. Monpesson, in a printed letter, had afterwards the confidence to deny that hee had ever made any such confession" ("Letters of the Second Earl of Chesterfield," p. 24, 1829, 8vo.). Joseph Glanville published a relation of the famous disturbance at the house of Mr. Monpesson, at Tedworth, Wilts, occasioned by the beating of an invisible drum every night for a year. This story, which was believed at the time, furnished the plot for Addison's play of "The Drummer," or the "Haunted House." In the "Mercurius Publicus," April 16-23, 1663, there is a curious examination on this subject, by which it appears that one William Drury, of Uscut, Wilts, was the invisible drummer.—B.]

in Wiltshire, much of late talked of, who beats a drum up and down. There are books of it, and, they say, very true; but my Lord observes, that though he do answer to any tune that you will play to him upon another drum, yet one tune he tried to play and could not; which makes him suspect the whole; and I think it is a good argument. Sometimes they talked of handsome women, and Sir J. Minnes saying that there was no beauty like what he sees in the country-markets, and specially at Bury, in which I will agree with him that there is a prettiest women I ever saw. My Lord replied thus: "Sir John, what do you think of your neighbour's wife?" looking upon me. "Do you not think that he hath a great beauty to his wife? Upon my word he hath." Which I was not a little proud of. Thence by barge with my Lord to Blackfriars, where we landed and I thence walked home, where vexed to find my boy (whom I boxed at his coming for it) and Will abroad, though he was but upon Tower Hill a very little while. My head akeing with the healths I was forced to drink to-day I sent for the barber, and he having done, I up to my wife's closett, and there played on my viallin a good while, and without supper anon to bed, sad for want of my wife, whom I love with all my heart, though of late she has given me some troubled thoughts.

16th. Up, but not so early as I intend now, and to my office, where doing business all the morning. At noon by desire I dined with Sir W. Batten, who tells me that the House have voted the supply, intended for the King, shall be by subsidy. After dinner with Sir J. Minnes to see some pictures at Brewer's, said to be of good hands, but I do not like them. So I to the office and thence to Stacy's, his Tar merchant, whose servant with whom I agreed yesterday for some tar do by combination with Bowyer and Hill fall from our agreement, which vexes us all at the office, even Sir W. Batten, who was so earnest for it. So to the office, where we sat all the afternoon till night, and then to Sir W. Pen, who continues ill, and so to bed about 10 o'clock.

17th. Up before 4 o'clock, which is the hour I intend now to rise at, and to my office a while, and with great pleasure I fell to my business again. Anon went with money to my tar merchant to pay for the tar, which he refuses to sell me; but now the master is come home, and so he speaks very civilly, and I believe we shall have it with peace. I brought back my money to my office, and thence to White Hall, and in the garden spoke to my Lord Sandwich, who is in his gold-buttoned suit, as the mode is, and looks nobly. Captain Ferrers, I see, is come home from France. I only spoke one word to him, my Lord being there. He tells me the young gentlemen are well there; so my Lord went to my Lord Albemarle's to dinner, and I by water home and dined alone, and at the office (after half an hour's viallin practice after dinner) till late at night, and so home and to bed. This day I sent my cozen Edward Pepys his Lady, at my cozen Turner's, a piece of venison given me yesterday, and Madam Turner I sent for a dozen bottles of her's, to fill with wine for her. This day I met with Pierce the surgeon, who tells me that the King has made peace between Mr. Edward Montagu and his father Lord Montagu, and that all is well again; at which; for the family's sake, I am very glad, but do not think it will hold long.

18th. Up by four o'clock and to my office, where all the morning writing out in my Navy collections the ordinary estimate of the Navy, and did it neatly. Then dined at home alone, my mind pleased with business, but sad for the absence of my wife. After dinner half an hour at my viallin, and then all the afternoon sitting at the office late, and so home and to bed. This morning Mr. Cutler came and sat in my closet half an hour with me, his discourse very excellent, being a wise man, and I do perceive by him as well as many others that my diligence is taken notice of in the world, for which I bless God and hope to continue doing so. Before I went into my house this night I called at Sir W. Batten's, where finding some great ladies at table at supper with him and his lady, I retreated and went home, though they called to me again and again, and afterwards sent for me. So I went, and who should it be but Sir Fr. Clerke and his lady and another proper lady at supper there, and great cheer, where I staid till 11 o'clock at night, and so home and to bed.

19th. Lay till 6 o'clock, and then up and to my office, where all the morning, and at noon to the Exchange, and coming home met Mr. Creed, and took him back, and he dined with me, and by and by came Mr. Moore, whom I supplied with L30, and then abroad with them by water to Lambeth, expecting to have seen the Archbishop lie in state; but it seems he is not laid out yet. And so over to White Hall, and at the Privy Seal Office examined the books, and found the grant of increase of salary to the principall officers in the year 1639, L300 among the Controller, Surveyor, and Clerk of the Shippes. Thence to Wilkinson's after a good walk in the Park, where we met on horseback Captain Ferrers; who tells us that the King of France is well again, and that he saw him train his Guards, all brave men, at Paris; and that when he goes to his mistress, Madame la Valiere, a pretty little woman, now with child by him, he goes with his guards with him publiquely, and his trumpets and kettle-drums with him, who stay before the house while he is with her; and yet he says that, for all this, the Queen do not know of it, for that nobody dares to tell her; but that I dare not believe. Thence I to Wilkinson's, where we had bespoke a dish of pease, where we eat them very merrily, and there being with us the little gentleman, a friend of Captain Ferrers, that was with my wife and I at a play a little while ago, we went thence to the Rhenish wine-house, where we called for a red Rhenish wine called Bleahard, a pretty wine, and not mixed, as they say. Here Mr. Moore showed us the French manner, when a health is drunk, to bow to him that drunk to you, and then apply yourself to him, whose lady's health is drunk, and then to the person that you drink to, which I never knew before; but it seems it is now the fashion. Thence by water home and to bed, having played out of my chamber window on my pipe before I went to bed, and making Will read a part of a Latin chapter, in which I perceive in a little while he will be pretty ready, if he spends but a little pains in it.

20th. Up and to my office, where all the morning, and dined at home, Mr. Deane, of Woolwich, with me, and he and I all the afternoon down by water, and in a timber yard, measuring of timber, which I now understand thoroughly, and shall be able in a little time to do the King great service. Home in the evening, and after Will's reading a little in the Latin Testament, to bed.

21st (Lord's day). Up betimes, and fell to reading my Latin grammar, which I perceive I have great need of, having lately found it by my calling Will to the reading of a chapter in Latin, and I am resolved to go through it. After being trimmed, I by water to White Hall, and so over the Park, it raining hard, to Mr. Coventry's chamber, where I spent two hours with him about business of the Navy, and how by his absence things are like to go with us, and with good content from my being with him he carried me by coach and set me down at Whitehall, and thence to right home by water. He shewed me a list, which he hath prepared for the Parliament's view, if the business of his selling of offices should be brought to further hearing, wherein he reckons up, as I remember, 236 offices of ships which have been disposed of without his taking one farthing. This, of his own accord, he opened his cabinet on purpose to shew me, meaning, I suppose, that I should discourse abroad of it, and vindicate him therein, which I shall with all my power do. At home, being wet, shifted my band and things, and then to dinner, and after dinner went up and tried a little upon my tryangle, which I understand fully, and with a little use I believe could bring myself to do something. So to church, and slept all the sermon, the Scot, to whose voice I am not to be reconciled, preaching. Thence with Sir J. Minnes (who poor man had forgot that he carried me the other day to the painter's to see some pictures which he has since bought and are brought home) to his Jodgings to see some base things he calls them of great masters of painting. So I said nothing that he had shown me them already, but commended them, and I think they are indeed good enough. Thence to see Sir W. Pen, who continues ill of the gout still. Here we staid a good while, and then I to my office, and read my vows seriously and with content, and so home to supper, to prayers, and to bed.

22nd. Up betimes and to my office, reading over all our letters of the office that we have wrote since I came into the Navy, whereby to bring the whole series of matters into my memory, and to enter in my manuscript some of them that are needful and of great influence. By and by with Sir W. Batten by coach to Westminster, where all along I find the shops evening with the sides of the houses, even in the broadest streets; which will make the City very much better than it was. I walked in the Hall from one man to another. Hear that the House is still divided about the manner of levying the subsidys which they intend to give the King, both as to the manner, the time, and the number. It seems the House do consent to send to the King to desire that he would be graciously pleased to let them know who it was that did inform him of what words Sir Richard Temple should say, which were to this purpose: "That if the King would side with him, or be guided by him and his party, that he should not lack money:" but without knowing who told it, they do not think fit to call him to any account for it. Thence with Creed and bought a lobster, and then to an alehouse, where the maid of the house is a confident merry lass, and if modest is very pleasant to the customers that come thither. Here we eat it, and thence to walk in the Park a good while. The Duke being gone a-hunting, and by and by came in and shifted himself; he having in his hunting, rather than go about, 'light and led his horse through a river up to his breast, and came so home: and when we were come, which was by and by, we went on to him, and being ready he retired with us, and we had a long discourse with him. But Mr. Creed's accounts stick still through the perverse ignorance of Sir G. Carteret, which I cannot safely control as I would. Thence to the Park again, and there walked up and down an hour or two till night with Creed, talking, who is so knowing, and a man of that reason, that I cannot but love his company, though I do not love the man, because he is too wise to be made a friend of, and acts all by interest and policy, but is a man fit to learn of. So to White Hall, and by water to the Temple, and calling at my brother's and several places, but to no purpose, I came home, and meeting Strutt, the purser, he tells me for a secret that he was told by Field that he had a judgment against me in the Exchequer for L400. So I went to Sir W. Batten, and taking Mr. Batten, his son the counsellor, with me, by coach, I went to Clerke, our Solicitor, who tells me there can be no such thing, and after conferring with them two together, who are resolved to look well after the business, I returned home and to my office, setting down this day's passages, and having a letter that all is well in the country I went home to supper, and then a Latin chapter of Will and to bed.

23rd. Up by four o'clock, and so to my office; but before I went out, calling, as I have of late done, for my boy's copybook, I found that he had not done his task; so I beat him, and then went up to fetch my rope's end, but before I got down the boy was gone. I searched the cellar with a candle, and from top to bottom could not find him high nor low. So to the office; and after an hour or two, by water to the Temple, to my cozen Roger; who, I perceive, is a deadly high man in the Parliament business, and against the Court, showing me how they have computed that the King hath spent, at least hath received, about four millions of money since he came in: and in Sir J. Winter's case, in which I spoke to him, he is so high that he says he deserves to be hanged, and all the high words he could give, which I was sorry to see, though I am confident he means well. Thence by water home, and to the 'Change; and by and by comes the King and the Queen by in great state, and the streets full of people. I stood in Mr.--------'s balcone. They dine all at my Lord Mayor's; but what he do for victuals, or room for them, I know not. So home to dinner alone, and there I found that my boy had got out of doors, and came in for his hat and band, and so is gone away to his brother; but I do resolve even to let him go away for good and all. So I by and by to the office, and there had a great fray with Sir W. Batten and Sir J. Minnes, who, like an old dotard, is led by the nose by him. It was in Captain Cocke's business of hemp, wherein the King is absolutely abused; but I was for peace sake contented to be quiet and to sign to his bill, but in my manner so as to justify myself, and so all was well; but to see what a knave Sir W. Batten is makes my heart ake. So late at my office, and then home to supper and to bed, my man Will not being well.

24th. Up before 4 o'clock, and so to my lute an hour or more, and then by water, drinking my morning draft alone at an alehouse in Thames Street, to the Temple, and thence after a little discourse with my cozen Roger about some business, away by water to St. James's, and there an hour's private discourse with Mr. Coventry, where he told me one thing to my great joy, that in the business of Captain Cocke's hemp, disputed before him the other day, Mr. Coventry absent, the Duke did himself tell him since, that Mr. Pepys and he did stand up and carry it against the rest that were there, Sir G. Carteret and Sir W. Batten, which do please me much to see that the Duke do take notice of me. We did talk highly of Sir W. Batten's corruption, which Mr. Coventry did very kindly say that it might be only his heaviness and unaptness for business, that he do things without advice and rashly, and to gratify people that do eat and drink and play with him, and that now and then he observes that he signs bills only in anger and fury to be rid of men. Speaking of Sir G. Carteret, of whom I perceive he speaks but slightly, and diminishing of him in his services for the King in Jersey; that he was well rewarded, and had good lands and rents, and other profits from the King, all the time he was there; and that it was always his humour to have things done his way. He brought an example how he would not let the Castle there be victualled for more than a month, that so he might keep it at his beck, though the people of the town did offer to supply it more often themselves, which, when one did propose to the King, Sir George Carteret being by, says Sir George, "Let me know who they are that would do it, I would with all my heart pay them." "Ah, by God," says the Commander that spoke of it, "that is it that they are afeard of, that you would hug them," meaning that he would not endure them. Another thing he told me, how the Duke of York did give Sir G. Carteret and the Island his profits as Admirall, and other things, toward the building of a pier there. But it was never laid out, nor like to be. So it falling out that a lady being brought to bed, the Duke was to be desired to be one of the godfathers; and it being objected that that would not be proper, there being no peer of the land to be joyned with him, the lady replied, "Why, let him choose; and if he will not be a godfather without a peer, then let him even stay till he hath made a pier of his own."

[In the same spirit, long after this, some question arising as to the best material to be used in building Westminster Bridge, Lord Chesterfield remarked, that there were too many wooden piers (peers) at Westminster already.—B.]

He tells me, too, that he hath lately been observed to tack about at Court, and to endeavour to strike in with the persons that are against the Chancellor; but this he says of him, that he do not say nor do anything to the prejudice of the Chancellor. But he told me that the Chancellor was rising again, and that of late Sir G. Carteret's business and employment hath not been so full as it used to be while the Chancellor stood up. From that we discoursed of the evil of putting out men of experience in business as the Chancellor, and from that to speak of the condition of the King's party at present, who, as the Papists, though otherwise fine persons, yet being by law kept for these fourscore years out of employment, they are now wholly uncapable of business; and so the Cavaliers for twenty years, who, says he, for the most part have either given themselves over to look after country and family business, and those the best of them, and the rest to debauchery, &c.; and that was it that hath made him high against the late Bill brought into the House for the making all men incapable of employment that had served against the King. Why, says he, in the sea-service, it is impossible to do any thing without them, there being not more than three men of the whole King's side that are fit to command almost; and these were Captain Allen, Smith, and Beech; and it may be Holmes, and Utber, and Batts might do something. I desired him to tell me if he thought that I did speak anything that I do against Sir W. Batten and Sir J. Minnes out of ill will or design. He told me quite the contrary, and that there was reason enough. After a good deal of good and fine discourse, I took leave, and so to my Lord Sandwich's house, where I met my Lord, and there did discourse of our office businesses, and how the Duke do show me kindness, though I have endeavoured to displease more or less of my fellow officers, all but Mr. Coventry and Pett; but it matters not. Yes, says my Lord, Sir J. Minnes, who is great with the Chancellor; I told him the Chancellor I have thought was declining, and however that the esteem he has among them is nothing but for a jester or a ballad maker; at which my Lord laughs, and asks me whether I believe he ever could do that well. Thence with Mr. Creed up and down to an ordinary, and, the King's Head being full, went to the other over against it, a pretty man that keeps it, and good and much meat, better than the other, but the company and room so small that he must break, and there wants the pleasure that the other house has in its company. Here however dined an old courtier that is now so, who did bring many examples and arguments to prove that seldom any man that brings any thing to Court gets any thing, but rather the contrary; for knowing that they have wherewith to live, will not enslave themselves to the attendance, and flattery, and fawning condition of a courtier, whereas another that brings nothing, and will be contented to cog, and lie, and flatter every man and woman that has any interest with the persons that are great in favour, and can cheat the King, as nothing is to be got without offending God and the King, there he for the most part, and he alone, saves any thing. Thence to St. James Park, and there walked two or three hours talking of the difference between Sir G. Carteret and Mr. Creed about his accounts, and how to obviate him, but I find Creed a deadly cunning fellow and one that never do any thing openly, but has intrigues in all he do or says. Thence by water home to see all well, and thence down to Greenwich, and there walked into a pretty common garden and there played with him at nine pins for some drink, and to make the fellows drink that set up the pins, and so home again being very cold, and taking a very great cold, being to-day the first time in my tabby doublet this year. Home, and after a small supper Creed and I to bed. This day I observed the house, which I took to be the new tennis-court, newly built next my Lord's lodgings, to be fallen down by the badness of the foundation or slight working, which my cozen Roger and his discontented party cry out upon, as an example how the King's work is done, which I am sorry to see him and others so apt to think ill of things. It hath beaten down a good deal of my Lord's lodgings, and had like to have killed Mrs. Sarah, she having but newly gone out of it.

25th. Up both of us pretty early and to my chamber, where he and I did draw up a letter to Sir G. Carteret in excuse and preparation for Creed against we meet before the Duke upon his accounts, which I drew up and it proved very well, but I am pleased to see with what secret cunning and variety of artifice this Creed has carried on his business even unknown to me, which he is now forced by an accident to communicate to me. So that taking up all the papers of moment which lead to the clearing of his accounts unobserved out of the Controller's hand, which he now makes great use of; knowing that the Controller has not wherewith to betray him. About this all the morning, only Mr. Bland came to me about some business of his, and told me the news, which holds to be true, that the Portuguese did let in the Spaniard by a plot, and they being in the midst of the country and we believing that they would have taken the whole country, they did all rise and kill the whole body, near 8,000 men, and Don John of Austria having two horses killed under him, was forced with one man to flee away. Sir George Carteret at the office (after dinner, and Creed being gone, for both now and yesterday I was afraid to have him seen by Sir G. Carteret with me, for fear that he should increase his doubt that I am of a plot with Creed in the business of his accounts) did tell us that upon Tuesday last, being with my Lord Treasurer, he showed him a letter from Portugall speaking of the advance of the Spaniards into their country, and yet that the Portuguese were never more courageous than now; for by an old prophecy, from France, sent thither some years, though not many since, from the French King, it is foretold that the Spaniards should come into their country, and in such a valley they should be all killed, and then their country should be wholly delivered from the Spaniards. This was on Tuesday last, and yesterday came the very first news that in this very valley they had thus routed and killed the Spaniards, which is very strange but true. So late at the office, and then home to supper and to bed. This noon I received a letter from the country from my wife, wherein she seems much pleased with the country; God continue that she may have pleasure while she is there. She, by my Lady's advice, desires a new petticoat of the new silk striped stuff, very pretty. So I went to Paternoster Row' presently, and bought her one, with Mr. Creed's help, a very fine rich one, the best I did see there, and much better than she desires or expects, and sent it by Creed to Unthanke to be made against tomorrow to send by the carrier, thinking it had been but Wednesday to-day, but I found myself mistaken, and also the taylor being out of the way, it could not be done, but the stuff was sent me back at night by Creed to dispose of some other way to make, but now I shall keep it to next week.

26th. Up betimes, and Mr. Moore coming to see me, he and

[Paternoster Row, now famous as the headquarters of the publishing houses, was at this time chiefly inhabited by mercers. "This street, before the Fire of London, was taken up by eminent Mercers, Silkmen and Lacemen; and their shops were so resorted to by the nobility and gentry in their coaches, that oft times the street was so stop'd up that there was no passage for foot passengers" (Strype's "Stow," book iii., p. 195)].

I discoursed of going to Oxford this Commencement, Mr. Nathaniel Crew being Proctor and Mr. Childe commencing Doctor of Musique this year, which I have a great mind to do, and, if I can, will order my matters so that I may do it. By and by, he and I to the Temple, it raining hard, my cozen Roger being got out, he and I walked a good while among the Temple trees discoursing of my getting my Lord to let me have security upon his estate for L100 per ann. for two lives, my own and my wife, for my money. But upon second thoughts Mr. Moore tells me it is very likely my Lord will think that I beg something, and may take it ill, and so we resolved not to move it there, but to look for it somewhere else. Here it raining hard he and I walked into the King's Bench Court, where I never was before, and there staid an hour almost, till it had done raining, which is a sad season, that it is said there hath not been one fair day these three months, and I think it is true, and then by water to Westminster, and at the Parliament House I spoke with Roger Pepys. The House is upon the King's answer to their message about Temple, which is, that my Lord of Bristol did tell him that Temple did say those words; so the House are resolved upon sending some of their members to him to know the truth, and to demand satisfaction if it be not true. So by water home, and after a little while getting me ready, Sir W. Batten, Sir J. Minnes, my Lady Batten, and I by coach to Bednall Green, to Sir W. Rider's to dinner, where a fine place, good lady mother, and their daughter, Mrs. Middleton, a fine woman. A noble dinner, and a fine merry walk with the ladies alone after dinner in the garden, which is very pleasant; the greatest quantity of strawberrys I ever saw, and good, and a collation of great mirth, Sir J. Minnes reading a book of scolding very prettily. This very house

[Sir William Rider's house was known as Kirby Castle, and was supposed to have been built in 1570 by John Thorpe for John Kirby. It was associated in rhyme with other follies of the time in bricks and mortar, as recorded by Stow

> "Kirkebyes Castell, and Fisher's Follie,
> Spinila's pleasure, and Megse's glorie."

The place was known in Strype's time as the "Blind Beggar's House," but he knew nothing of the ballad, "The Beggar's Daughter of Bednall Green," for he remarks, "perhaps Kirby beggared himself by it." Sr. William Rider died at this house in 1669.]

was built by the Blind Beggar of Bednall Green, so much talked of and sang in ballads; but they say it was only some of the outhouses of it. We drank great store of wine, and a beer glass at last which made me almost sick. At table, discoursing of thunder and lightning, they told many stories of their own knowledge at table of their masts being shivered from top to bottom, and sometimes only within and the outside whole, but among the rest Sir W. Rider did tell a story of his own knowledge, that a Genoese gaily in Leghorn Roads was struck by thunder, so as the mast was broke a-pieces, and the shackle upon one of the slaves was melted clear off of his leg without hurting his leg. Sir William went on board the vessel, and would have contributed towards the release of the slave whom Heaven had thus set free, but he could not compass it, and so he was brought to his fetters again. In the evening home, and a little to my Tryangle, and so to bed.

27th. Up by 4 o'clock and a little to my office. Then comes by agreement Sir W. Warren, and he and I from ship to ship to see deals of all sorts, whereby I have encreased my knowledge and with great pleasure. Then to his yard and house, where I staid two hours or more discoursing of the expense of the navy and the corruption of Sir W. Batten and his man Wood that he brings or would bring to sell all that is to be sold by the Navy. Then home to the office, where we sat a little, and at noon home to dinner, alone, and thence, it raining hard, by water to the Temple, and so to Lincoln's Inn, and there walked up and down to see the new garden which they are making, and will be very pretty, and so to walk under the Chappell by agreement, whither Mr. Clerke our Solicitor came to me, and he fetched Mr. Long, our Attorney in the Exchequer in the business against Field, and I directed him to come to the best and speediest composition he could, which he will do. So home on foot, calling upon my brother's and elsewhere upon business, and so home to my office, and there wrote letters to my father and wife, and so home to bed, taking three pills overnight.

28th (Lord's day). Early in the morning my last night's physic worked and did give me a good stool, and then I rose and had three or four stools, and walked up and down my chamber. Then up, my maid rose and made me a posset, and by and by comes Mr. Creed, and he and I spent all the morning discoursing against to-morrow before the Duke the business of his pieces of eight, in which the Treasurer makes so many queries. At noon, my physic having done working, I went down to dinner, and then he and I up again and spent most of the afternoon reading in Cicero and other books of good discourse, and then he went away, and then came my brother Tom to see me, telling me how the Joyces do make themselves fine clothes against Mary is brought to bed. He being gone I went to cast up my monthly accounts, and to my great trouble I find myself L7 worse than I was the last month, but I confess it is by my reckoning beforehand a great many things, yet however I am troubled to see that I can hardly promise myself to lay up much from month's end to month's end, about L4 or L5 at most, one month with another, without some extraordinary gettings, but I must and I hope I shall continue to have a care of my own expenses. So to the reading my vows seriously and then to supper. This evening there came my boy's brother to see for him, and tells me he knows not where he is, himself being out of town this week and is very sorry that he is gone, and so am I, but he shall come no more. So to prayers, and to bed.

29th. Up betimes and to my office, and by and by to the Temple, and there appointed to meet in the evening about my business, and thence I walked home, and up and down the streets is cried mightily the great victory got by the Portugalls against the Spaniards, where 10,000 slain, 3 or 4,000 taken prisoners, with all the artillery, baggage, money, &c., and Don John of Austria

[He was natural son of Philip IV., King of Spain, who, after his
father's death in 1665, exerted his whole influence to overthrow the
Regency appointed during the young king's minority.—B.]

forced to flee with a man or two with him, which is very great news. Thence home and at my office all the morning, and then by water to St. James's, but no meeting to-day being holy day, but met Mr. Creed in the Park, and after a walk or two, discoursing his business, took leave of him in Westminster Hall, whither we walked, and then came again to the Hall and fell to talk with Mrs. Lane, and after great talk that she never went abroad with any man as she used heretofore to do, I with one word got her to go with me and to meet me at the further Rhenish wine-house, where I did give her a Lobster and do so touse her and feel her all over, making her believe how fair and good a skin she has, and indeed she has a very white thigh and leg, but monstrous fat. When weary I did give over and somebody, having seen some of our dalliance, called aloud in the street, "Sir! why do you kiss the gentlewoman so?" and flung a stone at the window, which vexed me, but I believe they could not see my touzing her, and so we broke up and I went out the back way, without being observed I think, and so she towards the Hall and I to White Hall, where taking water I to the Temple with my cozen Roger and Mr. Goldsborough to Gray's Inn to his counsel, one Mr. Rawworth, a very fine man, where it being the question whether I as executor should give a warrant to Goldsborough in my reconveying her estate back again, the mortgage being performed against all acts of the testator, but only my own, my cozen said he never heard it asked before; and the other that it was always asked, and he never heard it denied, or scrupled before, so great a distance was there in their opinions, enough to make a man forswear ever having to do with the law; so they agreed to refer it to Serjeant Maynard. So we broke up, and I by water home from the Temple, and there to Sir W. Batten and eat with him, he and his lady and Sir J. Minnes having been below to-day upon the East India men that are come in, but never tell me so, but that they have been at Woolwich and Deptford, and done great deal of business. God help them. So home and up to my lute long, and then, after a little Latin chapter with Will, to bed. But I have used of late, since my wife went, to make a bad use of my fancy with whatever woman I have a mind to, which I am ashamed of, and shall endeavour to do so no more. So to sleep.

30th. Up betimes yesterday and to-day, the sun rising very bright and glorious; and yet yesterday, as it hath been these two months and more, was a foul day the most part of the day. By and by by water to White Hall, and there to my Lord's lodgings by appointment, whither Mr. Creed comes to me, having been at Chelsey this morning to fetch my Lord to St. James's. So he and I to the Park, where we understand that the King and Duke are gone out betimes this morning on board the East India ships lately come in, and so our meeting appointed is lost. But he and I walked at the further end of the Park, not to be observed, whither by and by comes my Lord Sandwich, and he and we walked two hours and more in the Park and then

111

in White Hall Gallery, and lastly in White Hall garden, discoursing of Mr. Creed's accounts, and how to answer the Treasurer's objections. I find that the business is L500 deep, the advantage of Creed, and why my Lord and I should be concerned to promote his profit with so much dishonour and trouble to us I know not, but however we shall do what we can, though he deserves it not, for there is nothing even to his own advantage that can be got out of him, but by mere force. So full of policy he is in the smallest matters, that I perceive him to be made up of nothing but design. I left him here, being in my mind vexed at the trouble that this business gets me, and the distance that it makes between Sir G. Carteret and myself, which I ought to avoyd. Thence by water home and to dinner, and afterwards to the office, and there sat till evening, and then I by water to Deptford to see Sir W. Pen, who lies ill at Captain Rooth's, but in a way to be well again this weather, this day being the only fair day we have had these two or three months. Among other discourse I did tell him plainly some of my thoughts concerning Sir W. Batten. and the office in general, upon design for him to understand that I do mind things and will not balk to take notice of them, that when he comes to be well again he may know how to look upon me. Thence homeward walked, and in my way met Creed coming to meet me, and then turned back and walk a while, and so to boat and home by water, I being not very forward to talk of his business, and he by design the same, to see how I would speak of it, but I did not, but in general terms, and so after supper with general discourse to bed and sleep. Thus, by God's blessing, ends this book of two years; I being in all points in good health and a good way to thrive and do well. Some money I do and can lay up, but not much, being worth now above L700, besides goods of all sorts. My wife in the country with Ashwell, her woman, with my father; myself at home with W. Hewer and my cooke-maid Hannah, my boy Wayneman being lately run away from me. In my office, my repute and understanding good, especially with the Duke and Mr. Coventry; only the rest of the officers do rather envy than love me, I standing in most of their lights, specially Sir W. Batten, whose cheats I do daily oppose to his great trouble, though he appears mighty kind and willing to keep friendship with me, while Sir J. Minnes, like a dotard, is led by the nose by him. My wife and I, by my late jealousy, for which I am truly to be blamed, have not the kindness between us which we used and ought to have, and I fear will be lost hereafter if I do not take course to oblige her and yet preserve my authority. Publique matters are in an ill condition; Parliament sitting and raising four subsidys for the King, which is but a little, considering his wants; and yet that parted withal with great hardness. They being offended to see so much money go, and no debts of the publique's paid, but all swallowed by a luxurious Court: which the King it is believed and hoped will retrench in a little time, when he comes to see the utmost of the revenue which shall be settled on him: he expecting to have his L1,200,000 made good to him, which is not yet done by above L150,000, as he himself reports to the House. My differences with my uncle Thomas at a good quiett, blessed be God! and other matters. The town full of the great overthrow lately given to the Spaniards by the Portugalls, they being advanced into the very middle of Portugall. The weather wet for two or three months together beyond belief, almost not one fair day coming between till this day, which has been a very pleasant [day] and the first pleasant [day] this summer. The charge of the Navy intended to be limited to L200,000 per annum, the ordinary charge of it, and that to be settled upon the Customs. The King yet greatly taken up with Madam Castlemaine and Mrs. Stewart, which God of Heaven put an end to! Myself very studious to learn what I can of all things necessary for my place as an officer of the Navy, reading lately what concerns measuring of timber and knowledge of the tides. I have of late spent much time with Creed, being led to it by his business of his accounts, but I find him a fellow of those designs and tricks, that there is no degree of true friendship to be made with him, and therefore I must cast him off, though he be a very understanding man, and one that much may be learned of as to cunning and judging of other men. Besides, too, I do perceive more and more that my time of pleasure and idleness of any sort must be flung off to attend to getting of some money and the keeping of my family in order, which I fear by my wife's liberty may be otherwise lost.

A woman sober, and no high-flyer, as he calls it
After awhile I caressed her and parted seeming friends
Book itself, and both it and them not worth a turd
But a woful rude rabble there was, and such noises
Did find none of them within, which I was glad of
Did so watch to see my wife put on drawers, which (she did)
Duodecimal arithmetique
Employed by the fencers to play prizes at
Enquiring into the selling of places do trouble a great many
Every small thing is enough now-a-days to bring a difference
Give her a Lobster and do so touse her and feel her all over
God knows that I do not find honesty enough in my own mind
Goes with his guards with him publiquely, and his trumpets
Great plot which was lately discovered in Ireland
He hoped he should live to see her "ugly and willing"
He is too wise to be made a friend of
I calling her beggar, and she me pricklouse, which vexed me
I slept most of the sermon
In some churches there was hardly ten people in the whole church
It must be the old ones that must do any good
Jealous, though God knows I have no great reason
John has got a wife, and for that he intends to part with him
Keep at interest, which is a good, quiett, and easy profit
Lay long in bed talking and pleasing myself with my wife
My wife and her maid Ashwell had between them spilled the pot. . .

No sense nor grammar, yet in as good words that ever I saw
Nor would become obliged too much to any
Nothing is to be got without offending God and the King
Nothing of any truth and sincerity, but mere envy and design
Reading my Latin grammar, which I perceive I have great need
Sad for want of my wife, whom I love with all my heart
Saw his people go up and down louseing themselves
See whether my wife did wear drawers to-day as she used to do
Sent me last night, as a bribe, a barrel of sturgeon
She begins not at all to take pleasure in me or study to please
She used the word devil, which vexed me

So home, and after supper did wash my feet, and so to bed
Softly up to see whether any of the beds were out of order or no
Statute against selling of offices
The goldsmith, he being one of the jury to-morrow
Thence by coach, with a mad coachman, that drove like mad
Therefore ought not to expect more justice from her
They say now a common mistress to the King
Through the Fleete Ally to see a couple of pretty [strumpets]
Upon a small temptation I could be false to her
Waked this morning between four and five by my blackbird
Whose voice I am not to be reconciled
Wife and the dancing-master alone above, not dancing but talking
Would not make my coming troublesome to any

THE DIARY OF SAMUEL PEPYS M.A. F.R.S.

CLERK OF THE ACTS AND SECRETARY TO THE ADMIRALTY

Transcribed from the shorthand manuscript in the PEPYSIAN *library Magdalene College Cambridge by the Rev.* MYNORS *bright* M.A. *Late fellow and President of the College*

(Unabridged)

WITH LORD BRAYBROOKE'S NOTES

EDITED WITH ADDITIONS BY

HenryB. Wheatley F.S.A.

Diaryof Samuel Pepys.
July & August
1663

July 1st. This morning it rained so hard (though it was fair yesterday, and we thereupon in hopes of having some fair weather, which we have wanted these three months) that it wakened Creed, who lay with me last night, and me, and so we up and fell to discourse of the business of his accounts now under dispute, in which I have taken much trouble upon myself and raised a distance between Sir G. Carteret and myself, which troubles me, but I hope we have this morning light on an expedient that will right all, that will answer their queries, and yet save Creed the L500 which he did propose to make of the exchange abroad of the pieces of eight which he disbursed. Being ready, he and I by water to White Hall, where I left him before we came into the Court, for fear I should be seen by Sir G. Carteret with him, which of late I have been forced to avoid to remove suspicion. I to St. James's, and there discoursed a while with Mr. Coventry, between whom and myself there is very good understanding and friendship, and so to Westminster Hall, and being in the Parliament lobby, I there saw my Lord of Bristol come to the Commons House to give his answer to their question, about some words he should tell the King that were spoke by Sir Richard Temple, a member of their House. A chair was set at the bar of the House for him, which he used but little, but made an harangue of half an hour bareheaded, the House covered. His speech being done, he came out and withdrew into a little room till the House had concluded of an answer to his speech; which they staying long upon, I went away. And by and by out comes Sir W. Batten; and he told me that his Lordship had made a long and a comedian-like speech, and delivered with such action as was not becoming his Lordship. He confesses he did tell the King such a thing of Sir Richard Temple, but that upon his honour they were not spoke by Sir Richard, he having taken a liberty of enlarging to the King upon the discourse which had been between Sir Richard and himself lately; and so took upon himself the whole blame, and desired their pardon, it being not to do any wrong to their fellow-member, but out of zeal to the King. He told them, among many other things, that as to his religion he was a Roman Catholique, but such a one as thought no man to have right to the Crown of England but the Prince that hath it; and such a one as, if the King should desire his counsel as to his own, he would not advise him to another religion than the old true reformed religion of this country, it being the properest of this kingdom as it now stands; and concluded with a submission to what the House shall do with him, saying, that whatever they shall do, says he, "thanks be to God, this head, this heart, and this sword (pointing to them all), will find me a being in any place in Europe." The House hath hereupon voted clearly Sir Richard Temple to be free from the imputation of saying those words; but when Sir William Batten came out, had not concluded what to say to my Lord, it being argued that to own any satisfaction as to my Lord from his speech, would be to lay some fault upon the King for the message he should upon no better accounts send to the impeaching of one of their members. Walking out, I hear that the House of Lords are offended that my Lord Digby should come to this House and make a speech there without leave first asked of the House of Lords. I hear also of another difficulty now upon him; that my Lord of Sunderland (whom I do not know) was so near to the marriage of his daughter as that the wedding-clothes were made, and portion and every thing agreed on and ready; and the other day he goes away nobody yet knows whither, sending her the next morning a release of his right or claim to her, and advice to his friends not to enquire into the reason of this doing, for he hath enough for it; but that he gives them liberty to say and think what they will of him, so they do not demand the reason of his leaving her, being resolved never to have her, but the reason desires and resolves not to give. Thence by water with Sir W. Batten to Trinity House, there to dine with him, which we did; and after dinner we fell talking, Sir J. Minnes, Mr. Batten and I; Mr. Batten telling us of a late triall of Sir Charles Sydly the other day, before my Lord Chief Justice Foster and the whole bench, for his debauchery a little while since at Oxford Kate's,

[The details in the original are very gross. Dr. Johnson relates the story in the "Lives of the Poets," in his life of Sackville, Lord Dorset "Sackville, who was then Lord Buckhurst, with Sir Charles Sedley and Sir Thomas Ogle, got drunk at the Cock, in Bow Street, by Covent Garden, and going into the balcony exposed themselves to the populace in very indecent postures. At last, as they grew warmer, Sedley stood forth naked, and harangued the populace in such profane language, that the publick indignation was awakened; the crowd attempted to force the door, and being repulsed, drove in the performers with stones, and broke the windows of the house. For this misdemeanour they were indicted, and Sedley was fined five hundred pounds; what was the sentence of the others is not known. Sedley employed [Henry] Killigrew and another to procure a remission from the King, but (mark the friendship of the dissolute!) they begged the fine for themselves, and exacted it to the last groat." The woman known as Oxford Kate appears to have kept the notorious Cock Tavern in Bow Street at this date.]

coming in open day into the Balcone and showed his nakedness, ... and abusing of scripture and as it were from thence preaching a mountebank sermon from the pulpit, saying that there he had to sell such a powder as should make all the [women] in town run after him, 1000 people standing underneath to see and hear him, and that being done he took a glass of wine . . . . and then drank it off, and then took another and drank the King's health. It seems my Lord and the rest of the judges did all of them round give him a most high reproof; my Lord Chief justice saying, that it was for him, and such wicked wretches as he was, that God's anger and judgments hung

117

over us, calling him sirrah many times. It's said they have bound him to his good behaviour (there being no law against him for it) in L5000. It being told that my Lord Buckhurst was there, my Lord asked whether it was that Buckhurst that was lately tried for robbery; and when answered Yes, he asked whether he had so soon forgot his deliverance at that time, and that it would have more become him to have been at his prayers begging God's forgiveness, than now running into such courses again . . . . Thence home, and my clerks being gone by my leave to see the East India ships that are lately come home, I staid all alone within my office all the afternoon. This day I hear at dinner that Don John of Austria, since his flight out of Portugall, is dead of his wounds:—[not true]—so there is a great man gone, and a great dispute like to be ended for the crown of Spayne, if the King should have died before him. I received this morning a letter from my wife, brought by John Gower to town, wherein I find a sad falling out between my wife and my father and sister and Ashwell upon my writing to my father to advise Pall not to keep Ashwell from her mistress, or making any difference between them. Which Pall telling to Ashwell, and she speaking some words that her mistress heard, caused great difference among them; all which I am sorry from my heart to hear of, and I fear will breed ill blood not to be laid again. So that I fear my wife and I may have some falling out about it, or at least my father and I, but I shall endeavour to salve up all as well as I can, or send for her out of the country before the time intended, which I would be loth to do. In the evening by water to my coz. Roger Pepys' chamber, where he was not come, but I found Dr. John newly come to town, and is well again after his sickness; but, Lord! what a simple man he is as to any public matter of state, and talks so sillily to his brother Dr. Tom. What the matter is I know not, but he has taken (as my father told me a good while since) such displeasure that he hardly would touch his hat to me, and I as little to him. By and by comes Roger, and he told us the whole passage of my Lord Digby to-day, much as I have said here above; only that he did say that he would draw his sword against the Pope himself, if he should offer any thing against his Majesty, and the good of these nations; and that he never was the man that did either look for a Cardinal's cap for himself, or any body else, meaning Abbot Montagu; and the House upon the whole did vote Sir Richard Temple innocent; and that my Lord Digby hath cleared the honour of his Majesty, and Sir Richard Temple's, and given perfect satisfaction of his own respects to the House. Thence to my brother's, and being vexed with his not minding my father's business here in getting his Landscape done, I went away in an anger, and walked home, and so up to my lute and then to bed.

2d. Up betimes to my office, and there all the morning doing business, at noon to the Change, and there met with several people, among others Captain Cox, and with him to a Coffee [House], and drank with him and some other merchants. Good discourse. Thence home and to dinner, and, after a little alone at my viol, to the office, where we sat all the afternoon, and so rose at the evening, and then home to supper and to bed, after a little musique. My mind troubled me with the thoughts of the difference between my wife and my father in the country. Walking in the garden this evening with Sir G. Carteret and Sir J. Minnes, Sir G. Carteret told us with great contempt how like a stage-player my Lord Digby spoke yesterday, pointing to his head as my Lord did, and saying, "First, for his head," says Sir G. Carteret, "I know what a calf's head would have done better by half for his heart and his sword, I have nothing to say to them." He told us that for certain his head cost the late King his, for it was he that broke off the treaty at Uxbridge. He told us also how great a man he was raised from a private gentleman in France by Monsieur Grandmont,

[Antoine, Duc de Gramont, marshal of France, who died July 12th, 1678, aged seventy-four. His memoirs have been published.]

and afterwards by the Cardinall,—[Mazarin]—who raised him to be a Lieutenant-generall, and then higher; and entrusted by the Cardinall, when he was banished out of France, with great matters, and recommended by him to the Queen as a man to be trusted and ruled by: yet when he came to have some power over the Queen, he begun to dissuade her from her opinion of the Cardinal; which she said nothing to till the Cardinal was returned, and then she told him of it; who told my Lord Digby, "Eh bien, Monsieur, vous estes un fort bon amy donc:" but presently put him out of all; and then he was, from a certainty of coming in two or three years' time to be Mareschall of France (to which all strangers, even Protestants, and those as often as French themselves, are capable of coming, though it be one of the greatest places in France), he was driven to go out of France into Flanders; but there was not trusted, nor received any kindness from the Prince of Conde, as one to whom also he had been false, as he had been to the Cardinal and Grandmont. In fine, he told us how he is a man of excellent parts, but of no great faith nor judgment, and one very easy to get up to great height of preferment, but never able to hold it. So home and to my musique; and then comes Mr. Creed to me giving me an account of his accounts, how he has now settled them fit for perusal the most strict, at which I am glad. So he and I to bed together.

3d. Up and he home, and I with Sir J. Minnes and Sir W. Batten by coach to Westminster, to St. James's, thinking to meet Sir G. Carteret, and to attend the Duke, but he not coming we broke up, and so to Westminster Hall, and there meeting with Mr. Moore he tells me great news that my Lady Castlemaine is fallen from Court, and this morning retired. He gives me no account of the reason of it, but that it is so: for which I am sorry: and yet if the King do it to leave off not only her but all other mistresses, I should be heartily glad of it, that he may fall to look after business. I hear my Lord Digby is condemned at Court for his speech, and that my Lord Chancellor grows great again. Thence with Mr. Creed, whom I called at his chamber, over the water to Lambeth; but could not, it being morning, get to see the Archbishop's hearse: so he and I walked over the fields to Southwark, and there parted, and I spent half an hour in Mary Overy's Church, where are fine monuments of great antiquity, I believe, and has been a fine church. Thence to the Change, and meeting Sir J. Minnes there, he and I walked to look upon Backwell's design of making another alley from his shop through over against the Exchange door, which will be very noble and quite put down the other two.

So home to dinner and then to the office, and entered in my manuscript book the Victualler's contract, and then over the water and walked to see Sir W. Pen, and sat with him a while, and so home late, and to my viall. So up comes Creed again to me and stays all night, to-morrow morning being a hearing before the Duke. So to bed full of discourse of his business.

4th. Up by 4 o'clock and sent him to get matters ready, and I to my office looking over papers and mending my manuscript by scraping out the blots and other things, which is now a very fine book. So to St. James's by water with Sir J. Minnes and Sir W. Batten, I giving occasion to a wager about the tide, that it did flow through bridge, by which Sir W. Batten won 5s. of Sir J. Minnes. At St. James's we staid while the Duke made himself ready. Among other things Sir Allen Apsley showed the Duke the Lisbon Gazette in Spanish, where the late victory is set down particularly, and to the great honour of the English beyond measure. They have since taken back Evora, which was lost to the Spaniards, the English making the assault, and lost not more than three men. Here I learnt that the English foot are highly esteemed all over the world, but the horse not so much, which yet we count among ourselves the best; but they abroad have had no great knowledge of our horse, it seems. The Duke being ready, we retired with him, and there fell upon Mr. Creed's business, where the Treasurer did, like a mad coxcomb, without reason or method run over a great many things against the account, and so did Sir J. Minnes and Sir W. Batten, which the Duke himself and Mr. Coventry and my Lord Barkely and myself did remove, and Creed being called in did answer all with great method and excellently to the purpose (myself I am a little conscious did not speak so well as I purposed and do think I used to do, that is, not so intelligibly and persuasively, as I well hoped I should), not that what I said was not well taken, and did carry the business with what was urged and answered by Creed and Mr. Coventry, till the Duke himself did declare that he was satisfied, and my Lord Barkely offered to lay L100 that the King would receive no wrong in the account, and the two last knights held their tongues, or at least by not understanding it did say what made for Mr. Creed, and so Sir G. Carteret was left alone, but yet persisted to say that the account was not good, but full of corruption and foul dealing. And so we broke up to his shame, but I do fear to the loss of his friendship to me a good while, which I am heartily troubled for. Thence with Creed to the King's Head ordinary; but, coming late, dined at the second table very well for 12d.; and a pretty gentleman in our company, who confirms my Lady Castlemaine's being gone from Court, but knows not the reason; he told us of one wipe the Queen a little while ago did give her, when she came in and found the Queen under the dresser's hands, and had been so long:

"I wonder your Majesty," says she, "can have the patience to sit so long a-dressing?"—"I have so much reason to use patience," says the Queen, "that I can very well bear with it." He thinks that it may be the Queen hath commanded her to retire, though that is not likely. Thence with Creed to hire a coach to carry us to Hide Park, to-day there being a general muster of the King's Guards, horse and foot: but they demand so high, that I, spying Mr. Cutler the merchant, did take notice of him, and he going into his coach, and telling me that he was going to shew a couple of Swedish strangers the muster, I asked and went along with him; where a goodly sight to see so many fine horses and officers, and the King, Duke, and others come by a-horseback, and the two Queens in the Queen-Mother's coach, my Lady Castlemaine not being there. And after long being there, I 'light, and walked to the place where the King, Duke, &c., did stand to see the horse and foot march by and discharge their guns, to show a French Marquisse (for whom this muster was caused) the goodness of our firemen; which indeed was very good, though not without a slip now and then; and one broadside close to our coach we had going out of the Park, even to the nearness as to be ready to burn our hairs. Yet methought all these gay men are not the soldiers that must do the King's business, it being such as these that lost the old King all he had, and were beat by the most ordinary fellows that could be. Thence with much ado out of the Park, and I 'lighted and through St. James's down the waterside over, to Lambeth, to see the Archbishop's corps (who is to be carried away to Oxford on Monday), but came too late, and so walked over the fields and bridge home (calling by the way at old George's), but find that he is dead, and there wrote several letters, and so home to supper and to bed. This day in the Duke's chamber there being a Roman story in the hangings, and upon the standards written these four letters—S. P. Q. R., Sir G. Carteret came to me to know what the meaning of those four letters were; which ignorance is not to be borne in a Privy Counsellor, methinks, that a schoolboy should be whipt for not knowing.

5th (Lord's day). Lady Batten had sent twice to invite me to go with them to Walthamstow to-day, Mrs. Martha' being married already this morning to Mr. Castle, at this parish church. I could not rise soon enough to go with them, but got myself ready, and so to Games's, where I got a horse and rode thither very pleasantly, only coming to make water I found a stopping, which makes me fearful of my old pain. Being come thither, I was well received, and had two pair of gloves, as the rest, and walked up and down with my Lady in the garden, she mighty kind to me, and I have the way to please her. A good dinner and merry, but methinks none of the kindness nor bridall respect between the bridegroom and bride, that was between my wife and I, but as persons that marry purely for convenience. After dinner to church by coach, and there my Lady, Mrs. Turner, Mrs. Lemon, and I only, we, in spite to one another, kept one another awake; and sometimes I read in my book of Latin plays, which I took in my pocket, thinking to have walked it. An old doting parson preached. So home again, and by and by up and homewards, calling in our way (Sir J. Minnes and I only) at Mr. Batten's (who with his lady and child went in another coach by us), which is a very pretty house, and himself in all things within and without very ingenious, and I find a very fine study and good books. So set out, Sir J. Minnes and I in his coach together, talking all the way of chymistry, wherein he do know something, at least, seems so to me, that cannot correct him, Mr. Batten's man riding my horse, and so home and to my office a while to read my vows, then home to prayers and to bed.

6th. Up pretty early and to my office all the morning, writing out a list of the King's ships in my Navy collections with great pleasure. At noon Creed comes to me, who tells me how well he has sped with Sir G. Carteret after all our trouble, that he had his tallys up and all the kind words possible from him, which I believe is out of an apprehension what a fool he has made of himself hitherto in making so great a stop therein. But I find, and so my Lord Sandwich may, that Sir G. Carteret had a design to do him a disgrace, if he could possibly, otherwise he would never have carried the business so far after that manner, but would first have consulted my Lord and given him advice what to do therein for his own honour, which he thought endangered. Creed dined with me and then walked a while, and so away, and I to my office at my morning's work till dark night, and so with good content home. To supper, a little musique, and then to bed.

7th. Up by 4 o'clock and to my office, and there continued all the morning upon my Navy book to my great content. At noon down by barge with Sir J. Minnes (who is going to Chatham) to Woolwich, in our way eating of some venison pasty in the barge, I having neither eat nor drank to-day, which fills me full of wind. Here also in Mr. Pett's garden I eat some and the first cherries I have eat this year, off the tree where the King himself had been gathering some this morning. Thence walked alone, only part of the way Deane walked with me, complaining of many abuses in the Yard, to Greenwich, and so by water to Deptford, where I found Mr. Coventry, and with him up and down all the stores, to the great trouble of the officers, and by his help I am resolved to fall hard to work again, as I used to do. So thence he and I by water talking of many things, and I see he puts his trust most upon me in the Navy, and talks, as there is reason, slightly of the two old knights, and I should be glad by any drudgery to see the King's stores and service looked to as they ought, but I fear I shall never understand half the miscarriages and tricks that the King suffers by. He tells me what Mr. Pett did to-day, that my Lord Bristol told the King that he will impeach the Chancellor of High Treason: but I find that my Lord Bristol hath undone himself already in every body's opinion, and now he endeavours to raise dust to put out other men's eyes, as well as his own; but I hope it will not take, in consideration merely that it is hard for a Prince to spare an experienced old officer, be he never so corrupt; though I hope this man is not so, as some report him to be. He tells me that Don John is yet alive, and not killed, as was said, in the great victory against the Spaniards in Portugall of late. So home, and late at my office. Thence home and to my musique. This night Mr. Turner's house being to be emptied out of my cellar, and therefore I think to sit up a little longer than ordinary. This afternoon, coming from the waterside with Mr. Coventry, I spied my boy upon Tower Hill playing with the rest of the boys; so I sent W. Griffin to take him, and he did bring him to me, and so I said nothing to him, but caused him to be stripped (for he was run away with his best suit), and so putting on his other, I sent him going, without saying one word hard to him, though I am troubled for the rogue, though he do not deserve it. Being come home I find my stomach not well for want of eating to-day my dinner as I should do, and so am become full of wind. I called late for some victuals, and so to bed, leaving the men below in the cellar emptying the vats up through Mr. Turner's own house, and so with more content to bed late.

8th. Being weary, and going to bed late last night, I slept till 7 o'clock, it raining mighty hard, and so did every minute of the day after sadly. But I know not what will become of the corn this year, we having had but two fair days these many months. Up and to my office, where all the morning busy, and then at noon home to dinner alone upon a good dish of eeles, given me by Michell, the Bewpers' man, and then to my viall a little, and then down into the cellar and up and down with Mr. Turner to see where his vault may be made bigger, or another made him, which I think may well be. And so to my office, where very busy all day setting things in order my contract books and preparing things against the next sitting. In the evening I received letters out of the country, among others from my wife, who methinks writes so coldly that I am much troubled at it, and I fear shall have much ado to bring her to her old good temper. So home to supper and musique, which is all the pleasure I have of late given myself, or is fit I should, others spending too much time and money. Going in I stepped to Sir W. Batten, and there staid and talked with him (my Lady being in the country), and sent for some lobsters, and Mrs. Turner came in, and did bring us an umble pie hot out of her oven, extraordinary good, and afterwards some spirits of her making, in which she has great judgment, very good, and so home, merry with this night's refreshment.

9th. Up. Making water this morning, which I do every morning as soon as I am awake, with greater plenty and freedom than I used to do, which I think I may impute to last night's drinking of elder spirits. Abroad, it raining, to Blackfriars, and there went into a little alehouse and staid while I sent to the Wardrobe, but Mr. Moore was gone out. Here I kissed three or four times the maid of the house, who is a pretty girl, but very modest, and, God forgive me, had a mind to something more. Thence to my lawyer's; up and down to the Six Clerks' Office, where I found my bill against Tom Trice dismissed, which troubles me, it being through my neglect, and will put me to charges. So to Mr. Phillips, and discoursed with him about finding me out somebody that will let me have for money an annuity of about L100 per annum for two lives. So home, and there put up my riding things against the evening, in case Mr. Moore should continue his mind to go to Oxford, which I have little mind to do, the weather continuing so bad and the waters high. Dined at home, and Mr. Moore in the afternoon comes to me and concluded not to go. Sir W. Batten and I sat a little this afternoon at the office, and thence I by water to Deptford, and there mustered the Yard, purposely, God forgive me, to find out Bagwell, a carpenter, whose wife is a pretty woman, that I might have some occasion of knowing him and forcing her to come to the office again, which I did so luckily that going thence he and his wife did of themselves meet me in the way to thank me for my old kindness, but I spoke little to her, but shall give occasion for her coming to me. Her husband went along with me to show me Sir W. Pen's lodging, which I knew before, but only to have a time of speaking to him and sounding him. So left and I went in to Sir W. Pen, who continues ill, and worse, I think, than before. He tells me my Lady Castlemaine was at Court, for all this talk this week, which I am glad to hear; but it seems the King is stranger than ordinary to her. Thence walked home as I used to do, and to bed presently, having taken great cold in my feet by walking in the dirt this day in thin shoes or some other way, so that I begun to be in pain, and with warm clothes made myself better by morning, but yet in pain.

10th. Up late and by water to Westminster Hall, where I met Pierce the chirurgeon, who tells me that for certain the King is grown colder to my Lady Castlemaine than ordinary, and that he believes he begins to love the Queen, and do make much of her, more than he used to do. Up to the Lobby, and there sent out for Mr. Coventry and Sir W. Batten, and told them if they thought convenient I would go to Chatham today, Sir John Minnes being already there at a Pay, and I would do such and such business there, which they thought well of, and so I went home and prepared myself to go after, dinner with Sir W. Batten. Sir W. Batten and Mr. Coventry tell me that my Lord Bristol hath this day impeached my Lord Chancellor in the House of Lords of High Treason. The chief of the articles are these: 1st. That he should be the occasion of the peace made with Holland lately upon such disadvantageous terms, and that he was bribed to it. 2d. That Dunkirke was also sold by his advice chiefly, so much to the damage of England. 3d. That he had L6000 given him for the drawing-up or promoting of the Irish declaration lately, concerning the division of the lands there. 4th. He did carry on the design of the Portugall match, so much to the prejudice of the Crown of England, notwithstanding that he knew the Queen is not capable of bearing children. 5th. That the Duke's marrying of his daughter was a practice of his, thereby to raise his family; and that it was done by indirect courses. 6th. That the breaking-off of the match with Parma, in which he was employed at the very time when the match with Portugall was made up here, which he took as a great slur to him, and so it was; and that, indeed, is the chief occasion of all this fewde. 7th. That he hath endeavoured to bring in Popery, and wrote to the Pope for a cap for a subject of the King of England's (my Lord Aubigny); and some say that he lays it to the Chancellor, that a good Protestant Secretary (Sir Edward Nicholas) was laid aside, and a Papist, Sir H. Bennet, put in his room: which is very strange, when the last of these two is his own creature, and such an enemy accounted to the Chancellor, that they never did nor do agree; and all the world did judge the Chancellor to be falling from the time that Sir H. Bennet was brought in. Besides my Lord Bristoll being a Catholique himself, all this is very strange. These are the main of the Articles. Upon which my Lord Chancellor desired that the noble Lord that brought in these Articles, would sign to them with his hand; which my Lord Bristoll did presently. Then the House did order that the judges should, against Monday next, bring in their opinion, Whether these articles are treason, or no? and next, they would know, Whether they were brought in regularly or no, without leave of the Lords' House? After dinner I took boat (H. Russell) and down to Gravesend in good time, and thence with a guide post to Chatham, where I found Sir J. Minnes and Mr. Wayth walking in the garden, whom I told all this day's news, which I left the town full of, and it is great news, and will certainly be in the consequence of it. By and by to supper, and after long discourse, Sir J. Minnes and I, he saw me to my chamber, which not pleasing me, I sent word so to Mrs. Bradford, that I should be crowded into such a hole, while the clerks and boarders of her own take up the best rooms. However I lay there and slept well.

11th. Up early and to the Dock, and with the Storekeeper and other officers all the morning from one office to another. At noon to the Hill-house in Commissioner Pett's coach, and after seeing the guard-ships, to dinner, and after dining done to the Dock by coach, it raining hard, to see "The Prince" launched, which hath lain in the Dock in repairing these three years. I went into her and was launched in her. Thence by boat ashore, it raining, and I went to Mr. Barrow's, where Sir J. Minnes and Commissioner Pett; we staid long eating sweetmeats and drinking, and looking over some antiquities of Mr. Barrow's, among others an old manuscript Almanac, that I believe was made for some monastery, in parchment, which I could spend much time upon to understand. Here was a pretty young lady, a niece of Barrow's, which I took much pleasure to look on. Thence by barge to St. Mary Creek; where Commissioner Pett (doubtful of the growing greatness of Portsmouth by the finding of those creeks there), do design a wett dock at no great charge, and yet no little one; he thinks towards L10,000. And the place, indeed, is likely to be a very fit place, when the King hath money to do it with. Thence, it raining as hard as it could pour down, home to the Hillhouse, and anon to supper, and after supper, Sir J. Minnes and I had great discourse with Captain Cox and Mr. Hempson about business of the yard, and particularly of pursers' accounts with Hempson, who is a cunning knave in that point. So late to bed and, Mr. Wayth being gone, I lay above in the Treasurer's bed and slept well. About one or two in the morning the curtains of my bed being drawn waked me, and I saw a man stand there by the inside of my bed calling me French dogg 20 times, one after another, and I starting, as if I would get out of the bed, he fell a-laughing as hard as he could drive, still calling me French dogg, and laid his hand on my shoulder. At last, whether I said anything or no I cannot tell, but I perceived the man, after he had looked wistly upon me, and found that I did not answer him to the names that he called me by, which was Salmon, Sir Carteret's clerk, and Robt. Maddox, another of the clerks, he put off his hat on a suddaine, and forebore laughing, and asked who I was, saying, "Are you Mr. Pepys?" I told him yes, and now being come a little better to myself, I found him to be Tom Willson, Sir W. Batten's clerk, and fearing he might be in some melancholy fit, I was at a loss what to do or say. At last I asked him what he meant. He desired my pardon for that he was mistaken, for he thought verily, not knowing of my coming to lie there, that it had been Salmon, the Frenchman, with whom he intended to have made some sport. So I made nothing of it, but bade him good night, and I, after a little pause, to sleep again, being well pleased that it ended no worse, and being a little the better pleased with it, because it was the Surveyor's clerk, which will make sport when I come to tell Sir W. Batten of it, it being a report that old Edgeborough, the former Surveyor, who died here, do now and then walk.

12th (Lord's day). Up, and meeting Tom Willson he asked my pardon again, which I easily did give him, telling him only that it was well I was not a woman with child, for it might have made me miscarry. With Sir J. Minnes to church, where an indifferent good sermon. Here I saw Mrs. Becky Allen, who hath been married, and is this day churched, after her bearing a child. She is grown tall, but looks very white and thin, and I can find no occasion while I am here to come to have her company, which I desire and expected in my coming, but only coming out of the church I kissed her and her sister and mother-in-law. So to dinner, Sir J. Minnes, Commissioner Pett, and I, &c., and after dinner walked in the garden, it being a very fine day, the best we have had this great while, if not this whole summer. To church again, and after that walked through the Rope-ground to the Dock, and there over and over the Dock and grounds about it, and storehouses, &c., with the officers of the Yard, and then to Commissioner Pett's and had a good sullybub and other good things, and merry. Commissioner Pett showed me alone his bodys as a secrett, which I found afterwards by discourse with Sir J. Minnes that he had shown them him, wherein he seems to suppose great mystery in the nature of Lynes to be hid, but I do not understand it at all. Thence walked to the Hill-house, being myself much dissatisfied, and more than I thought I should have been with Commissioner Pett, being, by what I saw since I came hither, convinced that he is not able to exercise the command in the Yard over the officers that he ought to do, or somebody else, if ever the service be well looked after there. Sat up and with Sir J. Minnes talking, and he speaking his mind in slighting of the Commissioner, for which I wish there was not so much reason. For I do see he is but a man of words, though indeed he is the ablest man that we have to do service if he would or durst. Sir J. Minnes being gone to bed, I took Mr. Whitfield, one of the clerks, and walked to the Dock about eleven at night, and there got a boat and a crew, and rowed down to the guard-ships, it being a most pleasant moonshine evening that ever I saw almost. The guard-ships were very ready to hail us, being no doubt commanded thereto by their Captain, who remembers how I surprised them the last time I was here. However, I found him ashore, but the ship in pretty good order, and the arms well fixed, charged, and primed. Thence to the Soveraign, where I found no officers aboard, no arms fixed, nor any powder to prime their few guns, which were charged, without bullet though. So to the London, where neither officers nor any body awake; I boarded her, and might have done what I would, and at last could find but three little boys; and so spent the whole night in visiting all the ships, in which I found, for the most part, neither an officer aboard, nor any men so much as awake, which I was grieved to find, specially so soon after a great Larum, as Commissioner Pett brought us word that he [had] provided against, and put all in a posture of defence but a week ago, all which I am resolved to represent to the Duke.

13th. So, it being high day, I put in to shore and to bed for two hours just, and so up again, and with the Storekeeper and Clerk of the Rope-yard up and down the Dock and Rope-house, and by and by mustered the Yard, and instructed the Clerks of the Cheque in my new way of Callbook, and that and other things done, to the Hill-house, and there we eat something, and so by barge to Rochester, and there took coach hired for our passage to London, and Mrs. Allen, the clerk of the Rope-yard's wife with us, desiring her passage, and it being a most pleasant and warm day, we got by four o'clock home. In our way she telling us in what condition Becky Allen is married against all expectation a fellow that proves to be a coxcomb and worth little if any thing at all, and yet are entered into a way of living above their condition that will ruin them presently, for which, for the lady's sake, I am much troubled. Home I found all well there, and after dressing myself, I walked to the Temple; and there, from my cozen Roger, hear that the judges have this day brought in their answer to the Lords, That the articles against my Lord Chancellor are not Treason; and to-morrow they are to bring in their arguments to the House for the same. This day also the King did send by my Lord Chamberlain to the Lords, to tell them from him, that the most of the articles against my Lord Chancellor he himself knows to be false. Thence by water to Whitehall, and so walked to St. James's, but missed Mr. Coventry. I met the Queen-Mother walking in the Pell Mell, led by my Lord St. Alban's. And finding many coaches at the Gate, I found upon enquiry that the Duchess is brought to bed of a boy; and hearing that the King and Queen are rode abroad with the Ladies of Honour to the Park, and seeing a great crowd of gallants staying here to see their return, I also staid walking up and down, and among others spying a man like Mr. Pembleton (though I have little reason to think it should be he, speaking and discoursing long with my Lord D'Aubigne), yet how my blood did rise in my face, and I fell into a sweat from my old jealousy and hate, which I pray God remove from me. By and by the King and Queen, who looked in this dress (a white laced waistcoat and a crimson short pettycoat, and her hair dressed ci la negligence) mighty pretty; and the King rode hand in hand with her. Here was also my Lady Castlemaine rode among the rest of the ladies; but the King took, methought, no notice of her; nor when they 'light did any body press (as she seemed to expect, and staid for it) to take her down, but was taken down by her own gentleman. She looked mighty out of humour, and had a yellow plume in her hat (which all took notice of), and yet is very handsome, but very melancholy: nor did any body speak to her, or she so much as smile or speak to any body. I followed them up into White Hall, and into the Queen's presence, where all the ladies walked, talking and fiddling with their hats and feathers, and changing and trying one another's by one another's heads, and laughing. But it was the finest sight to me, considering their great beautys and dress, that ever I did see in all my life. But, above all, Mrs. Stewart in this dress, with her hat cocked and a red plume, with her sweet eye, little Roman nose, and excellent taille, is now the greatest beauty I ever saw, I think, in my life; and, if ever woman can, do exceed my Lady Castlemaine, at least in this dress nor do I wonder if the King changes, which I verily believe is the reason of his coldness to my Lady Castlemaine. Here late, with much ado I left to look upon them, and went away, and by water, in a boat with other strange company, there being no other to be had, and out of him into a sculler half to the bridge, and so home and to Sir W. Batten, where I staid telling him and Sir J. Minnes and Mrs. Turner, with great mirth, my being frighted at Chatham by young Edgeborough, and so home to supper and to bed, before I sleep fancying myself to sport with Mrs. Stewart with great pleasure.

14th. Up a little late, last night recovering my sleepiness for the night before, which was lost, and so to my office to put papers and things to right, and making up my journal from Wednesday last to this day. All the morning at my office doing of business; at noon Mr. Hunt came to me, and he and I to the Exchange, and a Coffee House, and drank there, and thence to my house to dinner, whither my uncle Thomas came, and he tells me that he is going down to Wisbech, there to try what he can recover of my uncle Day's estate, and seems to have good arguments for what he do go about, in which I wish him good speed. I made him almost foxed, the poor man having but a bad head, and not used I believe nowadays to drink much wine. So after dinner, they being gone, I to my office, and so home to bed. This day I hear the judges, according to order yesterday, did bring into the Lords' House their reasons of their judgment in the business between my Lord Bristoll and the Chancellor; and the Lords do concur with the Judges that the articles are not treason, nor regularly brought into the House, and so voted that a Committee should be chosen to examine them; but nothing to be done therein till the next sitting of this Parliament (which is like to be adjourned in a day or two), and in the mean time the two Lords to, remain without prejudice done to either of them.

15th. Up and all the morning at the office, among other things with Cooper the Purveyor, whose dullness in his proceeding in his work I was vexed at, and find that though he understands it may be as much as other men that profess skill in timber, yet I perceive that many things, they do by rote, and very dully. Thence home to dinner, whither Captain Grove came and dined with me, he going into the country to-day; among other discourse he told me of discourse very much to my honour, both as to my care and ability, happening at the Duke of Albemarle's table the other day, both from the Duke, and the Duchess themselves; and how I paid so much a year to him whose place it was of right, and that Mr. Coventry did report thus of me; which was greatly to my content, knowing how against their minds I was brought into the Navy. Thence by water to Westminster, and there spent a good deal of time walking in the Hall, which is going to be repaired, and, God forgive me, had a mind to have got Mrs. Lane abroad, or fallen in with any woman else (in that hot humour). But it so happened she could not go out, nor I meet with any body else, and so I walked homeward, and in my way did many and great businesses of my own at the Temple among my lawyers and others to my great content, thanking God that I did not fall into any company to occasion spending time and money. To supper, and then to a little viall and to bed, sporting in my fancy with the Queen.

16th. Up and dispatched things into the country and to my father's, and two keggs of Sturgeon and a dozen bottles of wine to Cambridge for my cozen Roger Pepys, which I give him. By and by down by water on several Deall ships, and stood upon a stage in one place seeing calkers sheathing of a ship. Then at Wapping to my carver's about my Viall head. So home, and thence to my Viall maker's in Bishops, gate Street; his name is Wise, who is a pretty fellow at it. Thence to the Exchange, and so home to dinner, and then to my office, where a full board, and busy all the afternoon, and among other things made a great contract with Sir W. Warren for 40,000 deals Swinsound, at L3 17s. od. per hundred. In the morning before I went on the water I was at Thames Street about some pitch, and there meeting Anthony Joyce, I took him and Mr. Stacy, the Tarr merchant, to the tavern, where Stacy told me many old stories of my Lady Batten's former poor condition, and how her former husband broke, and how she came to her state. At night, after office done, I went to Sir W. Batten's, where my Lady and I [had] some high words about emptying our house of office, where I did tell her my mind, and at last agreed that it should be done through my office, and so all well. So home to bed.

17th. Up, and after doing some business at my office, Creed came to me, and I took him to my viall maker's, and there I heard the famous Mr. Stefkins play admirably well, and yet I found it as it is always, I over expected. I took him to the tavern and found him a temperate sober man, at least he seems so to me. I commit the direction of my viall to him. Thence to the Change, and so home, Creed and I to dinner, and after dinner Sir W. Warren came to me, and he and I in my closet about his last night's contract, and from thence to discourse of measuring of timber, wherein I made him see that I could understand the matter well, and did both learn of and teach him something. Creed being gone through my staying talking to him so long, I went alone by water down to Redriffe, and so to sit and talk with Sir W. Pen, where I did speak very plainly concerning my thoughts of Sir G. Carteret and Sir J. Minnes. So as it may cost me some trouble if he should tell them again, but he said as much or more to me concerning them both, which I may remember if ever it should come forth, and nothing but what is true and my real opinion of them, that they neither do understand to this day Creed's accounts, nor do deserve to be employed in their places without better care, but that the King had better give them greater salaries to stand still and do nothing. Thence coming home I was saluted by Bagwell and his wife (the woman I have a kindness for), and they would have me into their little house, which I was willing enough to, and did salute his wife. They had got wine for me, and I perceive live prettily, and I believe the woman a virtuous modest woman. Her husband walked through to Redriffe with me, telling me things that I asked of in the yard, and so by water home, it being likely to rain again to-night, which God forbid. To supper and to bed.

18th. Up and to my office, where all the morning, and Sir J. Minnes and I did a little, and but a little business at the office. So I eat a bit of victuals at home, and so abroad to several places, as my bookseller's, and then to Thomson the instrument maker's to bespeak a ruler for my pocket for timber, &c., which I believe he will do to my mind. So to the Temple, Wardrobe, and lastly to Westminster Hall, where I expected some bands made me by Mrs. Lane, and while she went to the starchers for them, I staid at Mrs. Howlett's, who with her husband were abroad, and only their daughter (which I call my wife) was in the shop, and I took occasion to buy a pair of gloves to talk to her, and I find her a pretty spoken girl, and will prove a mighty handsome wench. I could love her very well. By and by Mrs. Lane comes, and my bands not being done she and I posted and met at the Crown in the Palace Yard, where we eat a chicken I sent for, and drank, and were mighty merry, and I had my full liberty of towzing her and doing what I would, but the last thing of all . . . . Of which I am heartily ashamed, but I do resolve never to do more so. But, Lord! to see what a mind she has to a husband, and how she showed me her hands to tell her her fortune, and every thing that she asked ended always whom and when she was to marry. And I pleased her so well, saying as. I know she would have me, and then she would say that she had been with all the artists in town, and they always told her the same things, as that she should live long, and rich, and have a good husband, but few children, and a great fit of sickness, and 20 other things, which she says she has always been told by others. Here I staid late before my bands were done, and then they came, and so I by water to the Temple, and thence walked home, all in a sweat with my tumbling of her and walking, and so a little supper and to bed, fearful of having taken cold.

19th (Lord's day). Lay very long in pleasant dreams till Church time, and so up, and it being foul weather so that I cannot walk as I intended to meet my Cozen Roger at Thomas Pepys's house (whither he rode last night), to Hatcham, I went to church, where a sober Doctor made a good sermon. So home to dinner alone, and then to read a little, and so to church again, where the Scot made an ordinary sermon, and so home to my office, and there read over my vows and increased them by a vow against all strong drink till November next of any sort or quantity, by which I shall try how I can forbear it. God send it may not prejudice my health, and then I care not. Then I fell to read over a silly play writ by a person of honour (which is, I find, as much as to say a coxcomb), called "Love a la Mode,"' and that being ended, home, and played on my lute and sung psalms till bedtime, then to prayers and to bed.

20th. Up and to my office, and then walked to Woolwich, reading Bacon's "Faber fortunae,"

[Pepys may here refer either to Essay XLI. (of Fortune) or to a chapter' in the "Advancement of Learning." The sentence, "Faber quisque fortunae propria," said to be by Appius Claudian, is quoted more than once in the "De Augmentis Scientiarum," lib. viii., cap. 2.]

which the oftener I read the more I admire. There found Captain Cocke, and up and down to many places to look after matters, and so walked back again with him to his house, and there dined very finely. With much ado obtained an excuse from drinking of wine, and did only taste a drop of Sack which he had for his lady, who is, he fears, a little consumptive, and her beauty begins to want its colour. It was Malago Sack, which, he says, is certainly 30 years old, and I tasted a drop of it, and it was excellent wine, like a spirit rather than wine. Thence by water to the office, and taking some papers by water to White Hall and St. James's, but there being no meeting with the Duke to-day, I returned by water and down to Greenwich, to look after some blocks that I saw a load carried off by a cart from Woolwich, the King's Yard. But I could not find them, and so returned, and being heartily weary I made haste to bed, and being in bed made Will read and construe three or four Latin verses in the Bible, and chide him for forgetting his grammar. So to sleep, and sleep ill all the night, being so weary, and feverish with it.

21st. And so lay long in the morning, till I heard people knock at my door, and I took it to be about 8 o'clock (but afterwards found myself a little mistaken), and so I rose and ranted at Will and the maid, and swore I could find my heart to kick them down stairs, which the maid mumbled at mightily. It was my brother, who staid and talked with me, his chief business being about his going about to build his house new at the top, which will be a great charge for him, and above his judgment. By and by comes Mr. Deane, of Woolwich, with his draught of a ship, and the bend and main lines in the body of a ship very finely, and which do please me mightily, and so am resolved to study hard, and learn of him to understand a body, and I find him a very pretty fellow in it, and rational, but a little conceited, but that's no matter to me. At noon, by my Lady Batten's desire, I went over the water to Mr. Castle's, who brings his wife home to his own house to-day, where I found a great many good old women, and my Lady, Sir W. Batten, and Sir J. Minnes. A good, handsome, plain dinner, and then walked in the garden; which is pleasant enough, more than I expected there, and so Sir J. Minnes, Sir W. Batten, and I by water to the office, and there sat, and then I by water to the Temple about my law business, and back again home and wrote letters to my father and wife about my desire that they should observe the feast at Brampton, and have my Lady and the family, and so home to supper and bed, my head aching all the day from my last night's bad rest, and yesterday's distempering myself with over walking, and to-day knocking my head against a low door in Mr. Castle's house. This day the Parliament kept a fast for the present unseasonable weather.

22nd. Up, and by and by comes my uncle Thomas, to whom I paid L10 for his last half year's annuity, and did get his and his son's hand and seal for the confirming to us Piggott's mortgage, which was forgot to be expressed in our late agreement with him, though intended, and therefore they might have cavilled at it, if they would. Thence abroad calling at several places upon some errands, among others to my brother Tom's barber and had my hair cut, while his boy played on the viallin, a plain boy, but has a very good genius, and understands the book very well, but to see what a shift he made for a string of red silk was very pleasant. Thence to my Lord Crew's. My Lord not being come home, I met and staid below with Captain Ferrers, who was come to wait upon my Lady Jemimah to St. James's, she being one of the four ladies that hold up the mantle at the christening this afternoon of the Duke's child (a boy). In discourse of the ladies at Court, Captain Ferrers tells me that my Lady Castlemaine is now as great again as ever she was; and that her going away was only a fit of her own upon some slighting words of the King, so that she called for her coach at a quarter of an hour's warning, and went to Richmond; and the King the next morning, under pretence of going a-hunting, went to see her and make friends, and never was a-hunting at all. After which she came back to Court, and commands the King as much as ever, and hath and doth what she will. No longer ago than last night, there was a private entertainment made for the King and Queen at the Duke of Buckingham's, and she: was not invited: but being at my Lady Suffolk's, her aunt's (where my Lady Jemimah and Lord Sandwich dined) yesterday, she was heard to say, "Well; much good may it do them, and for all that I will be as merry as they:" and so she went home and caused a great supper to be prepared. And after the King had been with the Queen at Wallingford House, he came to my Lady Castlemaine's, and was there all night, and my Lord Sandwich with him, which was the reason my Lord lay in town all night, which he has not done a great while before. He tells me he believes that, as soon as the King can get a husband for Mrs. Stewart however, my Lady Castlemaine's nose will be out of joynt; for that she comes to be in great esteem, and is more handsome than she. I found by his words that my Lord Sandwich finds some pleasure in the country where he now is, whether he means one of the daughters of the house or no I know not, but hope the contrary, that he thinks he is very well pleased with staying there, but yet upon breaking up of the Parliament, which the King by a message to-day says shall be on Monday next, he resolves to go. Ned Pickering, the coxcomb, notwithstanding all his hopes of my Lord's assistance, wherein I am sorry to hear my Lord has much concerned himself, is defeated of the place he expected under the Queen. He came hither by and by and brought some jewells for my Lady Jem. to put on, with which and her other clothes she looks passing well. I staid and dined with my Lord Crew, who whether he was not so well pleased with me as he used to be, or that his head was full of business, as I believe it was, he hardly spoke one word to me all dinner time, we dining alone, only young Jack Crew, Sir Thomas's son, with us. After dinner I bade him farewell. Sir Thomas I hear has gone this morning ill to bed, so I had no mind to see him. Thence homewards, and in the way first called at Wotton's, the shoemaker's, who tells me the reason of Harris's' going from Sir Wm. Davenant's house, that he grew very proud and demanded L20 for himself extraordinary, more than Betterton or any body else, upon every new play, and L10 upon every revive; which with other things Sir W. Davenant would not give him, and so he swore he would never act there more, in expectation of being received in the other House; but the King will not suffer it, upon Sir W. Davenant's desire that he would not, for then he might shut up house, and that is true. He tells me that his going is at present a great loss to the House, and that he fears he hath a stipend from the other House privately. He tells the that the fellow grew very proud of late, the King and every body else crying him up so high, and that above Betterton, he being a more ayery man, as he is indeed. But yet Betterton, he says, they all say do act: some parts that none but himself can do. Thence to my bookseller's, and found my Waggoners done. The very binding cost me 14s., but they are well done, and so with a porter home with them, and so by water to Ratcliffe, and there went to speak with Cumberford the platt-maker, and there saw his manner of working, which is very fine and laborious. So down to

Deptford, reading Ben Jonson's "Devil is an asse," and so to see Sir W. Pen, who I find walking out of doors a little, but could not stand long; but in doors and I with him, and staid a great while talking, I taking a liberty to tell him my thoughts in things of the office; that when he comes abroad again, he may know what to think of me, and to value me as he ought. Walked home as I used to do, and being weary, and after some discourse with Mr. Barrow, who came to see and take his leave of me, he being to-morrow to set out toward the Isle of Man, I went to bed. This day I hear that the Moores have made some attaques upon the outworks of Tangier; but my Lord Tiviott; with the loss of about 200 men, did beat them off, and killed many of them. To-morrow the King and Queen for certain go down to Tunbridge. But the King comes hack again against Monday to raise the Parliament.

23rd. Up and to my office, and thence by information from, Mr. Ackworth I went down to Woolwich, and mustered the three East India ships that lie there, believing that there is great-juggling between the Pursers and Clerks of the Cheque in cheating the King of the wages and victuals of men that do not give attendance, and I found very few on board. So to the yard, and there mustered the yard, and found many faults, and discharged several fellows that were absent from their business. I staid also at Mr. Ackworth's desire at dinner with him and his wife, and there was a simple fellow, a gentleman I believe of the Court, their kinsmen, that threatened me I could have little discourse or begin, acquaintance with Ackworth's wife, and so after dinner away, with all haste home, and there found Sir J. Minnes and Sir W. Batten at the office, and by Sir W. Batten's testimony and Sir G. Carteret's concurrence was forced to consent to a business of Captain Cocke's timber, as bad as anything we have lately disputed about, and all through Mr. Coventry's not being with us. So up and to supper with Sir W. Batten upon a soused mullett, very good meat, and so home and to bed.

24th. Up pretty early (though of late I have been faulty by an hour or two every morning of what I should do) and by water to the Temple, and there took leave of my cozen Roger Pepys, who goes out of town to-day. So to Westminster Hall, and there at Mrs. Michell's shop sent for beer and sugar and drink, and made great cheer with it among her and Mrs. Howlett, her neighbour, and their daughters, especially Mrs. Howlett's daughter, Betty, which is a pretty girl, and one I have long called wife, being, I formerly thought, like my own wife. After this good neighbourhood, which I do to give them occasion of speaking well and commending me in some company that now and then I know comes to their shop, I went to the Six clerks' office, and there had a writ for Tom Trice, and paid 20s. for it to Wilkinson, and so up and down to many places, among others to the viall maker's, and there saw the head, which now pleases me mightily, and so home, and being sent for presently to Mr. Bland's, where Mr. Povy and Gauden and I were invited to dinner, which we had very finely and great plenty, but for drink, though many and good, I drank nothing but small beer and water, which I drank so much that I wish it may not do me hurt. They had a kinswoman, they call daughter, in the house, a short, ugly, red-haired slut, that plays upon the virginalls, and sings, but after such a country manner I was weary of it, but yet could not but commend it. So by and by after dinner comes Monsr. Gotier, who is beginning to teach her, but, Lord! what a droll fellow it is to make her hold open her mouth, and telling this and that so drolly would make a man burst, but himself I perceive sings very well. Anon we sat dawn again to a collacon of cheesecakes, tarts, custards, and such like, very handsome, and so up and away home, where I at the office a while, till disturbed by, Mr. Hill, of Cambridge, with whom I walked in the garden a while, and thence home and then in my dining room walked, talking of several matters of state till 11 at night, giving him a glass of wine. I was not unwilling to hear him talk, though he is full of words, yet a man of large conversation, especially among the Presbyters and Independents; he tells me that certainly, let the Bishops alone, and they will ruin themselves, and he is confident that the King's declaration about two years since will be the foundation of the settlement of the Church some time or other, for the King will find it hard to banish all those that will appear Nonconformists upon this Act that is coming out against them. He being gone, I to bed.

25th. Up and to my office setting papers in order for these two or three days, in which I have been hindered a little, and then having intended this day to go to Banstead Downs to see a famous race, I sent Will to get himself ready to go with me, and I also by and by home and put on my riding suit, and being ready came to the office to Sir J. Minnes and Sir W. Batten, and did a little of course at the office this morning, and so by boat to White Hall, where I hear that the race is put off, because the Lords do sit in Parliament to-day. However, having appointed Mr. Creed to come to me to Fox Hall, I went over thither, and after some debate, Creed and I resolved to go to Clapham, to Mr. Gauden's, who had sent his coach to their place for me because I was to have my horse of him to go to the race. So I went thither by coach and my Will by horse with me; Mr. Creed he went over back again to Westminster to fetch his horse. When I came to Mr. Gauden's one first thing was to show me his house, which is almost built, wherein he and his family live. I find it very regular and finely contrived, and the gardens and offices about it as convenient and as full of good variety as ever I saw in my life. It is true he hath been censured for laying out so much money; but he tells me that he built it for his brother, who is since dead (the Bishop), who when he should come to be Bishop of Winchester, which he was promised (to which bishoprick at present there is no house), he did intend to dwell here. Besides, with the good husbandry in making his bricks and other things I do not think it costs him so much money as people think and discourse. By and by to dinner, and in comes Mr. Creed. I saluted Mr. Gauden's lady, and the young ladies, he having many pretty children, and his sister, the Bishop's widow; who was, it seems, Sir W. Russel's daughter, the Treasurer of the Navy; who by her discourse at dinner I find to be very well-bred, and a woman of excellent discourse, even so much as to have my attention all dinner with much more pleasure than I did give to Mr. Creed, whose discourse was mighty merry in inveighing at Mr. Gauden's victuals that they had at sea the last voyage that he prosecuted, till methought the woman began to take it seriously. After dinner by Mr. Gauden's motion we got Mrs. Gauden and her sister to sing to a viall, on which Mr. Gauden's eldest son (a pretty man, but a simple one methinks) played but very poorly, and the musique bad, but yet I commended it. Only I do find that the ladies have been taught to sing and do sing well now, but that the viall puts them out. I took the viall and played some things from one of their books, Lyra lessons, which they seemed to like well. Thus we pass an hour or two after dinner and towards the evening we bade them Adieu! and took horse; being resolved that, instead of the race which fails us, we would go to Epsum. So we set out, and being gone a little way I sent home Will to look to the house, and Creed and I rode forward; the road being full of citizens going and coming toward Epsum, where, when we came, we could hear of no lodging, the town so full; but which was better, I went towards Ashted, my old place of pleasure; and there by direction of one goodman Arthur, whom we met on the way, we went to Farmer Page's, at which direction he and I made good sport, and there we got a lodging in a little hole we could not stand upright in, but rather than go further to look we staid there, and while supper was getting ready I took him to walk up and down behind my cozen Pepys's house that was, which I find comes little short of what I took it to be when I was a little boy, as things use commonly to appear greater than then when one comes to be a man and knows more, and so up and down in the closes, which I know so well methinks, and account it good fortune that I lie here that I may have opportunity to renew my old walks. It seems there is one Mr. Rouse, they call him the Queen's Tailor, that lives there now. So to our lodging to supper, and among other meats had a brave dish of cream, the best I ever eat in my life, and with which we pleased ourselves much, and by and by to bed, where, with much ado yet good sport, we made shift to lie, but with little ease, and a little spaniel by us, which has followed us all the way, a pretty dogg, and we believe that follows my horse, and do belong to Mrs. Gauden, which we, therefore, are very careful of.

26th (Lord's-day). Up and to the Wells,

[Epsom medicinal wells were discovered about 1618, but they did not become fashionable until the Restoration. John Toland, in his "Description of Epsom," says that he often counted seventy coaches in the Ring (the present racecourse on the Downs) on a Sunday evening; but by the end of the eighteenth century Epsom had entirely lost its vogue.]

where great store of citizens, which was the greatest part of the company, though there were some others of better quality. I met many that I knew, and we drank each of us two pots and so walked away, it being very pleasant to see how everybody turns up his tail, here one and there another, in a bush, and the women in their quarters the like. Thence I walked with Creed to Mr. Minnes's house, which has now a very good way made to it, and thence to Durdans and walked round it and within the Court Yard and to the Bowling-green, where I have seen so much mirth in my time; but now no family in it (my Lord Barkeley, whose it is, being with his family at London), and so up and down by Minnes's wood, with great pleasure viewing my old walks, and where Mrs. Hely and I did use to walk and talk, with whom I had the first sentiments of love and pleasure in woman's company, discourse, and taking her by the hand, she being a pretty woman. So I led him to Ashted Church (by the place where Peter, my cozen's man, went blindfold and found a certain place we chose for him upon a wager), where we had a dull Doctor, one Downe, worse than I think even parson King was, of whom we made so much scorn, and after sermon home, and staid while our dinner, a couple of large chickens, were dressed, and a good mess of cream, which anon we had with good content, and after dinner (we taking no notice of other lodgers in the house, though there was one that I knew, and knew and spoke to me, one Mr. Rider, a merchant), he and I to walk, and I led him to the pretty little wood behind my cozens house, into which we got at last by clambering, and our little dog with us, but when we were among the hazel trees and bushes, Lord! what a course did we run for an hour together, losing ourselves, and indeed I despaired I should ever come to any path, but still from thicket to thicket, a thing I could hardly have believed a man could have been lost so long in so small a room. At last I found out a delicate walk in the middle that goes quite through the wood, and then went out of the wood, and holloed Mr. Creed, and made him hunt me from place to place, and at last went in and called him into my fine walk, the little dog still hunting with us through the wood. In this walk being all bewildered and weary and sweating, Creed he lay down upon the ground, which I did a little, but I durst not long, but walked from him in the fine green walk, which is half a mile long, there reading my vows as I used to on Sundays. And after that was done, and going and lying by Creed an hour, he and I rose and went to our lodging and paid our reckoning, and so mounted, whether to go toward London home or to find a new lodging, and so rode through Epsum, the whole town over, seeing the various companys that were there walking; which was very pleasant to see how they are there without knowing almost what to do, but only in the morning to drink waters. But, Lord! to see how many I met there of citizens, that I could not have thought to have seen there, or that they had ever had it in their heads or purses to go down thither. We rode out of the town through Yowell beyond Nonesuch House a mile, and there our little dogg, as he used to do, fell a-running after a flock of sheep feeding on the common, till he was out of sight, and then endeavoured to come back again, and went to the last gate that he parted with us at, and there the poor thing mistakes our scent, instead of coming forward he hunts us backward, and runs as hard as he could drive back towards Nonesuch, Creed and I after him, and being by many told of his going that way and the haste he made, we rode still and passed him through Yowell, and there we lost any further information of him. However, we went as far as Epsum almost, hearing nothing of him, we went back to Yowell, and there was told that he did pass through the town. We rode back to Nonesuch to see whether he might be gone back again, but hearing nothing we with great trouble and discontent for the loss of our dogg came back once more to Yowell, and there set up our horses and selves for all night, employing people to look for the dogg in the town, but can hear nothing of him. However, we gave order for supper, and while that was dressing walked out through Nonesuch Park to the house, and there viewed as much as we could of the outside, and looked through the great gates, and found a noble court; and altogether believe it to have been a very noble house, and a delicate park about it, where just now there was a doe killed, for the King to carry up to Court. So walked back again, and by and by our supper being ready, a good leg of mutton boiled, we supped and to bed, upon two beds in the same room, wherein we slept most excellently all night.

27th. Up in the morning about 7 o'clock, and after a little study, resolved of riding to the Wells to look for our dogg, which we did, but could hear nothing; but it being much a warmer day than yesterday there was great store of gallant company, more than then, to my greater pleasure. There was at a distance, under one of the trees on the common, a company got together that sung. I, at the distance, and so all the rest being a quarter of a mile off, took them for the Waytes, so I rode up to them, and found them only voices, some citizens met by chance, that sung four or five parts excellently. I have not been more pleased with a snapp of musique, considering the circumstances of the time and place, in all my life anything so pleasant. We drank each of us, three cupps, and so, after riding up to the horsemen upon the hill, where they were making of matches to run, we went away and to Yowell, where we found our breakfast, the remains of our supper last night hashed, and by and by, after the smith had set on two new shoes to Creed's horse, we mounted, and with little discourse, I being intent upon getting home in time, we rode hard home, observing Mr. Gauden's house, but not calling there (it being too late for me to stay, and wanting their dog too). The house stands very finely, and has a graceful view to the highway. Set up our horses at Fox Hall, and I by water (observing the King's barge attending his going to the House this day) home, it being about one o'clock. So got myself ready and shifting myself, and so by water to Westminster, and there came most luckily to the Lords' House as the House of Commons were going into the Lord's House, and there I crowded in along with the Speaker, and got to stand close behind him, where he made his speech to the King (who sat with his crown on and robes, and so all the Lords in their robes, a fine sight); wherein he told his Majesty what they have done this Parliament, and now offered for his royall consent. The greatest matters were a bill for the Lord's day (which it seems the Lords have lost, and so cannot be passed, at which the Commons are displeased); the bills against Conventicles and Papists (but it seems the Lords have not passed them), and giving his Majesty four entire subsidys; which last, with about twenty smaller Acts, were passed with this form: The Clerk of the House reads the title of the bill, and then looks at the end and there finds (writ by the King I suppose) "Le Roy le veult," and that he reads. And to others he reads, "Soit fait comme vous desirez." And to the Subsidys, as well that for the Commons, I mean the layety, as for the Clergy, the King writes, "Le Roy remerciant les Seigneurs, &c., Prelats, &c., accepte leur benevolences." The Speaker's speech was far from any oratory, but was as plain (though good matter) as any thing could be, and void of elocution. After the bills passed, the King, sitting on his throne, with his speech writ in a paper which he held in his lap, and scarce looked off of it, I thought, all the time he made his speech to them, giving them thanks for their subsidys, of which, had he not need, he would not have asked or received them; and that need, not from any extravagancys of his, he was sure, in any thing, but the disorders of the times compelling him to be at greater charge than he hoped for the future, by their care in their country, he should be: and that for his family expenses and others, he would labour however to retrench in many things convenient, and would have all others to do so too. He desired that nothing of old faults should be remembered, or severity for the same used to any in the country, it being his desire to have all forgot as well as forgiven. But, however, to use all care in suppressing any tumults, &c.; assuring them that the restless spirits of his and their adversaries have great expectations of something to be done this summer. And promised that though the Acts about Conventicles and Papists were not ripe for passing this Session, yet he would take care himself that neither of them should in this intervall be encouraged to the endangering of the peace; and that at their next meeting he would himself prepare two bills for them concerning them. So he concluded, that for the better proceeding of justice he did think fit to make this a

Session, and to prorogue them to the 16th of March next. His speech was very plain, nothing at all of spirit in it, nor spoke with any; but rather on the contrary imperfectly, repeating many times his words though he read all which I was sorry to see, it having not been hard for him to have got all the speech without book. So they all went away, the King out of the House at the upper end, he being by and by to go to Tunbridge to the Queen; and I in the Painted Chamber spoke with my Lord Sandwich while he was putting off his robes, who tells me he will now hasten down into the country, as soon as he can get some money settled on the Wardrobe. Here meeting Creed, he and I down to the Hall, and I having at Michell's shop wrote a little letter to Mr. Gauden, to go with his horse, and excusing my not taking leave or so much as asking after the old lady the widow when we came away the other day from them, he and I over the water to Fox Hall, and there sent away the horse with my letter, and then to the new Spring Garden, walking up and down, but things being dear and little attendance to be had we went away, leaving much brave company there, and so to a less house hard by, where we liked very well their Codlin tarts, having not time, as we intended, to stay the getting ready of a dish of pease. And there came to us an idle boy to show us some tumbling tricks, which he did very well, and the greatest bending of his body that ever I observed in my life. Thence by water to White Hall, and walked over the Park to St. James's; but missed Mr. Coventry, he not being within; and so out again, and there the Duke was coming along the Pell-Mell. It being a little darkish, I staid not to take notice of him, but we went directly back again. And in our walk over the Park, one of the Duke's footmen came running behind us, and came looking just in our faces to see who we were, and went back again. What his meaning is I know not, but was fearful that I might not go far enough with my hat off, though methinks that should not be it, besides, there were others covered nearer than myself was, but only it was my fear. So to White Hall and by water to the Bridge, and so home to bed, weary and well pleased with my journey in all respects. Only it cost me about 20s., but it was for my health, and I hope will prove so, only I do find by my riding a little swelling to rise just by my anus. I had the same the last time I rode, and then it fell again, and now it is up again about the bigness of the bag of a silkworm, makes me fearful of a rupture. But I will speak to Mr. Hollyard about it, and I am glad to find it now, that I may prevent it before it goes too far.

28th. Up after sleeping very well, and so to my office setting down the Journall of this last three days, and so settled to business again, I hope with greater cheerfulness and success by this refreshment. At the office all the morning, and at noon to Wise's about my viall that is a-doing, and so home to dinner and then to the office, where we sat all the afternoon till night, and I late at it till after the office was risen. Late came my Jane and her brother Will: to entreat for my taking of the boy again, but I will not hear her, though I would yet be glad to do anything for her sake to the boy, but receive him again I will not, nor give him anything. She would have me send him to sea; which if I could I would do, but there is no ship going out. The poor girl cried all the time she was with me, and would not go from me, staying about two hours with me till 10 or 11 o'clock, expecting that she might obtain something of me, but receive him I will not. So the poor girl was fain to go away crying and saying little. So from thence home, where my house of office was emptying, and I find they will do, it with much more cleanness than I expected. I went up and down among them a good while, but knowing that Mr. Coventry was to call me in the morning, I went to bed and left them to look after the people. So to bed.

29th. Up about 6 o'clock, and found the people to have just done, and Hannah not gone to bed yet, but was making clean of the yard and kitchen. Will newly gone to bed. So I to my office, and having given some order to Tom Hater, to whom I gave leave for his recreation to go down to Portsmouth this Pay, I went down to Wapping to Sir W. Warren, and there staid an hour or two discoursing of some of his goods and then things in general relating to this office, &c., and so home, and there going to Sir William Batten (having no stomach to dine at home, it being yet hardly clean of last night's [mess])and there I dined with my Lady and her daughter and son Castle, and mighty kind she is and I kind to her, but, Lord! how freely and plainly she rails against Commissioner Pett, calling him rogue, and wondering that the King keeps such a fellow in the Navy. Thence by and by walked to see Sir W. Pen at Deptford, reading by the way a most ridiculous play, a new one, called "The Politician Cheated." After a little sitting with him I walked to the yard a little and so home again, my Will with me, whom I bade to stay in the yard for me, and so to bed. This morning my brother Tom was with me, and we had some discourse again concerning his country mistress, but I believe the most that is fit for us to condescend to, will not content her friends.

30th. Up and to the office to get business ready for our sitting, this being the first day of altering it from afternoon during the Parliament sitting to the fore-noon again. By and by Mr. Coventry only came (Sir John Minnes and Sir William Batten being gone this morning to Portsmouth to pay some ships and the yard there), and after doing a little business he and I down to Woolwich, and there up and down the yard, and by and by came Sir G. Carteret and we all looked into matters, and then by water back to Deptford, where we dined with him at his house, a very good dinner and mightily tempted with wines of all sorts and brave French Syder, but I drunk none. But that which is a great wonder I find his little daughter Betty, that was in hanging sleeves but a month or two ago, and is a very little young child; married, and to whom, but to young Scott, son to Madam Catharine Scott, that was so long in law, and at whose triall I was with her husband; he pleading that it was unlawfully got and would not own it, she, it seems, being brought to bed of it, if not got by somebody else at Oxford, but it seems a little before his death he did own the child, and hath left him his estate, not long since. So Sir G. Carteret hath struck up of a sudden a match with him for his little daughter. He hath about L2000 per annum; and it seems Sir G. Carteret hath by this means over-reached Sir H. Bennet, who did endeavour to get this gentleman for a sister of his, but Sir G. Carteret I say has over-reached him. By this means Sir G. Carteret hath married two daughters this year both very well. After dinner into Deptford yard, but our bellies being full we could do no great business, and so parted, and Mr. Coventry and I to White Hall by water, where we also parted, and I to several places about business, and so calling for my five books of the Variorum print bound according to my common binding instead of the other which is more gaudy I went home. The town talk this day is of nothing but the great foot-race run this day on Banstead Downes, between Lee, the Duke of Richmond's footman, and a tyler, a famous runner. And Lee hath beat him; though the King and Duke of York and all men almost did bet three or four to one upon the tyler's head.

31st. Up early to my accounts this month, and I find myself worth clear L730, the most I ever had yet, which contents me though I encrease but very little. Thence to my office doing business, and at noon to my viall maker's, who has begun it and has a good appearance, and so to the Exchange, where I met Dr. Pierce, who tells me of his good luck to get to be groom of the Privy-Chamber to the Queen, and without my Lord Sandwich's help; but only by his good fortune, meeting a man that hath let him have his right for a small matter, about L60, for which he can every day have L400. But he tells me my Lord hath lost much honour in standing so long and so much for that coxcomb Pickering, and at last not carrying it for him; but hath his name struck out by the King and Queen themselves after he had been in ever since the Queen's coming. But he tells me he believes that either Sir H. Bennet, my Lady Castlemaine, or Sir Charles Barkeley had received some money for the place, and so the King could not disappoint them, but was forced to put out this fool rather than a better man. And I am sorry to hear what he tells me that Sir Charles Barkeley hath still such power over the King, as to be able to fetch him from the Council-table to my Lady Castlemaine when he pleases. He tells me also, as a friend, the great injury that he thinks I do myself by being so severe in the Yards, and contracting the ill-will of the whole Navy for those offices, singly upon myself. Now I discharge a good conscience therein, and I tell him that no man can (nor do he say any say it) charge me with doing wrong; but rather do as many good offices as any man. They think, he says, that I have a mind to get a good name with the King and Duke, who he tells me do not consider any such thing; but I shall have as good thanks to let all alone, and do as the rest. But I believe the contrary; and yet I told him I never go to the Duke alone, as others do, to talk of my own services. However, I will make use of his council, and take some course to prevent having the single ill-will of the office. Before I went to the office I went to the Coffee House, where Sir J. Cutler and Mr. Grant were, and there Mr. Grant showed me letters of Sir William Petty's, wherein he says, that his vessel which he hath built upon two keeles (a modell whereof, built for the King, he showed me) hath this month won a wager of L50 in sailing between Dublin and Holyhead with the pacquett-boat, the best ship or vessel the King hath there; and he offers to lay with any vessel in the world. It is about thirty ton in burden, and carries thirty men, with good accommodation, (as much more as any ship of her burden,) and so any vessel of this figure shall carry more men, with better accommodation by half, than any other ship. This carries also ten guns, of about five tons weight. In their coming back from Holyhead they started together, and this vessel came to Dublin by five at night, and the pacquett-boat not before eight the next morning; and when they came they did believe that, this vessel had been drowned, or at least behind, not thinking she could have lived in that sea. Strange things are told of this vessel, and he concludes his letter with this position, "I only affirm that the perfection of sayling lies in my principle, finde it out who can." Thence home, in my way meeting Mr. Rawlinson, who tells me that my uncle Wight is off of his Hampshire purchase and likes less of the Wights, and would have me to be kind and study to please him, which I am resolved to do. Being at home he sent for me to dinner to meet Mr. Moore, so I went thither and dined well, but it was strange for me to refuse, and yet I did without any reluctancy to drink wine in a tavern, where nothing else almost was drunk, and that excellent good. Thence with Mr. Moore to the Wardrobe, and there sat while my Lord was private with Mr. Townsend about his accounts an hour or two, we reading of a merry book against the Presbyters called Cabbala, extraordinary witty. Thence walked home and to my office, setting papers of all sorts and writing letters and putting myself into a condition to go to Chatham with Mr. Coventry to-morrow. So, at almost 12 o'clock, and my eyes tired with seeing to write, I went home and to bed. Ending the month with pretty good content of mind, my wife in the country and myself in good esteem, and likely by pains to become considerable, I think, with God's blessing upon my diligence.

Diaryof Samuel Pepys.
August
1663

Aug. 1st. Up betimes and got me ready, and so to the office and put things in order for my going. By and by comes Sir G. Carteret, and he and I did some business, and then Mr. Coventry sending for me, he staying in the boat, I got myself presently ready and down to him, he and I by water to Gravesend (his man Lambert with us), and there eat a bit and so mounted, I upon one of his horses which met him there, a brave proud horse, all the way talking of businesses of the office and other matters to good purpose. Being come to Chatham, we put on our boots and so walked to the yard, where we met Commissioner Pett, and there walked up and down looking and inquiring into many businesses, and in the evening went to the Commissioner's and there in his upper Arbor sat and talked, and there pressed upon the Commissioner to take upon him a power to correct and suspend officers that do not their duty and other things, which he unwillingly answered he would if we would own him in it. Being gone thence Mr. Coventry and I did discourse about him, and conclude that he is not able to do the same in that yard that he might and can and it maybe will do in another, what with his old faults and the relations that he has to most people that act there. After an hour or two's discourse at the Hill-house before going to bed, I see him to his and he me to my chamber, he lying in the Treasurer's and I in the Controller's chambers.

2nd (Lord's day). Up and after the barber had done he and I walked to the Docke, and so on board the Mathias, where Commissioner Pett and he and I and a good many of the officers and others of the yard did hear an excellent sermon of Mr. Hudson's upon "All is yours and you are God's," a most ready, learned, and good sermon, such as I have not heard a good while, nor ever thought he could have preached. We took him with us to the Hill-house, and there we dined, and an officer or two with us. So after dinner the company withdrew, and we three to private discourse and laid the matters of the yard home again to the Commissioner, and discoursed largely of several matters. Then to the parish church, and there heard a poor sermon with a great deal of false Greek in it, upon these words, "Ye are my friends, if ye do these things which I command you." Thence to the Docke and by water to view St. Mary Creeke, but do not find it so proper for a wet docks as we would have it, it being uneven ground and hard in the bottom and no, great depth of water in many places. Returned and walked from the Docke home, Mr. Coventry and I very much troubled to see how backward Commissioner Pett is to tell any of the faults of the officers, and to see nothing in better condition here for his being here than they are in other yards where there is none. After some discourse to bed. But I sat up an hour after Mr. Coventry was gone to read my vows, it raining a wonderful hard showre about 11 at night for an hour together. So to bed.

3rd. Up both of us very betimes and to the Yard, and see the men called over and choose some to be discharged. Then to the Ropehouses and viewed them all and made an experiment which was the stronger, English or Riga hemp, the latter proved the stronger, but the other is very good, and much better we believe than any but Riga. We did many other things this morning, and I caused the Timber measurer to measure some timber, where I found much fault and with reason, which we took public notice of, and did give them admonition for the time to come. At noon Mr. Pett did give us a very great dinner, too big in all conscience, so that most of it was left untouched. Here was Collonell Newman and several other gentlemen of the country and officers of the yard. After dinner they withdrew and Commissioner Pett, Mr. Coventry and I sat close to our business all the noon in his parler, and there run through much business and answered several people. And then in the evening walked in the garden, where we conjured him to look after the yard, and for the time to come that he would take the whole faults and ill management of the yard upon himself, he having full power and our concurrence to suspend or do anything else that he thinks fit to keep people and officers to their duty. He having made good promises, though I fear his performance, we parted (though I spoke so freely that he could have been angry) good friends, and in some hopes that matters will be better for the time to come. So walked to the Hillhouse (which we did view and the yard about it, and do think to put it off as soon as we can conveniently) and there made ourselves ready and mounted and rode to Gravesend (my riding Coate not being to be found I fear it is stole) on our way being overtaken by Captain Browne that serves the office of the Ordnance at Chatham. All the way, though he was a rogue and served the late times all along, yet he kept us in discourse of the many services that he did for many of the King's party, lords and Dukes, and among others he recovered a dog that was stolne from Mr. Cary (head-keeper of the buck-hounds to the King) and preserved several horses of the Duke of Richmond's, and his best horse he was forst to put out his eyes and keep him for a stallion to preserve him from being carried away. But he gone at last upon my enquiry to tell us how (he having been here too for survey of the Ropeyard) the day's work of the Rope-makers become settled, which pleased me very well. Being come to our Inn Mr. Coventry and I sat, and talked till 9 or 10 a-clock and then to bed.

4th. We were called up about four a-clock, and being ready went and took a Gravesend boat, and to London by nine a-clock. By the way talking of several businesses of the navy. So to the office, where Sir Wm. Pen (the first time that he has been with us a great while, he having been long sick) met us, and there we sat all the morning. My brother John I find come to town to my house, as I sent for him, on Saturday last; so at noon home and dined with him, and after dinner and the barber been with me I walked out with him to my viall maker's and other places and then left him, and I by water to Blackbury's, and there talked with him about some masts (and by the way he tells me that Paul's is now going to be repaired in good earnest), and so with him to his garden close by his house, where I eat some peaches and apricots; a very pretty place. So over the water to Westminster hall, and not finding Mrs. Lane, with whom I purposed to be merry, I went to Jervas's and took him and his wife over the water to their mother Palmer's (the woman that speaks in the belly, and with whom I have two or three years ago made good sport with Mr. Mallard), thinking because I had heard that she is a woman of that sort that I might there have lit upon some lady of pleasure (for which God forgive me), but blest be God there was none, nor anything that pleased me, but a poor little house that she has set out as fine as she can, and for her singing which she pretends to is only some old body songs and those sung abominably, only she pretends to be able to sing both bass and treble, which she do something like, but not what I thought formerly and expected now; nor do her speaking in her belly take me now as it did then, but it may be that is because I know it and see her mouth when she speaks, which should not be. After I had spent a shilling there in wine I took boat with Jervas and his wife and set them at Westminster, and it being late forbore Mrs. Lane and went by water to the Old Swan by a boat, where I had good sport with one of the young men about his travells as far as Voxhall, in mockery, which yet the fellow answered me most prettily and traveller-like unto my very good mirth. So home, and with my brother eat a bit of bread and cheese, and so to bed, he with me. This day I received a letter from my wife, which troubles me mightily, wherein she tells me how Ashwell did give her the lie to her teeth, and that thereupon my wife giving her a box on the eare, the other struck her again, and a deal of stir which troubles me, and that my Lady has been told by my father or mother something of my wife's carriage, which altogether vexes me, and I fear I shall find a trouble of my wife when she comes home to get down her head again, but if Ashwell goes I am resolved to have no more, but to live poorly and low again for a good while, and save money and keep my wife within bounds if I can, or else I shall bid Adieu to all content in the world. So to bed, my mind somewhat disturbed at this, but yet I shall take care, by prudence, to avoid the ill consequences which I fear, things not being gone too far yet, and this height that my wife is come to being occasioned from my own folly in giving her too much head heretofore for the year past.

5th. All the morning at the office, whither Deane of Woolwich came to me and discoursed of the body of ships, which I am now going about to understand, and then I took him to the coffee-house, where he was very earnest against Mr. Grant's report in favour of Sir W. Petty's vessel, even to some passion on both sides almost. So to the Exchange, and thence home to dinner with my brother, and in the afternoon to Westminster hall, and there found Mrs. Lane, and by and by by agreement we met at the Parliament stairs (in my way down to the boat who should meet us but my lady Jemimah, who saw me lead her but said nothing to me of her, though I ought to speak to her to see whether she would take notice of it or no) and off to Stangate and so to the King's Head at Lambeth marsh, and had variety of meats and drinks, but I did so towse her and handled her, but could get nothing more from her though I was very near it; but as wanton and bucksome as she is she dares not adventure upon the business, in which I very much commend and like her. Staid pretty late, and so over with her by water, and being in a great sweat with my towsing of her durst not go home by water, but took coach, and at home my brother and I fell upon Des Cartes, and I perceive he has studied him well, and I cannot find but he has minded his book, and do love it. This evening came a letter about business from Mr. Coventry, and with it a silver pen he promised me to carry inke in, which is very necessary. So to prayers and to bed.

6th. Up and was angry with my maid Hannah for keeping the house no better, it being more dirty now-a-days than ever it was while my whole family was together. So to my office, whither Mr. Coventry came and Sir William Pen, and we sat all the morning. This day Mr. Coventry borrowed of me my manuscript of the Navy. At noon I to the 'Change, and meeting with Sir W. Warren, to a coffee-house, and there finished a contract with him for the office, and so parted, and I to my cozen Mary Joyce's at a gossiping, where much company and good cheer. There was the King's Falconer, that lives by Paul's, and his wife, an ugly pusse, but brought him money. He speaking of the strength of hawkes, which will strike a fowle to the ground with that force that shall make the fowle rebound a great way from ground, which no force of man or art can do, but it was very pleasant to hear what reasons he and another, one Ballard, a rich man of the same Company of Leathersellers of which the Joyces are, did give for this. Ballard's wife, a pretty and a very well-bred woman, I took occasion to kiss several times, and she to carve, drink, and show me great respect. After dinner to talk and laugh. I drank no wine, but sent for some water; the beer not being good. A fiddler was sent for, and there one Mrs. Lurkin, a neighbour, a good, and merry poor woman, but a very tall woman, did dance and show such tricks that made us all merry, but above all a daughter of Mr. Brumfield's, black, but well-shaped and modest, did dance very well, which pleased me mightily. I begun the Duchess with her, but could not do it; but, however, I came off well enough, and made mighty much of her, kissing and leading her home, with her cozen Anthony and Kate Joyce (Kate being very handsome and well, that is, handsomely dressed to-day, and I grew mighty kind and familiar with her, and kissed her soundly, which she takes very well) to their house, and there I left them, having in our way, though nine o'clock at night, carried them into a puppet play in Lincolnes Inn Fields, where there was the story of Holofernes, and other clockwork, well done. There was at this house today Mr. Lawrence, who did give the name, it seems, to my cozen Joyce's child, Samuel, who is a very civil gentleman, and his wife a pretty woman, who, with Kate Joyce, were stewards of the feast to-day, and a double share cost for a man and a woman came to 16s., which I also would pay, though they would not by any means have had me do so. I walked home very well contented with this afternoon's work, I thinking it convenient to keep in with the Joyces against a bad day, if I should have occasion to make use of them. So I walked home, and after a letter to my wife by the post and my father, I home to supper, and after a little talk with my brother to bed.

7th. Up and to my office a little, and then to Brown's for my measuring rule, which is made, and is certainly the best and the most commodious for carrying in one's pocket, and most useful that ever was made, and myself have the honour of being as it were the inventor of this form of it. Here I staid discoursing an hour with him and then home, and thither came Sir Fairbrother to me, and we walked a while together in the garden and then abroad into the cittie, and then we parted for a while and I to my Viall, which I find done and once varnished, and it will please me very well when it is quite varnished. Thence home and to study my new rule till my head aked cruelly. So by and by to dinner and the Doctor and Mr. Creed came to me. The Doctor's discourse, which (though he be a very good-natured man) is but simple, was some sport to me and Creed, though my head akeing I took no great pleasure in it. We parted after dinner, and I walked to Deptford and there found Sir W. Pen, and I fell to measuring of some planks that was serving into the yard, which the people took notice of, and the measurer himself was amused at, for I did it much more ready than he, and I believe Sir W. Pen would be glad I could have done less or he more. By and by he went away and I staid walking up and down, discoursing with the officers of the yard of several things, and so walked back again, and on my way young Bagwell and his wife waylayd me to desire my favour about getting him a better ship, which I shall pretend to be willing to do for them, but my mind is to know his wife a little better. They being parted I went with Cadbury the mast maker to view a parcel of good masts which I think it were good to buy, and resolve to speak to the board about it. So home, and my brother John and I up and I to my musique, and then to discourse with him, and I find him not so thorough a philosopher, at least in Aristotle, as I took him for, he not being able to tell me the definition of final nor which of the 4 Qualitys belonged to each of the 4 Elements. So to prayers, and to bed, among other things being much satisfied with my new rule.

8th. Up and to my office, whither I search for Brown the mathematical instrument maker, who now brought me a ruler for measuring timber and other things so well done and in all things to my mind that I do set up my trust upon it that I cannot have a better, nor any man else have so good for this purpose, this being of my own ordering. By and by we sat all the morning dispatching of business, and then at noon rose, and I with Mr. Coventry down to the water-side, talking, wherein I see so much goodness and endeavours of doing the King service, that I do more and more admire him. It being the greatest trouble to me, he says, in the world to see not only in the Navy, but in the greatest matters of State, where he can lay his finger upon the soare (meaning this man's faults, and this man's office the fault lies in), and yet dare or can not remedy matters. Thence to the Exchange about several businesses, and so home to dinner, and in the afternoon took my brother John and Will down to Woolwich by water, and after being there a good while, and eating of fruit in Sheldon's garden, we began our walk back again, I asking many things in physiques of my brother John, to which he gives me so bad or no answer at all, as in the regions of the ayre he told me that he knew of no such thing, for he never read Aristotle's philosophy and Des Cartes ownes no such thing, which vexed me to hear him say. But I shall call him to task, and see what it is that he has studied since his going to the University. It was late before we could get from Greenwich to London by water, the tide being against us and almost past, so that to save time and to be clear of anchors I landed at Wapping, and so walked home weary enough, walking over the stones. This night Sir W. Batten and Sir J. Minnes returned [from] Portsmouth, but I did not go see them.

9th (Lord's day). Up, and leaving my brother John to go somewhere else, I to church, and heard Mr. Mills (who is lately returned out of the country, and it seems was fetched in by many of the parishioners, with great state,) preach upon the authority of the ministers, upon these words, "We are therefore embassadors of

Christ." Wherein, among other high expressions, he said, that such a learned man used to say, that if a minister of the word and an angell should meet him together, he would salute the minister first; which methought was a little too high. This day I begun to make use of the silver pen (Mr. Coventry did give me) in writing of this sermon, taking only the heads of it in Latin, which I shall, I think, continue to do. So home and at my office reading my vowes, and so to Sir W. Batten to dinner, being invited and sent for, and being willing to hear how they left things at Portsmouth, which I found but ill enough, and are mightily for a Commissioner to be at seat there to keep the yard in order. Thence in the afternoon with my Lady Batten, leading her through the streets by the hand to St. Dunstan's Church, hard by us (where by Mrs. Russell's means we were set well), and heard an excellent sermon of one Mr. Gifford, the parson there, upon "Remember Lot's wife." So from thence walked back to Mrs. Russell's, and there drank and sat talking a great while. Among other things talked of young Dawes that married the great fortune, who it seems has a Baronet's patent given him, and is now Sir Thos. Dawes, and a very fine bred man they say he is. Thence home, and my brother being abroad I walked to my uncle Wight's and there staid, though with little pleasure, and supped, there being the husband of Mrs. Anne Wight, who it seems is lately married to one Mr. Bentley, a Norwich factor. Home, and staid up a good while examining Will in his Latin below, and my brother along with him in his Greeke, and so to prayers and to bed. This afternoon I was amused at the tune set to the Psalm by the Clerke of the parish, and thought at first that he was out, but I find him to be a good songster, and the parish could sing it very well, and was a good tune. But I wonder that there should be a tune in the Psalms that I never heard of.

10th. Up, though not so early this summer as I did all the last, for which I am sorry, and though late am resolved to get up betimes before the season of rising be quite past. To my office to fit myself to wait on the Duke this day. By and by by water to White Hall, and so to St. James's, and anon called into the Duke's chamber, and being dressed we were all as usual taken in with him and discoursed of our matters, and that being done, he walked, and I in the company with him, to White Hall, and there he took barge for Woolwich, and, I up to the Committee of Tangier, where my Lord Sandwich, pay Lord Peterborough, (whom I have not seen before since his coming back,) Sir W. Compton, and Mr. Povy. Our discourse about supplying my Lord Teviott with money, wherein I am sorry to see, though they do not care for him, yet they are willing to let him for civility and compliment only have money almost without expecting any account of it; but by this means, he being such a cunning fellow as he is, the King is like to pay dear for our courtiers' ceremony. Thence by coach with my Lords Peterborough and Sandwich to my Lord Peterborough's house; and there, after an hour's looking over some fine books of the Italian buildings, with fine cuts; and also my Lord Peterborough's bowes and arrows, of which he is a great lover, we sat down to dinner, my Lady coming down to dinner also, and there being Mr. Williamson, that belongs to Sir H. Bennet, whom I find a pretty understanding and accomplished man, but a little conceited. After dinner I took leave and went to Greatorex's, whom I found in his garden, and set him to work upon my ruler, to engrave an almanac and other things upon the brasses of it, which a little before night he did, but the latter part he slubbered over, that I must get him to do it over better, or else I shall not fancy my rule, which is such a folly that I am come to now, that whereas before my delight was in multitude of books, and spending money in that and buying alway of other things, now that I am become a better husband, and have left off buying, now my delight is in the neatness of everything, and so cannot be pleased with anything unless it be very neat, which is a strange folly. Hither came W. Howe about business, and he and I had a great deal of discourse about my Lord Sandwich, and I find by him that my Lord do dote upon one of the daughters of Mrs. [Becke] where he lies, so that he spends his time and money upon her. He tells me she is a woman of a very bad fame and very impudent, and has told my Lord so, yet for all that my Lord do spend all his evenings with her, though he be at court in the day time, and that the world do take notice of it, and that Pickering is only there as a blind, that the world may think that my Lord spends his time with him when he do worse, and that hence it is that my Lord has no more mind to go into the country than he has. In fine, I perceive my Lord is dabbling with this wench, for which I am sorry, though I do not wonder at it, being a man amorous enough, and now begins to allow himself the liberty that he says every body else at Court takes. Here I am told that my Lord Bristoll is either fled or concealed himself; having been sent for to the King, it is believed to be sent to the Tower, but he is gone out of the way. Yesterday, I am told also, that Sir J. Lenthall, in Southwarke, did apprehend about one hundred Quakers, and other such people, and hath sent some of them to the gaole at Kingston, it being now the time of the Assizes. Hence home and examined a piece of, Latin of Will's with my brother, and so to prayers and to bed. This evening I had a letter from my father that says that my wife will come to town this week, at which I wonder that she should come to town without my knowing more of it. But I find they have lived very ill together since she went, and I must use all the brains I have to bring her to any good when she do come home, which I fear will be hard to do, and do much disgust me the thoughts of it.

11th. Up and to my office, whither, by and by, my brother Tom came, and I did soundly rattle him for his neglecting to see and please the Joyces as he has of late done. I confess I do fear that he do not understand his business, nor will do any good in his trade, though he tells me that he do please every body and that he gets money, but I shall not believe it till I see a state of his accounts, which I have ordered him to bring me before he sees me any more. We met and sat at the office all the morning, and at noon I to the 'Change, where I met Dr. Pierce, who tells me that the King comes to towne this day, from Tunbridge, to stay a day or two, and then fetch the Queen from thence, who he says is grown a very debonnaire lady, and now hugs him, and meets him gallopping upon the road, and all the actions of a fond and pleasant lady that can be, that he believes has a chat now and then of Mrs. Stewart, but that there is no great danger of her, she being only an innocent, young, raw girl; but my Lady Castlemaine, who rules the King in matters of state, and do what she list with him, he believes is now falling quite out of favour. After the Queen is come back she goes to the Bath; and so to Oxford, where great entertainments are making for her. This day I am told that my Lord Bristoll hath warrants issued out against him, to have carried him to the Tower; but he is fled away, or hid himself. So much the Chancellor hath got the better of him. Upon the 'Change my brother, and Will bring me word that Madam Turner would come and dine with me to-day, so I hasted home and found her and Mrs. Morrice there (The. Joyce being gone into the country), which is the reason of the mother rambling. I got a dinner for them, and after dinner my uncle Thomas and aunt Bell came and saw me, and I made them almost foxed with wine till they were very kind (but I did not carry them up to my ladies). So they went away, and so my two ladies and I in Mrs. Turner's coach to Mr. Povy's, who being not within, we went in and there shewed Mrs. Turner his perspective and volary,

> [A large birdcage, in which the birds can fly about; French 'voliere'. Ben Jonson uses the word volary.]

and the fine things that he is building of now, which is a most neat thing. Thence to the Temple and by water to Westminster; and there Morrice and I went to Sir R. Ling's to have fetched a niece of his, but she was not within, and so we went to boat again and then down to the bridge, and there tried to find a sister of Mrs. Morrice's, but she was not within neither, and so we went through bridge, and I carried them on board the King's pleasure-boat, all the way reading in a book of Receipts of making fine meats and sweetmeats, among others to make my own sweet water, which made us good sport. So I landed them at Greenwich, and there to a garden, and gave them fruit and wine, and so to boat again, and finally, in the cool of the evening, to Lyon Kee,

> [Lion Key, Lower Thames Street, where the famous Duchess of Suffolk in the time of Bishop Gardiner's persecution took boat for the continent. James, Duke of York, also left the country from this same place on the night of April 20th, 1648, when he escaped from St. James's Palace.]

the tide against us, and so landed and walked to the Bridge, and there took a coach by chance passing by, and so I saw them home, and there eat some cold venison with them, and drunk and bade them good night, having been mighty merry with them, and I think it is not amiss to preserve, though it cost me a little, such a friend as Mrs. Turner. So home and to bed, my head running upon what to do to-morrow to fit things against my wife's coming, as to buy a bedstead, because my brother John is here, and I have now no more beds than are used.

12th. A little to my office, to put down my yesterday's journall, and so abroad to buy a bedstead and do other things. So home again, and having put up the bedstead and done other things in order to my wife's coming, I went out to several places and to Mrs. Turner's, she inviting me last night, and there dined; with her and Madam Morrice and a stranger we were very merry and had a fine dinner, and thence I took leave and to White Hall, where my Lords Sandwich, Peterborough, and others made a Tangier Committee; spent the afternoon in reading and ordering with a great deal of alteration, and yet methinks never a whit the better, of a letter drawn by Creed to my Lord Rutherford. The Lords being against anything that looked to be rough, though it was in matter of money and accounts, wherein their courtship may cost the King dear. Only I do see by them, that speaking in matters distasteful to him that we write to, it is best to do it in the plainest way and without ambages or reasoning, but only say matters of fact, and leave the party to collect your meaning. Thence by water to my brother's, and there I hear my wife is come and gone home, and my father is come to town also, at which I wondered. But I discern it is to give my brother advice about his business, and it may be to pacify me about the differences that have been between my wife and him and my mother at her late being with them. Though by and by he coming to Mr. Holden's (where I was buying a hat) he took no notice to me of anything. I talked to him a little while and left him to lie at the end of the town, and I home, where methought I found my wife strange, not knowing, I believe, in what temper she could expect me to be in, but I fell to kind words, and so we were very kind, only she could not forbear telling me how she had been used by them and her mayde, Ashwell, in the country, but I find it will be best not to examine it, for I doubt she's in fault too, and therefore I seek to put it off from my hearing, and so to bed and there entertained her with great content, and so to sleep.

13th. Lay long in bed with my wife talking of family matters, and so up and to the office, where we sat all the' morning, and then home to dinner, and after dinner my wife and I to talk again about getting of a couple of good mayds and to part with Ashwell, which troubles me for her father's sake, though I shall be glad to have the charge taken away of keeping a woman. Thence a little to the office, and so abroad with my wife by water to White Hall, and there at my Lord's lodgings met my Lady Jemimah, with whom we staid a good while. Thence to Mrs. Hunt's, where I left my wife, and I to walk a little in St. James's Park, while Mrs. Harper might come home, with whom we came to speak about her kinswoman Jane Gentleman to come and live with us as a chamber mayde, and there met with Mr. Hoole my old acquaintance of Magdalen, and walked with him an hour in the Parke, discoursing chiefly of Sir Samuel Morland, whose lady is gone into France. It seems he buys ground and a farm in the country, and lays out money upon building, and God knows what! so that most of the money he sold his pension of L500 per annum for, to Sir Arthur Slingsby, is believed is gone. It seems he hath very great promises from the King, and Hoole hath seen some of the King's letters, under his own hand, to Morland, promising him great things (and among others, the order of the Garter, as Sir Samuel says); but his lady thought it below her to ask any thing at the King's first coming, believing the King would do it of himself, when as Hoole do really think if he had asked to be Secretary of State at the King's first coming, he might have had it. And the other day at her going into France, she did speak largely to the King herself, how her husband hath failed of what his Majesty had promised, and she was sure intended him; and the King did promise still, as he is a King and a gentleman, to be as good as his word in a little time, to a tittle: but I never believe it. Here in the Park I met with Mr. Coventry, where he sent for a letter he had newly writ to me, wherein he had enclosed one from Commissioner Pett complaining of his being defeated in his attempt to suspend two pursers, wherein the manner of his doing it, and complaint of our seeing him (contrary to our promises the other day), deserted, did make us laugh mightily, and was good sport to think how awkwardly he goes about a thing that he has no courage of his own nor mind to do. Mr. Coventry answered it very handsomely, but I perceive Pett has left off his corresponding with me any more. Thence to fetch my wife from Mrs. Hunt's, where now he was come in, and we eat and drunk, and so away (their child being at home, a very lively, but not pretty at all), by water to Mrs. Turner's, and there made a short visit, and so home by coach, and after supper to prayers and to bed, and before going to bed Ashwell began to make her complaint, and by her I do perceive that she has received most base usage from my wife, which my wife sillily denies, but it is impossible the wench could invent words and matter so particularly, against which my wife has nothing to say but flatly to deny, which I am sorry to see, and blows to have past, and high words even at Hinchinbrooke House among my Lady's people, of which I am mightily ashamed. I said nothing to either of them, but let them talk till she was gone and left us abed, and then I told my wife my mind with great sobriety of grief, and so to sleep.

14th. Awake, and to chide my wife again, and I find that my wife has got too great head to be brought down soon, nor is it possible with any convenience to keep Ashwell longer, my wife is so set and convinced, as she was in Sarah, to make her appear a Lyer in every small thing that we shall have no peace while she stays. So I up and to my office doing several businesses in my study, and so home to dinner. The time having outslipt me and my stomach, it being past, two a-clock, and yet before we could sit down to dinner Mrs. Harper and her cousin Jane came, and we treated and discoursed long about her coming to my wife for a chamber mayd, and I think she will do well. So they went away expecting notice when she shall come, and so we sat down to dinner at four a-clock almost, and then I walked forth to my brother's, where I found my father very discontented, and has no mind to come to my house, and would have begun some of the differences between my wife and him, but I desired to hear none of them, and am sorry at my folly in forcing it and theirs in not telling me of it at the beginning, and therefore am resolved to make the best of a bad market, and to bring my wife to herself again as soon and as well as I can. So we parted very kindly, and he will dine with me to-morrow or next day. Thence walked home, doing several errands by the way, and at home took my wife to visit Sir W. Pen, who is still lame, and after an hour with him went home and supped, and with great content to bed.

15th. Lay pretty long in bed, being a little troubled with some pain got by wind and cold, and so up with good peace of mind, hoping that my wife will mind her house and servants, and so to the office, and being too soon to sit walked to my viail, which is well nigh done, and I believe I may have it home to my mind next week. So back to my office, and there we sat all the morning, I till 2 o'clock before I could go to dinner again. After dinner walked forth to my instrument maker, and there had my rule he made me lay now so perfected, that I think in all points I have never need or desire a better, or think that any man yet had one so good in all the several points of it for my use. So by water down to Deptford, taking into my boat with me Mr. Palmer, one whom I knew and his wife when I was first married, being an acquaintance of my wife's and her friends lodging at Charing Cross during our differences. He joyed me in my condition, and himself it seems is forced to follow the law in a common ordinary way, but seems to do well, and is a sober man, enough by his discourse. He landed with me at Deptford, where he saw by the officers' respect to me a piece of my command, and took notice of it, though God knows I hope I shall not be elated with that, but rather desire to be known for serving the King well, and doing my duty. He gone I walked up and down the yard a while discoursing with the officers, and so by water home meditating on my new Rule with great pleasure. So to my office, and there by candle light doing business, and so home to supper and to bed.

16th (Lord's day). Up and with my wife to church, and finding her desirous to go to church, I did suspect her meeting of Pembleton, but he was not there, and so I thought my jealousy in vain, and treat the sermon with great quiet. And home to dinner very pleasant, only some angry, notwithstanding my wife could not forbear to give Ashwell, and after dinner to church again, and there, looking up and down, I found Pembleton to stand in the isle against us, he coming too late to get a pew. Which, Lord! into what a sweat did it put me! I do not think my wife did see him, which did a little satisfy me. But it makes me mad to see of what a jealous temper I am and cannot helpe it, though let him do what he can I do not see, as I am going to reduce my family, what hurt he can do me, there being no more occasion now for my wife to learn of him. Here preached a confident young coxcomb. So home, and I staid a while with Sir J. Minnes, at Mrs. Turner's, hearing his parrat talk, laugh, and crow, which it do to admiration. So home and with my wife to see Sir W. Pen, and thence to my uncle Wight, and took him at supper and sat down, where methinks my uncle is more kind than he used to be both to me now, and my father tell me to him also, which I am glad at. After supper home, it being extraordinary dark, and by chance a lanthorn came by, and so we hired it to light us home, otherwise were we no sooner within doors but a great showre fell that had doused us cruelly if we had not been within, it being as dark as pitch. So to prayers and to bed.

17th. Up, and then fell into discourse, my wife and I to Ashwell, and much against my will I am fain to express a willingness to Ashwell that she should go from us, and yet in my mind I am glad of it, to ease me of the charge. So she is to go to her father this day. And leaving my wife and her talking highly, I went away by coach with Sir J. Minnes and Sir W. Batten to St. James's, and there attended of course the Duke. And so to White Hall, where I met Mr. Moore, and he tells me with great sorrow of my lord's being debauched he fears by this woman at Chelsey, which I am troubled at, and resolve to speak to him of it if I can seasonably. Thence home, where I dined, and after dinner comes our old mayde Susan to look for a gorgett that she says she has lost by leaving it here, and by many circumstances it being clear to me that Hannah, our present cook-mayde, not only has it, but had it on upon her necke when Susan came in, and shifted it off presently upon her coming in, I did charge her so home with it (having a mind to have her gone from us), that in a huff she told us she would be gone to-night if I would pay her her wages, which I was glad and my wife of, and so fetched her her wages, and though I am doubtful that she may convey some things away with her clothes, my wife searching them, yet we are glad of her being so gone, and so she went away in a quarter of an hour's time. Being much amused at this to have never a maid but Ashwell, that we do not intend to keep, nor a boy, and my wife and I being left for an hour, till my brother came in, alone in the house, I grew very melancholy, and so my brother being come in I went forth to Mrs. Holden's, to whom I formerly spoke about a girle to come to me instead of a boy, and the like I did to Mrs. Standing and also to my brother Tom, whom I found at an alehouse in Popinjay ally drinking, and I standing with him at the gate of the ally, Ashwell came by, and so I left Tom and went almost home with her, talking of her going away. I find that she is willing to go, and told her (though behind my back my wife has told her that it was more my desire than hers that she should go, which was not well), that seeing my wife and she could not agree I did choose rather (was she my sister) have her gone, it would be better for us and for her too. To which she willing agreed, and will not tell me anything but that she do believe that my wife would have some body there that might not be so liable to give me information of things as she takes her to be. But, however, I must later to prevent all that. I parted with her near home, agreeing to take no notice of my coming along with her, and so by and by came home after her. Where I find a sad distracted house, which troubles me. However, to supper and prayers and to bed. And while we were getting to bed my wife began to discourse to her, and plainly asked whether she had got a place or no. And the other answered that she could go if we would to one of our own office, to which we agreed if she would. She thereupon said no; she would not go to any but where she might teach children, because of keeping herself in use of what things she had earnt, which she do not here nor will there, but only dressing. By which I perceive the wench is cunning, but one very fit for such a place, and accomplished to be woman to any lady in the land. So quietly to sleep, it being a cold night. But till my house is settled, I do not see that I can mind my business of the office, which grieves me to the heart. But I hope all will over in a little time, and I hope to the best. This day at Mrs. Holden's I found my new low crowned beaver according to the present fashion made, and will be sent home to-morrow.

18th. Up and to my office, where we sat all the morning. And at noon home, and my father came and dined with me, Susan being come and helped my wife to dress dinner. After dinner my father and I talked about our country-matters, and in fine I find that he thinks L50 per ann. will go near to keep them all, which I am glad of. He having taken his leave of me and my wife without any mention of the differences between them and my wife in the country, I went forth to several places about businesses, and so home again, and after prayers to bed.

19th. Up betimes, and my wife up and about the house, Susan beginning to have her drunken tricks, and put us in mind of her old faults and folly and distractednesse, which we had forgot, so that I became mightily troubled with her. This morning came my joyners to new lay the floors, and begun with the dining room. I out and see my viall again, and it is very well, and to Mr. Hollyard, and took some pills of him and a note under his hand to drink wine with my beere, without which I was obliged, by my private vowe, to drink none a good while, and have strictly observed it, and by my drinking of small beere and not eating, I am so mightily troubled with wind, that I know not what to do almost. Thence to White Hall, and there met Mr. Moore, and fell a-talking about my Lord's folly at Chelsey, and it was our discourse by water to London and to the great coffee house against the Exchange, where we sat a good while talking; and I find that my lord is wholly given up to this wench, who it seems has been reputed a common strumpett. I have little encouragement from Mr. Moore to meddle with it to tell my Lord, for fear it may do him no good, but me hurt. Thence homewards, taking leave of him, and met Tom Marsh, my old acquaintance at Westminster, who talks mightily of the honour of his place, being Clerke Assistant to the Clerke of the House of Commons, and I take him to be a coxcombe, and so did give him half a pint of wine, but drink none myself, and so got shut of him. So home, and there found my wife almost mad with Susan's tricks, so as she is forced to let her go and leave the house all in dirt and the clothes all wet, and gets Goody Taylour to do the business for her till another comes. Here came Will Howe, and he and I alone in my chamber talking of my Lord, who drives me out of love to my Lord to tell my Lord of the matter we discoursed of, which tend so much to the ruin of his state, and so I resolved to take a good heart and do whatever comes of it. He gone, we sat down and eat a bit of dinner fetched from the cooke's, and so up again and to my joyners, who will make my floors very handsome. By and by comes in Pembleton, which begun to make me sweat, but I did give him so little countenance, and declared at one word against dancing any more, and bid him a short (God be with you) myself, and so he took as short a leave of my wife and so went away, and I think without any time of receiving any great satisfaction from my wife or invitation to come again. To my office till it was dark doing business, and so home by candle light to make up my accounts for my Lord and Mr. Moore. By and by comes Mr. Moore to me, and staid a good while with me making up his accounts and mine, and we did not come to any end therein for want of his papers, and so put it off to another time. He supped with me in all my dirt and disorder, and so went away and we to bed. I discoursed with him a great while about my speaking to my Lord of his business, and I apprehend from him that it is likely to prove perhaps of bad effect to me and no good to him, and therefore I shall even let it alone and let God do his will, at least till my Lord is in the country, and then we shall see whether he resolves to come to Chelsey again or no, and so order the stopping of him therein if we can.

20th. Up betimes and to my office (having first been angry with my brother John, and in the heat of my sudden passion called him Asse and coxcomb, for which I am sorry, it being but for leaving the key of his chamber with a spring lock within side of his door), and there we sat all the morning, and at noon dined at home, and there found a little girl, which she told my wife her name was Jinny, by which name we shall call her. I think a good likely girl, and a parish child of St. Bride's, of honest parentage, and recommended by the churchwarden. After dinner among my joyners laying my floors, which please me well, and so to my office, and we sat this afternoon upon an extraordinary business of victualling. In the evening came Commissioner Pett, who fell foule on mee for my carriage to him at Chatham, wherein, after protestation of my love and good meaning to him, he was quiet; but I doubt he will not be able to do the service there that any other man of his ability would. Home in the evening my viall (and lute new strung being brought home too), and I would have paid Mr. Hunt for it, but he did not come along with it himself, which I expected and was angry for it, so much is it against my nature to owe anything to any body. This evening the girle that was brought to me to-day for so good a one, being cleansed of lice this day by my wife, and good, new clothes put on her back, she run away from Goody Taylour that was shewing her the way to the bakehouse, and we heard no more of her. So to supper and to bed.

21st. Up betimes and among my joyners, and to my office, where the joyners are also laying mouldings in the inside of my closet. Then abroad and by water to White Hall, and there got Sir G. Carteret to sign me my last quarter's bills for my wages, and meeting with Mr. Creed he told me how my Lord Teviott hath received another attaque from Guyland at Tangier with 10,000 men, and at last, as is said, is come, after a personal treaty with him, to a good understanding and peace with him. Thence to my brother's, and there told him how my girl has served us which he sent me, and directed him to get my clothes again, and get the girl whipped. So to other places by the way about small businesses, and so home, and after looking over all my workmen, I went by water and land to Deptford, and there found by appointment Sir W. Batten, but he was got to Mr. Waith's to dinner, where I dined with him, a good dinner and good discourse, and his wife, I believe, a good woman. We fell in discourse of Captain Cocke, and how his lady has lost all her fine linen almost, but besides that they say she gives out she had L3000 worth of linen, which we all laugh at, and Sir W. Batten (who I perceive is not so fond of the Captain as he used to be, and less of her, from her slight receiving of him and his lady it seems once) told me how he should say that he see he must spend L700 per ann. get it how he could, which was a high speech, and by all men's discover, his estate not good enough to spend so much. After dinner altered our design to go to Woolwich, and put it off to to-morrow morning, and so went all to Greenwich (Mrs. Waith excepted, who went thither, but not to the same house with us, but to her father's, that lives there), to the musique-house, where we had paltry musique, till the master organist came, whom by discourse I afterwards knew, having employed him for my Lord Sandwich, to prick out something (his name Arundell), and he did give me a fine voluntary or two, and so home by water, and at home I find my girl that run away brought by a bedel of St. Bride's Parish, and stripped her and sent her away, and a newe one come, of Griffin's helping to, which I think will prove a pretty girl. Her name, Susan, and so to supper after having this evening paid Mr. Hunt L3 for my viall (besides the carving which I paid this day 10s. for to the carver), and he tells me that I may, without flattery, say, I have as good a Theorbo viall and viallin as is in England. So to bed.

22nd. Up by four o'clock to go with Sir W. Batten to Woolwich and Sir J. Minnes, which we did, though not before 6 or 7 by their laying a-bed. Our business was to survey the new wharf building there, in order to the giving more to him that do it (Mr. Randall) than contracted for, but I see no reason for it, though it be well done, yet no better than contracted to be. Here we eat and drank at the Clerke of the Cheques, and in taking water at the Tower gate, we drank a cup of strong water, which I did out of pure conscience to my health, and I think is not excepted by my oaths, but it is a thing I shall not do again, hoping to have no such occasion. After breakfast Mr. Castle and I walked to Greenwich, and in our way met some gypsys, who would needs tell me my fortune, and I suffered one of them, who told me many things common as others do, but bade me beware of a John and a Thomas, for they did seek to do me hurt, and that somebody should be with me this day se'nnight to borrow money of me, but I should lend him none. She got ninepence of me. And so I left them and to Greenwich and so to Deptford, where the two knights were come, and thence home by water, where I find my closet done at my office to my mind and work gone well on at home; and Ashwell gone abroad to her father, my wife having spoken plainly to her. After dinner to my office, getting my closet made clean and setting some papers in order, and so in the evening home and to bed. This day Sir W. Batten tells me that Mr. Newburne (of whom the nickname came up among us forarse Tom Newburne) is dead of eating cowcumbers, of which, the other day, I heard another, I think Sir Nicholas Crisp's son.

23rd (Lord's day). Up and to church without my wife, she being all dirty, as my house is. God forgive me, I looked about to see if I could spy Pembleton, but I could not, which did please me not a little. Home to dinner, and then to walk up and down in my house with my wife, discoursing of our family matters, and I hope, after all my troubles of mind and jealousy, we shall live happily still. To church again, and so home to my wife; and with her read "Iter Boreale," a poem, made just at the King's coming home; but I never read it before, and now like it pretty well, but not so as it was cried up. So to supper. No pleasure or discourse with Ashwell, with whom for her neglect and unconcernment to do any thing in this time of dirt and trouble in the house, but gadding abroad as she has been all this afternoon, I know not whither. After supper to prayers and to bed, having been, by a sudden letter coming to me from Mr. Coventry, been with Sir W. Pen, to discourse with him about sending 500 soldiers into Ireland. I doubt matters do not go very right there.

24th. Up very early, and my joyners came to work. I to Mr. Moore; from him came back home again, and drew up an account to my Lord, and that being done met him at my Lord Sandwich's, where I was a good while alone with my Lord; and I perceive he confides in me and loves me as he uses to do, and tells me his condition, which is now very well all I fear is that he will not live within compass, for I am told this morning of strange dotages of his upon the slut at Chelsea, even in the presence of his daughter, my Lady Jem, and Mrs. Ferrets, who took notice of it. There come to him this morning his prints of the river Tagus and the City of Lisbon, which he measured with his own hand, and printed by command of the King. My Lord pleases himself with it, but methinks it ought to have been better done than by jobing. Besides I put him upon having some took off upon white sattin, which he ordered presently. I offered my Lord my accounts, and did give him up his old bond for L500 and took a new one of him for L700, which I am by lending him more money to make up: and I am glad of it. My Lord would have had me dine with him, but I had a mind to go home to my workmen, and so took a kind good bye of him, and so with Creed to St. James's, and, missing Mr. Coventry, walked to the New Exchange, and there drank some whey, and so I by water home, and found my closett at my office made very clean and neat to my mind mightily, and home to dinner, and then to my office to brush my books, and put them and my papers in order again, and all the afternoon till late at night doing business there, and so home to supper, and then to work in my chamber, making matters of this day's accounts clear in my books, they being a little extraordinary, and so being very late I put myself to bed, the rest being long ago gone.

25th. Up very early and removed the things out of my chamber into the dining room, it being to be new floored this day. So the workmen being come and falling to work there, I to the office, and thence down to Lymehouse to Phin. Pett's about masts, and so back to the office, where we sat; and being rose, and Mr. Coventry being gone, taking his leave, for that he is to go to the Bath with the Duke to-morrow, I to the 'Change and there spoke with several persons, and lastly with Sir W. Warren, and with him to a Coffee House, and there sat two hours talking of office business and Mr. Wood's knavery, which I verily believe, and lastly he tells me that he hears that Captain Cocke is like to become a principal officer, either a Controller or a Surveyor, at which I am not sorry so either of the other may be gone, and I think it probable enough that it may be so. So home at 2 o'clock, and there I found Ashwell gone, and her wages come to 50s., and my wife, by a mistake from me, did give her 20s. more; but I am glad that she is gone and the charge saved. After dinner among my joyners, and with them till dark night, and this night they made an end of all; and so having paid them 40s. for their six days' work, I am glad they have ended and are gone, for I am weary and my wife too of this dirt. My wife growing peevish at night, being weary, and I a little vexed to see that she do not retain things in her memory that belong to the house as she ought and I myself do, I went out in a little seeming discontent to the office, and after being there a while, home to supper and to bed. To-morrow they say the King and the Duke set out for the Bath. This noon going to the Exchange, I met a fine fellow with trumpets before him in Leadenhall-street, and upon enquiry I find that he is the clerk of the City Market; and three or four men carried each of them an arrow of a pound weight in their hands. It seems this Lord Mayor begins again an old custome, that upon the three first days of Bartholomew Fayre, the first, there is a match of wrestling, which was done, and the Lord Mayor there and Aldermen in Moorefields yesterday: to-day, shooting: and to-morrow, hunting. And this officer of course is to perform this ceremony of riding through the city, I think to proclaim or challenge any to shoot. It seems that the people of the fayre cry out upon it as a great hindrance to them.

26th. Up, and after doing something in order to the putting of my house in order now the joynery is done, I went by water to White Hall, where the Court full of waggons and horses, the King and Court going this day out towards the Bath, and I to St. James's, where I spent an hour or more talking of many things to my great content with Mr. Coventry in his chamber, he being ready to set forth too with the Duke to-day, and so left him, and I meeting Mr. Gauden, with him to our offices and in Sir W. Pen's chamber did discourse by a meeting on purpose with Mr. Waith about the victualling business and came to some issue in it. So home to dinner, and Mr. Moore came and dined with me, and after dinner I paid him some money which evened all reckonings between him and me to this day, and for my Lord also I paid him some money, so that now my Lord owes me, for which I have his bond, just L700. After long discourse with him of the fitness of his giving me a receipt for this money, which I for my security think necessary and he otherwise do not think so, at last, after being a little angry, and I resolving not to let go my money without it, he did give me one. Thence I took him, and he and I took a pleasant walk to Deptford and back again, I doing much business there. He went home and I home also, indoors to supper, being very glad to see my house begin to look like itself again, hoping after this is over not to be in any dirt a great while again, but it is very handsome, and will be more when the floors come to be of one colour. So weary to bed. Pleased this day to see Captain Hickes come to me with a list of all the officers of Deptford Yard, wherein he, being a high old Cavalier, do give me an account of every one of them to their reproach in all respects, and discovers many of their knaverys; and tells me, and so I thank God I hear every where, that my name is up for a good husband for the King, and a good man, for which I bless God; and that he did this by particular direction of Mr. Coventry.

27th. Up, after much pleasant talke with my wife and a little that vexes me, for I see that she is confirmed in it that all that I do is by design, and that my very keeping of the house in dirt, and the doing of this and any thing else in the house, is but to find her employment to keep her within and from minding of her pleasure, in which, though I am sorry to see she minds it, is true enough in a great degree. To my office, and there we sat and despatched much business. Home and dined with my wife well, and then up and made clean my closet of books, and had my chamber a third time made very clean, so that it is now in a very fine condition. Thence down to see some good plank in the river with Sir W. Batten and back again, it being a very cold day and a cold wind. Home again, and after seeing Sir W. Pen, to my office, and there till late doing of business, being mightily encouraged by every body that I meet withal upon the 'Change and every where else, that I am taken notice of for a man that do the King's business wholly and well. For which the Lord be praised, for I know no honour I desire more. Home to supper, where I find my house very clean from top to bottom again to my great content. I found a feacho (as he calls it) of fine sugar and a case of orange-flower water come from Mr. Cocke, of Lisbon, the fruits of my last year's service to him, which I did in great justice to the man, a perfect stranger. He sends it me desiring that I would not let Sir J. Minnes know it, from whom he expected to have found the service done that he had from me, from whom he could expect nothing, and the other failed him, and would have done I am sure to this day had not I brought it to some end. After supper to bed.

28th. At the office betimes (it being cold all night and this morning, and a very great frost they say abroad, which is much, having had no summer at all almost), where we sat, and in the afternoon also about settling the establishment of the number of men borne on ships, &c., till the evening, and after that in my closet till late, and quite tired with business, home to supper and to bed.

29th. Abroad with my wife by water to Westminster, and there left her at my Lord's lodgings, and I to Jervas the barber's, and there was trimmed, and did deliver back a periwigg, which he brought by my desire the other day to show me, having some thoughts, though no great desire or resolution yet to wear one, and so I put it off for a while. Thence to my wife, and calling at both the Exchanges, buying stockings for her and myself, and also at Leadenhall, where she and I, it being candlelight, bought meat for to-morrow, having never a mayde to do it, and I myself bought, while my wife was gone to another shop, a leg of beef, a good one, for six pense, and my wife says is worth my money. So walked home with a woman carrying our things. I am mightily displeased at a letter Tom sent me last night, to borrow L20 more of me, and yet gives me no account, as I have long desired, how matters stand with him in the world. I am troubled also to see how, contrary to my expectation, my brother John neither is the scholler nor minds his studies as I thought would have done, but loiters away his time, so that I must send him soon to Cambridge again.

31st. Up and to my office all the morning, where Sir W. Batten and Sir J. Minnes did pay the short allowance money to the East India companies, and by the assistance of the City Marshall and his men, did lay hold of two or three of the chief of the companies that were in the mutiny the other day, and sent them to prison. This noon came Jane Gentleman to serve my wife as her chamber mayde. I wish she may prove well. So ends this month, with my mind pretty well in quiett, and in good disposition of health since my drinking at home of a little wine with my beer; but no where else do I drink any wine at all. The King and Queen and the Court at the Bath, my Lord Sandwich in the country newly gone.

And so to bed and there entertained her with great content
Apprehend about one hundred Quakers
Being cleansed of lice this day by my wife
Conceited, but that's no matter to me
Fear it may do him no good, but me hurt
Fearful that I might not go far enough with my hat off
He having made good promises, though I fear his performance
My wife has got too great head to be brought down soon
So much is it against my nature to owe anything to any body
Sporting in my fancy with the Queen
Things being dear and little attendance to be had we went away
Towzing her and doing what I would, but the last thing of all. . . .

THE DIARY OF SAMUEL PEPYS M.A. F.R.S.

CLERK OF THE ACTS AND SECRETARY TO THE ADMIRALTY

Transcribed from the shorthand manuscript in the PEPYSIAN *library Magdalene College Cambridge by the Rev.* MYNORS *bright* M.A. *Late fellow and President of the College*

(Unabridged)

WITH LORD BRAYBROOKE'S NOTES

EDITED WITH ADDITIONS BY

*Henry*B. *Wheatley* F.S.A.

Diary of Samuel Pepys.
September & *October*
1663

Sept. 1st. Up pretty betimes, and after a little at my viall to my office, where we sat all the morning, and I got my bill among others for my carved work (which I expected to have paid for myself) signed at the table, and hope to get the money back again, though if the rest had not got it paid by the King, I never intended nor did desire to have him pay for my vanity. In the evening my brother John coming to me to complain that my wife seems to be discontented at his being here, and shows him great disrespect; so I took and walked with him in the garden, and discoursed long with him about my affairs, and how imprudent it is for my father and mother and him to take exceptions without great cause at my wife, considering how much it concerns them to keep her their friend and for my peace; not that I would ever be led by her to forget or desert them in the main, but yet she deserves to be pleased and complied with a little, considering the manner of life that I keep her to, and how convenient it were for me to have Brampton for her to be sent to when I have a mind or occasion to go abroad to Portsmouth or elsewhere. So directed him how to behave himself to her, and gave him other counsel; and so to my office, where late.

2nd. Up betimes and to my office, and thence with Sir J. Minnes by coach to White Hall, where met us Sir W. Batten, and there staid by the Council Chamber till the Lords called us in, being appointed four days ago to attend them with an account of the riott among the seamen the other day, when Sir J. Minnes did as like a coxcomb as ever I saw any man speak in my life, and so we were dismissed, they making nothing almost of the matter. We staid long without, till by and by my Lord Mayor comes, who also was commanded to be there, and he having, we not being within with him, an admonition from the Lords to take better care of preserving the peace, we joyned with him, and the Lords having commanded Sir J. Minnes to prosecute the fellows for the riott, we rode along with my Lord Mayor in his coach to the Sessions House in the Old Bayley, where the Sessions are now sitting. Here I heard two or three ordinary tryalls, among others one (which, they say, is very common now-a-days, and therefore in my now taking of mayds I resolve to look to have some body to answer for them) a woman that went and was indicted by four names for entering herself a cookemayde to a gentleman that prosecuted her there, and after 3 days run away with a silver tankard, a porringer of silver, and a couple of spoons, and being now found is found guilty, and likely will be hanged. By and by up to dinner with my Lord Mayor and the Aldermen, and a very great dinner and most excellent venison, but it almost made me sick by not daring to drink wine. After dinner into a withdrawing room; and there we talked, among other things, of the Lord Mayor's sword. They tell me this sword, they believe, is at least a hundred or two hundred years old; and another that he hath, which is called the Black Sword, which the Lord Mayor wears when he mournes, but properly is their Lenten sword to wear upon Good Friday and other Lent days, is older than that. Thence I, leaving Sir J. Minnes to look after his indictment drawing up, I home by water, and there found my wife mightily pleased with a present of shells, fine shells given her by Captain Hickes, and so she and I up and look them over, and indeed they are very pleasant ones. By and by in comes Mr. Lewellin, lately come from Ireland, to see me, and he tells me how the English interest falls mightily there, the Irish party being too great, so that most of the old rebells are found innocent, and their lands, which were forfeited and bought or given to the English, are restored to them; which gives great discontent there among the English. He being gone, I to my office, where late, putting things in order, and so home to supper and to bed. Going through the City, my Lord Mayor told me how the piller set up by Exeter House is only to show where the pipes of water run to the City; and observed that this City is as well watered as any city in the world, and that the bringing the water to the City hath cost it first and last above L300,000; but by the new building, and the building of St. James's by my Lord St. Albans,

[It was at this time that the Earl of St. Albans planned St. James's Square, which was first styled "The Piazza." The "Warrant for a grant to Baptist May and Abraham Cowley on nomination of the Earl of St. Albans of several parcels of ground in Pall Mall described, on rental of L80, for building thereon a square of 13 or 14 great and good houses," was dated September 24th, 1664.]

which is now about (and which the City stomach I perceive highly, but dare not oppose it), were it now to be done, it would not be done for a million of money.

3rd. Up betimes, and for an hour at my viall before my people rise. Then up and to the office a while, and then to Sir W. Batten, who is going this day for pleasure down to the Downes. I eat a breakfast with them, and at my Lady's desire with them by coach to Greenwich, where I went aboard with them on the Charlotte yacht. The wind very fresh, and I believe they will be all sicke enough, besides that she is mighty troublesome on the water. Methinks she makes over much of her husband's ward, young Mr. Griffin, as if she expected some service from him when he comes to it, being a pretty young boy. I left them under sayle, and I to Deptford, and, after a word or two with Sir J. Minnes, walked to Redriffe and so home. In my way, it coming into my head, overtaking of a beggar or two on the way that looked like Gypsys, what the Gypsys 8 or 9 days ago had foretold, that somebody that day se'nnight should be with me to borrow money, but I should lend none; and looking, when I came to my office, upon my journall, that my brother John had brought a letter that day from my brother Tom to borrow L20 more of me, which had vexed me so that I had sent the letter to my father into the country, to acquaint him of it, and how little he is beforehand that he is still forced to borrow. But it pleased me mightily to see how, contrary to my expectations, having so lately lent him L20, and belief that he had money by him to spare, and that after some days not thinking of it,

I should look back and find what the Gypsy had told me to be so true. After dinner at home to my office, and there till late doing business, being very well pleased with Mr. Cutler's coming to me about some business, and among other things tells me that they value me as a man of business, which he accounts the best virtuoso, and I know his thinking me so, and speaking where he comes, may be of good use to me. Home to supper, and to bed.

4th. Up betimes, and an hour at my viall, and then abroad by water to White Hall and Westminster Hall, and there bought the first newes-books of L'Estrange's writing;

[Roger L'Estrange, a voluminous writer of pamphlets and periodical papers, and translator of classics, &c. Born 1616. He was Licenser of the Press to Charles *ii.* and James *ii.*; and M.P. for Winchester in James *ii.*'s parliament. L'Estrange was knighted in the reign of James *ii.*, and died 1704. In 1663 L'Estrange set up a paper called "The Public Intelligencer," which came out on August 31st, and continued to be published twice a week till January 19th, 1665, when it was superseded by the scheme of publishing the "London Gazette," the first number of which appeared on February 4th following.]

he beginning this week; and makes, methinks, but a simple beginning. Then to speak to Mrs. Lane, who seems desirous to have me come to see her and to have her company as I had a little while ago, which methinks if she were very modest, considering how I tumbled her and tost her, she should not. Thence to Mrs. Harper, and sent for Creed, and there Mrs. Harper sent for a maid for me to come to live with my wife. I like the maid's looks well enough, and I believe may do well, she looking very modestly and speaking so too. I directed her to speak with my wife, and so Creed and I away to Mr. Povy's, and he not being at home, walked to Lincoln's Inn walks, which they are making very fine, and about one o'clock went back to Povy's; and by and by in comes he, and so we sat and down to dinner, and his lady, whom I never saw before (a handsome old woman that brought him money that makes him do as he does), and so we had plenty of meat and drink, though I drunk no wine, though mightily urged to it, and in the exact manner that I never saw in my life any where, and he the most full and satisfied in it that man can be in this world with any thing. After dinner done, to see his new cellars, which he has made so fine with so noble an arch and such contrivances for his barrels and bottles, and in a room next to it such a grotto and fountayne, which in summer will be so pleasant as nothing in the world can be almost. But to see how he himself do pride himself too much in it, and command and expect to have all admiration, though indeed everything do highly deserve it, is a little troublesome. Thence Creed and I away, and by his importunity away by coach to Bartholomew Fayre, where I have no mind to go without my wife, and therefore rode through the fayre without 'lighting, and away home, leaving him there; and at home made my wife get herself presently ready, and so carried her by coach to the fayre, and showed her the monkeys dancing on the ropes, which was strange, but such dirty sport that I was not pleased with it. There was also a horse with hoofs like rams hornes, a goose with four feet, and a cock with three. Thence to another place, and saw some German Clocke works, the Salutation of the Virgin Mary, and several Scriptural stories; but above all there was at last represented the sea, with Neptune, Venus, mermaids, and Ayrid on a dolphin, the sea rocking, so well done, that had it been in a gaudy manner and place, and at a little distance, it had been admirable. Thence home by coach with my wife, and I awhile to the office, and so to supper and to bed. This day I read a Proclamation for calling in and commanding every body to apprehend my Lord Bristoll.

5th. Up betimes and to my viall awhile, and so to the office, and there sat, and busy all the morning. So at noon to the Exchange, and so home to dinner, where I met Creed, who dined with me, and after dinner mightily importuned by Captain Hicks, who came to tell my wife the names and story of all the shells, which was a pretty present he made her the other day. He being gone, Creed, my wife, and I to Cornhill, and after many tryalls bought my wife a chintz, that is, a painted Indian callico, for to line her new study, which is very pretty. So home with her, and then I away (Creed being gone) to Captain Minors upon Tower Hill, and there, abating only some impertinence of his, I did inform myself well in things relating to the East Indys; both of the country and the disappointment the King met with the last voyage, by the knavery of the Portugall Viceroy, and the inconsiderablenesse of the place of Bombaim,

> [Bombay, which was transferred to the East India Company in 1669.
> The seat of the Western Presidency of India was removed from Surat
> to Bombay in 1685-87.]

if we had had it. But, above all things, it seems strange to me that matters should not be understood before they went out; and also that such a thing as this, which was expected to be one of the best parts of the Queen's portion, should not be better understood; it being, if we had it, but a poor place, and not really so as was described to our King in the draught of it, but a poor little island; whereas they made the King and Lord Chancellor, and other learned men about the King, believe that that, and other islands which are near it, were all one piece; and so the draught was drawn and presented to the King, and believed by the King and expected to prove so when our men came thither; but it is quite otherwise. Thence to my office, and after several letters writ, home to supper and to bed, and took a pill. I hear this day that Sir W. Batten was fain to put ashore at Queenborough with my Lady, who has been so sick she swears never to go to sea again. But it happens well that Holmes is come home into the Downes, where he will meet my Lady, and it may be do her more good than she looked for. He brings news of the peace between Tangier and the Moors, but the particulars I know not. He is come but yesterday.

6th (Lord's day). My pill I took last night worked very well, and I lay long in bed and sweat to get away the itching all about my body from head to foot, which is beginning again as it did the last winter, and I find after I am up that it is abated. I staid at home all day and my wife also, whom, God forgive me, I staid along with me for fear of her seeing of Pembleton. But she and I entertained one another all day long with great pleasure, contriving about my wife's closet and the bedchamber, whither we intend to go up she and I to-day. We dined alone and supped also at night, my brother John with us, and so to prayers and to bed.

7th. Up pretty betimes, and awhile to my vyall, and then abroad to several places, to buy things for the furnishing my house and my wife's closet, and then met my uncle Thomas, by appointment, and he and I to the Prerogative Office in Paternoster Row, and there searched and found my uncle Day's will, end read it over and advised upon it, and his wife's after him, and though my aunt Perkins testimony is very good, yet I fear the estate being great, and the rest that are able to inform us in the matter are all possessed of more or less of the estate, it will be hard for us ever to do anything, nor will I adventure anything till I see what part will be given to us by my uncle Thomas of all that is gained. But I had another end of putting my uncle into some doubt, that so I might keep him: yet from going into the country that he may be there against the Court at his own charge, and so I left him and his son at a loss what to do till I see them again. And so I to my Lord Crew's, thinking to have dined there, but it was too late, and so back and called at my brother's and Mr. Holden's about several businesses, and went all alone to the Black Spread Eagle in Bride Lane, and there had a chopp of veale and some bread, cheese, and beer, cost me a shilling to my dinner, and so through Fleet Ally, God forgive me, out of an itch to look upon the sluts there, against which when I saw them my stomach turned, and so to Bartholomew Fayre, where I met with Mr. Pickering, and he and I to see the monkeys at the Dutch house, which is far beyond the other that my wife and I saw the other day; and thence to see the dancing on the ropes, which was very poor and tedious. But he and I fell in discourse about my Lord Sandwich. He tells me how he is sorry for my Lord at his being at Chelsey, and that his but seeming so to my Lord without speaking one word, had put him clear out of my Lord's favour, so as that he was fain to leave him before he went into the country, for that he was put to eat with his servants; but I could not fish from him, though I knew it, what was the matter; but am very sorry to see that my Lord hath thus much forgot his honour, but am resolved not to meddle with it. The play being done, I stole from him and hied home, buying several things at the ironmonger's—dogs, tongs, and shovels—for my wife's closett and the rest of my house, and so home, and thence to my office awhile, and so home to supper and to bed. By my letters from Tangier today I hear that it grows very strong by land, and the Mole goes on. They have lately killed two hundred of the Moores, and lost about forty or fifty. I am mightily afeard of laying out too much money in goods upon my house, but it is not money flung away, though I reckon nothing money but when it is in the bank, till I have a good sum beforehand in the world.

8th. Up and to my viall a while, and then to my office on Phillips having brought me a draught of the Katherine yacht, prettily well done for the common way of doing it. At the office all the morning making up our last half year's account to my Lord Treasurer, which comes to L160,000 or there abouts, the proper expense of this half year, only with an addition of L13,000 for the third due of the last account to the Treasurer for his disbursements, and L1100 for this half year's; so that in three years and a half his thirds come to L14,100. Dined at home with my wife. It being washing day, we had a good pie baked of a leg of mutton; and then to my office, and then abroad, and among other places to Moxon's, and there bought a payre of globes cost me L3 10s., with which I am well pleased, I buying them principally for my wife, who has a mind to understand them, and I shall take pleasure to teach her. But here I saw his great window in his dining room, where there is the two Terrestrial Hemispheres, so painted as I never saw in my life, and nobly done and to good purpose, done by his own hand. Thence home to my office, and there at business late, and then to supper home and to bed, my people sitting up longer than ordinary before they had done their washing.

9th. Up by break of day, and then to my vials a while, and so to Sir W. Warren's by agreement, and after talking and eating something with him, he and I down by water to Woolwich, and there I did several businesses, and had good discourse, and thence walked to Greenwich; in my way a little boy overtook us with a fine cupp turned out of Lignum Vitae, which the poor child confessed was made in the King's yard by his father, a turner there, and that he do often do it, and that I might have one, and God knows what, which I shall examine. Thence to Sir W. Warren's again, and there drew up a contract for masts which he is to sell us, and so home to dinner, finding my poor wife busy. I, after dinner, to the office, and then to White Hall, to Sir G. Carteret's, but did not speak with him, and so to Westminster Hall, God forgive me, thinking to meet Mrs. Lane, but she was not there, but here I met with Ned Pickering, with whom I walked 3 or 4 hours till evening, he telling me the whole business of my Lord's folly with this Mrs. Becke, at Chelsey, of all which I am ashamed to see my Lord so grossly play the beast and fool, to the flinging off of all honour, friends, servants, and every thing and person that is good, and only will have his private lust undisturbed with this common . . . . his sitting up night after night alone, suffering nobody to come to them, and all the day too, casting off Pickering, basely reproaching him with his small estate, which yet is a good one, and other poor courses to obtain privacy beneath his honour, and with his carrying her abroad and playing on his lute under her window, and forty other poor sordid things, which I am grieved to hear; but believe it to no purpose for me to meddle with it, but let him go on till God Almighty and his own conscience and thoughts of his lady and family do it. So after long discourse, to my full satisfaction but great trouble, I home by water and at my office late, and so to supper to my poor wife, and so to bed, being troubled to think that I shall be forced to go to Brampton the next Court, next week.

10th. Up betimes and to my office, and there sat all the morning making a great contract with Sir W. Warren for L3,000 worth of masts; but, good God! to see what a man might do, were I a knave, the whole business from beginning to end being done by me out of the office, and signed to by them upon the once reading of it to them, without the least care or consultation either of quality, price, number, or need of them, only in general that it was good to have a store. But I hope my pains was such, as the King has the best bargain of masts has been bought these 27 years in this office. Dined at home and then to my office again, many people about business with me, and then stepped a little abroad about business to the Wardrobe, but missed Mr. Moore, and elswhere, and in my way met Mr. Moore, who tells me of the good peace that is made at Tangier with the Moores, but to continue but from six months to six months, and that the Mole is laid out, and likely to be done with great ease and successe, we to have a quantity of ground for our cattle about the town to our use.

To my office late, and then home to supper, after writing letters, and to bed. This day our cook maid (we having no luck in maids now-adays), which was likely to prove a good servant, though none of the best cooks, fell sick and is gone to her friends, having been with us but 4 days.

11th. This morning, about two or three o'clock, knocked up in our back yard, and rising to the window, being moonshine, I found it was the constable and his watch, who had found our back yard door open, and so came in to see what the matter was. So I desired them to shut the door, and bid them good night, and so to bed again, and at 6 o'clock up and a while to my vyall, and then to the office, where all the morning upon the victualler's accounts, and then with him to dinner at the Dolphin, where I eat well but drank no wine neither; which keeps me in such good order that I am mightily pleased with myself for it. Hither Mr. Moore came to me, and he and I home and advised about business, and so after an hour's examining the state of the Navy debts lately cast up, I took coach to Sir Philip Warwick's, but finding Sir G. Carteret there I did not go in, but directly home, again, it raining hard, having first of all been with Creed and Mrs. Harper about a cook maid, and am like to have one from Creed's lodging. In my way home visited my Lord Crew and Sir Thomas, thinking they might have enquired by the by of me touching my Lord's matters at Chelsey, but they said nothing, and so after some slight common talk I bid them good night. At home to my office, and after a while doing business home to supper and bed.

12th. Up betimes, and by water to White Hall; and thence to Sir Philip Warwick, and there had half an hour's private discourse with him; and did give him some good satisfaction in our Navy matters, and he also me, as to the money paid and due to the Navy; so as he makes me assured by particulars, that Sir G. Carteret is paid within L80,000 every farthing that we to this day, nay to Michaelmas day next have demanded; and that, I am sure, is above L50,000 snore than truly our expenses have been, whatever is become of the money. Home with great content that I have thus begun an acquaintance with him, who is a great man, and a man of as much business as any man in England; which I will endeavour to deserve and keep. Thence by water to my office, in here all the morning, and so to the 'Change at noon, and there by appointment met and bring home my uncle Thomas, who resolves to go with me to Brampton on Monday next. I wish he may hold his mind. I do not tell him, and yet he believes that there is a Court to be that he is to do some business for us there. The truth is I do find him a much more cunning fellow than I ever took him for, nay in his very drink he has his wits about him. I took him home to dinner, and after dinner he began, after a glass of wine or two, to exclaim against Sir G. Carteret and his family in Jersey, bidding me to have a care of him, and how high, proud, false, and politique a fellow he is, and how low he has been under his command in the island. After dinner, and long discourse, he went away to meet on Monday morning, and I to my office, and thence by water to White Hall and Westminster Hall about several businesses, and so home, and to my office writing a laborious letter about our last account to my Lord Treasurer, which took me to one o'clock in the morning,

13th (Lord's day). So that Griffin was fain to carry it to Westminster to go by express, and my other letters of import to my father and elsewhere could not go at all. To bed between one and two and slept till 8, and lay talking till 9 with great pleasure with my wife. So up and put my clothes in order against tomorrow's journey, and then at noon at dinner, and all the afternoon almost playing and discoursing with my wife with great content, and then to my office there to put papers in order against my going. And by and by comes my uncle Wight to bid us to dinner to-morrow to a haunch of venison I sent them yesterday, given me by Mr. Povy, but I cannot go, but my wife will. Then into the garden to read my weekly vows, and then home, where at supper saying to my wife, in ordinary fondness, "Well! shall you and I never travel together again?" she took me up and offered and desired to go along with me. I thinking by that means to have her safe from harm's way at home here, was willing enough to feign, and after some difficulties made did send about for a horse and other things, and so I think she will go. So, in a hurry getting myself and her things ready, to bed.

14th. Up betimes, and my wife's mind and mine holding for her going, so she to get her ready, and I abroad to do the like for myself, and so home, and after setting every thing at my office and at home in order, by coach to Bishop's Gate, it being a very promising fair day. There at the Dolphin we met my uncle Thomas and his son-in-law, which seems a very sober man, and Mr. Moore. So Mr. Moore and my wife set out before, and my uncle and I staid for his son Thomas, who, by a sudden resolution, is preparing to go with us, which makes me fear something of mischief which they design to do us. He staying a great while, the old man and I before, and about eight miles off, his son comes after us, and about six miles further we overtake Mr. Moore and my wife, which makes me mightily consider what a great deal of ground is lost in a little time, when it is to be got up again by another, that is to go his own ground and the other's too; and so after a little bayte (I paying all the reckonings the whole journey) at Ware, to Buntingford, where my wife, by drinking some cold beer, being hot herself, presently after 'lighting, begins to be sick, and became so pale, and I alone with her in a great chamber there, that I thought she would have died, and so in great horror, and having a great tryall of my true love and passion for her, called the mayds and mistresse of the house, and so with some strong water, and after a little vomit, she came to be pretty well again; and so to bed, and I having put her to bed with great content, I called in my company, and supped in the chamber by her, and being very merry in talk, supped and then parted, and I to bed and lay very well. This day my cozen Thomas dropped his hanger, and it was lost.

15th. Up pretty betimes and rode as far as Godmanehester, Mr. Moore having two falls, once in water and another in dirt, and there 'light and eat and drunk, being all of us very weary, but especially my uncle and wife. Thence to Brampton to my father's, and there found all well, but not sensible how they ought to treat my uncle and his son, at least till the Court be over, which vexed me, but on my counsel they carried it fair to them; and so my father, cozen Thomas, and I up to Hinchingbroke, where I find my Lord and his company gone to Boughton, which vexed me; but there I find my Lady and the young ladies, and there I alone with my Lady two hours, she carrying me through every part of the house and gardens, which are, and will be, mighty noble indeed. Here I saw Mrs. Betty Pickering, who is a very well-bred and comely lady, but very fat. Thence, without so much as drinking, home with my father and cozen, who staid for me, and to a good supper; after I had had an hour's talk with my father abroad in the fields, wherein he begun to talk very highly of my promises to him of giving him the profits of Sturtlow, as if it were nothing that I give him out of my purse, and that he would have me to give this also from myself to my brothers and sister; I mean Brampton and all, I think: I confess I was angry to hear him talk in that manner, and took him up roundly in it, and advised him if he could not live upon L50 per ann., which was another part of his discourse, that he would think to come and live at Tom's again, where L50 per ann. will be a good addition to Tom's trade, and I think that must be done when all is done. But my father spoke nothing more of it all the time I was in the country, though at the time he seemed to like it well enough. I also spoke with Piggott too this evening before I went in to supper, and doubt that I shall meet with some knots in my business to-morrow before I can do it at the Court, but I shall do my best. After supper my uncle and his son to Stankes's to bed, which troubles me, all our father's beds being lent to Hinchingbroke, and so my wife and I to bed, she very weary.

16th. Up betimes, and with my wife to Hinchingbroke to see my Lady, she being to go to my Lord this morning, and there I left her, and so back to the Court, and heard Sir R. Bernard's charges to the Courts Baron and Leete, which took up till noon, and were worth hearing, and after putting my business into some way, went home to my father's to dinner, and after dinner to the Court, where Sir Robert and his son came again by and by, and then to our business, and my father and I having given bond to him for the L21 Piggott owed him, my uncle Thomas did quietly admit himself and surrender to us the lands first mortgaged for our whole debt, and Sir Robert added to it what makes it up L209, to be paid in six months. But when I came to give him an account of more lands to be surrendered to us, wherein Piggott's wife was concerned, and she there to give her consent, Sir Robert would not hear of it, but began to talk very high that we were very cruel, and we had caution enough for our money, and he could not in conscience let the woman do it, and reproached my uncle, both he and his son, with taking use upon use for this money. To all which I did give him such answers and spoke so well, and kept him so to it, that all the Court was silent to hear us, and by report since do confess they did never hear the like in the place. But he by a wile had got our bond, and I was content to have as much as I could though I could not get all, and so took Piggott's surrender of them without his wife, and by Sir Robert's own consent did tell the Court that if the money were not paid in the time, and the security prove not sufficient, I would conclude myself wronged by Sir Robert, which he granted I should do. This kept us till night, but am heartily glad it ended so well on my uncle's part, he doing that and Prior's little house very willingly. So the Court broke up, and my father and Mr. Shepley and I to Gorrum's to drink, and then I left them, and to the Bull, where my uncle was to .hear what he and the people said of our business, and here nothing but what liked me very well. So by and by home and to supper, and with my mind in pretty good quiett, to bed.

17th. Up, and my father being gone to bed ill last night and continuing so this morning, I was forced to come to a new consideration, whether it was fit for to let my uncle and his son go to Wisbeach about my uncle Day's estate alone or no, and concluded it unfit; and so resolved to go with them myself, leaving my wife there, I begun a journey with them, and with much ado, through the fens, along dikes, where sometimes we were ready to have our horses sink to the belly, we got by night, with great deal of stir and hard riding, to Parson's Drove, a heathen place, where I found my uncle and aunt Perkins, and their daughters, poor wretches! in a sad, poor thatched cottage, like a poor barn, or stable, peeling of hemp, in which I did give myself good content to see their manner of preparing of hemp; and in a poor condition of habitt took them to our miserable inn, and there, after long stay, and hearing of Frank, their son, the miller, play, upon his treble, as he calls it, with which he earns part of his living, and singing of a country bawdy song, we sat down to supper; the whole crew, and Frank's wife and child, a sad company, of which I was ashamed, supped with us. And after supper I, talking with my aunt about her report concerning my uncle Day's will and surrender, I found her in such different reports from what she writes and says to the people, and short of what I expected, that I fear little will be done of good in it. By and by newes is brought to us that one of our horses is stole out of the stable, which proves my uncle's, at which I am inwardly glad—I mean, that it was not mine; and at this we were at a great loss; and they doubting a person that lay at next door, a Londoner, some lawyer's clerk, we caused him to be secured in his bed, and other care to be taken to seize the horse; and so about twelve at night or more, to bed in a sad, cold, nasty chamber, only the mayde was indifferent handsome, and so I had a kiss or two of her, and I to bed, and a little after I was asleep they waked me to tell me that the horse was found, which was good newes, and so to sleep till the morning, but was bit cruelly, and nobody else of our company, which I wonder at, by the gnatts.

18th. Up, and got our people together as soon as we could; and after eating a dish of cold cream, which was my supper last night too, we took leave of our beggarly company, though they seem good people, too; and over most sad Fenns, all the way observing the sad life which the people of the place which if they be born there, they do call the Breedlings' of the place, do live, sometimes rowing from one spot to another, and then wadeing, to Wisbeach, a pretty town, and a fine church and library, where sundry very old abbey manuscripts; and a fine house, built on the church ground by Secretary Thurlow, and a fine gallery built for him in the church, but now all in the Bishop of Ely's hands. After visiting the church, &c., we went out of the towne, by the help of a stranger, to find out one Blinkhorne, a miller, of whom we might inquire something of old Day's disposal of his estate, and in whose hands it now is; and by great chance we met him, and brought him to our inn to dinner; and instead of being informed in his estate by this fellow, we find that he is the next heir to the estate, which was matter, of great sport to my cozen Thomas and me, to see such a fellow prevent us in our hopes, he being Day's brother's, daughter's son, whereas we are but his sister's sons and grandsons; so that, after all, we were fain to propose our matter to him, and to get him to give us leave to look after the business, and so he to have one-third part, and we two to have the other two-third parts, of what should be recovered of the estate, which he consented to; and after some discourse and paying the reckoning, we mounted again, and rode, being very merry at our defeat, to Chatteris, my uncle very weary, and after supper, and my telling of three stories, to their good liking, of spirits, we all three in a chamber went to bed.

19th. Up pretty betimes, and after eating something, we set out and I (being willing thereto) went by a mistake with them to St. Ives, and there, it being known that it was their nearer way to London, I took leave of them there, they going straight to London and I to Brampton, where I find my father ill in bed still, and Madam Norbery (whom and her fair daughter and sister I was ashamed to kiss, but did, my lip being sore with riding in the wind and bit with the gnatts), lately come to town, come to see my father and mother, and they after a little stay being gone, I told my father my success. And after dinner my wife and I took horse, and rode with marvellous, and the first and only hour of, pleasure, that ever I had in this estate since I had to do with it, to Brampton woods; and through the wood rode, and gathered nuts in my way, and then at Graffam to an old woman's house to drink, where my wife used to go; and being in all circumstances highly pleased, and in my wife's riding and good company at this time, I rode, and she showed me the river behind my father's house, which is very pleasant, and so saw her home, and I straight to Huntingdon, and there met Mr. Shepley and to the Crown (having sent home my horse by Stankes), and there a barber came and trimmed me, and thence walked to Hinchingbroke, where my Lord and ladies all are just alighted. And so I in among them, and my Lord glad to see me, and the whole company. Here I staid and supped with them, and after a good stay talking, but yet observing my Lord not to be so mightily ingulphed in his pleasure in the country as I expected and hoped, I took leave of them, and after a walk in the courtyard in the dark with Mr. Howe, who tells me that my Lord do not enjoy himself and please himself as he used to do, but will hasten up to London, and that he is resolved to go to Chelsey again, which we are heartily grieved for and studious how to prevent if it be possible, I took horse, there being one appointed for me, and a groom to attend me, and so home, where my wife: staid up and sister for me, and so to bed, troubled for what I hear of my Lord.

20th (Lord's day). Up, and finding my father somewhat better, walked to Huntingdon church, where in my Lord's pew, with the young ladies, by my Lord's own showing me the place, I stayed the sermon, and so to Hinchingbroke, walking with Mr. Shepley and Dr. King, whom they account a witty man here, as well as a good physician, and there my Lord took me with the rest of the company, and singly demanded my opinion in the walks in his garden, about the bringing of the crooked wall on the mount to a shape; and so to dinner, there being Collonel Williams and much other company, and a noble dinner. But having before got my Lord's warrant for travelling to-day, there being a proclamation read yesterday against it at Huntingdon, at which I am very glad, I took leave, leaving them at dinner, and walked alone to my father's, and there, after a word or two to my father and mother, my wife and I mounted, and, with my father's boy, upon a horse I borrowed of Captain Ferrers, we rode to Bigglesworth by the help of a couple of countrymen, that led us through the very long and dangerous waters, because of the ditches on each side, though it begun to be very dark, and there we had a good breast of mutton roasted for us, and supped, and to bed.

21st. Up very betimes by break of day, and got my wife up, whom the thought of this day's long journey do discourage; and after eating something, and changing of a piece of gold to pay the reckoning, we mounted, and through Baldwicke, where a fayre is kept to-day, and a great one for cheese and other such commodities, and so to Hatfield, it being most curious weather from the time we set out to our getting home, and here we dined, and my wife being very weary, and believing that it would be hard to get her home to-night, and a great charge to keep her longer abroad, I took the opportunity of an empty coach that was to go to London, and left her to come in it to London, for half-a-crown, and so I and the boy home as fast as we could drive, and it was even night before we got home. So that I account it very good fortune that we took this course, being myself very weary, much more would my wife have been. At home found all very well and my house in good order. To see Sir W. Pen, who is pretty well, and Sir J. Minnes, who is a little lame on one foot, and the rest gone to Chatham, viz.: Sir G. Carteret and Sir W. Batten, who has in my absence inveighed against my contract the other day for Warren's masts, in which he is a knave, and I shall find matter of tryumph, but it vexes me a little. So home, and by and by comes my wife by coach well home, and having got a good fowl ready for supper against her coming, we eat heartily, and so with great content and ease to our own bed, there nothing appearing so to our content as to be at our own home, after being abroad awhile.

22nd. I up, well refreshed after my journey, and to my office and there set some things in order, and then Sir W. Pen and I met and held an office, and at noon to dinner, and so by water with my wife to Westminster, she to see her father and mother, and we met again at my Lord's lodgings, and thence by water home again, where at the door we met Sir W. Pen and his daughter coming to visit us, and after their visit I to my office, and after some discourse to my great satisfaction with Sir W. Warren about our bargain of masts, I wrote my letters by the post, and so home to supper and to bed. This day my wife showed me bills printed, wherein her father, with Sir John Collidon and Sir Edward Ford, have got a patent for curing of smoky chimneys.

[The Patent numbered 138 is printed in the appendix to Wheatley's "Samuel Pepys and the World he lived in" (p. 241). It is drawn in favour of John Colladon, Doctor in Physicke, and of Alexander Marchant, of St. Michall, and describes "a way to prevent and cure the smoakeing of Chimneys, either by stopping the tunnell towards the top, and altering the former course of the smoake, or by setting tunnells with checke within the chimneyes." Sir Edward Ford's name does not appear in the patent.]

I wish they may do good thereof, but fear it will prove but a poor project. This day the King and Queen are to come to Oxford. I hear my Lady Castlemaine is for certain gone to Oxford to meet him, having lain within here at home this week or two, supposed to have miscarried; but for certain is as great in favour as heretofore;

[According to Collins, Henry Fitzroy, Lady Castlemaine's second son by Charles *ii.*, was born on September 20th, 1663. He was the first Duke of Grafton.—B.]

at least Mrs. Sarah at my Lord's, who hears all from their own family, do say so. Every day brings newes of the Turke's advance into Germany, to the awakeing of all the Christian Princes thereabouts, and possessing himself of Hungary. My present care is fitting my wife's closett and my house, and making her a velvet coate, and me a new black cloth suit, and coate and cloake, and evening my reckoning as well as I can against Michaelmas Day, hoping for all that to have my balance as great or greater than ever I had yet.

23rd. Up betimes and to my office, where setting down my journall while I was in the country to this day, and at noon by water to my Lord Crew's, and there dined with him and Sir Thomas, thinking to have them inquire something about my Lord's lodgings at Chelsey, or any thing of that sort, but they did not, nor seem to take the least notice of it, which is their discretion, though it might be better for my Lord and them too if they did, that so we might advise together for the best, which cannot be while we seem ignorant one to another, and it is not fit for me to begin the discourse. Thence walked to several places about business and to Westminster Hall, thinking to meet Mrs. Lane, which is my great vanity upon me at present, but I must correct it. She was not in the way. So by water home and to my office, whither by and by came my brother John, who is to go to Cambridge to-morrow, and I did give him a most severe reprimand for his bad account he gives me of his studies. This I did with great passion and sharp words, which I was sorry to be forced to say, but that I think it for his good, forswearing doing anything for him, and that which I have yet, and now do give him, is against my heart, and will also be hereafter, till I do see him give me a better account of his studies. I was sorry to see him give me no answer, but, for aught I see, to hear me without great resentment, and such as I should have had: in his condition. But I have done my duty, let him do his, for I am resolved to be as good as my word. After two hours walking in the garden, till after it was dark, I ended with him and to my office, and there set some papers in order, and so to supper, and my poor wife, who is mighty busy at home; fitting her closet. So to bed.

24th. Up betimes, and after taking leave of my brother, John, who went from me to my father's this day, I went forth by water to Sir Philip Warwick's, where I was with him a pretty while; and in discourse he tells me, and made it; appear to me, that the King cannot be in debt to the Navy at this time L5,000; and it is my opinion that Sir G. Carteret do owe the King money, and yet the whole Navy debt paid. Thence I parted, being doubtful of myself that I have not, spoke with the gravity and weight that I ought to do in so great a business. But I rather hope it is my doubtfulness of myself, and the haste which he was in, some very great personages waiting for him without, while he was with me, that made him willing to be gone. To the office by water, where we sat doing little, now Mr. Coventry is not here, but only vex myself to see what a sort of coxcombs we are when he is not here to undertake such a business as we do. In the afternoon telling my wife that I go to Deptford, I went, by water to Westminster Hall, and there finding Mrs. Lane, took her over to Lambeth, where we were lately, and there, did what I would with her, but only the main thing, which she; would not consent to, for which God be praised . . . . . But, trust in the Lord, I shall never do so again while I live. After being tired with her company I landed her at White; Hall, and so home and at my office writing letters till 12 at night almost, and then home to supper and bed, and there found my poor wife hard at work, which grieved my heart to see that I should abuse so good a wretch, and that is just with God to make her bad with me for my wrongin of her, but I do resolve never to do the like again. So to bed.

25th. Lay pretty long in bed, and so to my office all the morning till by and by called out by Sir J. Minnes and Sir W. Batten, with them by water to Deptford, where it of a sudden did lighten, thunder, and rain so as we could do nothing but stay in Davis's house, and by and by Sir J. Minnes and I home again by water, and I home to dinner, and after dinner to the office, and there till night all alone, even of my clerks being there, doing of business, and so home and to bed.

26th. Up and to my office, and there we sat till noon, and then I to the Exchange, but did little there, but meeting Mr. Rawlinson he would needs have me home to dinner, and Mr. Deane of Woolwich being with me I took him with me, and there we dined very well at his own dinner, only no invitation, but here I sat with little pleasure, considering my wife at home alone, and so I made what haste home I could, and was forced to sit down again at dinner with her, being unwilling to neglect her by being known to dine abroad. My doing so being only to keep Deane from dining at home with me, being doubtful what I have to eat. So to the office, and there till late at night, and so home to supper and bed, being mightily pleased to find my wife so mindful of her house.

27th (Lord's day). Lay chatting with my wife a good while, then up and got me ready and to church, without my man William, whom I have not seen to-day, nor care, but would be glad to have him put himself far enough out of my favour that he may not wonder to have me put him away. So home to dinner, being a little troubled to see Pembleton out again, but I do not discern in my wife the least memory of him. Dined, and so to my office a little, and then to church again, where a drowsy sermon, and so home to spend the evening with my poor wife, consulting about her closett, clothes, and other things. At night to supper, though with little comfort, I finding myself both head and breast in great pain, and what troubles me most my right ear is almost deaf. It is a cold, which God Almighty in justice did give me while I sat lewdly sporting with Mrs. Lane the other day with the broken window in my neck. I went to bed with a posset, being very melancholy in consideration of the loss of my hearing.

28th. Up, though with pain in my head, stomach, and ear, and that deaf so as in my way by coach to White Hall with Sir J. Minnes I called at Mr. Holliard's, who did give me some pills, and tells me I shall have my hearing again and be well. So to White Hall, where Sir J. Minnes and I did spend an hour in the Gallery, looking upon the pictures, in which he hath some judgment. And by and by the Commissioners for Tangier met: and there my Lord Teviott, together with Captain Cuttance, Captain Evans, and Jonas Moore, sent to that purpose, did bring us a brave draught of the Mole to be built there; and report that it is likely to be the most considerable place the King of England hath in the world; and so I am apt to think it will. After discourse of this, and of supplying the garrison with some more horse, we rose; and

Sir J. Minnes and I home again, finding the street about our house full, Sir R. Ford beginning his shrievalty to-day and, what with his and our houses being new painted, the street begins to look a great deal better than it did, and more gracefull. Home and eat one bit of meat, and then by water with him and Sir W. Batten to a sale of old provisions at Deptford, which we did at Captain Boddily's house, to the value of L600 or L700, but I am not satisfied with the method used in this thing. Then home again by water, and after a little at my office, and visit Sir W. Pen, who is not very well again, with his late pain, home to supper, being hungry, and my ear and cold not so bad I think as it was. So to bed, taking one of my pills. Newes that the King comes to town for certain on Thursday next from his progresse.

29th. Took two pills more in the morning and they worked all day, and I kept the house. About noon dined, and then to carry several heavy things with my wife up and down stairs, in order to our going to lie above, and Will to come down to the Wardrobe, and that put me into a violent sweat, so I had a fire made, and then, being dry again, she and I to put up some paper pictures in the red chamber, where we go to lie very pretty, and the map of Paris. Then in the evening, towards night, it fell to thunder, lighten, and rain so violently that my house was all afloat, and I in all the rain up to the gutters, and there dabbled in the rain and wet half an hour, enough to have killed a man. That done downstairs to dry myself again, and by and by come Mr. Sympson to set up my wife's chimney-piece in her closett, which pleases me, and so that being done, I to supper and to bed, shifting myself from top to toe, and doubtful of my doing myself hurt.

30th. Rose very well, and my hearing pretty well again, and so to my office, by and by Mr. Holliard come, and at my house he searched my ear, and I hope all will be well, though I do not yet hear so well as I used to do with my right ear. So to my office till noon, and then home to dinner, and in the afternoon by water to White Hall, to the Tangier Committee; where my Lord Tiviott about his accounts; which grieves me to see that his accounts being to be examined by us, there are none of the great men at the Board that in compliment will except against any thing in his accounts, and so none of the little persons dare do it: so the King is abused. Thence home again by water with Sir W. Rider, and so to my office, and there I sat late making up my month's accounts, and, blessed be God, do find myself L760 creditor, notwithstanding that for clothes for myself and wife, and layings out on her closett, I have spent this month L47. So home, where I found our new cooke-mayde Elizabeth, whom my wife never saw at all, nor I but once at a distance before, but recommended well by Mr. Creed, and I hope will prove well. So to supper, prayers, and bed. This evening Mr. Coventry is come to St. James's, but I did not go see him, and tomorrow the King, Queen, Duke and his Lady, and the whole Court comes to towne from their progresse. Myself and family well, only my father sicke in the country. All the common talke for newes is the Turke's advance in Hungary, &c.

Diaryof Samuel Pepys.
October
1663

October 1st. Up and betimes to my office, and then to sit, where Sir G. Carteret, Sir W. Batten, Sir W. Pen, Sir J. Minnes, Mr. Coventry and myself, a fuller board than by the King's progresse and the late pays and my absence has been a great while. Sat late, and then home to dinner. After dinner I by water to Deptford about a little business, and so back again, buying a couple of good eeles by the way, and after writing by the post, home to see the painter at work, late, in my wife's closet, and so to supper and to bed, having been very merry with the painter, late, while he was doing his work. This day the King and Court returned from their progress.

2nd. Up betimes and by water to St. James's, and there visited Mr. Coventry as a compliment after his new coming to town, but had no great talk with him, he being full of business. So back by foot through London, doing several errands, and at the 'Change met with Mr. Cutler, and he and I to a coffee-house, and there discoursed, and he do assure me that there is great likelyhood of a war with Holland, but I hope we shall be in good condition before it comes to break out. I like his company, and will make much of his acquaintance. So home to dinner with my wife, who is over head and eares in getting her house up, and so to the office, and with Mr. Lewes, late, upon some of the old victuallers' accounts, and so home to supper and to bed, up to our red chamber, where we purpose always to lie. This day I received a letter from Mr. Barlow, with a Terella,

[Professor Silvanus P. Thompson, F.R.S., has kindly supplied me with the following interesting note on the terrella (or terella): The name given by Dr. William Gilbert, author of the famous treatise, "De Magnete" (Lond. 1600), to a spherical loadstone, on account of its acting as a model, magnetically, of the earth; compass-needles pointing to its poles, as mariners' compasses do to the poles of the earth. The term was adopted by other writers who followed Gilbert, as the following passage from Wm. Barlowe's "Magneticall Advertisements" (Lond. 1616) shows: "Wherefore the round Loadstone is significantly termed by Doct. Gilbert Terrella, that is, a little, or rather a very little Earth: For it representeth in an exceeding small model (as it were) the admirable properties magneticall of the huge Globe of the earth" (op. cit, p. 55). Gilbert set great store by his invention of the terrella, since it led him to propound the true theory of the mariners' compass. In his portrait of himself which he had painted for the University of Oxford he was represented as holding in his hand a globe inscribed terella. In the Galileo Museum in Florence there is a terrella twenty-seven inches in diameter, of loadstone from Elba, constructed for Cosmo de' Medici. A smaller one contrived by Sir Christopher Wren was long preserved in the museum of the Royal Society (Grew's "Rarities belonging to the Royal Society," p. 364).

Evelyn was shown "a pretty terrella described with all ye circles and skewing all y magnetic deviations" (Diary, July 3rd, 1655).]

which I had hoped he had sent me, but to my trouble I find it is to present from him to my Lord Sandwich, but I will make a little use of it first, and then give it him.

3rd. Up, being well pleased with my new lodging and the convenience of having our mayds and none else about us, Will lying below. So to the office, and there we sat full of business all the morning. At noon I home to dinner, and then abroad to buy a bell to hang by our chamber door to call the mayds. Then to the office, and met Mr. Blackburne, who came to know the reason of his kinsman (my Will) his being observed by his friends of late to droop much. I told him my great displeasure against him and the reasons of it, to his great trouble yet satisfaction, for my care over him, and how every thing I said was for the good of the fellow, and he will take time to examine the fellow about all, and to desire my pleasure concerning him, which I told him was either that he should became a better servant or that we would not have him under my roof to be a trouble. He tells me in a few days he will come to me again and we shall agree what to do therein. I home and told my wife all, and am troubled to see that my servants and others should be the greatest trouble I have in the world, more than for myself. We then to set up our bell with a smith very well, and then I late at the office. So home to supper and to bed.

4th (Lord's day). Up and to church, my house being miserably overflooded with rayne last night, which makes me almost mad. At home to dinner with my wife, and so to talk, and to church again, and so home, and all the evening most pleasantly passed the time in good discourse of our fortune and family till supper, and so to bed, in some pain below, through cold got.

5th. Up with pain, and with Sir J. Minnes by coach to the Temple, and then I to my brother's, and up and down on business, and so to the New Exchange, and there met Creed, and he and I walked two or three hours, talking of many businesses, especially about Tangier, and my Lord Tiviot's bringing in of high accounts, and yet if they were higher are like to pass without exception, and then of my Lord Sandwich sending a messenger to know whether the King intends to come to Newmarket, as is talked, that he may be ready to entertain him at Hinchingbroke. Thence home and dined, and my wife all day putting up her hangings in her closett, which she do very prettily herself with her own hand, to my great content. So I to the office till night, about several businesses, and then went and sat an hour or two with Sir W. Pen, talking very largely of Sir J. Minnes's simplicity and unsteadiness, and of Sir W. Batten's suspicious dealings, wherein I was open, and he sufficiently, so that I do not care for his telling of tales, for he said as much, but whether that were so or no I said nothing but what is my certain knowledge and belief concerning him. Thence home to bed in great pain.

6th. Slept pretty well, and my wife waked to ring the bell to call up our mayds to the washing about 4 o'clock, and I was and she angry that our bell did not wake them sooner, but I will get a bigger bell. So we to sleep again till 8 o'clock, and then I up in some ease to the office, where we had a full board, where we examined Cocke's second account, when Mr. Turner had drawn a bill directly to be paid the balance thereof, as Mr. Cocke demanded, and Sir J. Minnes did boldly assert the truth of it, and that he had examined it, when there is no such thing, but many vouchers, upon examination, missing, and we saw reason to strike off several of his demands, and to bring down his 5 per cent. commission to 3 per cent. So we shall save the King some money, which both the Comptroller and his clerk had absolutely given away. There was also two occasions more of difference at the table; the one being to make out a bill to Captain Smith for his salary abroad as commander-in-chief in the Streights. Sir J. Minnes did demand an increase of salary for his being Vice-Admiral in the Downes, he having received but 40s. without an increase, when Sir J. Lawson, in the same voyage, had L3, and others have also had increase, only he, because he was an officer of the board, was worse used than any body else, and particularly told Sir W. Batten that he was the opposer formerly of his having an increase, which I did wonder to hear him so boldly lay it to him. So we hushed up the dispute, and offered, if he would, to examine precedents, and report them, if there was any thing to his advantage to be found, to the Duke. The next was, Mr. Chr. Pett and Deane were summoned to give an account of some knees

["Naturally grown timber or bars of iron bent to a right angle or to fit the surfaces and to secure bodies firmly together as hanging knees secure the deck beams to the sides."—Smyth's Sailor's Word- Book. There are several kinds of knees.]

which Pett reported bad, that were to be served in by Sir W. Warren, we having contracted that none should be served but such as were to be approved of by our officers. So that if they were bad they were to be blamed for receiving them. Thence we fell to talk of Warren's other goods, which Pett had said were generally bad, and falling to this contract again, I did say it was the most cautious and as good a contract as had been made here, and the only [one] that had been in such terms. Sir J. Minnes told me angrily that Winter's timber, bought for 33s. per load, was as good and in the same terms. I told him that it was not so, but that he and Sir W. Batten were both abused, and I would prove it was as dear a bargain as had been made this half year, which occasioned high words between them and me, but I am able to prove it and will. That also was so ended, and so to other business. At noon Lewellin coming to me I took him and Deane, and there met my uncle Thomas, and we dined together, but was vexed that, it being washing-day, we had no meat dressed, but sent to the Cook's, and my people had so little witt to send in our meat from abroad in that Cook's dishes, which were marked with the name of the Cook upon them, by which, if they observed anything, they might know it was not my own dinner. After dinner we broke up, and I by coach, setting down Luellin in Cheapside. So to White Hall, where at the Committee of Tangier, but, Lord! how I was troubled to see my Lord Tiviott's accounts of L10,000 paid in that manner, and wish 1000 times I had not been there. Thence rose with Sir G. Carteret and to his lodgings, and there discoursed of our frays at the table to-day, and particularly of that of the contract, and the contract of masts the other day, declaring my fair dealing, and so needing not any man's good report of it, or word for it, and that I would make it so appear to him, if he desired it, which he did, and I will do it. Thence home by water in great pain, and at my office a while, and thence a little to Sir W. Pen, and so home to bed, and finding myself beginning to be troubled with wind as I used to be, and in pain in making water, I took a couple of pills that I had by me of Mr. Hollyard's.

7th. They wrought in the morning, and I did keep my bed, and my pain continued on me mightily that I kept within all day in great pain, and could break no wind nor have any stool after my physic had done working. So in the evening I took coach and to Mr. Holliard's, but he was not at home, and so home again, and whether the coach did me good or no I know not . . . . So to bed and lay in good ease all night, and . . . . pretty well to the morning . . . . .

[Pepys's prescription for the colic:

"Balsom of Sulphur, 3 or 4 drops in a spoonfull of Syrrup of Colts foote, not eating or drinking two hours before or after.

"The making of this Balsom:

"2/3ds of fine Oyle, and 1/3d of fine Brimstone, sett 13 or 14 houres upon yt fire, simpring till a thicke Stufte lyes at ye Bottome, and ye Balsom at ye topp. Take this off &c.

"Sir Rob. Parkhurst for ye Collique."—M. B.]

8th. So, keeping myself warm, to the office, and at noon home to dinner, my pain coming again by breaking no wind nor having any stool. So to Mr. Holliard, and by his direction, he assuring me that it is nothing of the stone, but only my constitution being costive, and that, and cold from without, breeding and keeping the wind, I took some powder that he did give me in white wine, and sat late up, till past eleven at night, with my wife in my chamber till it had done working, which was so weakly that I could hardly tell whether it did work or no. My mayds being at this time in great dirt towards getting of all my house clean, and weary and having a great deal of work to do therein to-morrow and next day, were gone to bed before my wife and I, who also do lie in our room more like beasts than Christians, but that is only in order to having of the house shortly in a cleaner, or rather very clean condition. Some ease I had so long as this did keep my body loose, and I slept well.

9th. And did keep my bed most of this morning, my body I find being still bound and little wind, and so my pain returned again, though not so bad, but keeping my body with warm clothes very hot I made shift to endure it, and at noon sent word to Mr. Hollyard of my condition, that I could neither have a natural stool nor break wind, and by that means still in pain and frequent offering to make water. So he sent me two bottles of drink and some syrup, one bottle to take now and the other to-morrow morning. So in the evening, after Commissioner Pett, who came to visit me, and was going to Chatham, but methinks do talk to me in quite another manner, doubtfully and shyly, and like a stranger, to what he did heretofore. After I saw he was gone I did drink one of them, but it was a most loathsome draught, and did keep myself warm after it, and had that afternoon still a stool or two, but in no plenty, nor any wind almost carried away, and so to bed. In no great pain, but do not think myself likely to be well till I have a freedom of stool and wind. Most of this day and afternoon my wife and I did spend together in setting things now up and in order in her closet, which indeed is, and will be, when I can get her some more things to put in it, a very pleasant place, and is at present very pretty, and such as she, I hope, will find great content in. So to bed.

10th. Up, and not in any good ease yet, but had pain in making water, and some course. I see I must take besides keeping myself warm to make myself break wind and go freely to stool before I can be well, neither of which I can do yet, though I have drank the other bottle of Mr. Hollyard's against my stomach this morning. I did, however, make shift to go to the office, where we sat, and there Sir J. Minnes and Sir W. Batten did advise me to take some juniper water, and Sir W. Batten sent to his Lady for some for me, strong water made of juniper. Whether that or anything else of my draught this morning did it I cannot tell, but I had a couple of stools forced after it . . . . but whether I shall grow better upon it I cannot tell. Dined at home at noon, my wife and house in the dirtiest pickle that ever she and it was in almost, but in order, I hope, this night to be very clean. To the office all the afternoon upon victualling business, and late at it, so after I wrote by the post to my father, I home. This evening Mr. Hollyard sends me an electuary to take (a walnut quantity of it) going to bed, which I did. 'Tis true I slept well, and rose in a little ease in the morning.

11th (Lord's day). And was mightily pleased to see my house clean and in good condition, but something coming into my wife's head, and mine, to be done more about bringing the green bed into our chamber, which is handsomer than the red one, though not of the colour of our hangings, my wife forebore to make herself clean to-day, but continued in a sluttish condition till to-morrow. I after the old passe, all the day within doors, ... the effect of my electuary last night, and the greatest of my pain I find to come by my straining . . . . For all this I eat with a very good stomach, and as much as I use to do, and so I did this noon, and staid at home discoursing and doing things in my chamber, altering chairs in my chamber, and set them above in the red room, they being Turkey work, and so put their green covers upon those that were above, not so handsome. At night fell to reading in the Church History of Fuller's, and particularly Cranmer's letter to Queen Elizabeth, which pleases me mightily for his zeal, obedience, and boldness in a cause of religion. After supper to bed as I use to be, in pain . . . . .

12th. Up (though slept well) and made some water in the morning [as] I used to do, and a little pain returned to me, and some fears, but being forced to go to the Duke at St. James's, I took coach and in my way called upon Mr. Hollyard and had his advice to take a glyster. At St. James's we attended the Duke all of us. And there, after my discourse, Mr. Coventry of his own accord begun to tell the Duke how he found that discourse abroad did run to his prejudice about the fees that he took, and how he sold places and other things; wherein he desired to appeal to his Highness, whether he did any thing more than what his predecessors did, and appealed to us all. So Sir G. Carteret did answer that some fees were heretofore taken, but what he knows not; only that selling of places never was nor ought to be countenanced. So Mr. Coventry very hotly answered to Sir G. Carteret, and appealed to himself whether he was not one of the first that put him upon looking after this taking of fees, and that he told him that Mr. Smith should say that he made L5000 the first year, and he believed he made L7000. This Sir G. Carteret denied, and said, that if he did say so he told a lie, for he could not, nor did know, that ever he did make that profit of his place; but that he believes he might say L2500 the first year. Mr. Coventry instanced in another thing, particularly wherein Sir G. Carteret did advise with him about the selling of the Auditor's place of the stores, when in the beginning there was an intention of creating such an office. This he confessed, but with some lessening of the tale Mr. Coventry told, it being only for a respect to my Lord Fitz-Harding. In fine, Mr. Coventry did put into the Duke's hand a list of above 250 places that he did give without receiving one farthing, so much as his ordinary fees for them, upon his life and oath; and that since the Duke's establishment of fees he had never received one token more of any man; and that in his whole life he never conditioned or discoursed of any consideration from any commanders since he came to the Navy. And afterwards, my Lord Barkeley merrily discoursing that he wished his profit greater than it was, and that he did believe that he had got L50,000 since he came in, Mr. Coventry did openly declare that his Lordship, or any of us, should have not only all he had got, but all that he had in the world (and yet he did not come a beggar into the Navy, nor would yet be thought to speak in any contempt of his Royall Highness's bounty), and should have a year to consider of it too, for L25,000. The Duke's answer was, that he wished we all had made more profit than he had of our places, and that we had all of us got as much as one man below stayres in the Court, which he presently named, and it was Sir George Lane! This being ended, and the list left in the Duke's hand, we parted, and I with Sir G. Carteret, Sir J. Minnes, and Sir W. Batten by coach to the Exchange, and there a while, and so home, and whether it be the jogging, or by having my mind more employed (which I believe is a great matter) I know not, but . . . . I begin to be suddenly well, at least better than I was. So home and to dinner, and thence by coach to the Old Exchange, and there cheapened some laces for my wife, and then to Mr.-----the great laceman in Cheapside, and bought one cost me L4. more by 20s. than I intended, but when I came to see them I was resolved to buy one worth wearing with credit, and so to the New Exchange, and there put it to making, and so to my Lord's lodgings and left my wife, and so I to the Committee of Tangier, and then late home with my wife again by coach, beginning to be very well, and yet when I came home . . . . the little straining which I thought was no strain at all at the present did by and by bring me some pain for a good while. Anon, about 8 o'clock, my wife did give me a clyster which Mr. Hollyard directed, *viz.*, a pint of strong ale, 4 oz. of sugar, and 2 oz. of butter. It lay while I lay upon the bed above an hour, if not two, and then thinking it quite lost I rose, and by and by it began with my walking to work, and gave me three or four most excellent stools and carried away wind, put me in excellent ease, and taking my usual walnut quantity of electuary at my going into bed I had about two stools in the night . . . . .

13th. And so rose in the morning in perfect good ease . . . . continued all the morning well, and in the afternoon had a natural easily and dry stoole, the first I have had these five days or six, for which God be praised, and so am likely to continue well, observing for the time to come when any of this pain comes again

(1) To begin to keep myself as warm as I can.

(2) Strain as little as ever I can backwards, remembering that my pain will come by and by, though in the very straining I do not feel it.

(3) Either by physic forward or by clyster backward or both ways to get an easy and plentiful going to stool and breaking of wind.

(4) To begin to suspect my health immediately when I begin to become costive and bound, and by all means to keep my body loose, and that to obtain presently after I find myself going the contrary.

This morning at the office, and at noon with Creed to the Exchange, where much business, but, Lord! how my heart, though I know not reason for it, began to doubt myself, after I saw Stint, Field's one-eyed solicitor, though I know not any thing that they are doing, or that they endeavour any thing further against us in the business till the terme. Home, and Creed with me to dinner, and after dinner John Cole, my old friend, came to see and speak with me about a friend. I find him ingenious, but more and more discern his city pedantry; but however, I will endeavour to have his company now and then, for that he knows much of the temper of the City, and is able to acquaint therein as much as most young men, being of large acquaintance, and himself, I think, somewhat unsatisfied with the present state of things at Court and in the Church. Then to the office, and there busy till late, and so home to my wife, with some ease and pleasure that I hope to be able to follow my business again, which by God's leave I am resolved to return to with more and more eagerness. I find at Court, that either the King is doubtfull of some disturbance, or else would seem so (and I have reason to hope it is no worse), by his commanding all commanders of castles, &c., to repair to their charges; and mustering the Guards the other day himself, where he found reason to dislike their condition to my Lord Gerard, finding so many absent men, or dead pays.

> [This is probably an allusion to the practice of not reporting the deaths of soldiers, that the officers might continue to draw their pay.—B.]

My Lady Castlemaine, I hear, is in as great favour as ever, and the King supped with her the very first night he came from Bath: and last night and the night before supped with her; when there being a chine of beef to roast, and the tide rising into their kitchen that it could not be roasted there, and the cook telling her of it, she answered, "Zounds! she must set the house on fire but it should be roasted!" So it was carried to Mrs. Sarah's husband's, and there it was roasted. So home to supper and to bed, being mightily pleased with all my house and my red chamber, where my wife and I intend constantly to lie, and the having of our dressing room and mayds close by us without any interfering or trouble.

14th. Up and to my office, where all the morning, and part of it Sir J. Minnes spent, as he do every thing else, like a fool, reading the Anatomy of the body to me, but so sillily as to the making of me understand any thing that I was weary of him, and so I toward the 'Change and met with Mr. Grant, and he and I to the Coffee-house, where I understand by him that Sir W. Petty and his vessel are coming, and the King intends to go to Portsmouth to meet it. Thence home and after dinner my wife and I, by Mr. Rawlinson's conduct, to the Jewish Synagogue: where the men and boys in their vayles, and the women behind a lattice out of sight; and some things stand up, which I believe is their Law, in a press to which all coming in do bow; and at the putting on their vayles do say something, to which others that hear him do cry Amen, and the party do kiss his vayle. Their service all in a singing way, and in Hebrew. And anon their Laws that they take out of the press are carried by several men, four or five several burthens in all, and they do relieve one another; and whether it is that every one desires to have the carrying of it, I cannot tell, thus they carried it round about the room while such a service is singing. And in the end they had a prayer for the King, which they pronounced his name in Portugall; but the prayer, like the rest, in Hebrew. But, Lord! to see the disorder, laughing, sporting, and no attention, but confusion in all their service, more like brutes than people knowing the true God, would make a man forswear ever seeing them more and indeed I never did see so much, or could have imagined there had been any religion in the whole world so absurdly performed as this. Away thence with my mind strongly disturbed with them, by coach and set down my wife in Westminster Hall, and I to White Hall, and there the Tangier Committee met, but the Duke and the Africa Committee meeting in our room, Sir G. Carteret; Sir W. Compton, Mr. Coventry, Sir W. Rider, Cuttance and myself met in another room, with chairs set in form but no table, and there we had very fine discourses of the business of the fitness to keep Sally, and also of the terms of our King's paying the Portugees that deserted their house at Tangier, which did much please me, and so to fetch my wife, and so to the New Exchange about her things, and called at Thomas Pepys the turner's and bought something there, an so home to supper and to bed, after I had been a good while with Sir W. Pen, railing and speaking freely our minds against Sir W. Batten and Sir J. Minnes, but no more than the folly of one and the knavery of the other do deserve.

15th. Up, I bless God being now in pretty good condition, but cannot come to make natural stools yet . . . . . So up and to the office, where we sat all the morning, and at noon dined at home, my head full of business, and after stepping abroad to buy a thing or two, compasses and snuffers for my wife, I returned to my office and there mighty busy till it was late, and so home well contented with the business that I had done this afternoon, and so to supper and to bed.

16th. Up and to my office, where all the morning doing business, and at noon home to dinner, and then up to remove my chest and clothes up stairs to my new wardrobe, that I may have all my things above where I lie, and so by coach abroad with my wife, leaving her at my Lord's till I went to the Tangier Committee, where very good discourse concerning the Articles of peace to be continued with Guyland, and thence took up my wife, and with her to her tailor's, and then to the Exchange and to several places, and so home and to my office, where doing some business, and then home to supper and to bed.

17th. Up and to my office, and there we sat a very full board all the morning upon some accounts of Mr. Gauden's. Here happened something concerning my Will which Sir W. Batten would fain charge upon him, and I heard him mutter something against him of complaint for his often receiving people's money to Sir G. Carteret, which displeased me much, but I will be even with him. Thence to the Dolphin Tavern, and there Mr. Gauden did give us a great dinner. Here we had some discourse of the Queen's being very sick, if not dead, the Duke and Duchess of York being sent for betimes this morning to come to White Hall to her. So to my office and there late doing business, and so home to supper, my house being got mighty clean to my great content from top to toe, and so to bed, myself beginning to be in good condition of health also, but only my laying out so much money upon clothes for myself and wife and her closet troubles me.

18th (Lord's day). Up, and troubled at a distaste my wife took at a small thing that Jane did, and to see that she should be so vexed that I took part with Jane, wherein I had reason; but by and by well again, and so my wife in her best gown and new poynt that I bought her the other day, to church with me, where she has not been these many weeks, and her mayde Jane with her. I was troubled to see Pembleton there, but I thought it prudence to take notice myself first of it and show my wife him, and so by little and little considering that it mattered not much his being there I grew less concerned and so mattered it not much, and the less when, anon, my wife showed me his wife, a pretty little woman, and well dressed, with a good jewel at her breast. The parson, Mr. Mills, I perceive, did not know whether to pray for the Queen or no, and so said nothing about her; which makes me fear she is dead. But enquiring of Sir J. Minnes, he told me that he heard she was better last night. So home to dinner, and Tom came and dined with me, and so, anon, to church again, and there a simple coxcomb preached worse than the Scot, and no Pembleton nor his wife there, which pleased me not a little, and then home and spent most of the evening at Sir W. Pen's in complaisance, seeing him though he deserves no respect from me. This evening came my uncle Wight to speak with me about my uncle Thomas's business, and Mr. Moore came, 4 or 5 days out of the country and not come to see me before, though I desired by two or three messengers that he would come to me as soon as he came to town. Which do trouble me to think he should so soon forget my kindness to him, which I am afraid he do. After walking a good while in the garden with these, I went up again to Sir W. Pen, and took my wife home, and after supper to prayers, and read very seriously my vowes, which I am fearful of forgetting by my late great expenses, but I hope in God I do not, and so to bed.

19th. Waked with a very high wind, and said to my wife, "I pray God I hear not of the death of any great person, this wind is so high!" fearing that the Queen might be dead. So up; and going by coach with Sir W. Batten and Sir J. Minnes to St.

James's, they tell me that Sir W. Compton, who it is true had been a little sickly for a week or fortnight, but was very well upon Friday at night last at the Tangier Committee with us, was dead—died yesterday: at which I was most exceedingly surprised, he being, and so all the world saying that he was, one of the worthyest men and best officers of State now in England; and so in my conscience he was: of the best temper, valour, abilities of mind, integrity, birth, fine person, and diligence of any one man he hath left behind him in the three kingdoms; and yet not forty years old, or if so, that is all.

[Sir William Compton (1625-1663) was knighted at Oxford, December 12th, 1643. He was called by Cromwell "the sober young man and the godly cavalier." After the Restoration he was M.P. for Cambridge (1661), and appointed Master of the Ordnance. He died in Drury Lane, suddenly, as stated in the text, and was buried at Compton Wynyates, Warwickshire.]

I find the sober men of the Court troubled for him; and yet not so as to hinder or lessen their mirth, talking, laughing, and eating, drinking, and doing every thing else, just as if there was no such thing, which is as good an instance for me hereafter to judge of death, both as to the unavoidableness, suddenness, and little effect of it upon the spirits of others, let a man be never so high, or rich, or good; but that all die alike, no more matter being made of the death of one than another, and that even to die well, the praise of it is not considerable in the world, compared to the many in the world that know not nor make anything of it, nor perhaps to them (unless to one that like this poor gentleman, who is one of a thousand, there nobody speaking ill of him) that will speak ill of a man. Coming to St. James's, I hear that the Queen did sleep five hours pretty well to-night, and that she waked and gargled her mouth, and to sleep again; but that her pulse beats fast, beating twenty to the King's or my Lady Suffolk's eleven; but not so strong as it was. It seems she was so ill as to be shaved and pidgeons put to her feet, and to have the extreme unction given her by the priests, who were so long about it that the doctors were angry. The King, they all say; is most fondly disconsolate for her, and weeps by her, which makes her weep;

["The queen was given over by her physicians, . . . , and the good nature of the king was much affected with the situation in which he saw! a princess whom, though he did not love her, yet he greatly esteemed. She loved him tenderly, and thinking that it was the last time she should ever speak to him, she told him 'That the concern he showed for her death was enough to make her quit life with regret; but that not possessing charms sufficient to merit his tenderness, she had at least the consolation in dying to give place to a consort who might be more worthy, of it and to whom heaven, perhaps, might grant a blessing that had been refused to her.' At these words she bathed his hands with some tears which he thought would be her last; he mingled his own with hers, and without supposing she would take him at his word, he conjured her to live for his sake."—Grammont Memoirs, chap. vii.]

which one this day told me he reckons a good sign, for that it carries away some rheume from the head. This morning Captain Allen tells me how the famous Ned Mullins, by a slight fall, broke his leg at the ancle, which festered; and he had his leg cut off on Saturday, but so ill done, notwithstanding all the great chyrurgeons about the town at the doing of it, that they fear he will not live with it, which is very strange, besides the torment he was put to with it. After being a little with the Duke, and being invited to dinner to my Lord Barkeley's, and so, not knowing how to spend our time till noon, Sir W. Batten and I took coach, and to the Coffee-house in Cornhill;

[This may be the Coffee House in Exchange Alley, which had for a sign, Morat the Great, or The Great Turk, where coffee was sold in berry, in powder, and pounded in a mortar. There is a token of the house, see "Boyne's Tokens," ed. Williamson, vol. i., p. 592.]

where much talk about the Turk's proceedings, and that the plague is got to Amsterdam, brought by a ship from Argier; and it is also carried to Hambrough. The Duke says the King purposes to forbid any of their ships coming into the river. The Duke also told us of several Christian commanders (French) gone over to the Turks to serve them; and upon inquiry I find that the King of France do by this aspire to the Empire, and so to get the Crown of Spayne also upon the death of the King, which is very probable, it seems. Back to St. James's, and there dined with my Lord Barkeley and his lady, where Sir G. Carteret, Sir W. Batten, and myself, with two gentlemen more; my Lady, and one of the ladies of honour to the Duchesse (no handsome woman, but a most excellent hand). A fine French dinner, and so we after dinner broke up and to Creed's new lodgings in Axe-yard, which I like very well and so with him to White Hall and walked up and down in the galleries with good discourse, and anon Mr. Coventry and Povy, sad for the loss of one of our number we sat down as a Committee for Tangier and did some business and so broke up, and I down with Mr. Coventry and in his chamber discoursing of business of the office and Sir J. Minnes and Sir W. Batten's carriage, when he most ingeniously tells me how they have carried themselves to him in forbearing to speak the other day to the Duke what they know they have so largely at other times said to him, and I told him what I am put to about the bargain for masts. I perceive he thinks of it all and will remember it. Thence took up my wife at Mrs. Harper's where she and Jane were, and so called at the New Exchange for some things for her, and then at Tom's went up and saw his house now it is finished, and indeed it is very handsome, but he not within and so home and to my office; and then to supper and to bed.

20th. Up and to the office, where we sat; and at noon Sir G. Carteret, Sir J. Minnes, and I to dinner to my Lord Mayor's, being invited, where was the Farmers of the Customes, my Lord Chancellor's three sons, and other great and much company, and a very great noble dinner, as this Mayor—[Sir John Robinson.]—is good for nothing else. No extraordinary discourse of any thing, every man being intent upon his dinner, and myself willing to have drunk some wine to have warmed my belly, but I did for my oath's sake willingly refrain it, but am so well pleased and satisfied afterwards thereby, for it do keep me always in so good a frame of mind that I hope I shall not ever leave this practice. Thence home, and took my wife by coach to White Hall, and she set down at my Lord's lodgings, I to a Committee of Tangier, and thence with her homeward, calling at several places by the way. Among others at Paul's Churchyard, and while I was in Kirton's shop, a fellow came to offer kindness or force to my wife in the coach, but she refusing, he went away, after the coachman had struck him, and he the coachman. So I being called, went thither, and the fellow coming out again of a shop, I did give him a good cuff or two on the chops, and seeing him not oppose me, I did give him another; at last found him drunk, of which I was glad, and so left him, and home, and so to my office awhile, and so home to supper and to bed. This evening, at my Lord's lodgings, Mrs. Sarah talking with my wife and I how the Queen do, and how the King tends her being so ill. She tells us that the Queen's sickness is the spotted fever; that she was as full of the spots as a leopard which is very strange that it should be no more known; but perhaps it is not so. And that the King do seem to take it much to heart, for that he hath wept before her; but, for all that; that he hath not missed one night since she was sick, of supping with my Lady Castlemaine; which I believe is true, for she [Sarah] says that her husband hath dressed the suppers every night; and I confess I saw him myself coming through the street dressing of a great supper to-night, which Sarah says is also for the King and her; which is a very strange thing.

21st. Up, and by and by comes my brother Tom to me, though late (which do vex me to the blood that I could never get him to come time enough to me, though I have spoke a hundred times; but he is very sluggish, and too negligent ever to do well at his trade I doubt), and having lately considered with my wife very much of the inconvenience of my going in no better plight, we did resolve of putting me into a better garb, and, among other things, to have a good velvet cloake; that is, of cloth lined with velvet and other things modish, and a perruque, and so I sent him and her out to buy me velvet, and I to the Exchange, and so to Trinity House, and there dined with Sir W. Batten, having some business to speak with him, and Sir W. Rider. Thence, having my belly full, away on foot to my brother's, all along Thames Streete, and my belly being full of small beer, I did all alone, for health's sake, drink half a pint of Rhenish wine at the Still-yard, mixed with beer. From my brother's with my wife to the Exchange, to buy things for her and myself, I being in a humour of laying out money, but not prodigally, but only in clothes, which I every day see that I suffer for want of, I so home, and after a little at my office, home to supper and to bed. Memorandum: This morning one Mr. Commander, a scrivener, came to me from Mr. Moore with a deed of which. Mr. Moore had told me, that my Lord had made use of my name, and that I was desired by my Lord to sign it. Remembering this very well, though understanding little of the particulars, I read it over, and found it concern Sir Robt. Bernard and Duckinford, their interest in the manor of Brampton. So I did sign it, declaring to Mr. Commander that I am only concerned in having my name at my Lord Sandwich's desire used therein, and so I sealed it up after I had signed and sealed the deed, and desired him to give it so sealed to Mr.

Moore. I did also call at the Wardrobe this afternoon to have told Mr. Moore of it, but he was not within, but knowing Mr. Commander to have the esteem of a good and honest man with my Lord Crew, I did not doubt to intrust him with the deed after I had signed it. This evening after I came home I begun to enter my wife in arithmetique, in order to her studying of the globes, and she takes it very well, and, I hope, with great pleasure, I shall bring her to understand many fine things.

22nd. Up to the office, where we sat till noon and then I home to dinner, and after dinner with my wife to her study and there read some more arithmetique, which she takes with great ease and pleasure. This morning, hearing that the Queen grows worse again, I sent to stop the making of my velvet cloake, till I see whether she lives or dies. So a little abroad about several businesses, and then home and to my office till night, and then home to supper, teach my wife, and so to bed.

23rd. Up, and this morning comes Mr. Clerke, and tells me that the Injunction against Trice is dismissed again, which troubles me much. So I am to look after it in the afternoon. There comes also by appointment my uncle Thomas, to receive the first payment of his daughter's money. But showing of me the original of the deed by which his daughter gives her right to her legacy to him, and the copy of it attested by the Scrivener, for me to keep by me, I did find some difference, and thereupon did look more into it, and at last did find the whole thing a forgery; yet he maintained it again and again, upon oath, that it had been signed and sealed by my cozen Mary ever since before her marriage. So I told him to his teeth he did like a knave, and so he did, and went with him to the Scrivener at Bedlam, and there found how it came to pass, viz., that he had lost, or pretends to have lost, the true original, and that so he was forced to take this course; but a knave, at least a man that values not what he swears to, I perceive he is. But however I am now better able to see myself fully secured before I part with the money, for I find that his son Charles has right to this legacy till the first L100 of his daughter's portion be paid, he being bond for it. So I put him upon getting both his sons to be bound for my security, and so left him and so home, and then abroad to my brother's, but found him abroad at the young couple that was married yesterday, and he one of the Br[ide's] men, a kinswoman (Brumfield) of the Joyces married to an upholster. Thence walked to the King's Head at Charing Cross and there dined, and hear that the Queen slept pretty well last night, but her fever continues upon her still. It seems she hath never a Portuguese doctor here. Thence by appointment to the Six Clerks' office to meet Mr. Clerke, which I did and there waited all the afternoon for Wilkinson my attorney, but he came not, and so vexed and weary we parted, and I endeavoured but in vain to have found Dr. Williams, of whom I shall have use in Trice's business, but I could not find him. So weary walked home; in my way bought a large kitchen knife and half dozen oyster knives. Thence to Mr. Holliard, who tells me that Mullins is dead of his leg cut off the other day, but most basely done. He tells me that there is no doubt but that all my slyme do come away in my water, and therefore no fear of the stone; but that my water being so slymy is a good sign. He would have me now and then to take a clyster, the same I did the other day, though I feel no pain, only to keep me loose, and instead of butter, which he would have to be salt butter, he would have me sometimes use two or three ounces of honey, at other times two or three ounces of Linseed oil. Thence to Mr. Rawlinson's and saw some of my new bottles made, with my crest upon them, filled with wine, about five or six dozen. So home and to my office a little, and thence home to prepare myself against T. Trice, and also to draw a bond fit for my uncle and his sons to enter into before I pay them the money. That done to bed.

24th. Up and to my office, where busy all the morning about Mr. Gauden's account, and at noon to dinner with him at the Dolphin, where mighty merry by pleasant stories of Mr. Coventry's and Sir J. Minnes's, which I have put down some of in my book of tales. Just as I was going out my uncle Thomas came to the with a draught of a bond for him and his sons to sign to me about the payment of the L20 legacy, which I agreed to, but he would fain have had from me the copy of the deed, which he had forged and did bring me yesterday, but I would not give him it. Says [he] I perceive then you will keep it to defame me with, and desired me not to speak of it, for he did it innocently. Now I confess I do not find any great hurt in the thing, but only to keep from me a sight of the true original deed, wherein perhaps there was something else that may touch this business of the legacy which he would keep from me, or it may be, it is really lost as he says it is. But then he need not have used such a slight, but confess it without danger. Thence by coach with Mr. Coventry to the Temple, and thence I to the Six Clerks' office, and discoursed with my Attorney and Solicitor, and he and I to Mr. Turner, who puts me in great fear that I shall not get retayned again against Tom Trice; which troubles me. Thence, it being night, homewards, and called at Wotton's and tried some shoes, but he had none to fit me. He tells me that by the Duke of York's persuasion Harris is come again to Sir W. Davenant upon his terms that he demanded, which will make him very high and proud. Thence to another shop, and there bought me a pair of shoes, and so walked home and to my office, and dispatch letters by the post, and so home to supper and to bed, where to my trouble I find my wife begin to talk of her being alone all day, which is nothing but her lack of something to do, for while she was busy she never, or seldom, complained . . . . . The Queen is in a good way of recovery; and Sir Francis Pridgeon hath got great honour by it, it being all imputed to his cordiall, which in her dispaire did give her rest and brought her to some hopes of recovery. It seems that, after the much talk of troubles and a plot, something is found in the North that a party was to rise, and some persons that were to command it are found, as I find in a letter that Mr. Coventry read to-day about it from those parts.

[This refers to a rising in the West Riding of Yorkshire, which took place on October 12th, and was known as the Farneley Wood Plot. The rising was easily put down, and several prisoners were taken. A special commission of oyer and terminer was sent down to York to try the prisoners in January, 1663-64, when twenty-one were convicted and executed. (See Whitaker's "Loidis and Elmete," 1816.)]

25th (Lord's day). Up, and my wife and I to church, where it is strange to see how the use and seeing Pembleton come with his wife thither to church, I begin now to make too great matter of it, which before was so terrible to me. Dined at home, my wife and I alone, a good dinner, and so in the afternoon to church again, where the

Scot preached, and I slept most of the afternoon. So home, and my wife and I together all the evening discoursing, and then after reading my vowes to myself, and my wife with her mayds (who are mighty busy to get it dispatched because of their mistress's promise, that when it is done they shall have leave all to go see their friends at Westminster, whither my wife will carry them) preparing for their washing to-morrow, we hastened to supper and to bed.

26th. Waked about one o'clock in the morning . . . . My wife being waked rung her bell, and the mayds rose and went to washing, we to sleep again till 7 o'clock, and then up, and I abroad to look out Dr. Williams, but being gone out I went to Westminster, and there seeing my Lord Sandwich's footman knew he was come to town, and so I went in and saw him, and received a kind salute from him, but hear that my father is very ill still. Thence to Westminster Hall with Creed, and spent the morning walking there, where, it being Terme time, I met several persons, and talked with them, among others Dr. Pierce, who tells me that the Queen is in a way to be pretty well again, but that her delirium in her head continues still; that she talks idle, not by fits, but always, which in some lasts a week after so high a fever, in some more, and in some for ever; that this morning she talked mightily that she was brought to bed, and that she wondered that she should be delivered without pain and without spueing or being sicke, and that she was troubled that her boy was but an ugly boy. But the King being by, said, "No, it is a very pretty boy."—"Nay," says she, "if it be like you it is a fine boy indeed, and I would be very well pleased with it." The other day she talked mightily of Sir H. Wood's lady's great belly, and said if she should miscarry he would never get another, and that she never saw such a man as this Sir H. Wood in her life, and seeing of Dr. Pridgeon, she said, "Nay, Doctor, you need not scratch your head, there is hair little enough already in the place." But methinks it was not handsome for the weaknesses of Princes to be talked of thus. Thence Creed and I to the King's Head ordinary, where much and very good company, among others one very talking man, but a scholler, that would needs put in his discourse and philosophy upon every occasion, and though he did well enough, yet his readiness to speak spoilt all. Here they say that the Turkes go on apace, and that my Lord Castlehaven is going to raise 10,000 men here for to go against him; that the King of France do offer to assist the Empire upon condition that he may be their Generalissimo, and the Dolphin chosen King of the Romans: and it is said that the King of France do occasion this difference among the Christian Princes of the Empire, which gives the Turke such advantages. They say also that the King of Spayne is making all imaginable force against Portugall again. Thence Creed and I to one or two periwigg shops about the Temple, having been very much displeased with one that we saw, a head of greasy and old woman's hair, at Jervas's in the morning; and there I think I shall fit myself of one very handsomely made. Thence by coach, my mind being troubled for not meeting with Dr. Williams, to St. Catharine's to look at a Dutch ship or two for some good handsome maps, but met none, and so back to Cornhill to Moxon's, but it being dark we staid not to see any, then to coach again, and presently spying Sir W. Batten; I 'light and took him in and to the Globe in Fleete Streete, by appointment, where by and by he and I with our solicitor to Sir F. Turner about Field's business, and back to the Globe, and thither I sent for Dr. Williams, and he is willing to swear in my behalf against T. Trice, *viz.*, that at T. Trice's desire we have met to treat about our business. Thence (I drinking no wine) after an hour's stay Sir W. Batten and another, and he drinking, we home by coach, and so to my office and set down my Journall, and then home to supper and to bed, my washing being in a good condition over. I did give Dr. Williams 20s. tonight, but it was after he had answered me well to what I had to ask him about this business, and it was only what I had long ago in my petty bag book allotted for him besides the bill of near L4 which I paid him a good while since by my brother Tom for physique for my wife, without any consideration to this business that he is to do for me, as God shall save me. Among the rest, talking of the Emperor at table to-day one young gentleman, a pretty man, and it seems a Parliament man, did say that he was a sot;

[Leopold I, the Holy Roman Emperor, was born June 9th, 1640. He became King of Hungary in 1655, and King of Bohemia in 1658, in which year he received the imperial crown. The Princes of the German Empire watched for some time the progress of his struggle with the Turks with indifference, but in 1663 they were induced to grant aid to Leopold after he had made a personal appeal to them in the diet at Ratisbon.]

for he minded nothing of the Government, but was led by the Jesuites. Several at table took him up, some for saying that he was a sot in being led by the Jesuites, [who] are the best counsel he can take. Another commander, a Scott[ish] Collonell, who I believe had several under him, that he was a man that had thus long kept out the Turke till now, and did many other great things, and lastly Mr. Progers, one of our courtiers, who told him that it was not a thing to be said of any Soveraigne Prince, be his weaknesses what they will, to be called a sot, which methinks was very prettily said.

27th. Up, and my uncle Thomas and his scrivener bringing me a bond and affidavit to my mind, I paid him his L20 for his daughter's legacy, and L5 more for a Quarter's annuity, in the manner expressed in each acquittance, to which I must be referred on any future occasion, and to the bond and affidavit. Thence to the office and there sat till noon, and then home to dinner, and after dinner (it being a foul house to-day among my maids, making up their clothes) abroad with my Will with me by coach to Dr, Williams, and with him to the Six Clerks's office, and there, by advice of his acquaintance, I find that my case, through my neglect and the neglect of my lawyers, is come to be very bad, so as that it will be very hard to get my bill retayned again. However, I got him to sign and swear an affidavit that there was treaties between T. Trice and me with as much advantage as I could for me, but I will say that for him he was most exact as ever I saw man in my life, word by word what it was that he swore to, and though, God forgive me, I could have been almost naturally willing to have let him ignorantly have sworn to something that was not of itself very certain, either or no, yet out of his own conscience and care he altered the words himself so as to make them very safe for him to swear. This I carrying to my clerk Wilkinson, and telling him how I heard matters to stand, he, like a conceited fellow, made nothing of it but advised me to offer Trice's clerks the cost of the dismission, *viz.*, 46s. 8d., which I did, but they would not take it without his client. Immediately thereupon we parted, and met T. Trice coming into the room, and he came to me and served me with a subpoena for these very costs, so I paid it him, but Lord! to see his resolution, and indeed discretion, in the wording of his receipt, he would have it most express to my greatest disadvantage that could be, yet so as I could not deny to give it him. That being paid, my clerke, and then his began to ask why we could not think, being friends, of referring it, or stating it, first ourselves, and then put it to some good lawyer to judge in it. From one word to more we were resolved to try, and to that end to step to the Pope's Head Taverne, and there he and his Clerke and Attorney and I and my Clerke, and sent for Mr. Smallwood, and by and by comes Mr. Clerke, my Solicitor, and after I had privately discoursed with my men and seen how doubtfully they talked, and what future certain charge and trouble it would be, with a doubtful victory, I resolved to condescend very low, and after some talke all together Trice and I retired, and he came to L150 the lowest, and I bid him L80. So broke off and then went to our company, and they putting us to a second private discourse, at last I was contented to give him L100, he to spend 40s. of it among this good company that was with us. So we went to our company, both seeming well pleased that we were come to an end, and indeed I am in the respects above said, though it be a great sum for us to part with. I am to pay him by giving him leave to buy about L40 worth of Piggott's land and to strike off so much of Piggott's debt, and the other to give him bond to pay him in 12 months after without interest, only giving him a power to buy more land of Piggott and paying him that way as he did for the other, which I am well enough contented with, or at least to take the land at that price and give him the money. This last I did not tell him, but I shall order it so. Having agreed upon to-morrow come se'nnight for the spending of the 40s. at Mr. Rawlinson's, we parted, and I set T. Trice down in Paul's Churchyard and I by coach home and to my office, and there set down this day's passages, and so home to supper and to bed. Mr. Coventry tells me to-day that the Queen had a very good night last night; but yet it is strange that still she raves and talks of little more than of her having of children, and fancys now that she hath three children, and that the girle is very like the King. And this morning about five o'clock waked (the physician feeling her pulse, thinking to be better able to judge, she being still and asleep, waked her) and the first word she said was, "How do the children?"

28th. Up and at my office all the morning, and at noon Mr. Creed came to me and dined with me, and after dinner Murford came to me and he and I discoursed wholly upon his breach of contract with us. After that Mr. Creed and I abroad, I doing several errands, and with him at last to the great coffee-house, and there after some common discourse we parted and I home, paying what I owed at the Mitre in my way, and at home Sympson the joyner coming he set up my press for my cloaks and other small things, and so to my office a little, and to supper, and to bed. This morning Mr. Blackburne came to me, and telling me what complaints Will made of the usage he had from my wife and other discouragements, and, I seeing him, instead of advising, rather favouring his kinsman, I told him freely my mind, but friendlily, and so we have concluded to have him have a lodging elsewhere, and that I will spare him L15 of his salary, and if I do not need to keep another L20.

29th. Up, it being my Lord Mayor's day, Sir Anthony Bateman. This morning was brought home my new velvet cloake, that is, lined with velvet, a good cloth the outside, the first that ever I had in my life, and I pray God it may not be too soon now that I begin to wear it. I had it this day brought, thinking to have worn it to dinner, but I thought it would be better to go without it because of the crowde, and so I did not wear it. We met a little at the office, and then home again and got me ready to go forth, my wife being gone forth by my consent before to see her father and mother, and taken her cooke mayde and little girle to Westminster with her for them to see their friends. This morning in dressing myself and wanting a band,

> [The band succeeded the ruff as the ordinary civil costume. The lawyers, who now retain bands, and the clergy, who have only lately left them off, formerly wore ruffs.]

I found all my bands that were newly made clean so ill smoothed that I crumpled them, and flung them all on the ground, and was angry with Jane, which made the poor girle mighty sad, so that I were troubled for it afterwards. At noon I went forth, and by coach to Guild Hall (by the way calling at Mr. Rawlinson's), and there was admitted, and meeting with Mr. Proby (Sir R. Ford's son), and Lieutenant-Colonel Baron, a City commander, we went up and down to see the tables; where under every salt there was a bill of fare, and at the end of the table the persons proper for the table. Many were the tables, but none in the Hall but the Mayor's and the Lords of the Privy Council that had napkins

> [As the practice of eating with forks gradually was introduced from Italy into England, napkins were not so generally used, but considered more as an ornament than a necessary.
>
> > "The laudable use of forks,
> > Brought into custom here, as they are in Italy,
> > To the sparing of napkins."
>
> Ben Jonson, The Devil is an Ass, act v., sc. 3.
>
> The guests probably brought their own knife and fork with them in a case.—M.B.]

or knives, which was very strange. We went into the Buttry, and there stayed and talked, and then into the Hall again: and there wine was offered and they drunk, I only drinking some hypocras, which do not break my vowe, it being, to the best of my present judgement, only a mixed compound drink, and not any wine.

[A drink, composed usually of red wine, but sometimes of white, with the addition of sugar and spices. Sir Walter Scott ("Quarterly Review," vol. xxxiii.) says, after quoting this passage of Pepys,

"Assuredly his pieces of bacchanalian casuistry can only be matched by that of Fielding's chaplain of Newgate, who preferred punch to wine, because the former was a liquor nowhere spoken against in Scripture."]

If I am mistaken, God forgive me! but I hope and do think I am not. By and by met with Creed; and we, with the others, went within the several Courts, and there saw the tables prepared for the Ladies and Judges and Bishopps: all great sign of a great dinner to come. By and by about one o'clock, before the Lord Mayor came, come into the Hall, from the room where they were first led into, the Lord Chancellor (Archbishopp before him), with the Lords of the Council, and other Bishopps, and they to dinner. Anon comes the Lord Mayor, who went up to the lords, and then to the other tables to bid wellcome; and so all to dinner. I sat near Proby, Baron, and Creed at the Merchant Strangers' table; where ten good dishes to a messe, with plenty of wine of all sorts, of which I drunk none; but it was very unpleasing that we had no napkins nor change of trenchers, and drunk out of earthen pitchers and wooden dishes.—[The City plate was probably melted during the Civil War.- M.B.]—It happened that after the lords had half dined, came the French Embassador, up to the lords' table, where he was to have sat; but finding the table set, he would not sit down nor dine with the Lord Mayor, who was not yet come, nor have a table to himself, which was offered; but in a discontent went away again. After I had dined, I and Creed rose and went up and down the house, and up to the lady's room, and there stayed gazing upon them. But though there were many and fine, both young and old, yet I could not discern one handsome face there; which was very strange, nor did I find the lady that young Dawes married so pretty as I took her for, I having here an opportunity of looking much upon her very near. I expected musique, but there was none but only trumpets and drums, which displeased me. The dinner, it seems, is made by the Mayor and two Sheriffs for the time being, the Lord Mayor paying one half, and they the other. And the whole, Proby says, is reckoned to come to about 7 or L800 at most. Being wearied with looking upon a company of ugly women, Creed and I went away, and took coach and through Cheapside, and there saw the pageants, which were very silly, and thence to the Temple, where meeting Greatorex, he and we to Hercules Pillars, there to show me the manner of his going about of draining of fenns, which I desired much to know, but it did not appear very satisfactory to me, as he discoursed it, and I doubt he will faile in it. Thence I by coach home, and there found my wife come home, and by and by came my brother Tom, with whom I was very angry for not sending me a bill with my things, so as that I think never to have more work done by him if ever he serves me so again, and so I told him. The consideration of laying out L32 12s. this very month in his very work troubles me also, and one thing more, that is to say, that Will having been at home all the day, I doubt is the occasion that Jane has spoken to her mistress tonight that she sees she cannot please us and will look out to provide herself elsewhere, which do trouble both of us, and we wonder also at her, but yet when the rogue is gone I do not fear but the wench will do well. To the office a little, to set down my Journall, and so home late to supper and to bed. The Queen mends apace, they say; but yet talks idle still.

30th. Lay long in bed with my wife, and then up and a while at my office, and so to the Change, and so [home] again, and there I found my wife in a great passion with her mayds. I upstairs to set some things in order in our chamber and wardrobe, and so to dinner upon a good dish of stewed beef, then up again about my business. Then by coach with my wife to the New Exchange, and there bought and paid for several things, and then back, calling at my periwigg-makers, and there showed my wife the periwigg made for me, and she likes it very well, and so to my brother's, and to buy a pair of boddice for her, and so home, and to my office late, and then home to my wife, purposing to go on to a new lesson in arithmetique with her. So to supper and to bed. The Queen mends apace, but her head still light. My mind very heavy thinking of my great layings out lately, and what they must still be for clothes, but I hope it is in order to getting of something the more by it, for I perceive how I have hitherto suffered for lack of going as becomes my place. After a little discourse with my wife upon arithmetique, to bed.

31st. Up and to the office, where we sat all the morning, and at noon home to dinner, where Creed came and dined with me, and after dinner he and I upstairs, and I showed him my velvet cloake and other things of clothes, that I have lately bought, which he likes very well, and I took his opinion as to some things of clothes, which I purpose to wear, being resolved to go a little handsomer than I have hitherto. Thence to the office; where busy till night, and then to prepare my monthly account, about which I staid till 10 or 11 o'clock at night, and to my great sorrow find myself L43 worse than I was the last month, which was then L760, and now it is but L717. But it hath chiefly arisen from my layings-out in clothes for myself and wife; *viz.*, for her about L12, and for myself L55, or thereabouts; having made myself a velvet cloake, two new cloth suits, black, plain both; a new shagg

[Shag was a stuff similar to plush. In 1703 a youth who was missing is described in an advertisement as wearing "red shag breeches, striped with black stripes." (Planche's "Cyclopxdia of Costume ").]

gowne, trimmed with gold buttons and twist, with a new hat, and, silk tops for my legs, and many other things, being resolved henceforward to go like myself. And also two perriwiggs, one whereof costs me L3, and the other 40s.—I have worn neither yet, but will begin next week, God willing. So that I hope I shall not need now to lay out more money a great while, I having laid out in clothes for myself and wife, and for her closett and other things without, these two months, this and the last, besides household expenses of victuals, &c., above L110. But I hope I shall with more comfort labour to get more, and with better successe than when, for want of clothes, I was forced to sneake like a beggar. Having done this I went home, and after supper to bed, my mind being eased in knowing my condition, though troubled to think that I have been forced to spend so much.

Thus I end this month worth L717, or thereabouts, with a good deal of good goods more than I had, and a great deal of new and good clothes. My greatest trouble and my wife's is our family, mighty out of order by this fellow Will's corrupting the mayds by his idle talke and carriage, which we are going to remove by hastening him out of the house, which his uncle Blackburne is upon doing, and I am to give him L20 per annum toward his maintenance. The Queene continues lightheaded, but in hopes to recover. The plague is much in Amsterdam, and we in fears of it here, which God defend.

    [Defend is used in the sense of forbid. It is a Gallicism from the
    French "defendre."]

The Turke goes on mightily in the Emperor's dominions, and the Princes cannot agree among themselves how to go against him. Myself in pretty good health now, after being ill this month for a week together, but cannot yet come to . . . . well, being so costive, but for this month almost I have not had a good natural stool, but to this hour am forced to take physic every night, which brings me neither but one stool, and that in the morning as soon as I am up, all the rest of the day very costive. My father has been very ill in the country, but I hope better again now. I am lately come to a conclusion with Tom Trice to pay him L100, which is a great deale of money, but I hope it will save a great deale more. But thus everything lessens, which I have and am like to have, and therefore I must look about me to get something more than just my salary, or else I may resolve to live well and die a beggar.

    And so to sleep till the morning, but was bit cruelly
    And there, did what I would with her
    Content as to be at our own home, after being abroad awhile
    Found guilty, and likely will be hanged (for stealing spoons)
    Half a pint of Rhenish wine at the Still-yard, mixed with beer
    His readiness to speak spoilt all
    No more matter being made of the death of one than another
    Out of an itch to look upon the sluts there
    Plague is much in Amsterdam, and we in fears of it here
    Pride himself too much in it
    Reckon nothing money but when it is in the bank
    Resolve to live well and die a beggar
    Scholler, that would needs put in his discourse (every occasion)
    She was so ill as to be shaved and pidgeons put to her feet
    The plague is got to Amsterdam, brought by a ship from Argier
    We having no luck in maids now-a-days
    Who is over head and eares in getting her house up

THE DIARY OF SAMUEL PEPYS M.A. F.R.S.

CLERK OF THE ACTS AND SECRETARY TO THE ADMIRALTY

Transcribed from the shorthand manuscript in the PEPYSIAN *library Magdalene College Cambridge by the Rev.* MYNORS *bright* M.A. *Late fellow and President of the College*

(Unabridged)

WITH LORD BRAYBROOKE'S NOTES

EDITED WITH ADDITIONS BY

HenryB. Wheatley F.S.A.

Diary of Samuel Pepys.
November & December
1663

November 1st (Lord's day). This morning my brother's man brought me a new black baize waistecoate, faced with silke, which I put on from this day, laying by half-shirts for this winter. He brought me also my new gowne of purple shagg, trimmed with gold, very handsome; he also brought me as a gift from my brother, a velvet hat, very fine to ride in, and the fashion, which pleases me very well, to which end, I believe, he sent it me, for he knows I had lately been angry with him. Up and to church with my wife, and at noon dined at home alone, a good calves head boiled and dumplings, an excellent dinner methought it was. Then to church again, whither Sir W. Pen came, the first time he has been at church these several months, he having been sicke all the while. Home and to my office, where I taught my wife some part of subtraction, and then fell myself to set some papers of my last night's accounts in order, and so to supper home, and after supper another bout at arithmetique with my wife, and then to my office again and made an end of my papers, and so home to prayers, and then to read my vowes, and to bed.

2d. Up, and by coach to White Hall, and there in the long Matted Gallery I find Sir G. Carteret, Sir J. Minnes, and Sir W. Batten—and by and by comes the King to walk there with three or four with him; and soon as he saw us, says he, "Here is the Navy Office," and there walked twenty turns the length of the gallery, talking, methought, but ordinary talke. By and by came the Duke, and he walked, and at last they went into the Duke's lodgings. The King staid so long that we could not discourse with the Duke, and so we parted. I heard the Duke say that he was going to wear a perriwigg; and they say the King also will. I never till this day observed that the King is mighty gray. Thence, meeting with Creed, walked with him to Westminster Hall, and thence by coach took up Mrs. Hunt, and carried her towards my house, and we light at the 'Change, and sent her to my house, Creed and I to the Coffeehouse, and then to the 'Change, and so home, and carried a barrel of oysters with us, and so to dinner, and after a good dinner left Mrs. Hunt and my wife making marmalett of quinces, and Creed and I to the perriwigg makers, but it being dark concluded of nothing, and so Creed went away, and I with Sir W. Pen, who spied me in the street, in his coach home. There found them busy still, and I up to my vyall. Anon, the comfiture being well done, my wife and I took Mrs. Hunt at almost 9 at night by coach and carried Mrs. Hunt home, and did give her a box of sugar and a haunch of venison given me by my Lady the other day. We did not 'light, but saw her within doors, and straight home, where after supper there happening some discourse where my wife thought she had taken Jane in a lie, she told me of it mighty triumphantly, but I, not seeing reason to conclude it a lie, was vexed, and my wife and I to very high words, wherein I up to my chamber, and she by and by followed me up, and to very bad words from her to me, calling me perfidious and man of no conscience, whatever I pretend to, and I know not what, which troubled me mightily, and though I would allow something to her passion, yet I see again and again that she spoke but somewhat of what she had in her heart. But I tempered myself very well, so as that though we went to bed with discontent she yielded to me and began to be fond, so that being willing myself to peace, we did before we sleep become very good friends, it being past 12 o'clock, and so with good hearts and joy to rest.

3rd. Up and to the office, where busy all the morning, and at noon to the Coffee-house, and there heard a long and most passionate discourse between two doctors of physique, of which one was Dr. Allen, whom I knew at Cambridge, and a couple of apothecarys; these maintaining chymistry against them Galenicall physique; and the truth is, one of the apothecarys whom they charged most, did speak very prettily, that is, his language and sense good, though perhaps he might not be so knowing a physician as to offer to contest with them. At last they came to some cooler terms, and broke up. I home, and there Mr. Moore coming by my appointment dined with me, and after dinner came Mr. Goldsborough, and we discoursed about the business of his mother, but could come to no agreement in it but parted dissatisfied. By and by comes Chapman, the periwigg-maker, and upon my liking it, without more ado I went up, and there he cut off my haire, which went a little to my heart at present to part with it; but, it being over, and my periwigg on, I paid him L3 for it; and away went he with my owne haire to make up another of, and I by and by, after I had caused all my mayds to look upon it; and they conclude it do become me; though Jane was mightily troubled for my parting of my own haire, and so was Besse, I went abroad to the Coffeehouse, and coming back went to Sir W. Pen and there sat with him and Captain Cocke till late at night, Cocke talking of some of the Roman history very well, he having a good memory. Sir W. Pen observed mightily, and discoursed much upon my cutting off my haire, as he do of every thing that concerns me, but it is over, and so I perceive after a day or two it will be no great matter.

4th. Up and to my office, shewing myself to Sir W. Batten, and Sir J. Minnes, and no great matter made of my periwigg, as I was afeard there would be. Among other things there came to me Shales of Portsmouth, by my order, and I began to discourse with him about the arrears of stores belonging to the Victualling Office there, and by his discourse I am in some hopes that if I can get a grant from the King of such a part of all I discover I may chance to find a way to get something by the by, which do greatly please me the very thoughts of. Home to dinner, and very pleasant with my wife, who is this day also herself making of marmalett of quince, which she now do very well herself. I left her at it and by coach I to the New Exchange and several places to buy and bring home things, among others a case I bought of the trunk maker's for my periwigg, and so home and to my office late, and among other things wrote a letter to Will's uncle to hasten his removal from me, and so home to supper and to bed. This morning Captain Cocke did give me a good account of the Guinny trade. The Queene is in a great way to recovery. This noon came John Angier to me in a pickle, I was sad to see him, desiring my good word for him to go a trooper to Tangier, but I did schoole him and sent him away with good advice, but no present encouragement. Presently after I had a letter from his poor father at Cambridge, who is broke, it seems, and desires me to get him a protection, or a place of employment; but, poor man, I doubt I can helpe him, but will endeavour it.

5th. Lay long in bed, then up, called by Captain Cocke about business of a contract of his for some Tarre, and so to the office, and then to Sir W. Pen and there talked, and he being gone came Sir W. Warren and discoursed about our business with Field, and at noon by agreement to the Miter to dinner upon T. Trice's 40s., to be spent upon our late agreement. Here was a very poor dinner and great company. All our lawyers on both sides, and several friends of his and some of mine brought by him, *viz*., Mr. Moore, uncle Wight, Dr. Williams, and my cozen Angier, that lives here in town, who t Captain John Shales after dinner carried me aside and showed me a letter from his poor brother at Cambridge to me of the same contents with that yesterday to me desiring help from me. Here I was among a sorry company without any content or pleasure, and at the last the reckoning coming to above 40s. by 15s., he would have me pay the 10s. and he would pay the 5s., which was so poor that I was ashamed of it, and did it only to save contending with him. There, after agreeing a day for him and I to meet and seal our agreement, I parted and home, and at the office by agreement came Mr. Shales, and there he and I discourse till late the business of his helping me in the discovery of some arrears of provisions and stores due to the stores at Portsmouth, out of which I may chance to get some money, and save the King some too, and therefore I shall endeavour to do the fellow some right in other things here to his advantage between Mr. Gauden and him. He gone my wife and I to her arithmetique, in which she pleases me well, and so to the office, there set down my Journall, and so home to supper and to bed. A little troubled to see how my family is out of order by Will's being there, and also to hear that Jane do not please my wife as I expected and would have wished.

6th. This morning waking, my wife was mighty-earnest with me to persuade me that she should prove with child since last night, which, if it be, let it come, and welcome. Up to my office, whither Commissioner Pett came, newly come out of the country, and he and I walked together in the garden talking of business a great while, and I perceive that by our countenancing of him he do begin to pluck up his head, and will do good things I hope in the yard. Thence, he being gone, to my office and there dispatched many people, and at noon to the 'Change to the coffee-house, and among other things heard Sir John Cutler say, that of his owne experience in time of thunder, so many barrels of beer as have a piece of iron laid upon them will not be soured, and the others will. Thence to the 'Change, and there discoursed with many people, and I hope to settle again to my business and revive my report of following of business, which by my being taken off for a while by sickness and, laying out of money has slackened for a little while. Home, and there found Mrs. Hunt, who dined very merry, good woman; with us. After dinner came in Captain Grove, and he and I alone to talk of many things, and among many others of the Fishery, in which he gives the such hopes that being at this time full of projects how to get a little honestly, of which some of them I trust in God will take, I resolved this afternoon to go and consult my Lord Sandwich about it, and so, being to carry home Mrs. Hunt, I took her and my wife by coach and set them at Axe Yard, and I to my Lord's and thither sent for Creed and discoursed with him about it, and he and I to White Hall, where Sir G. Carteret and my Lord met me very fortunately, and wondered first to see me in my perruque, and I am glad it is over, and then, Sir G. Carteret being gone, I took my Lord aside, who do give me the best advice he can, and telling me how there are some projectors, by name Sir Edward Ford, who would have the making of farthings,

[Sir Edward Ford, son of Sir William Ford of Harting, born at Up Park in 1605. "After the Restoration he invented a mode of coining farthings. Each piece was to differ minutely from another to prevent forgery. He failed in procuring a patent for these in England, but obtained one for Ireland. He died in Ireland before he could carry his design into execution, on September 3rd, 1670" ("Dictionary of National Biography ").]

and out of that give so much to the King for the maintenance of the Fishery; but my Lord do not like that, but would have it go as they offered the last year, and so upon my desire he promises me when it is seasonable to bring me into the commission with others, if any of them take, and I perceive he and Mr. Coventry are resolved to follow it hard. Thence, after walking a good while in the Long gallery, home to my Lord's lodging, my Lord telling me how my father did desire him to speak to me about my giving of my sister something, which do vex me to see that he should trouble my Lord in it, but however it is a good occasion for me to tell my Lord my condition, and so I was glad of it. After that we begun to talk of the Court, and he tells me how Mr. Edward Montagu begins to show respect to him again after his endeavouring to bespatter him all was, possible; but he is resolved never to admit him into his friendship again. He tells me how he and Sir H. Bennet, the Duke of Buckingham and his Duchesse, was of a committee with somebody else for the getting of Mrs. Stewart for the King; but that she proves a cunning slut, and is advised at Somerset House by the Queene-Mother, and by her mother, and so all the plot is spoiled and the whole committee broke. Mr. Montagu and the Duke of Buckingham fallen a-pieces, the Duchesse going to a nunnery; and so Montagu begins to enter friendship with my Lord, and to attend the Chancellor whom he had deserted. My Lord tells me that Mr. Montagu, among other things, did endeavour to represent him to the Chancellor's sons as one that did desert their father in the business of my Lord of Bristoll; which is most false, being the only man that hath several times dined with him when no soul hath come to him, and went with him that very day home when the Earl impeached him in the Parliament House, and hath refused ever to pay a visit to my Lord of Bristoll, not so much as in return to a visit of his. So that the Chancellor and my Lord are well known and trusted one by another. But yet my Lord blames the Chancellor for desiring to have it put off to the next Session of Parliament, contrary to my Lord Treasurer's advice, to whom he swore he would not do it: and, perhaps, my Lord Chancellor, for aught I see by my Lord's discourse, may suffer by it when the Parliament comes to sit. My Lord tells me that he observes the Duke of York do follow and understand business very well, and is mightily improved thereby. Here Mr. Pagett coming in I left my Lord and him, and thence I called my wife and her maid Jane and by coach home and to my office, where late writing some things against tomorrow, and so home to supper and to bed. This morning Mr. Blackburne came to me to let me know that he had got a lodging very commodious for his kinsman, and so he is ready at my pleasure to go when I would bid him, and so I told him that I would in a day or two send to speak with him and he and I would talk and advise Will what to do, of which I am very glad.

7th. Up and to the office, where we sat all the morning, and Sir W. Pen and I had a word or two, where by opposing him in not being willing to excuse a mulct put upon the purser of the James, absent from duty, he says, by his business and order, he was mighty angry, and went out of the office like an asse discontented: At which I am never a whit sorry; I would not have [him] think that I dare not oppose him, where I see reason and cause for it. Home to dinner, and then by coach abroad about several businesses to several places, among others to Westminster Hall, where, seeing Howlett's daughter going out of the other end of the Hall, I followed her if I would to have offered talk to her and dallied with her a little, but I could not overtake her. Then calling at Unthank's for something of my wife's not done, a pretty little gentlewoman, a lodger there, came out to tell me that it was not yet done, which though it vexed me yet I took opportunity of taking her by the hand with the boot, and so found matter to talk a little the longer to her, but I was ready to laugh at myself to see how my anger would not operate, my disappointment coming to me by such a messenger. Thence to Doctors' Commons and there consulted Dr. Turner about some differences we have with the officers of the East India ships about goods brought by them without paying freight, which we demand of them. So home to my office, and there late writing letters, and so home to supper and to bed, having got a scurvy cold by lying cold in my head the last night. This day Captain Taylor brought me a piece of plate, a little small state dish, he expecting that I should get him some allowance for demorage

["'Demurrage' is the compensation due to a shipowner from a freighter for unduly decaying his vessel in port beyond the time specified in the charter-party or bill of lading. It is in fact an extended freight. A ship, unjustly detained as a prize is entitled to 'demurrage.'"—Smyth's Sailor's Word-Book, 1867.]

of his ship "William," kept long at Tangier, which I shall and may justly do.

8th (Lord's day). Up, and it being late, to church without my wife, and there I saw Pembleton come into the church and bring his wife with him, a good comely plain woman, and by and by my wife came after me all alone, which I was a little vexed at. I found that my coming in a perriwigg did not prove so strange to the world as I was afear'd it would, for I thought that all the church would presently have cast their eyes all upon me, but I found no such thing. Here an ordinary lazy sermon of Mr. Mill's, and then home to dinner, and there Tom came and dined with us; and after dinner to talk about a new black cloth suit that I have a making, and so at church time to church again, where the Scott preached, and I slept most of the time. Thence home, and I spent most of the evening upon Fuller's "Church History" and Barckly's

"Argeny," and so after supper to prayers and to bed, a little fearing my pain coming back again, myself continuing as costive as ever, and my physic ended, but I had sent a porter to-day for more and it was brought me before I went to bed, and so with pretty good content to bed.

9th. Up and found myself very well, and so by coach to White Hall and there met all my fellow officers, and so to the Duke, where, when we came into his closett, he told us that Mr. Pepys was so altered with his new perriwigg that he did not know him. So to our discourse, and among and above other things we were taken up in talking upon Sir J. Lawson's coming home, he being come to Portsmouth; and Captain Berkely is come to towne with a letter from the Duana of Algier to the King, wherein they do demand again the searching of our ships and taking out of strangers, and their goods; and that what English ships are taken without the Duke's pass they will detain (though it be flat contrary to the words of the peace) as prizes, till they do hear from our King, which they advise him may be speedy. And this they did the very next day after they had received with great joy the Grand Seignor's confirmation of the Peace from Constantinople by Captain Berkely; so that there is no command nor certainty to be had of these people. The King is resolved to send his will by a fleete of ships; and it is thought best and speediest to send these very ships that are now come home, five sail of good ships, back again after cleaning, victualling, and paying them. But it is a pleasant thing to think how their Basha, Shavan Aga, did tear his hair to see the soldiers order things thus; for (just like his late predecessor) when they see the evil of war with England, then for certain they complain to the Grand Seignor of him, and cut his head off: this he is sure of, and knows as certain. Thence to Westminster Hall, where I met with Mr. Pierce, chyrurgeon; and among other things he asked me seriously whether I knew anything of my Lord's being out of favour with the King; and told me, that for certain the King do take mighty notice of my Lord's living obscurely in a corner not like himself, and becoming the honour that he is come to. I was sorry to hear, and the truth is, from my Lord's discourse among his people (which I am told) of the uncertainty of princes' favours, and his melancholy keeping from Court, I am doubtful of some such thing; but I seemed wholly strange to him in it, but will make my use of it. He told me also how loose the Court is, nobody looking after business, but every man his lust and gain; and how the King is now become besotted upon Mrs. Stewart, that he gets into corners, and will be with her half an houre together kissing her to the observation of all the world; and she now stays by herself and expects it, as my Lady Castlemaine did use to do; to whom the King, he says, is still kind, so as now and then he goes to have a chat with her as he believes; but with no such fondness as he used to do. But yet it is thought that this new wench is so subtle, that she lets him not do any thing than is safe to her, but yet his doting is so great that, Pierce tells me, it is verily thought if the Queene had died, he would have married her. The Duke of Monmouth is to have part of the Cockpitt new built for lodgings for him, and they say to be made Captain of the Guards in the room of my Lord Gerard. Having thus talked with him, there comes into the Hall Creed and Ned Pickering, and after a turne or two with them, it being noon, I walked with them two to the King's Head ordinary, and there we dined; little discourse but what was common, only that the Duke of Yorke is a very, desperate huntsman, but I was ashamed of Pickering, who could not forbear having up my Lord Sandwich now and then in the most paltry matters abominable. Thence I took leave of them, and so having taken up something at my wife's tailor's, I home by coach and there to my office, whither Shales came and I had much discourse with him about the business of the victualling, and thence in the evening to the Coffeehouse, and there sat till by and by, by appointment Will brought me word that his uncle Blackburne was ready to speak with me. So I went down to him, and he and I to a taverne hard by, and there I begun to speak to Will friendlily, advising him how to carry himself now he is going from under my roof, without any reflections upon the occasion from whence his removal arose. This his uncle seconded, and after laying down to him his duty to me, and what I expect of him, in a discourse of about a quarter of an houre or more, we agreed upon his going this week, towards the latter (end) of the week, and so dismissed him, and Mr. Blackburne and I fell to talk of many things, wherein I did speak so freely to him in many things agreeing with his sense that he was very open to me: first, in that of religion, he makes it great matter of prudence for the King and Council to suffer liberty of conscience; and imputes the losse of Hungary to the Turke from the Emperor's denying them this liberty of their religion. He says that many pious ministers of the word of God, some thousands of them, do now beg their bread: and told me how highly the present clergy carry themselves every where, so as that they are hated and laughed at by everybody; among other things, for their excommunications, which they send upon the least occasions almost that can be. And I am convinced in my judgement, not only from his discourse, but my thoughts in general, that the present clergy will never heartily go down with the generality of the commons of England; they have been so used to liberty and freedom, and they are so acquainted with the pride and debauchery of the present clergy. He did give me many stories of the affronts which the clergy receive in all places of England from the gentry and ordinary persons of the parish. He do tell me what the City thinks of General Monk, as of a most perfidious man that hath betrayed every body, and the King also; who, as he thinks, and his party, and so I have heard other good friends of the King say, it might have been better for the King to have had his hands a little bound for the present, than be forced to bring such a crew of poor people about him, and be liable to satisfy the demands of every one of them. He told me that to his knowledge (being present at every meeting at the Treaty at the Isle of Wight), that the old King did confess himself overruled and convinced in his judgement against the Bishopps, and would have suffered and did agree to exclude the service out of the churches, nay his own chappell; and that he did always say, that this he did not by force, for that he would never abate one inch by any vyolence; but what he did was out of his reason and judgement. He tells me that the King by name, with all his dignities, is prayed for by them that they call Fanatiques, as heartily and powerfully as in any of the other churches that are thought better: and that, let the King think what he will, it is them that must helpe him in the day of warr. For as they are the most, so generally they are the most substantial sort of people, and the soberest; and did desire me to observe it to my Lord Sandwich, among other things, that of all the old army now you cannot see a man begging about the street; but what? You shall have this captain turned a shoemaker; the lieutenant, a baker; this a brewer; that a haberdasher; this common soldier, a porter; and every man in his apron and frock, &c., as if they never had done anything else: whereas the others go with their belts and swords, swearing and cursing, and stealing; running into people's houses, by force oftentimes, to carry away something; and this is the difference between the temper of one and the other; and concludes (and I think with some reason,) that the spirits of the old parliament soldiers are so quiett and contented with God's providences, that the King is safer from any evil meant him by them one thousand times more than from his own discontented Cavalier. And then to the publique management of business: it is done, as he observes, so loosely and so carelessly, that the kingdom can never be happy with it, every man looking after himself, and his owne lust and luxury; among other things he instanced in the business of money, he do believe that half of what money the Parliament gives the King is not so much as gathered. And to the purpose he told me how the Bellamys (who had some of the Northern counties assigned them for their debt for the petty warrant victualling) have often complained to him that they cannot get it collected, for that nobody minds, or, if they do, they won't pay it in. Whereas (which is a very remarkable thing,) he hath been told by some of the Treasurers at Warr here of late, to whom the most of the L120,000 monthly was paid, that for most months the payments were gathered so duly, that they seldom had so much or more than 40s., or the like, short in the whole collection; whereas now the very Commissioners for Assessments and other publique payments are such persons, and those that they choose in the country so like themselves, that from top to bottom there is not a man carefull of any thing, or if he be, he is not solvent; that what between the beggar and the knave, the King is abused the best part of all his revenue. From thence we began to talk of the Navy, and particularly of Sir W. Pen, of whose rise to be a general I had a mind to be informed. He told me he was always a conceited man, and one that would put the best side outward, but that it was his pretence of sanctity that brought him into play. Lawson, and Portman, and the Fifth-monarchy men, among whom he was a great brother, importuned that he might be general; and it was pleasant to see how Blackburne himself did act it, how when the Commissioners of the Admiralty would enquire of the captains and admirals of such and such men, how they would with a sigh and casting up the eyes say, "Such a man fears the Lord," or, "I hope such a man hath the Spirit of God," and such things as that. But he tells me that there was a cruel articling against Pen after one fight, for cowardice, in putting himself within a coyle of cables, of which he had much ado to acquit himself: and by great friends did it, not without remains of guilt, but that his brethren had a mind to pass it by, and Sir H. Vane did advise him to search his heart, and see whether this fault or a greater sin was not the occasion of this so great tryall. And he tells me, that what Pen gives out about Cromwell's sending and entreating him to go to Jamaica, is very false; he knows the contrary: besides, the Protector never was a man that needed to send for any man, specially such a one as he, twice. He tells me that the business of Jamaica did miscarry absolutely by his pride, and that when he was in the Tower he would cry like a child. This he says of his own personal knowledge, and lastly tells me that just upon the turne, when Monk was come from the North to the City, and did begin to think of bringing in the King, Pen was then turned Quaker. This he is most certain of. He tells me that Lawson was never counted any thing but only a seaman, and a stout man, but a false man, and that now he appears the greatest hypocrite in the world. And Pen the same. He tells me that it is much talked of, that the King intends to legitimate the Duke of Monmouth; and that he has not, nor his friends of his persuasion, have any hopes of getting their consciences at liberty but by God Almighty's turning of the King's heart, which they expect, and are resolved to live and die in quiett hopes of it; but never to repine, or act any thing more than by prayers towards it. And that not only himself but all of them have, and are willing at any time to take the oaths of Allegiance and Supremacy. Thus far, and upon many more things, we had discoursed when some persons in a room hard by began to sing in three parts very finely and to play upon a flagilette so pleasantly that my discourse afterwards was but troublesome, and I could not attend it, and so, anon, considering of a sudden the time of night, we found it 11 o'clock, which I thought it had not been by two hours, but we were close in talk, and so we rose, he having drunk some wine and I some beer and sugar, and so by a fair moonshine home and to bed, my wife troubled with tooth ache. Mr. Blackburne observed further to me, some certain notice that he had of the present plot so much talked of; that he was told by Mr. Rushworth, how one Captain Oates, a great discoverer, did employ several to bring and seduce others into a plot, and that one of his agents met with one that would not listen to him, nor conceal what he had offered him, but so detected the trapan. This, he says, is most true. He also, among other instances how the King is served, did much insist upon the cowardice and corruption of the King's guards and militia, which to be sure will fail the King, as they have done already, when there will be occasion for them.

10th. Up and to the office, where we sat till noon, and then to the Exchange, where spoke with several and had my head casting about how to get a penny and I hope I shall, and then hone, and there Mr. Moore by appointment dined with me, and after dinner all the afternoon till night drawing a bond and release against to-morrow for T. Trice, and I to come to a conclusion in which I proceed with great fear and jealousy, knowing him to be a rogue and one that I fear has at this time got too great a hank—[hold]—over me by the neglect of my lawyers. But among other things I am come to an end with Mr. Moore for a L32, a good while lying in my hand of my Lord Privy Seal's which he for the odd L7 do give me a bond to secure me against, and so I got L25 clear. Then, he being gone, to the office and there late setting down yesterday's remarkable discourses, and so home to supper, late, and to bed. The Queene, I hear, is now very well again, and that she hath bespoke herself a new gowne.

11th. Up and to my office all the morning, and at noon to the Coffee-house, where with Dr. Allen some good discourse about physique and chymistry. And among other things, I telling him what Dribble the German Doctor do offer of an instrument to sink ships; he tells me that which is more strange, that something made of gold, which they call in chymistry Aurum fulminans, a grain, I think he said, of it put into a silver spoon and fired, will give a blow like a musquett, and strike a hole through the spoon downward, without the least force upward; and this he can make a cheaper experiment of, he says, with iron prepared. Thence to the 'Change, and being put off a meeting with T. Trice, he not coming, I home to dinner, and after dinner by coach with my wife to my periwigg maker's for my second periwigg, but it is not done, and so, calling at a place or two, home, and there to my office, and there taught my wife a new lesson in arithmetique and so sent her home, and I to several businesses; and so home to supper and to bed, being mightily troubled with a cold in my stomach and head, with a great pain by coughing.

12th. Lay long in bed, indeed too long, divers people and the officers staying for me. My cozen Thomas Pepys the executor being below, and I went to him and stated reckonings about our debt, for his payments of money to my uncle Thomas heretofore by the Captain's orders. I did not pay him but will soon do it if I can. To the office and there all the morning, where Sir W. Pen, like a coxcomb, was so ready to cross me in a motion I made unawares for the entering a man at Chatham into the works, wherein I was vexed to see his spleene, but glad to understand it, and that it was in no greater a matter, I being not at all concerned here. To the 'Change and did several businesses there and so home with Mr. Moore to dinner, my wife having dined, with Mr. Hollyard with her to-day, he being come to advise her about her hollow sore place. After dinner Mr. Moore and I discoursing of my Lord's negligence in attendance at Court, and the discourse the world makes of it, with the too great reason that I believe there is for it; I resolved and took coach to his lodgings, thinking to speak with my Lord about it without more ado. Here I met Mr. Howe, and he and I largely about it, and he very soberly acquainted me how things are with my Lord, that my Lord do not do anything like himself, but follows his folly, and spends his time either at cards at Court with the ladies, when he is there at all, or else at Chelsy with the slut to his great disgrace, and indeed I do see and believe that my Lord do apprehend that he do grow less too at Court. Anon my Lord do come in, and I begun to fall in discourse with him, but my heart did misgive me that my Lord would not take it well, and then found him not in a humour to talk, and so after a few ordinary words, my Lord not talking in the manner as he uses to do; I took leave, and spent some time with W. Howe again, and told him how I could not do what I had so great a mind and resolution to do, but that I thought it would be as well to do it in writing, which he approves of, and so I took leave of him, and by coach home, my mind being full of it, and in pain concerning it. So to my office busy very late, the nights running on faster than one thinks, and so to supper and to bed.

13th. Up and to my office, busy all the morning with Commissioner Pett; at noon I to the Exchange, and meeting Shales, he and I to the Coffee-house and there talked of our victualling matters, which I fear will come to little. However I will go on and carry it as far as I can. So home to dinner where I expected Commissioner Pett, and had a good dinner, but he came not. After dinner came my perriwigg-maker, and brings me a second periwigg, made of my own haire, which comes to 21s. 6d. more than the worth of my own haire, so that they both come to L4 1s. 6d., which he sayth will serve me two years, but I fear it. He being gone, I to my office, and put on my new shagg purple gowne, with gold buttons and loop lace, I being a little fearful of taking cold and of pain coming upon me. Here I staid making an end of a troublesome letter, but to my advantage, against Sir W. Batten, giving Sir G. Carteret an account of our late great contract with Sir W. Warren for masts, wherein I am sure I did the King L600 service. That done home to my wife to take a clyster, which I did, and it wrought very well and brought a great deal of wind, which I perceive is all that do trouble me. After that, about 9 or 10 o'clock, to supper in my wife's chamber, and then about 12 to bed.

14th. Up and to the office, where we sat, and after we had almost done, Sir W. Batten desired to have the room cleared, and there he did acquaint the board how he was obliged to answer to something lately said which did reflect upon the Comptroller and him, and to that purpose told how the bargain for Winter's timber did not prove so bad as I had reported to the board it would. After he had done I cleared the matter that I did not mention the business as a thing designed by me against them, but was led to it by Sir J. Minnes, and that I said nothing but what I was told by Mayers the surveyor as much as by Deane upon whom they laid all the fault, which I must confess did and do still trouble me, for they report him to be a fellow not fit to be employed, when in my conscience he deserves better than any officer in the yard. I thought it not convenient to vindicate him much now, but time will serve when I will do it, and I am bound to do it. I offered to proceed to examine and prove what I said if they please, but Mr. Coventry most discreetly advised not, it being to no purpose, and that he did believe that what I said did not by my manner of speaking it proceed from any design of reproaching them, and so it ended. But my great trouble is for poor Deane. At noon home and dined with my wife, and after dinner Will told me if I pleased he was ready to remove his things, and so before my wife I did give him good counsel, and that his going should not abate my kindnesse for him, if he carried himself well, and so bid "God bless him," and left him to remove his things, the poor lad weeping, but I am apt to think matters will be the better both for him and us. So to the office and there late busy. In the evening Mr. Moore came to tell me that he had no opportunity of speaking his mind to my Lord yesterday, and so I am resolved to write to him very suddenly. So after my business done I home, I having staid till 12 o'clock at night almost, making an end of a letter to Sir G. Carteret about the late contract for masts, wherein I have done myself right, and no wrong to Sir W. Batten. This night I think is the first that I have lain without ever a man in my house besides myself, since I came to keep any. Will being this night gone to his lodging, and by the way I hear to-day that my boy Waynman has behaved himself so with Mr. Davis that they have got him put into a Barbadoes ship to be sent away, and though he sends to me to get a release for him I will not out of love to the boy, for I doubt to keep him here were to bring him to the gallows.

15th (Lord's day). Lay very long in bed with my wife and then up and to my office there to copy fair my letter to Sir G. Carteret, which I did, and by and by most opportunely a footman of his came to me about other business, and so I sent it him by his own servant. I wish good luck with it. At noon home to dinner, my wife not being up, she lying to expect Mr. Holyard the surgeon. So I dined by myself, and in the afternoon to my office again, and there drew up a letter to my Lord, stating to him what the world talks concerning him, and leaving it to him and myself to be thought of by him as he pleases, but I have done but my duty in it. I wait Mr. Moore's coming for his advice about sending it. So home to supper to my wife, myself finding myself by cold got last night beginning to have some pain, which grieves me much in my mind to see to what a weakness I am come. This day being our Queene's birthday, the guns of the Tower went all off; and in the evening the Lord Mayor sent from church to church to order the constables to cause bonfires to be made in every streete, which methinks is a poor thing to be forced to be commanded. After a good supper with my wife, and hearing of the mayds read in the Bible, we to prayers, and to bed.

16th. Up, and being ready then abroad by coach to White Hall, and there with the Duke, where Mr. Coventry did a second time go to vindicate himself against reports and prove by many testimonies that he brought, that he did nothing but what had been done by the Lord Admiral's secretaries heretofore, though he do not approve of it, nor since he had any rule from the Duke hath he exceeded what he is there directed to take, and the thing I think is very clear that they always did take and that now he do take less than ever they did heretofore. Thence away, and Sir G. Carteret did call me to him and discourse with me about my letter yesterday, and did seem to take it unkindly that I should doubt of his satisfaction in the bargain of masts, and did promise me that hereafter whatever he do hear to my prejudice he would tell me before he would believe it, and that this was only Sir W. Batten's report in this business, which he says he did ever approve of, in which I know he lies. Thence to my Lord's lodgings thinking to find Mr. Moore, in order to the sending away my letter of reproof to my Lord, but I do not find him, but contrary do find my Lord come to Court, which I am glad to hear and should be more glad to hear that he do follow his business that I may not have occasion to venture upon his good nature by such a provocation as my letter will be to him. So by coach home, to the Exchange, where I talked about several businesses with several people, and so home to dinner with my wife, and then in the afternoon to my office, and there late, and in the evening Mr. Hollyard came, and he and I about our great work to look upon my wife's malady, which he did, and it seems her great conflux of humours, heretofore that did use to swell there, did in breaking leave a hollow which has since gone in further and further; till now it is near three inches deep, but as God will have it do not run into the bodyward, but keeps to the outside of the skin, and so he must be forced to cut it open all along, and which my heart I doubt will not serve for me to see done, and yet she will not have any body else to see it done, no, not her own mayds, and so I must do it, poor wretch, for her. To-morrow night he is to do it. He being gone, I to my office again a little while, and so home to supper and to bed.

17th. Up, and while I am dressing myself, Mr. Deane of Woolwich came to me, and I did tell him what had happened to him last Saturday in the office, but did encourage him to make no matter of it, for that I did not fear but he would in a little time be master of his enemies as much as they think to master him, and so he did tell me many instances of the abominable dealings of Mr. Pett of Woolwich towards him. So we broke up, and I to the office, where we sat all the forenoon doing several businesses, and at noon I to the 'Change where Mr. Moore came to me, and by and by Tom Trice and my uncle Wight, and so we out to a taverne (the New Exchange taverne over against the 'Change where I never was before, and I found my old playfellow Ben Stanley master of it), and thence to a scrivener to draw up a bond, and to another tavern (the King's Head) we went, and calling on my cozen Angier at the India House there we eat a bit of pork from a cookes together, and after dinner did seal the bond, and I did take up the old bond of my uncle's to my aunt, and here T. Trice before them do own all matters in difference between us is clear as to this business, and that he will in six days give me it under the hand of his attorney that there is no judgment against the bond that may give me any future trouble, and also a copy of their letters of his Administration to Godfrey, as much of it as concerns me to have. All this being done towards night we broke up, and so I home and with Mr. Moore to my office, and there I read to him the letter I have wrote to send to my

Lord to give him an account how the world, both city and court, do talk of him and his living as he do there in such a poor and bad house so much to his disgrace. Which Mr. Moore do conclude so well drawn: that he would not have me by any means to neglect sending it, assuring me in the best of his judgment that it cannot but endear me to my Lord instead of what I fear of getting his offence, and did offer to take the same words and send them as from, him with his hand to him, which I am not unwilling should come (if they are at all fit to go) from any body but myself, and so, he being gone, I did take a copy of it to keep by me in shorthand, and sealed them up to send to-morrow by my Will. So home, Mr. Hollyard being come to my wife, and there she being in bed, he and I alone to look again upon her . . . . and there he do find that, though it would not be much pain, yet she is so fearful, and the thing will be somewhat painful in the tending, which I shall not be able to look after, but must require a nurse and people about her; so that upon second thoughts he believes that a fomentation will do as well, and though it will be troublesome yet no pain, and what her mayd will be able to do without knowing directly what it is for, but only that it may be for the piles. For though it be nothing but what is fiery honest, yet my wife is loth to give occasion of discourse concerning it. By this my mind and my wife's is much eased, for I confess I should have been troubled to have had my wife cut before my face, I could not have borne to have seen it. I had great discourse with him about my disease. He tells me again that I must eat in a morning some loosening gruel, and at night roasted apples, that I must drink now and then ale with my wine, and eat bread and butter and honey, and rye bread if I can endure it, it being loosening. I must also take once a week a clyster of his last prescription, only honey now and then instead of butter, which things I am now resolved to apply myself to. He being gone I to my office again to a little business, and then home to supper and to bed, being in, a little pain by drinking of cold small beer to-day and being in a cold room at the Taverne I believe.

18th. Up, and after being ready, and done a little business at the office, I and Mr. Hater by water to Redriffe, and so walked to Deptford, where I have not been a very great, while, and there paid off the Milford in very good order, and all respect showed me in the office as much as there used to be to any of the rest or the whole board. That done at noon I took Captain Terne, and there coming in by chance Captain Berkeley, him also to dinner with me to the Globe. Captain Berkeley, who was lately come from Algier, did give us a good account of the place, and how the Basha there do live like a prisoner, being at the mercy of the soldiers and officers, so that there is nothing but a great confusion there. After dinner came Sir W. Batten, and I left him to pay off another ship, and I walked home again reading of a little book of new poems of Cowley's, given me by his brother. Abraham do lie, it seems, very sicke, still, but like to recover. At my office till late, and then came Mr. Hollyard so full of discourse and Latin that I think he hath got a cupp, but I do not know; but full of talke he is in defence of Calvin and Luther. He begun this night the fomentation to my wife, and I hope it will do well with her. He gone, I to the office again a little, and so to bed. This morning I sent Will with my great letter of reproof to my Lord Sandwich, who did give it into his owne hand. I pray God give a blessing to it, but confess I am afeard what the consequence may be to me of good or bad, which is according to the ingenuity that he do receive it with. However, I am satisfied that it will do him good, and that he needs it:

My lord,

I do verily hope that neither the manner nor matter of this advice will be condemned by your Lordship, when for my defence in the first I shall alledge my double attempt, since your return from Hinchinbroke, of doing it personally, in both of which your Lordship's occasions, no doubtfulnesse of mine, prevented me, and that being now fearful of a sudden summons to Portsmouth, for the discharge of some ships there, I judge it very unbecoming the duty which every bit of bread I eat tells me I owe to your Lordship to expose the safety of your honour to the uncertainty of my return. For the matter, my Lord, it is such as could I in any measure think safe to conceal from, or likely to be discovered to you by any other hand, I should not have dared so far to owne what from my heart I believe is false, as to make myself but the relater of other's discourse; but, sir, your Lordship's honour being such as I ought to value it to be, and finding both in city and court that discourses pass to your prejudice, too generally for mine or any man's controllings but your Lordship's, I shall, my Lord, without the least greatening or lessening the matter, do my duty in laying it shortly before you.

People of all conditions, my Lord, raise matter of wonder from your Lordship's so little appearance at Court: some concluding thence their disfavour thereby, to which purpose I have had questions asked me, and endeavouring to put off such insinuations by asserting the contrary, they have replied, that your Lordship's living so beneath your quality, out of the way, and declining of Court attendance, hath been more than once discoursed about the King. Others, my Lord, when the chief ministers of State, and those most active of the Council have been reckoned up, wherein your Lordship never used to want an eminent place, have said, touching your Lordship, that now your turn was served, and the King had given you a good estate, you left him to stand or fall as he would, and, particularly in that of the Navy, have enlarged upon your letting fall all service there.

Another sort, and those the most, insist upon the bad report of the house wherein your Lordship, now observed in perfect health again, continues to sojourne, and by name have charged one of the daughters for a common courtizan, alledging both places and persons where and with whom she hath been too well known, and how much her wantonnesse occasions, though unjustly, scandal to your Lordship, and that as well to gratifying of some enemies as to the wounding of more friends I am not able to tell.

Lastly, my Lord, I find a general coldness in all persons towards your Lordship, such as, from my first dependance on you, I never yet knew, wherein I shall not offer to interpose any thoughts or advice of mine, well knowing your Lordship needs not any. But with a most faithful assurance that no person nor papers under Heaven is privy to what I here write, besides myself and this, which I shall be careful to have put into your owne hands, I rest confident of your Lordship's just construction of my dutifull intents herein, and in all humility take leave, may it please your Lordship,

Your Lordship's most obedient Servant, S. P.

The foregoing letter was sealed up, and enclosed in this that follows

My lord,

If this finds your Lordship either not alone, or not at leisure, I beg the suspending your opening of the enclosed till you shall have both, the matter very well bearing such a delay, and in all humility remain, may it please your Lordship,

Your Lordship's most obedient Servant, S. P.

November 17, 1663.

My servant hath my directions to put this into your Lordship's owne hand, but not to stay for any answer.

19th. Up, and to the office, where (Sir J. Minnes and Sir W. Batten being gone this morning to Portsmouth) the rest of us met, and rode at noon. So I to the 'Change, where little business, and so home to dinner, and being at dinner Mr. Creed in and dined with us, and after dinner Mr. Gentleman, my Jane's father, to see us and her. And after a little stay with them, I was sent for by Sir G. Carteret by agreement, and so left them, and to him and with him by coach to my Lord Treasurer, to discourse with him about Mr. Gauden's having of money, and to offer to him whether it would not be necessary, Mr. Gauden's credit being so low as it is, to take security of him if he demands any great sum, such as L20,000, which now ought to be paid him upon his next year's declaration. Which is a sad thing, that being reduced to this by us, we should be the first to doubt his credit; but so it is. However, it will be managed with great tenderness to him. My Lord Treasurer we found in his bed-chamber, being laid up of the goute. I find him a very ready man, and certainly a brave servant to the

King: he spoke so quick and sensibly of the King's charge. Nothing displeased me in him but his long nails, which he lets grow upon a pretty thick white short hand, that it troubled me to see them. Thence with Sir G. Carteret by coach, and he set me down at the New Exchange. In our way he told me there is no such thing likely yet as a Dutch war, neither they nor we being in condition for it, though it will come certainly to that in some time, our interests lying the same way, that is to say, in trade. But not yet. Thence to the Temple, and there visited my cozen Roger Pepys and his brother Dr. John, a couple, methinks, of very ordinary men, and thence to speak [with] Mr. Moore, and met him by the way, who tells me, to my great content, that he believes my letter to my Lord Sandwich hath wrought well upon him, and that he will look after himself and his business upon it, for he begins already to do so. But I dare not conclude anything till I see him, which shall be to-morrow morning, that I may be out of my pain to know how he takes it of me. He and I to the Coffee-house, and there drank and talked a little, and so I home, and after a little at my office home to supper and to bed, not knowing how to avoid hopes from Mr. Moore's words to-night, and yet I am fearful of the worst.

20th. Up, and as soon as I could to my Lord Sandwich's lodgings, but he was gone out before, and so I am defeated of my expectation of being eased one way or other in the business of my Lord. But I went up to Mr. Howe, who I saw this day the first time in a periwigg, which becomes him very well, and discoursed with him. He tells me that my Lord is of a sudden much changed, and he do believe that he do take my letter well. However, we do both bless God that it hath so good an effect upon him. Thence I home again, calling at the Wardrobe, where I found my Lord, but so busy with Mr. Townsend making up accounts there that I was unwilling to trouble him, and so went away. By and by to the Exchange, and there met by agreement Mr. Howe, and took him with a barrel of oysters home to dinner, where we were very merry, and indeed I observe him to be a very hopeful young man, but only a little conceited. After dinner I took him and my wife, and setting her in Covent Garden at her mother's, he and I to my Lord's, and thence I with Mr. Moore to White Hall, there the King and Council being close, and I thinking it an improper place to meet my Lord first upon the business; I took coach, and calling my wife went home, setting Mr. Moore down by the way, and having been late at the office alone looking over some plates of the Northern seas, the White seas, and Archangell river, I went home, and, after supper, to bed. My wife tells me that she and her brother have had a great falling out to-night, he taking upon him to challenge great obligation upon her, and taxing her for not being so as she ought to be to her friends, and that she can do more with me than she pretends, and I know not what, but God be thanked she cannot. A great talke there is today of a crush between some of the Fanatiques up in arms, and the King's men in the North; but whether true I know not yet.

21st. At the office all the morning and at noon I receive a letter from Mr. Creed, with a token, *viz*., a very noble parti-coloured Indian gowne for my wife. The letter is oddly writ, over-prizing his present, and little owning any past service of mine, but that this was his genuine respects, and I know not what: I confess I had expectations of a better account from him of my service about his accounts, and so give his boy 12d., and sent it back again, and after having been at the pay of a ship this afternoon at the Treasury, I went by coach to Ludgate, and, by pricing several there, I guess this gowne may be worth about L12 or L15. But, however, I expect at least L50 of him. So in the evening I wrote him a letter telling him clearly my mind, a copy of which I keep and of his letter and so I resolve to have no more such correspondence as I used to have but will have satisfaction of him as I do expect. So to write my letters, and after all done I went home to supper and to bed, my mind being pretty well at ease from my letter to Creed, and more for my receipt this afternoon of L17 at the Treasury, for the L17 paid a year since to the carver for his work at my house, which I did intend to have paid myself, but, finding others to do it, I thought it not amisse to get it too, but I am afeard that we may hear of it to our greater prejudices hereafter.

22nd (Lord's day). Up pretty early, and having last night bespoke a coach, which failed me this morning, I walked as far as the Temple, and there took coach, and to my Lord's lodgings, whom I found ready to go to chappell; but I coming, he begun, with a very serious countenance, to tell me that he had received my late letter, wherein first he took notice of my care of him and his honour, and did give me thanks for that part of it where I say that from my heart I believe the contrary of what I do there relate to be the discourse of others; but since I intended it not a reproach, but matter of information, and for him to make a judgment of it for his practice, it was necessary for me to tell him the persons of whom I have gathered the several particulars which I there insist on. I would have made excuses in it; but, seeing him so earnest in it, I found myself forced to it, and so did tell him Mr. Pierce; the chyrurgeon, in that of his Lordship's living being discoursed of at Court; a mayd servant that-I kept, that lived at Chelsy school; and also Mr. Pickering, about the report touching the young woman; and also Mr. Hunt, in Axe Yard, near whom she lodged. I told him the whole city do discourse concerning his neglect of business; and so I many times asserting my dutifull intention in all this, and he owning his accepting of it as such. That that troubled me most in particular is, that he did there assert the civility of the people of the house, and the young gentlewoman, for whose reproach he was sorry. His saying that he was resolved how to live, and that though he was taking a house, meaning to live in another manner, yet it was not to please any people, or to stop report, but to please himself, though this I do believe he might say that he might not seem to me to be so much wrought upon by what I have writ; and lastly, and most of all, when I spoke of the tenderness that I have used in declaring this to him, there being nobody privy to it, he told me that I must give him leave to except one. I told him that possibly somebody might know of some thoughts of mine, I having borrowed some intelligence in this matter from them, but nobody could say they knew of the thing itself what I writ. This, I confess, however, do trouble me, for that he seemed to speak it as a quick retort, and it must sure be Will. Howe, who did not see anything of what I writ, though I told him indeed that I would write; but in this, I think, there is no great hurt. I find him, though he cannot but owne his opinion of my good intentions, and so, he did again and again profess it, that he is troubled in his mind at it; and I confess, I think I may have done myself an injury for his good, which, were it to do again, and that I believed he would take it no better, I think I should sit quietly without taking any notice of it, for I doubt there is no medium between his taking it very well or very ill. I could not forbear weeping before him at the latter end, which, since, I am ashamed of, though I cannot see what he can take it to proceed from but my tenderness and good will to him. After this discourse was ended, he began to talk very, cheerfully of other things, and I walked with him to White Hall, and we discoursed of the pictures in the gallery, which, it may be, he might do out of policy, that the boy might not see any, strangeness in him; but I rather think that his mind was somewhat eased, and hope that he will be to me as he was before. But, however, I doubt not when he sees that I follow my business, and become an honour to him, and not to be like to need him, or to be a burden to him, and rather able to serve him than to need him, and if he do continue to follow business, and so come to his right witts again, I do not doubt but he will then consider my faithfulnesse to him, and esteem me as he ought. At chappell I had room in the Privy Seale pew with other gentlemen, and there heard Dr. Killigrew, preach, but my mind was so, I know not whether troubled, or only full of thoughts of what had passed between my Lord and me that I could not mind it, nor can at this hour remember three words. The anthem was good after sermon, being the fifty-first psalme, made for five voices by one of Captain Cooke's boys, a pretty boy. And they say there are four or five of them that can do as much. And here I first perceived that the King is a little musicall, and kept good time with his hand all along the anthem. Up into the gallery after sermon and there I met Creed. We saluted one another and spoke but not one word of what had passed yesterday between us, but told me he was forced to such a place to dinner and so we parted. Here I met Mr. Povy, who tells me how Tangier had like to have been betrayed, and that one of the King's officers is come, to whom 8,000 pieces of eight were offered for his part. Hence I to the King's Head ordinary, and there dined, good and much company, and a good dinner: most of their discourse was about hunting, in a dialect I understand very little. Thence by coach to our own church, and there my mind being yet unsettled I could mind nothing, and after sermon home and there told my wife what had passed, and thence to my office, where doing business only to keep my mind employed till late; and so home to supper, to prayers, and to bed.

23rd: Up and to Alderman Backwell's, where Sir W. Rider, by appointment, met us to consult about the insuring of our hempe ship from Archangell, in which we are all much concerned, by my Lord Treasurer's command. That being put in a way I went to Mr. Beacham, one of our jury, to confer with him about our business with Field at our trial to-morrow, and thence to St. Paul's Churchyarde, and there bespoke "Rushworth's Collections," and "Scobell's Acts of the Long Parliament,"' &c., which I will make the King pay for as to the office; and so I do not break my vow at all. Back to the Coffee-house, and then to the 'Change, where Sir W. Rider and I did bid 15 per cent., and nobody will take it under 20 per cent., and the lowest was 15 per cent. premium, and 15 more to be abated in case of losse, which we did not think fit without order to give, and so we parted, and I home to a speedy, though too good a dinner to eat alone, *viz.*, a good goose and a rare piece of roast beef. Thence to the Temple, but being there too soon and meeting Mr. Moore I took him up and to my Lord Treasurer's, and thence to Sir Ph. Warwick's, where I found him and did desire his advice, who left me to do what I thought fit in this business of the insurance, and so back again to the Temple all the way telling Mr. Moore what had passed between my Lord and me yesterday, and indeed my fears do grow that my Lord will not reform as I hoped he would nor have the ingenuity to take my advice as he ought kindly. But however I am satisfied that the one person whom he said he would take leave to except is not Mr. Moore, and so W. Howe I am sure could tell him nothing of my letter that ever he saw it. Here Mr. Moore and I parted, and I up to the Speaker's chamber, and there met Mr. Coventry by appointment to discourse about Field's business, and thence we parting I homewards and called at the Coffeehouse, and there by great accident hear that a letter is come that our ship is safe come to Newcastle. With this news I went like an asse presently to Alderman Backewell and, told him of it, and he and I went to the African House in Broad Street to have spoke with Sir W. Rider to tell him of it, but missed him. Now what an opportunity had I to have concealed this and seemed to have made an insurance and got L100 with the least trouble and danger in the whole world. This troubles me to think I should be so oversoon. So back again with Alderman Backewell talking of the new money, which he says will never be counterfeited, he believes; but it is deadly inconvenient for telling, it is so thick, and the edges are made to turn up. I found him as full of business, and, to speak the truth, he is a very painfull man, and ever was, and now-a-days is well paid for it. So home and to my office, doing business late in order to the getting a little money, and so home to supper and to bed.

24th. Up and to the office, where we sat all the morning, and at noon to the 'Change, where everybody joyed me in our hemp ship's coming safe, and it seems one man, Middleburgh, did give 20 per cent. in gold last night, three or four minutes before the newes came of her being safe. Thence with Mr. Deane home and dined, and after dinner and a good deal of discourse of the business of Woolwich Yard, we opened his draught of a ship which he has made for me, and indeed it is a most excellent one and that that I hope will be of good use to me as soon as I get a little time, and much indebted I am to the poor man. Toward night I by coach to Whitehall to the Tangier committee, and there spoke with my Lord and he seems mighty kind to me, but I will try him to-morrow by a visit to see whether he holds it or no. Then home by coach again and to my office, where late with Captain Miners about the East India business. So home to supper and to bed, being troubled to find myself so bound as I am, notwithstanding all the physic that I take. This day our tryall was with Field, and I hear that they have given him L29 damage more, which is a strange thing, but yet not so much as formerly, nor as I was afeard of.

25th. Up and to Sir G. Carteret's house, and with him by coach to Whitehall. He uses me mighty well to my great joy, and in our discourse took occasion to tell me that as I did desire of him the other day so he desires of me the same favour that we may tell one another at any time any thing that passes among us at the office or elsewhere wherein we are either dissatisfied one with another, and that I should find him in all things as kind and ready to serve me as my own brother. This methinks-was very sudden and extraordinary and do please me mightily, and I am resolved by no means ever to lose him again if I can. He told me that he did still observe my care for the King's service in my office. He set me down in Fleet Street and thence I by another coach to my Lord Sandwich's, and there I did present him Mr. Barlow's "Terella," with which he was very much pleased, and he did show me great kindnesse, and by other discourse I have reason to think that he is not at all, as I feared he would be, discontented against me more than the trouble of the thing will work upon him. I left him in good humour, and I to White Hall, to the Duke of York and Mr. Coventry, and there advised about insuring the hempe ship at 12 per cent., notwithstanding her being come to Newcastle, and I do hope that in all my three places which are now my hopes and supports I may not now fear any thing, but with care, which through the Lord's blessing I will never more neglect, I don't doubt but to keep myself up with them all. For in the Duke, and Mr. Coventry, my Lord Sandwich and Sir G. Carteret I place my greatest hopes, and it pleased me yesterday that Mr. Coventry in the coach (he carrying me to the Exchange at noon from the office) did, speaking of Sir W. Batten, say that though there was a difference between them, yet he would embrace any good motion of Sir W. Batten to the King's advantage as well as of Mr. Pepys' or any friend he had. And when I talked that I would go about doing something of the Controller's work when I had time, and that I thought the Controller would not take it ill, he wittily replied that there was nothing in the world so hateful as a dog in the manger. Back by coach to the Exchange, there spoke with Sir W. Rider about insuring, and spoke with several other persons about business, and shall become pretty well known quickly. Thence home to dinner with my poor wife, and with great joy to my office, and there all the afternoon about business, and among others Mr. Bland came to me and had good discourse, and he has chose me a referee for him in a business, and anon in the evening comes Sir W. Warren, and he and I had admirable discourse. He advised me in things I desired about, bummary,—[bottomry]—and other ways of putting out money as in parts of ships, how dangerous they are, and lastly fell to talk of the Dutch management of the Navy, and I think will helpe me to some accounts of things of the Dutch Admiralty, which I am mighty desirous to know. He seemed to have been mighty privy with my Lord Albemarle in things before this great turn, and to the King's dallying with him and others for some years before, but I doubt all was not very true. However, his discourse is very useful in general, though he would seem a little more than ordinary in this. Late at night home to supper and to bed, my mind in good ease all but my health, of which I am not a little doubtful.

26th. Up and to the office, where we sat all the morning, and at noon I to the 'Change, and there met with Mr. Cutler the merchant, who would needs have me home to his house by the Dutch Church, and there in an old but good house, with his wife and mother, a couple of plain old women, I dined a good plain dinner, and his discourse after dinner with me upon matters of the navy victualling very good and worth my hearing, and so home to my office in the afternoon with my mind full of business, and there at it late, and so home to supper to my poor wife, and to bed, myself being in a little pain. . . . . by a stroke . . . . in pulling up my breeches yesterday over eagerly, but I will lay nothing to it till I see whether it will cease of itself or no. The plague, it seems, grows more and more at Amsterdam; and we are going upon making of all ships coming from thence and Hambrough, or any other infected places, to perform their Quarantine (for thirty days as Sir Rd. Browne expressed it in the order of the Council, contrary to the import of the word, though in the general acceptation it signifies now the thing, not the time spent in doing it) in Holehaven, a thing never done by us before.

27th. Up and to my office, where busy with great delight all the morning, and at noon to the 'Change, and so home to dinner with my poor wife, and with great content to my office again, and there hard at work upon stating the account of the freights due to the King from the East India Company till late at night, and so home to supper and to bed. My wife mightily pleased with my late discourse of getting a trip over to Calais, or some other port of France, the next summer, in one of the yachts, and I believe I shall do it, and it makes good sport that my mayde Jane dares not go, and Besse is wild to go, and is mad for joy, but yet will be willing to stay if Jane hath a mind, which is the best temper in this and all other things that ever I knew in my life.

28th. Up and at the office sat all the morning, and at noon by Mr. Coventry's coach to the 'Change, and after a little while there where I met with Mr. Pierce, the chyrurgeon, who tells me for good newes that my Lord Sandwich is resolved to go no more to Chelsy, and told me he believed that I had been giving my Lord some counsel, which I neither denied nor affirmed, but seemed glad with him that he went thither no more, and so I home to dinner, and thence abroad to Paul's Church Yard, and there looked upon the second part of Hudibras, which I buy not, but borrow to read, to see if it be as good as the first, which the world cry so mightily up, though it hath not a good liking in me, though I had tried by twice or three times reading to bring myself to think it witty. Back again home and to my office, and there late doing business and so home to supper and to bed. I have been told two or three times, but to-day for certain I am told how in Holland publickly they have pictured our King with reproach. One way is with his pockets turned the wrong side outward, hanging out empty; another with two courtiers picking of his pockets; and a third, leading of two ladies, while others abuse him; which amounts to great contempt.

29th (Lord's day). This morning I put on my best black cloth suit, trimmed with scarlett ribbon, very neat, with my cloake lined with velvett, and a new beaver, which altogether is very noble, with my black silk knit canons I bought a month ago. I to church alone, my wife not going, and there I found my Lady Batten in a velvet gown, which vexed me that she should be in it before my wife, or that I am able to put her into one, but what cannot be, cannot be. However, when I came home I told my wife of it, and to see my weaknesse, I could on the sudden have found my heart to have offered her one, but second thoughts put it by, and indeed it would undo me to think of doing as Sir W. Batten and his Lady do, who has a good estate besides his office. A good dinner we had of boeuf a la mode, but not roasted so well as my wife used to do it. So after dinner I to the French Church, but that being too far begun I came back to St. Dunstan's by six and heard a good sermon, and so home and to my office all, the evening making up my accounts of this month, and blessed be God I have got up my crumb again to L770, the most that ever I had yet, and good clothes a great many besides, which is a great mercy of God to me. So home to supper and to bed.

30th. Was called up by a messenger from Sir W. Pen to go with him by coach to White Hall. So I got up and went with him, and by the way he began to observe to me some unkind dealing of mine to him a weeke or two since at the table, like a coxcomb, when I answered him pretty freely that I would not think myself to owe any man the service to do this or that because they would have it so (it was about taking of a mulct upon a purser for not keeping guard at Chatham when I was there), so he talked and I talked and let fall the discourse without giving or receiving any great satisfaction, and so to other discourse, but I shall know him still for a false knave. At White Hall we met the Duke in the Matted Gallery, and there he discoursed with us; and by and by my Lord Sandwich came and stood by, and talked; but it being St. Andrew's, and a collar-day, he went to the Chappell, and we parted. From him and Sir W. Pen and I back again and 'light at the 'Change, and to the Coffee-house, where I heard the best story of a cheate intended by a Master of a ship, who had borrowed twice his money upon the bottomary, and as much more insured upon his ship and goods as they were worth, and then would have cast her away upon the coast of France, and there left her, refusing any pilott which was offered him; and so the Governor of the place took her and sent her over hither to find an owner, and so the ship is come safe, and goods and all; they all worth L500, and he had one way or other taken L3000. The cause is to be tried to-morrow at Guildhall, where I intend to be. Thence home to dinner, and then with my wife to her arithmetique. In the evening came W. Howe to see me, who tells me that my Lord hath been angry three or four days with him, would not speak to him; at last did, and charged him with having spoken to me about what he had observed concerning his Lordship, which W. Howe denying stoutly, he was well at ease; and continues very quiett, and is removing from Chelsy as fast as he can, but, methinks, both by my Lord's looks upon me to-day, or it may be it is only my doubtfulness, and by W. Howe's discourse, my Lord is not very well pleased, nor, it may be, will be a good while, which vexes me; but I hope all will over in time, or else I am but ill rewarded for my good service. Anon he and I to the Temple and there parted, and I to my cozen Roger Pepys, whom I met going to his chamber; he was in haste, and to go out of town tomorrow. He tells me of a letter from my father which he will keep to read to me at his coming to town again. I perceive it is about my father's jealousys concerning my wife's doing ill offices with me against him only from the differences they had when she was there, which he very unwisely continues to have and troubles himself and friends about to speak to me in, as my Lord Sandwich, Mr. Moore, and my cozen Roger, which vexes me, but I must impute it to his age and care for my mother and Pall and so let it go. After little discourse with him I took coach and home, calling upon my bookseller's for two books, Rushworth's and Scobell's Collections. I shall make the King pay for them. The first I spent some time at the office to read and it is an excellent book. So home and spent the evening with my wife in arithmetique, and so to supper and to bed. I end this month with my mind in good condition for any thing else, but my unhappy adventuring to disoblige my Lord by doing him service in representing to him the discourse of the world concerning him and his affairs.

Diaryof Samuel Pepys.
December
1663

December 1st. Up and to the office, where we sat all the morning. At noon I home to dinner with my poor wife, with whom now-a-days I enjoy great pleasure in her company and learning of Arithmetique. After dinner I to Guild Hall to hear a tryall at King's Bench, before Lord Chief Justice Hide, about the insurance of a ship, the same I mention in my yesterday's journall, where everything was proved how money was so taken up upon bottomary and insurance, and the ship left by the master and seamen upon rocks, where, when the sea fell at the ebb, she must perish. The master was offered helpe, and he did give the pilotts 20 sols to drink to bid them go about their business, saying that the rocks were old, but his ship was new, and that she was repaired for L6 and less all the damage that she received, and is now brought by one, sent for on purpose by the insurers, into the Thames, with her cargo, vessels of tallow daubed over with butter, instead of all butter, the whole not worth above L500, ship and all, and they had took up, as appeared, above L2,400. He had given his men money to content them; and yet, for all this, he did bring some of them to swear that it was very stormy weather, and [they] did all they could to save her, and that she was seven feete deep water in hold, and were fain to cut her main and foremast, that the master was the last man that went out, and they were fain to force [him] out when she was ready to sink; and her rudder broke off, and she was drawn into the harbour after they were gone, as wrecke all broken, and goods lost: that she could not be carried out again without new building, and many other things so contrary as is not imaginable more. There was all the great counsel in the kingdom in the cause; but after one witnesse or two for the plaintiff, it was cried down as a most notorious cheate; and so the jury, without going out, found it for the plaintiff. But it was pleasant to see what mad sort of testimonys the seamen did give, and could not be got to speak in order: and then their terms such as the judge could not understand; and to hear how sillily the Counsel and judge would speak as to the terms necessary in the matter, would make one laugh: and above all, a Frenchman that was forced to speak in French, and took an English oathe he did not understand, and had an interpreter sworn to tell us what he said, which was the best testimony of all. So home well satisfied with this afternoon's work, purposing to spend an afternoon or two every term so, and so to my office a while and then home to supper, arithmetique with my wife, and to bed. I heard other causes, and saw the course of pleading by being at this trial, and heard and learnt two things: one is that every man has a right of passage in, but not a title to, any highway. The next, that the judge would not suffer Mr. Crow, who hath fined for Alderman, to be called so, but only Mister, and did eight or nine times fret at it, and stop every man that called him so.

2nd. My wife troubled all last night with the toothache and this morning. I up and to my office, where busy, and so home to dinner with my wife, who is better of her tooth than she was, and in the afternoon by agreement called on by Mr. Bland, and with him to the Ship a neighbour tavern and there met his antagonist Mr. Custos and his referee Mr. Clarke a merchant also, and begun the dispute about the freight of a ship hired by Mr. Bland to carry provisions to Tangier, and the freight is now demanded, whereas he says that the goods were some spoiled, some not delivered, and upon the whole demands L1300 of the other, and their minds are both so high, their demands so distant, and their words so many and hot against one another that I fear we shall bring it to nothing. But however I am glad to see myself so capable of understanding the business as I find I do, and shall endeavour to do Mr. Bland all the just service I can therein. Here we were in a bad room, which vexed me most, but we. meet at another house next. So at noon I home and to my office till 9 o'clock, and so home to my wife to keep her company, arithmetique, then to supper, and to bed, she being well of her tooth again.

3rd. Up and to the office, where all the forenoon, and then (by Mr. Coventry's coach) to the 'Change, and so home to dinner, very pleasant with my poor wife.

Somebody from Portsmouth, I know not who, has this day sent me a Runlett of Tent. So to my office all the afternoon, where much business till late at night, and so home to my wife, and then to supper and to bed. This day Sir G. Carteret did tell us at the table, that the Navy (excepting what is due to the Yards upon the quarter now going on, and what few bills he hath not heard of) is quite out of debt; which is extraordinary good newes, and upon the 'Change to hear how our creditt goes as good as any merchant's upon the 'Change is a joyfull thing to consider, which God continue! I am sure the King will have the benefit of it, as well as we some peace and creditt.

4th. Up pretty betimes, that is about 7 o'clock, it being now dark then, and so got me ready, with my clothes, breeches and warm stockings, and by water with Henry Russell, cold and wet and windy to Woolwich, to a hempe ship there, and staid looking upon it and giving direction as to the getting it ashore, and so back again very cold, and at home without going on shore anywhere about 12 o'clock, being fearful of taking cold, and so dined at home and shifted myself, and so all the afternoon at my office till night, and then home to keep my poor wife company, and so to supper and to bed.

5th. Up and to the office, where we sat all the morning, and then with the whole board, *viz.*, Sir J. Minnes, Sir W. Batten, and myself along with Captain Allen home to dinner, where he lives hard by in Mark Lane, where we had a very good plain dinner and good welcome, in a pretty little house but so smoky that it was troublesome to us all till they put out the fire, and made one of charcoale. I was much pleased with this dinner for the many excellent stories told by Mr. Coventry, which I have put down in my book of tales and so shall not mention them here. We staid till night, and then Mr. Coventry away, and by and by I home to my office till 9 or 10 at night, and so home to supper and to bed after some talke and Arithmetique with my poor wife, with whom now-a-days I live with great content, out of all trouble of mind by jealousy (for which God forgive me), or any other distraction more than my fear of my Lord Sandwich's displeasure.

6th (Lord's day). Lay long in bed, and then up and to church alone, which is the greatest trouble that I have by not having a man or, boy to wait on me, and so home to dinner, my wife, it being a cold day, and it begun to snow (the first snow we have seen this year) kept her bed till after dinner, and I below by myself looking over my arithmetique books and timber rule. So my wife rose anon, and she and I all the afternoon at arithmetique, and she is come to do Addition, Subtraction, and Multiplicacion very well, and so I purpose not to trouble her yet with Division, but to begin with the Globes to her now. At night came Captain Grove to discourse with me about Field's business and of other matters, and so, he being gone, I to my office, and spent an houre or two reading Rushworth, and so to supper home, and to prayers and bed, finding myself by cold to have some pain begin with me, which God defend should increase.

7th. Up betimes, and, it being a frosty morning, walked on foot to White Hall, but not without some fear of my pain coming. At White Hall I hear and find that there was the last night the greatest tide that ever was remembered in England to have been in this river: all White Hall having been drowned, of which there was great discourse. Anon we all met, and up with the Duke and did our business, and by and by my Lord of Sandwich came in, but whether it be my doubt or no I cannot tell, but I do not find that he made any sign of kindnesse or respect to me, which troubles me more than any thing in the world. After done there Sir W. Batten and Captain Allen and I by coach to the Temple, where I 'light, they going home, and indeed it being my trouble of mind to try whether I could meet with my Lord Sandwich and try him to see how he will receive me. I took coach and back again to Whitehall, but there could not find him. But here I met Dr. Clerke, and did tell him my story of my health; how my pain comes to me now-a-days. He did write something for me which I shall take when there is occasion. I then fell to other discourse of Dr. Knapp, who tells me he is the King's physician, and is become a solicitor for places for people, and I am mightily troubled with him. He tells me he is the most impudent fellow in the world, that gives himself out to be the King's physician, but it is not so, but is cast out of the Court. From thence I may learn what impudence there is in the world, and how a man may be deceived in persons: Anon the King and Duke and Duchesse came to dinner in the Vane-roome, where I never saw them before; but it seems since the tables are done, he dines there all together. The Queene is pretty well, and goes out of her chamber to her little chappell in the house. The King of France, they say, is hiring of sixty sail of ships of the Dutch, but it is not said for what design. By and by, not hoping to see my Lord, I went to the King's Head ordinary, where a good dinner but no discourse almost, and after dinner by coach, home, and found my wife this cold day not yet out of bed, and after a little good talk with her to my office, and there spent my time till late. Sir W. Warren two or three hours with me talking of trade, and other very good discourse, which did please me very, well, and so, after reading in Rushworth, home to supper and to bed.

8th. Lay long in bed, and then up and to the office, where we sat all the morning, and among other things my Lord Barkely called in question his clerk Mr. Davy for something which Sir W. Batten and I did tell him yesterday, but I endeavoured to make the least of it, and so all was put up. At noon to the 'Change, and among other businesses did discourse with Captain Taylor, and I think I shall safely get L20 by his ship's freight at present, besides what it may be I may get hereafter. So home to dinner, and thence by coach to White Hall, where a great while walked with my Lord Tiviott, whom I find a most carefull, thoughtfull, and cunning man, as I also ever took him to be. He is this day bringing in an account where he makes the King debtor to him L10,000 already on the garrison of Tangier account; but yet demands not ready money to pay it, but offers such ways of paying it out of the sale of old decayed provisions as will enrich him finely. Anon came my Lord Sandwich, and then we fell to our business at the Committee about my Lord Tiviott's accounts, wherein I took occasion to speak now and then, so as my Lord Sandwich did well seem to like of it, and after we were up did bid me good night in a tone that, methinks, he is not so displeased with me as I did doubt he is; however, I will take a course to know whether he be or no. The Committee done, I took coach and home to my office, and there late, and so to supper at home, and to bed, being doubtful of my pain through the very cold weather which we have, but I will take all the care I can to prevent it.

9th. Lay very long in bed for fear of my pain, and then rose and went to stool (after my wife's way, who by all means would have me sit long and upright) very well, and being ready to the office. From thence I was called by and by to my wife, she not being well. So to her, and found her in great pain. . . . . . So by and by to my office again, and then abroad to look out a cradle to burn charcoal in at my office, and I found one to my mind in Newgate Market, and so meeting Hoby's man in the street, I spoke to him to serve it in to the office for the King. So home to dinner, and after talk with my wife, she in bed and pain all day, I to my office most of the evening, and then home to my wife. This day Mrs. Russell did give my wife a very fine St. George, in alabaster, which will set out my wife's closett mightily. This evening at the office, after I had wrote my day's passages, there came to me my cozen Angier of Cambridge, poor man, making his moan, and obtained of me that I would send his son to sea as a Reformado, which I will take care to do. But to see how apt every man is to forget friendship in time of adversity. How glad was I when he was gone, for fear he should ask me to be bond for him, or to borrow money of me.

10th. Up, pretty well, the weather being become pretty warm again, and to the office, where we sat all the morning, and I confess having received so lately a token from Mrs. Russell, I did find myself concerned for our not buying some tallow of her (which she bought on purpose yesterday most unadvisedly to her great losse upon confidence of putting it off to us). So hard it is for a man not to be warped against his duty and master's interest that receives any bribe or present, though not as a bribe, from any body else. But she must be contented, and I to do her a good turn when I can without wrong to the King's service. Then home to dinner (and did drink a glass of wine and beer, the more for joy that this is the shortest day in the year,—- [Old Style]—which is a pleasant consideration) with my wife. She in bed but pretty well, and having a messenger from my brother, that he is not well nor stirs out of doors, I went forth to see him, and found him below, he has not been well, but is not ill. I found him taking order for the distribution of Mrs. Ramsey's coals, a thing my father for many years did, and now he after him, which I was glad to see, as also to hear that Mr. Wheatly begins to look after him. I hope it is about his daughter. Thence to St. Paul's Church Yard, to my bookseller's, and having gained this day in the office by my stationer's bill to the King about 40s. or L3, I did here sit two or three hours calling for twenty books to lay this money out upon, and found myself at a great losse where to choose, and do see how my nature would gladly return to laying out money in this trade. I could not tell whether to lay out my money for books of pleasure, as plays, which my nature was most earnest in; but at last, after seeing Chaucer, Dugdale's History of Paul's, Stows London, Gesner, History of Trent, besides Shakespeare, Jonson, and Beaumont's plays, I at last chose Dr. Fuller's Worthys, the Cabbala or Collections of Letters of State, and a little book, Delices de Hollande, with another little book or two, all of good use or serious pleasure: and Hudibras, both parts, the book now in greatest fashion for drollery, though I cannot, I confess, see enough where the wit lies. My mind being thus settled, I went by linke home, and so to my office, and to read in Rushworth; and so home to supper and to bed. Calling at Wotton's, my shoemaker's, today, he tells me that Sir H. Wright is dying; and that Harris is come to the Duke's house again; and of a rare play to be acted this week of Sir William Davenant's: the story of Henry the Eighth with all his wives.

11th. Up and abroad toward the Wardrobe, and going out Mr. Clerke met me to tell me that Field has a writ against me in this last business of L30 10s., and that he believes he will get an execution against me this morning, and though he told me it could not be well before noon, and that he would stop it at the Sheriff's, yet it is hard to believe with what fear I did walk and how I did doubt at every man I saw and do start at the hearing of one man cough behind my neck. I to, the Wardrobe and there missed Mr. Moore. So to Mr. Holden's and evened all reckonings there for hats, and then walked to Paul's Churchyard and after a little at my bookseller's and bought at a shop Cardinall Mazarin's Will in French. I to the Coffeehouse and there among others had good discourse with an Iron Merchant, who tells me the great evil of discouraging our natural manufacture of England in that commodity by suffering the Swede to bring in three times more than ever they did and our owne Ironworks be lost, as almost half of them, he says, are already. Then I went and sat by Mr. Harrington, and some East country merchants, and talking of the country about Quinsborough, and thereabouts, he told us himself that for fish, none there, the poorest body, will buy a dead fish, but must be alive, unless it be in winter; and then they told us the manner of putting their nets into the water. Through holes made in the thick ice, they will spread a net of half a mile long; and he hath known a hundred and thirty and a hundred and seventy barrels of fish taken at one draught. And then the people come with sledges upon the ice, with snow at the bottome, and lay the fish in and cover them with snow, and so carry them to market. And he hath seen when the said fish have been frozen in the sledge, so as that he hath taken a fish and broke a-pieces, so hard it hath been; and yet the same fishes taken out of the snow, and brought into a hot room, will be alive and leap up and down. Swallows are often brought up in their nets out of the mudd from under water, hanging together to some twigg or other, dead in ropes, and brought to the fire will come to life. Fowl killed in December. (Alderman Barker said) he did buy, and putting into the box under his sledge, did forget to take them out to eate till Aprill next, and they then were found there, and were through the frost as sweet and fresh and eat as well as at first killed. Young beares are there; their flesh sold in market as ordinarily as beef here, and is excellent sweet meat. They tell us that beares there do never hurt any body, but fly away from you, unless you pursue and set upon them; but wolves do much mischief. Mr. Harrington told us how they do to get so much honey as they send abroad. They make hollow a great fir-tree, leaving only a small slitt down straight in one place, and this they close up again, only leave a little hole, and there the bees go in and fill the bodys of those trees as full of wax and honey as they can hold; and the inhabitants at times go and open the slit, and take what they please without killing the bees, and so let them live there still and make more. Fir trees are always planted close together, because of keeping one another from the violence of the windes; and when a fell is made, they leave here and there a grown tree to preserve the young ones coming up. The great entertainment and sport of the Duke of Corland, and the princes thereabouts, is hunting; which is not with dogs as we, but he appoints such a day, and summons all the country-people as to a campagnia; and by several companies gives every one their circuit, and they agree upon a place where the toyle is to be set; and so making fires every company as they go, they drive all the wild beasts, whether bears, wolves, foxes, swine, and stags, and roes, into the toyle; and there the great men have their stands in such and such places, and shoot at what they have a mind to, and that is their hunting. They are not very populous there, by reason that people marry women seldom till they are towards or above thirty; and men thirty or forty years old, or more oftentimes. Against a publique hunting the Duke sends that no wolves be killed by the people; and whatever harm they do, the Duke makes it good to the person that suffers it: as Mr. Harrington instanced in a house where he lodged, where a wolfe broke into a hog-stye, and bit three or four great pieces off the back of the hog, before the house could come to helpe it (it calling, and that did give notice to the people of the house); and the man of the house told him that there were three or four wolves thereabouts that did them great hurt; but it was no matter, for the Duke was to make it good to him, otherwise he would kill them. Hence home and upstairs, my wife keeping her bed, and had a very good dinner, and after dinner to my office, and there till late busy. Among other things Captain Taylor came to me about his bill for freight, and besides that I found him contented that I have the L30 I got, he do offer me to give me L6 to take the getting of the bill paid upon me, which I am ready to do, but I am loath to have it said that I ever did it. However, I will do him the service to get it paid if I can and stand to his courtesy what he will give me. Late to supper home, and to my great joy I have by my wife's good advice almost brought myself by going often and leisurely to the stool that I am come almost to have my natural course of stool as well as ever, which I pray God continue to me.

12th. Up and to the office where all the morning, and among other things got Sir G. Carteret to put his letters to Captain Taylor's bill by which I am in hopes to get L5, which joys my heart. We had this morning a great dispute between Mr. Gauden, Victualler of the Navy, and Sir J. Lawson, and the rest of the Commanders going against Argier, about their fish and keeping of Lent; which Mr. Gauden so much insists upon to have it observed, as being the only thing that makes up the loss of his dear bargain all the rest of the year. At noon went home and there I found that one Abrahall, who strikes in for the serving of the King with Ship chandlery ware, has sent my wife a Japan gowne, which pleases her very well and me also, it coming very opportune, but I know not how to carry myself to him, I being already obliged so far to Mrs. Russell, so that I am in both their pays. To the Exchange, where I had sent Luellin word I would come to him, and thence brought him home to dinner with me. He tells me that W. Symon's wife is dead, for which I am sorry, she being a good woman, and tells me an odde story of her saying before her death, being in good sense, that there stood her uncle Scobell. Then he began to tell me that Mr. Deering had been with him to desire him to speak to me that if I would get him off with these goods upon his hands, he would give me 50 pieces, and further that if I would stand his friend to helpe him to the benefit of his patent as the King's merchant, he could spare me L200 per annum out of his profits. I was glad to hear both of these, but answered him no further than that as I would not by any thing be bribed to be unjust in my dealings,

[Edward Dering was granted, August, 1660, "the office of King's merchant in the East, for buying and providing necessaries for apparelling the Navy" ("Calendar," Domestic, 1660-61, p. 212). There is evidence among the State Papers of some dissatisfaction with the

223

timber, &c., which he supplied to the Navy, and at this time he appears to have had some stores left on his hands.]

so I was not so squeamish as not to take people's acknowledgment where I had the good fortune by my pains to do them good and just offices, and so I would not come to be at any agreement with him, but I would labour to do him this service and to expect his consideration thereof afterwards as he thought fit. So I expect to hear more of it. I did make very much of Luellin in hopes to have some good by this business, and in the evening received some money from Mr. Moore, and so went and settled accounts in my books between him and me, and I do hope at Christmas not only to find myself as rich or more than ever I was yet, but also my accounts in less compass, fewer reckonings either of debts or moneys due to me, than ever I have been for some years, and indeed do so, the goodness of God bringing me from better to a better expectation and hopes of doing well. This day I heard my Lord Barkeley tell Sir G. Carteret that he hath letters from France that the King hath unduked twelve Dukes, only to show his power and to crush his nobility, who he said he did see had heretofore laboured to cross him. And this my Lord Barkeley did mightily magnify, as a sign of a brave and vigorous mind, that what he saw fit to be done he dares do. At night, after business done at my office, home to supper and to bed. I have forgot to set down a very remarkable passage that, Lewellen being gone, and I going into the office, and it begun to be dark, I found nobody there, my clerks being at the burial of a child of W. Griffin's, and so I spent a little time till they came, walking in the garden, and in the mean time, while I was walking Mrs. Pen's pretty maid came by my side, and went into the office, but finding nobody there I went in to her, being glad of the occasion. She told me as she was going out again that there was nobody there, and that she came for a sheet of paper. So I told her I would supply her, and left her in the office and went into my office and opened my garden door, thinking to have got her in, and there to have caressed her, and seeming looking for paper, I told her this way was as near a way for her, but she told me she had left the door open and so did not come to me. So I carried her some paper and kissed her, leading her by the hand to the garden door and there let her go. But, Lord! to see how much I was put out of order by this surprisal, and how much I could have subjected my mind to have treated and been found with this wench, and how afterwards I was troubled to think what if she should tell this and whether I had spoke or done any thing that might be unfit for her to tell. But I think there was nothing more passed than just what I here write.

13th (Lord's day). Up and made me ready for Church, but my wife and I had a difference about her old folly that she would fasten lies upon her mayds, and now upon Jane, which I did not see enough to confirm me in it, and so would not consent to her. To church, where after sermon home, and to my office, before dinner, reading my vowes, and so home to dinner, where Tom came to me and he and I dined together, my wife not rising all day, and after dinner I made even accounts with him, and spent all the afternoon in my chamber talking of many things with him, and about Wheately's daughter for a wife for him, and then about the Joyces and their father Fenner, how they are sometimes all honey one with another and then all turd, and a strange rude life there is among them. In the evening, he gone, I to my office to read Rushworth upon the charge and answer of the Duke of Buckingham, which is very fine, and then to do a little business against to-morrow, and so home to supper to my wife, and then to bed.

14th. Up by candlelight, which I do not use to do, though it be very late, that is to say almost 8 o'clock, and out by coach to White Hall, where we all met and to the Duke, where I heard a large discourse between one that goes over an agent from the King to Legorne and thereabouts, to remove the inconveniences his ships are put to by denial of pratique; which is a thing that is now-a-days made use of only as a cheat, for a man may buy a bill of health for a piece of eight, and my enemy may agree with the Intendent of the Sante for ten pieces of eight or so; that he shall not give me a bill of health, and so spoil me in my design, whatever it be. This the King will not endure, and so resolves either to have it removed, or to keep all ships from coming in, or going out there, so long as his ships are stayed for want hereof. Then, my Lord Sandwich being there, we all went into the Duke's closet and did our business. But among other things, Lord! what an account did Sir J. Minnes and Sir W. Batten make of the pulling down and burning of the head of the Charles, where Cromwell was placed with people under his horse, and Peter, as the Duke called him, is praying to him; and Sir J. Minnes would needs infer the temper of the people from their joy at the doing of this and their building a gibbet for the hanging of his head up, when God knows, it is even the flinging away of L100 out of the King's purse, to the building of another, which it seems must be a Neptune. Thence I through White Hall only to see what was doing, but meeting none that I knew I went through the garden to my Lord Sandwich's lodging, where I found my Lord got before me (which I did not intend or expect) and was there trying some musique, which he intends for an anthem of three parts, I know not whether for the King's chapel or no, but he seems mighty intent upon it. But it did trouble me to hear him swear before God and other oathes, as he did now and then without any occasion, which methinks did so ill become him, and I hope will be a caution for me, it being so ill a thing in him. The musique being done, without showing me any good or ill countenance, he did give me his hat and so adieu, and went down to his coach without saying anything to me. He being gone I and Mr. Howe talked a good while. He tells me that my Lord, it is true, for a while after my letter, was displeased, and did shew many slightings of me when he had occasion of mentioning me to his Lordship, but that now my Lord is in good temper and he do believe will shew me as much respect as ever, and would have me not to refrain to come to him. This news I confess did much trouble me, but when I did hear how he is come to himself, and hath wholly left Chelsy, and the slut, and that I see he do follow his business, and becomes in better repute than before, I am rejoiced to see it, though it do cost me some disfavour for a time, for if not his good nature and ingenuity, yet I believe his memory will not bear it always in his mind. But it is my comfort that this is the thing that after so many years good service that has made him my enemy. Thence to the King's Head ordinary, and there dined among a company of fine gentlemen; some of them discoursed of the King of France's greatness, and how he is come to make the Princes of the Blood to take place of all foreign Embassadors, which it seems is granted by them of Venice and other States, and expected from my Lord. Hollis, our King's Embassador there; and that either upon that score or something else he hath not had his entry yet in Paris, but hath received several affronts, and among others his harnesse cut, and his gentlemen of his horse killed, which will breed bad blood if true. They say also that the King of France hath hired threescore ships of Holland, and forty of the Swede, but nobody knows what to do; but some great designs he hath on foot against the next year. Thence by coach home and to my office, where I spent all the evening till night with Captain Taylor discoursing about keeping of masts, and when he was gone, with Sir W. Warren, who did give me excellent discourse about the same thing, which I have committed to paper, and then fell to other talk of his being at Chatham lately and there discoursing of his masts. Commissioner Pett did let fall several scurvy words concerning my pretending to know masts as well as any body, which I know proceeds ever since I told him I could measure a piece of timber as well as anybody employed by the King. But, however, I shall remember him for a black sheep again a good while, with all his fair words to me, and perhaps may let him know that my ignorance does the King as much good as all his knowledge, which would do more it is true if it were well used. Then we fell to talk of Sir J. Minnes's and Sir W. Batten's burning of Oliver's head, while he was there; which was done with so much insulting and folly as I never heard of, and had the Trayned Band of Rochester to come to the solemnity, which when all comes to all, Commissioner Pett says it never was made for him; but it troubles me the King should suffer L100 losse in his purse, to make a new one after it was forgot whose it was, or any words spoke of it. He being gone I mightily pleased with his discourse, by which I always learn something, I to read a little in Rushworth, and so home to supper to my wife, it having been washing day, and so to bed, my mind I confess a little troubled for my Lord Sandwich's displeasure. But God will give me patience to bear since it rises from so good an occasion.

15th. Before I was up, my brother's man came to tell me that my cozen, Edward Pepys, was dead, died at Mrs. Turner's, for which my wife and I are very sorry, and the more for that his wife was the only handsome woman of our name. So up and to the office, where the greatest business was Sir J. Minnes and Sir W. Batten against me for Sir W. Warren's contract for masts, to which I may go to my memorandum book to see what past, but came off with conquest, and my Lord Barkely and Mr. Coventry well convinced that we are well used. So home to dinner, and thither came to me Mr. Mount and Mr. Luellin, I think almost foxed, and there dined with me and very merry as I could be, my mind being troubled to see things so ordered at the Board, though with no disparagement to me at all. At dinner comes a messenger from the Counter with an execution against me for the L30 10s., given the last verdict to Field. The man's name is Thomas, of the Poultry Counter. I sent Griffin with him to the Dolphin, where Sir W. Batten was at dinner, and he being satisfied that I should pay the money, I did cause the money to be paid him, and Griffin to tell it out to him in the office. He offered to go along with me to Sir R. Ford, but I thought it not necessary, but let him go with it, he also telling me that there is never any receipt for it given, but I have good witness of the payment of it. They being gone, Luellin having again told me by myself that Deering is content to give me L50 if I can sell his deals for him to the King, not that I did ever offer to take it, or bid Luellin bargain for me with him, but did tacitly seem to be willing to do him what service I could in it, and expect his thanks, what he thought good. Thence to White Hall by coach, by the way overtaking Mr. Moore, and took him into the coach to me, and there he could tell me nothing of my Lord, how he stands as to his thoughts or respect to me, but concludes that though at present he may be angry yet he will come to be pleased again with me no doubt, and says that he do mind his business well, and keeps at Court. So to White Hall, and there by order found some of the Commissioners of Tangier met, and my Lord Sandwich among the rest, to whom I bowed, but he shewed me very little if any countenance at all, which troubles me mightily. Having soon done there, I took up Mr. Moore again and set him down at Pauls, by the way he proposed to me of a way of profit which perhaps may shortly be made by money by fines upon houses at the Wardrobe, but how I did not understand but left it to another discourse. So homeward, calling upon Mr. Fen, by Sir G. Carteret's desire, and did there shew him the bill of Captain Taylor's whereby I hope to get something justly. Home and to my office, and there very late with Sir W. Warren upon very serious discourse, telling him how matters passed to-day, and in the close he and I did fall to talk very openly of the business of this office, and (if I was not a little too open to tell him my interest, which is my fault) he did give me most admirable advice, and such as do speak him a most able and worthy man, and understanding seven times more than ever I thought to be in him. He did particularly run over every one of the officers and commanders, and shewed me how I had reason to mistrust every one of them, either for their falsenesse or their over-great power, being too high to fasten a real friendship in, and did give me a common but a most excellent saying to observe in all my life. He did give it in rhyme, but the sense was this, that a man should treat every friend in his discourse and opening his mind to him as of one that may hereafter be his foe. He did also advise me how I should take occasion to make known to the world my case, and the pains that I take in my business, and above all to be sure to get a thorough knowledge in my employment, and to that add all the interest at Court that I can, which I hope I shall do. He staid talking with me till almost 12 at night, and so good night, being sorry to part with him, and more sorry that he should have as far as Wapping to walk to-night. So I to my Journall and so home, to supper and to bed.

16th. Up, and with my head and heart full of my business, I to my office, and there all the morning, where among other things to my great content Captain Taylor brought me L40, the greater part of which I shall gain to myself after much care and pains out of his bill of freight, as I have at large set down in my book of Memorandums. At noon to the 'Change and there met with Mr. Wood by design, and got out of him to my advantage a condition which I shall make good use of against Sir W. Batten (vide my book of Memorandums touching the contract of masts of Sir W. Warren about which I have had so much trouble). So home to dinner and then to the Star Tavern hard by to our arbitration of Mr. Bland's business, and at it a great while, but I found no order like to be kept in our inquiry, and Mr. Clerke, the other arbitrator, one so far from being fit (though able as to his trade of a merchant) to inquire and to take pains in searching out the truth on both sides, that we parted without doing anything, nor do I believe we shall at all ever attain to anything in it. Then home and till 12 at night making up my accounts with great account of this day's receipt of Captain Taylor's money and some money reimbursed me which I have laid out on Field's business. So home with my mind in pretty good quiet, and to Supper and to bed.

17th. Up and to the office, where we sat all the morning. At noon home to my poor wife and dined, and then by coach abroad to Mrs. Turner's where I have not been for many a day, and there I found her and her sister Dike very sad for the death of their brother. After a little common expression of sorrow, Mrs. Turner told me that the trouble she would put me to was, to consult about getting an achievement prepared, scutcheons were done already, to set over the door. So I did go out to Mr. Smith's, where my brother tells me the scutcheons are made, but he not being within, I went to the Temple, and there spent my time in a Bookseller's shop, reading in a book of some Embassages into Moscovia, &c., where was very good reading, and then to Mrs. Turner's, and thither came Smith to me, with whom I did agree for L4 to make a handsome one, ell square within the frame. After he was gone I sat an houre talking of the suddennesse of his death within 7 days, and how by little and little death came upon him, neither he nor they thinking it would come to that. He died after a day's raveing, through lightness in his head for want of sleep. His lady did not know of his sickness, nor do they hear yet how she takes it. Hence home, taking some books by the way in Paul's Churchyard by coach to my office, where late doing business, and so home to supper and to bed.

18th. Up, and after being ready and done several businesses with people, I took water (taking a dram of the bottle at the waterside) with a gaily, the first that ever I had yet, and down to Woolwich, calling at Ham Creeke, where I met Mr. Deane, and had a great deal of talke with him about business, and so to the Ropeyarde and Docke, discoursing several things, and so back again and did the like at Deptford, and I find that it is absolutely necessary for me to do thus once a weeke at least all the yeare round, which will do me great good, and so home with great ease and content, especially out of the content which I met with in a book I bought yesterday, being a discourse of the state of Rome under the present Pope, Alexander the 7th, it being a very excellent piece. After eating something at home, then to my office, where till night about business to dispatch. Among other people came Mr. Primate, the leather seller, in Fleete Streete, to see me, he says, coming this way; and he tells me that he is upon a proposal to the King, whereby, by a law already in being, he will supply the King, without wrong to any man, or charge to the people in general, so much as it is now, above L200,000 per annum, and God knows what, and that the King do like the proposal, and hath directed that the Duke of Monmouth, with their consent, be made privy, and go along with him and his fellow proposer in the business, God knows what it is; for I neither can guess nor believe there is any such thing in his head. At night made an end of the discourse I read this morning, and so home to supper and to bed.

19th. Up and to the office, where we sat all the morning, and I laboured hard at Deering's business of his deals more than I would if I did not think to get something, though I do really believe that I did what is to the King's advantage in it, and yet, God knows, the expectation of profit will have its force and make a man the more earnest. Dined at home, and then with Mr. Bland to another meeting upon his arbitration, and seeing we were likely to do no good I even put them upon it, and they chose Sir W. Rider alone to end the matter, and so I am rid of it. Thence by coach to my shoemaker's and paid all there, and gave something to the boys' box against Christmas. To Mrs. Turner's, whom I find busy with Sir W. Turner, about advising upon going down to Norfolke with the corps, and I find him in talke a sober, considering man. So home to my office late, and then home to supper and to bed. My head full of business, but pretty good content.

20th (Lord's day). Up and alone to church, where a common sermon of Mr. Mills, and so home to dinner in our parler, my wife being clean, and the first time we have dined here a great while together, and in the afternoon went to church with me also, and there begun to take her place above Mrs. Pen, which heretofore out of a humour she was wont to give her as an affront to my Lady Batten. After a dull sermon of the Scotchman, home, and there I found my brother Tom and my two cozens Scotts, he and she, the first time they were ever here. And by and by in comes my uncle. Wight and Mr. Norbury, and they sat with us a while drinking, of wine, of which I did give them plenty. But the two would not stay supper, but the other two did. And we were as merry as I could be with people that I do wish well to, but know not what discourse either to give them or find from them. We showed them our house from top to bottom, and had a good Turkey roasted for our supper, and store of wine, and after supper sent them home on foot, and so we to prayers and to bed.

21st. Up betimes, my wife having a mind to have gone abroad with me, but I had not because of troubling me, and so left her, though against my will, to go and see her father and mother by herself, and I straight to my Lord Sandwich's, and there I had a pretty kind salute from my Lord, and went on to the Duke's, where my fellow officers by and by came, and so in with him to his closet, and did our business, and so broke up, and I with Sir W. Batten by coach to Salisbury Court, and there spoke with Clerk our Solicitor about Field's business, and so parted, and I to Mrs. Turner's, and there saw the achievement pretty well set up, and it is well done. Thence I on foot to Charing Crosse to the ordinary, and there, dined, meeting Mr. Gauden and Creed. Here variety of talk but to no great purpose. After dinner won a wager of a payre of gloves of a crowne of Mr. Gauden upon some words in his contract for victualling. There parted in the street with them, and I to my Lord's, but he not being within, took coach, and, being directed by sight of bills upon the walls, I did go to Shoe Lane to see a cocke-fighting at a new pit there, a sport I was never at in my life; but, Lord! to see the strange variety of people, from Parliament-man (by name Wildes, that was Deputy Governor of the Tower when Robinson was Lord Mayor) to the poorest 'prentices, bakers, brewers, butchers, draymen, and what not; and all these fellows one with another in swearing, cursing, and betting. I soon had enough of it, and yet I would not but have seen it once, it being strange to observe the nature of these poor creatures, how they will fight till they drop down dead upon the table, and strike after they are ready to give up the ghost, not offering to run away when they are weary or wounded past doing further, whereas where a dunghill brood comes he will, after a sharp stroke that pricks him, run off the stage, and then they wring off his neck without more ado, whereas the other they preserve, though their eyes be both out, for breed only of a true cock of the game. Sometimes a cock that has had ten to one against him will by chance give an unlucky blow, will strike the other starke dead in a moment, that he never stirs more; but the common rule is, that though a cock neither runs nor dies, yet if any man will bet L10 to a crowne, and nobody take the bet, the game is given over, and not sooner. One thing more it is strange to see how people of this poor rank, that look as if they had not bread to put in their mouths, shall bet three or four pounds at one bet, and lose it, and yet bet as much the next battle (so they call every match of two cocks), so that one of them will lose L10 or L20 at a meeting. Thence, having enough of it, by coach to my Lord Sandwich's, where I find him within with Captain Cooke and his boys, Dr. Childe, Mr. Madge, and Mallard, playing and singing over my Lord's anthem which he hath made to sing in the King's Chappell: my Lord saluted me kindly and took me into the withdrawing-room, to hear it at a distance, and indeed it sounds very finely, and is a good thing, I believe, to be made by him, and they all commend it. And after that was done Captain Cooke and his two boys did sing some Italian songs, which I must in a word say I think was fully the best musique that I ever yet heard in all my life, and it was to me a very great pleasure to hear them. After all musique ended, my Lord going to White Hall, I went along with him, and made a desire for to have his coach to go along with my cozen Edward Pepys's hearse through the City on Wednesday next, which he granted me presently, though he cannot yet come to speak to me in the familiar stile that he did use to do, nor can I expect it. But I was the willinger of this occasion to see whether he would deny me or no, which he would I believe had he been at open defyance against me. Being not a little pleased with all this, though I yet see my Lord is not right yet, I thanked his Lordship and parted with him in White Hall. I back to my Lord's, and there took up W. Howe in a coach, and carried him as far as the Half Moone, and there set him down. By the way, talking of my Lord, who is come another and a better man than he was lately, and God be praised for it, and he says that I shall find my Lord as he used to be to me, of which I have good hopes, but I shall beware of him, I mean W. Howe, how I trust him, for I perceive he is not so discreet as I took him for, for he has told Captain Ferrers (as Mr. Moore tells me) of my letter to my Lord, which troubles me, for fear my Lord should think that I might have told him. So called with my coach at my wife's brother's lodging, but she was gone newly in a coach homewards, and so I drove hard and overtook her at Temple Bar, and there paid off mine, and went home with her in her coach. She tells me how there is a sad house among her friends. Her brother's wife proves very unquiet, and so her mother is, gone back to be with her husband and leave the young couple to themselves, and great trouble, and I fear great want, will be among them, I pray keep me from being troubled with them. At home to put on my gowne and to my office, and there set down this day's Journall, and by and by comes Mrs. Owen, Captain Allen's daughter, and causes me to stay while the papers relating to her husband's place, bought of his father, be copied out because of her going by this morning's tide home to Chatham. Which vexes me, but there is no help for it. I home to supper while a young [man] that she brought with her did copy out the things, and then I to the office again and dispatched her, and so home to bed.

22nd. Up and there comes my she cozen Angier, of Cambridge, to me to speak about her son. But though I love them, and have reason so to do, yet, Lord! to consider how cold I am to speak to her, for fear of giving her too much hopes of expecting either money or anything else from me besides my care of her son. I let her go without drinking, though that was against my will, being forced to hasten to the office, where we sat all the morning, and at noon I to Sir R. Ford's, where Sir R. Browne (a dull but it seems upon action a hot man), and he and I met upon setting a price upon the freight of a barge sent to France to the Duchess of Orleans. And here by discourse I find them greatly crying out against the choice of Sir J. Cutler to be

Treasurer for Paul's upon condition that he give L1500 towards it, and it seems he did give it upon condition that he might be Treasurer for the work, which they say will be worth three times as much money, and talk as if his being chosen to the office will make people backward to give, but I think him as likely a man as either of them, or better. The business being done we parted, Sir R. Ford never inviting me to dine with him at all, and I was not sorry for it. Home and dined. I had a letter from W. Howe that my Lord hath ordered his coach and six horses for me to-morrow, which pleases me mightily to think that my Lord should do so much, hoping thereby that his anger is a little over. After dinner abroad with my wife by coach to Westminster, and set her at Mrs. Hunt's while I about my business, having in our way met with Captain Ferrers luckily to speak to him about my coach, who was going in all haste thither, and I perceive the King and Duke and all the Court was going to the Duke's playhouse to see "Henry *viii.*" acted, which is said to be an admirable play. But, Lord! to see how near I was to have broken my oathe, or run the hazard of 20s. losse, so much my nature was hot to have gone thither; but I did not go, but having spoke with W. Howe and known how my Lord did do this kindly as I would have it, I did go to Westminster Hall, and there met Hawley, and walked a great while with him. Among other discourse encouraging him to pursue his love to Mrs. Lane, while God knows I had a roguish meaning in it. Thence calling my wife home by coach, calling at several places, and to my office, where late, and so home to supper and to bed. This day I hear for certain that my Lady Castlemaine is turned Papist, which the Queene for all do not much like, thinking that she do it not for conscience sake. I heard to-day of a great fray lately between Sir H. Finch's coachman, who struck with his whip a coachman of the King's to the losse of one of his eyes; at which the people of the Exchange seeming to laugh and make sport with some words of contempt to him, my Lord Chamberlin did come from the King to shut up the 'Change, and by the help of a justice, did it; but upon petition to the King it was opened again.

23rd. Up betimes and my wife; and being in as mourning a dress as we could, at present, without cost, put ourselves into, we by Sir W. Pen's coach to Mrs. Turner's, at Salisbury Court, where I find my Lord's coach and six horses. We staid till almost eleven o'clock, and much company came, and anon, the corps being put into the hearse, and the scutcheons set upon it, we all took coach, and I and my wife and Auditor Beale in my Lord Sandwich's coach, and went next to Mrs. Turner's mourning coach, and so through all the City and Shoreditch, I believe about twenty coaches, and four or five with six and four horses. Being come thither, I made up to the mourners, and bidding them a good journey, I took leave and back again, and setting my wife into a hackney out of Bishopsgate Street, I sent her home, and I to the 'Change and Auditor Beale about his business. Did much business at the 'Change, and so home to dinner, and then to my office, and there late doing business also to my great content to see God bless me in my place and opening honest ways, I hope to get a little money to lay up and yet to live handsomely. So to supper and to bed. My wife having strange fits of the toothache, some times on this, and by and by on that side of her tooth, which is not common.

24th. Up betimes; and though it was a most foggy morning, and cold, yet with a gally down to Eriffe, several times being at a loss whither we went. There I mustered two ships of the King's, lent by him to the Guiny Company, which are manned better than ours at far less wages. Thence on board two of the King's, one of them the "Leopard," Captain Beech, who I find an able and serious man. He received me civilly, and his wife was there, a very well bred and knowing woman, born at Antwerp, but speaks as good English as myself, and an ingenious woman. Here was also Sir G. Carteret's son, who I find a pretty, but very talking man, but good humour. Thence back again, entertaining myself upon my sliding rule with great content, and called at Woolwich, where Mr. Chr. Pett having an opportunity of being alone did tell me his mind about several things he thought I was offended with him in, and told me of my kindness to his assistant. I did give him such an answer as I thought was fit and left him well satisfied, he offering to do me all the service, either by draughts or modells that I should desire. Thence straight home, being very cold, but yet well, I thank God, and at home found my wife making mince pies, and by and by comes in Captain Ferrers to see us, and, among other talke, tells us of the goodness of the new play of "Henry *viii.*," which makes me think [it] long till my time is out; but I hope before I go I shall set myself such a stint as I may not forget myself as I have hitherto done till I was forced for these months last past wholly to forbid myself the seeing of one. He gone I to my office and there late writing and reading, and so home to bed.

25th (Christmas day). Lay long talking pleasantly with my wife, but among other things she begun, I know not whether by design or chance, to enquire what she should do if I should by any accident die, to which I did give her some slight answer; but shall make good use of it to bring myself to some settlement for her sake, by making a will as soon as I can. Up and to church, where Mr. Mills made an ordinary sermon, and so home and dined with great pleasure with my wife, and all the afternoon first looking out at window and seeing the boys playing at many several sports in our back yard by Sir W. Pen's, which reminded me of my own former times, and then I began to read to my wife upon the globes with great pleasure and to good purpose, for it will be pleasant to her and to me to have her understand these things. In the evening at the office, where I staid late reading Rushworth, which is a most excellent collection of the beginning of the late quarrels in this kingdom, and so home to supper and to bed, with good content of mind.

26th. Up and walked forth first to the Minerys to Brown's, and there with great pleasure saw and bespoke several instruments, and so to Cornhill to Mr. Cades, and there went up into his warehouse to look for a map or two, and there finding great plenty of good pictures, God forgive me! how my mind run upon them, and bought a little one for my wife's closett presently, and concluded presently of buying L10 worth, upon condition he would give me the buying of them. Now it is true I did still within me resolve to make the King one way or other pay for them, though I saved it to him another way, yet I find myself too forward to fix upon the expense, and came away with a resolution of buying them, but do hope that I shall not upon second thoughts do it without a way made out before I buy them to myself how to do [it] without charge to my main stock. Thence to the Coffee-house, and sat long in good discourse with some gentlemen concerning the Roman Empire. So home and found Mr. Hollyard there, and he stayed and dined with us, we having a pheasant to dinner. He gone, I all the afternoon with my wife to cards, and, God forgive me! to see how the very discourse of plays, which I shall be at liberty to see after New Year's Day next, do set my mind upon them, but I must be forced to stint myself very strictly before I begin, or else I fear I shall spoil all. In the evening came my aunt Wight's kinswoman to see how my wife do, with a compliment from my aunt, which I take kindly as it is unusual for her to do it, but I do perceive my uncle is very kind to me of late. So to my office writing letters, and then to read and make an end of Rushworth, which I did, and do say that it is a book the most worth reading for a man of my condition or any man that hopes to come to any publique condition in the world that I do know. So home to supper and to bed.

27th. Up and to church alone and so home to dinner with my wife very pleasant and pleased with one another's company, and in our general enjoyment one of another, better we think than most other couples do. So after dinner to the French church, but came too late, and so back to our owne church, where I slept all the sermon the Scott preaching, and so home, and in the evening Sir J. Minnes and I met at Sir W. Pen's about ordering some business of the Navy, and so I home to supper, discourse, prayers, and bed.

28th. Up and by coach to my Lord's lodgings, but he was gone abroad, so I lost my pains, but, however, walking through White Hall I heard the King was gone to play at Tennis, so I down to the new Tennis Court; and saw him and Sir Arthur Slingsby play against my Lord of Suffolke and my Lord Chesterfield. The King beat three, and lost two sets, they all, and he particularly playing well, I thought. Thence went and spoke with the Duke of Albemarle about his wound at Newhall, but I find him a heavy dull man, methinks, by his answers to me. Thence to the King's Head ordinary and there dined, and found Creed there, but we met and dined and parted without any thing more than "How do you?" After dinner straight on foot to Mr. Hollyard's, and there paid him L3 in full for his physic and work to my wife . . . . but whether it is cured for ever or no I cannot tell, but he says it will never come to anything, though it may be it may ooze now and then a little. So home and found my wife gone out with Will (whom she sent for as she do now a days upon occasion) to have a tooth drawn, she having it seems been in great pain all day, and at night came home with it drawn, and pretty well. This evening I had a stove brought me to the office to try, but it being an old one it smokes as much as if there was nothing but a hearth as I had before, but it may be great new ones do not, and therefore I must enquire further. So at night home to supper and to bed. The Duchesse of York is fallen sicke of the meazles.

29th. Up and to the office, where all the morning sitting, at noon to the 'change, and there I found and brought home Mr. Pierse the surgeon to dinner. Where I found also Mr. Luellin and Mount, and merry at dinner, but their discourse so free . . . . that I was weary of them. But after dinner Luellin took me up to my chamber to give me L50 for the service I did him, though not so great as he expected and I intended. But I told him that I would not sell my liberty to any man. If he would give me any thing by another's hand I would endeavour to deserve it, but I will never give him himself thanks for it, not acknowledging the receiving of any, which he told me was reasonable. I did also tell him that neither this nor any thing should make me to do any thing that should not be for the King's service besides. So we parted and left them three at home with my wife going to cards, and I to my office and there staid late. Sir W. Pen came like a cunning rogue to sit and talk with me about office business and freely about the Comptroller's business of the office, to which I did give him free answers and let him make the best of them. But I know him to be a knave, and do say nothing that I fear to have said again. Anon came Sir W. Warren, and after talking of his business of the masts and helping me to understand some foul dealing in the business of Woods we fell to other talk, and particularly to speak of some means how to part this great familiarity between Sir W. Batten and Sir J. Minnes, and it is easy to do by any good friend of Sir J. Minnes to whom it will be a good service, and he thinks that Sir J. Denham will be a proper man for it, and so do I. So after other discourse we parted, and I home and to bed.

30th. Up betimes and by coach to my Lord Sandwich, who I met going out, and he did ask me how his cozen, my wife; did, the first time he hath done so since his being offended, and, in my conscience, he would be glad to be free with me again, but he knows not how to begin. So he went out, and I through the garden to Mr. Coventry, where I saw Mr. Ch. Pett bringing him a modell, and indeed it is a pretty one, for a New Year's gift; but I think the work not better done than mine. With him by coach to London, with good and friendly discourse of business and against Sir W. Batten and his foul dealings. So leaving him at the Guiny House I to the Coffee House, whither came Mr. Grant and Sir W. Petty, with whom I talked, and so did many, almost all the house there, about his new vessel, wherein he did give me such satisfaction in every point that I am almost confident she will prove an admirable invention. So home to dinner, and after being upon the 'Change awhile I dined with my wife, who took physique to-day, and so to my office, and there all the afternoon till late at night about office business, and so to supper and to bed.

31st. Up and to the office, where we sat all the morning, and among other things Sir W. Warren came about some contract, and there did at the open table, Sir W. Batten not being there; openly defy him, and insisted how Sir W. Batten did endeavour to oppose him in everything that he offered. Sir W. Pen took him up for it, like a counterfeit rogue, though I know he was as much pleased to hear him talk so as any man there. But upon his speaking no more was said but to the business. At noon we broke up and I to the 'Change awhile, and so home again to dinner, my head aching mightily with being overcharged with business. We had to dinner, my wife and I, a fine turkey and a mince pie, and dined in state, poor wretch, she and I, and have thus kept our Christmas together all alone almost, having not once been out, but to-morrow my vowes are all out as to plays and wine, but I hope I shall not be long before I come to new ones, so much good, and God's blessing, I find to have attended them. Thence to the office and did several businesses and answered several people, but my head aching and it being my great night of accounts, I went forth, took coach, and to my brother's, but he was not within, and so I back again and sat an hour or two at the Coffee [house], hearing some simple discourse about Quakers being charmed by a string about their wrists, and so home, and after a little while at my office, I home and supped, and so had a good fire in my chamber and there sat till 4 o'clock in the morning making up my accounts and writing this last Journall of the year. And first I bless God I do, after a large expense, even this month, by reason of Christmas, and some payments to my father, and other things extraordinary, find that I am worth in money, besides all my household stuff, or any thing of Brampton, above L800, whereof in my Lord Sandwich's hand, L700, and the rest in my hand. So that there is not above L5 of all my estate in money at this minute out of my hands and my Lord's. For which the good God be pleased to give me a thankful heart and a mind careful to preserve this and increase it. I do live at my lodgings in the Navy Office, my family being, besides my wife and I, Jane Gentleman, Besse, our excellent, good-natured cookmayde, and Susan, a little girle, having neither man nor boy, nor like to have again a good while, living now in most perfect content and quiett, and very frugally also; my health pretty good, but only that I have been much troubled with a costiveness which I am labouring to get away, and have hopes of doing it. At the office I am well, though envied to the devil by Sir William Batten, who hates me to death, but cannot hurt me. The rest either love me, or at least do not show otherwise, though I know Sir W. Pen to be a false knave touching me, though he seems fair. My father and mother well in the country; and at this time the young ladies of Hinchingbroke with them, their house having the small-pox in it. The Queene after a long and sore sicknesse is become well again; and the King minds his mistresse a little too much, if it pleased God! but I hope all things will go well, and in the Navy particularly, wherein I shall do my duty whatever comes of it. The great talke is the designs of the King of France, whether against the Pope or King of Spayne nobody knows; but a great and a most promising Prince he is, and all the Princes of Europe have their eye upon him. My wife's brother come to great unhappiness by the ill-disposition, my wife says, of his wife, and her poverty, which she now professes, after all her husband's pretence of a great fortune, but I see none of them, at least they come not to trouble me. At present I am concerned for my cozen Angier, of Cambridge, lately broke in his trade, and this day am sending his son John, a very rogue, to sea. My brother Tom I know not what to think of, for I cannot hear whether he minds his business or not; and my brother John at Cambridge, with as little hopes of doing good there, for when he was here he did give me great cause of dissatisfaction with his manner of life. Pall with my father, and God knows what she do there, or what will become of her, for I have not anything yet to spare her, and she grows now old, and must be disposed of one way or other. The Duchesse of York, at this time, sicke of the meazles, but is growing well again. The Turke very far entered into Germany, and all that part of the world at a losse what to expect from his proceedings. Myself, blessed be God! in a good way, and design and resolution of sticking to my business to get a little money with doing the best service I can to the King also; which God continue! So ends the old year.

    Again that she spoke but somewhat of what she had in her heart
    Better we think than most other couples do
    Compliment from my aunt, which I take kindly as it is unusual
    Did go to Shoe Lane to see a cocke-fighting at a new pit there
    Dined at home alone, a good calves head boiled and dumplings
    Every man looking after himself, and his owne lust and luxury
    Excommunications, which they send upon the least occasions
    Expectation of profit will have its force
    King was gone to play at Tennis

Opening his mind to him as of one that may hereafter be his foe
Pen was then turned Quaker
Persuade me that she should prove with child since last night
Pride and debauchery of the present clergy
Quakers being charmed by a string about their wrists
Taught my wife some part of subtraction
To bed with discontent she yielded to me and began to be fond

A woman sober, and no high-flyer, as he calls it
Academy was dissolved by order of the Pope
After oysters, at first course, a hash of rabbits, a lamb
After some pleasant talk, my wife, Ashwell, and I to bed
After awhile I caressed her and parted seeming friends
Again that she spoke but somewhat of what she had in her heart
And there, did what I would with her
And so to sleep till the morning, but was bit cruelly
And so to bed and there entertained her with great content
And so to bed, my father lying with me in Ashwell's bed
Apprehend about one hundred Quakers
At last we pretty good friends
Before I sent my boy out with them, I beat him for a lie
Being cleansed of lice this day by my wife
Better we think than most other couples do
Book itself, and both it and them not worth a turd
But a woful rude rabble there was, and such noises
Compliment from my aunt, which I take kindly as it is unusual
Conceited, but that's no matter to me
Content as to be at our own home, after being abroad awhile
Dare not oppose it alone for making an enemy and do no good
Did so watch to see my wife put on drawers, which (she did)
Did go to Shoe Lane to see a cocke-fighting at a new pit there
Did find none of them within, which I was glad of
Dined at home alone, a good calves head boiled and dumplings
Dinner was great, and most neatly dressed
Dog attending us, which made us all merry again
Dr. Calamy is this day sent to Newgate for preaching
Duodecimal arithmetique
Eat a mouthful of pye at home to stay my stomach
Employed by the fencers to play prizes at
Enquiring into the selling of places do trouble a great many
Every man looking after himself, and his owne lust and luxury
Every small thing is enough now-a-days to bring a difference
Excommunications, which they send upon the least occasions
Expectation of profit will have its force
Familiarity with her other servants is it that spoils them all
Fear it may do him no good, but me hurt
Fearful that I might not go far enough with my hat off
Feverish, and hath sent for Mr. Pierce to let him blood

Found guilty, and likely will be hanged (for stealing spoons)
Found him a fool, as he ever was, or worse
Galileo's air thermometer, made before 1597
Give her a Lobster and do so touse her and feel her all over
God knows that I do not find honesty enough in my own mind
Goes with his guards with him publiquely, and his trumpets
Goes down the wind in honour as well as every thing else
Great plot which was lately discovered in Ireland
Had a good supper of an oxe's cheek
Half a pint of Rhenish wine at the Still-yard, mixed with beer
Hanged with a silken halter
He is too wise to be made a friend of
He hoped he should live to see her "ugly and willing"
He having made good promises, though I fear his performance
His readiness to speak spoilt all
How highly the Presbyters do talk in the coffeehouses still
I calling her beggar, and she me pricklouse, which vexed me
I and she never were so heartily angry in our lives as to-day
I do not find other people so willing to do business as myself
I slept most of the sermon
I was very angry, and resolve to beat him to-morrow
Ill humour to be so against that which all the world cries up
In some churches there was hardly ten people in the whole church
Insurrection of the Catholiques there
It must be the old ones that must do any good
Jealous, though God knows I have no great reason
John has got a wife, and for that he intends to part with him
Justice of proceeding not to condemn a man unheard
Keep at interest, which is a good, quiett, and easy profit
King was gone to play at Tennis
Lady Castlemaine hath all the King's Christmas presents
Lay long in bed talking and pleasing myself with my wife
Lay very long with my wife in bed talking with great pleasure
Lay chiding, and then pleased with my wife in bed
Liability of a husband to pay for goods supplied his wife
Many thousands in a little time go out of England
Matters in Ireland are full of discontent
Money, which sweetens all things
Most flat dead sermon, both for matter and manner of delivery
Much discourse, but little to be learned
My maid Susan ill, or would be thought so
My wife has got too great head to be brought down soon
My wife and her maid Ashwell had between them spilled the pot. . .

No more matter being made of the death of one than another
No sense nor grammar, yet in as good words that ever I saw
Nor will yield that the Papists have any ground given them
Nor would become obliged too much to any

Nothing in the world done with true integrity
Nothing of any truth and sincerity, but mere envy and design
Nothing is to be got without offending God and the King
Once a week or so I know a gentleman must go . . . .
Opening his mind to him as of one that may hereafter be his foe
Out of an itch to look upon the sluts there
Pain of the stone, and makes bloody water with great pain
Parliament do agree to throw down Popery
Pen was then turned Quaker
Persuade me that she should prove with child since last night
Plague is much in Amsterdam, and we in fears of it here
Pride and debauchery of the present clergy
Pride himself too much in it
Quakers being charmed by a string about their wrists
Rabbit not half roasted, which made me angry with my wife
Railed bitterly ever and anon against John Calvin
Reading my Latin grammar, which I perceive I have great need
Reckon nothing money but when it is in the bank
Resolve to live well and die a beggar
Sad for want of my wife, whom I love with all my heart
Saw his people go up and down louseing themselves
Scholler, that would needs put in his discourse (every occasion)
Scholler, but, it may be, thinks himself to be too much so
See how time and example may alter a man
See whether my wife did wear drawers to-day as she used to do
Sent me last night, as a bribe, a barrel of sturgeon
Servant of the King's pleasures too, as well as business
She was so ill as to be shaved and pidgeons put to her feet
She is conceited that she do well already
She used the word devil, which vexed me
She begins not at all to take pleasure in me or study to please
So home, and mighty friends with my wife again
So much is it against my nature to owe anything to any body
So home to supper and bed with my father
So home, and after supper did wash my feet, and so to bed
So neat and kind one to another
Softly up to see whether any of the beds were out of order or no
Sorry for doing it now, because of obliging me to do the like
Sporting in my fancy with the Queen
Statute against selling of offices
Talk very highly of liberty of conscience
Taught my wife some part of subtraction
That I might say I saw no money in the paper
That he is not able to live almost with her
The plague is got to Amsterdam, brought by a ship from Argier
The goldsmith, he being one of the jury to-morrow
The house was full of citizens, and so the less pleasant
Thence by coach, with a mad coachman, that drove like mad

There is no passing but by coach in the streets, and hardly that
There is no man almost in the City cares a turd for him
Therefore ought not to expect more justice from her
These young Lords are not fit to do any service abroad
They were so false spelt that I was ashamed of them
They say now a common mistress to the King
Things being dear and little attendance to be had we went away
Though it be but little, yet I do get ground every month
Through the Fleete Ally to see a couple of pretty [strumpets]
To bed with discontent she yielded to me and began to be fond
Towzing her and doing what I would, but the last thing of all
Upon a small temptation I could be false to her
Vexed at my wife's neglect in leaving of her scarf
Waked this morning between four and five by my blackbird
We having no luck in maids now-a-days
Who is over head and eares in getting her house up
Whose voice I am not to be reconciled
Wife and the dancing-master alone above, not dancing but talking
Wine, new and old, with labells pasted upon each bottle
With much ado in an hour getting a coach home
Would not make my coming troublesome to any
Yet it was her fault not to see that I did take them

Made in the USA